Technology-mediated Crisis Response in Language Studies

Advances in CALL Research and Practice

Series Editor: Stephanie Link, Oklahoma State University

The *Advances in CALL Research and Practice* book series is published in partnership between the Computer Assisted Language Instruction Consortium (CALICO) and Equinox Publishing. While the series will typically include a single volume published annually, it is possible that two books are published in a year or that the series goes a year without a volume, depending on the response to calls for papers.

Founding Series Editor: Greg Kessler, Ohio University

Published

2016
Landmarks in CALL Research
Edited by Greg Kessler

2017
Learner Autonomy and Web 2.0
Edited by Marco Cappellini, Tim Lewis, and Annick Rivens Mompean

2018
Assessment Across Online Language Education
Edited by Stephanie Link and Jinrong Li

2019
Engaging Language Learners through CALL
Edited by Nike Arnold and Lara Ducate

2020
Understanding Attitude in Intercultural Virtual Communication
Edited by Ana Oskoz and Margarita Vinagre

2021
Project-Based Language Learning and CALL
From Virtual Exchange to Social Justice
Edited by Michael Thomas and Kasumi Yamazaki

2022
Identity, Multilingualism and CALL
Responding to New Global Realities
Edited by Liudmila Klimanova

Technology-mediated Crisis Response in Language Studies

Edited by Senta Goertler and Jesse Gleason

SHEFFIELD UK BRISTOL CT

Published by Equinox Publishing Ltd.

UK Office 415, The Workstation, 15 Paternoster Row, Sheffield,
South Yorkshire S1 2BX
USA ISD, 70 Enterprise Drive, Bristol, CT 06010

www.equinoxpub.com

First published 2024

British Library Cataloguing-in-Publication Data

A catalogue record for this book is available from the British Library.

ISBN-13 978 1 80050 456 1 (paperback)
978 1 80050 457 8 (ePDF)
978 1 80050 499 8 (ePub)

Library of Congress Cataloging-in-Publication Data

Names: Goertler, Senta, editor. | Gleason, Jesse, editor.
Title: Technology-mediated crisis response in language studies / edited by Senta Goertler and Jesse Gleason.
Description: Sheffield, South Yorkshire ; Bristol, CT : Equinox Publishing Ltd, 2024. | Series: Advances in call research and practice | Includes bibliographical references and index. | Summary: "In this volume, we capture some of the lessons learned during and as a result of the COVID-19 pandemic in order to move forward as a field with intention and purpose, and to take advantage of any crisis-prompted innovation. The volume aims to provide implications for other current and future challenges and crises that require our attention in language teaching and technology. Contributions will bring additional depth to the pandemic discussion in each of the four parts: (1) Emergency Response, (2) Problem Solving, (3) Outcomes, and (4) By-Products"-- Provided by publisher.
Identifiers: LCCN 2023050742 (print) | LCCN 2023050743 (ebook) | ISBN 9781800504561 (paperback) | ISBN 9781800504578 (pdf) | ISBN 9781800504998 (epub)
Subjects: LCSH: Language and languages--Study and teaching--Technological innovations. | COVID-19 Pandemic, 2020---Influence. | LCGFT: Essays.
Classification: LCC P53.855 .T446 2024 (print) | LCC P53.855 (ebook) | DDC 418.0078/5--dc23/eng/20231204
LC record available at https://lccn.loc.gov/2023050742
LC ebook record available at https://lccn.loc.gov/2023050743

Typeset by Sparks – www.sparkspublishing.com
Printed and bound by CPI Group (UK) Ltd, Croydon, CR0 4YY

Contents

Acknowledgments

We would like to take this opportunity to thank all of the scholars, who submitted work to our volume. We are grateful to the wonderful authors in this chapter. We look forward to reading the works of those scholars, who were not included in the final version of this topic, in other publication venues. The type of research included in this volume is only possible through the openness and time commitment of study participants. Thank you to all study participants. We would like to thank CALICO for giving us the opportunity to edit this volume. It would have been impossible to maintain the high standards of the edited volume without the support from the series editor, Stephanie Link, the editorial personnel at Equinox, and the Research Assistants, Mary Ellen Rutemeyer and Nolan Rachocki. The COVID-19 pandemic had an impact on people's willingness and ability to review manuscripts. Edited volumes and journals have struggled to find reviewers. Hence, we would like to especially thank the reviewers for the 2024 volume.

Leah Adelson	University of Cincinnati
Hope Anderson	Arizona State University
Katie Angus	University of Southern Mississippi
Zeynep Bilki	TED University, Ankara
Robert Blake	University of California, Davis
Joe Cunningham	Georgetown University
Elizabeth Deifell	Appalachian State University
Li Jin	DePaul University
Lara Ducate	University of South Carolina
Adam Gacs	Michigan State University
Marta Gonzalez-Lloret	University of Hawaii
Susan Hojnacki	Aquinas College
Greg Kessler	Ohio University
Liudmila Klimanova	University of Arizona
Amanda Lanier	Michigan State University
Lara Lomicka	University of South Carolina
Gillian Lord	University of Florida

Jeffrey Maloney	Brigham Young University, Hawaii
Mandy Menke	University of Minnesota
Shannon Quinn	Michigan State University
Marianna Ryshina-Pankova	Georgetown University
Shannon Sauro	University of Maryland, Baltimore County
Theresa Schenker	Yale University
Ursula Stickler	The Open University
Oksana Vorobel	Borough of Manhattan Community College, City University of New York
Chantelle Warner	University of Arizona
Lawrence Williams	University of North Texas
Yi Xu	University of Pittsburgh

Danke! Gracias! To our families for their patience and support as we worked on this volume!

1 Working Through Crises

Senta Goertler and Jesse Gleason

Responding to Crises: Emergency Remote Teaching and Learning

There have been many crises that have been responded to with technology: from offering online courses to address enrollment issues to developing app-based language modules for refugees to the use of technology to assist in language revitalization. In this volume, we will focus on the COVID-19 pandemic as an example of a crisis and the technological response to the crisis, which often involved moving instruction partially or fully online.

In spring of 2020, the global COVID-19 pandemic necessitated social isolation, which in many places around the globe prompted education to remote formats. Suddenly, Computer-Assisted Language Learning (CALL) practitioners and scholars were in high demand. While the CALL field has spent decades investigating the efficacy of technology-mediated language learning in general (Plonsky & Ziegler, 2016) and different delivery formats in particular (Grgurović et al., 2013), their work has not always been recognized, known, and/or accepted by language educators and scholars. Already prior to this sudden ubiquitous instruction in remote formats, researchers in CALL and syntheses of CALL research had concluded that technology-mediated language learning and online or hybrid delivery formats are at least not harmful to learners and may even have some benefits (Aldrich & Moneypenny, 2019; Blake et al., 2008; Goertler, 2019). Yet, what happened in educational institutions around the globe in 2020 was not planned online instruction, but rather emergency remote teaching and learning (Gacs et al., 2020). Emergency Remote Teaching and Learning (ERTL) was unplanned, unprecedented, and highly unpredictable; leading many institutions and language educators to rethink their pedagogies, policies, practices, technologies, strategies and more.

The COVID-19 crisis forced educational institutions to quickly adjust to new ways of doing their work. In the months and years following March 2020, adjustments were made and refined that could have long-term implications for language learning and teaching. The beginning under pandemic conditions forced many educational institutions to triage some form of distance education with limited planning, the subsequent semesters provided opportunities to refine their fully or partially online delivery, while still managing a global health crisis, which prompted other crises (e.g., financial crisis, isolation, temporary school closures, etc.) and disruptions (British Academy, 2021). Much of the early research on the COVID-19 pandemic has focused on its negative effects, such as the lack of infrastructure and preparedness (Tao & Gao, 2022), issues in equitable access for educators and learners (Back et al., 2022), perceived lowered outcomes (Moser et al., 2021), and the emotional burdens (MacIntyre et al., 2020). In this volume, we aim to capture some of the lessons learned during and as a result of the COVID-19 pandemic and other co-occurring crises in order to move forward as a field with intention and purpose and to take advantage of the crisis-prompted innovation and the questions the disruptions raised. The volume aims to provide implications for other current and future crises that require our attention in language teaching and technology.

The Making of the Book

The motivation for this edited volume was fourfold: (1) COVID-19 was a global phenomenon, yet it was experienced differently in different communities; (2) the COVID-19 pandemic was an ever-evolving crisis that changed throughout time; (3) the crisis was a lesson in crisis-preparedness; and (4) the disruptions experienced were an opportunity for innovation, and made inequities and other crises more visible. The global COVID-19 health crisis required emergency responses (i.e., solutions with very little notice) and sustainable problem-solving (i.e., purposeful and innovative solutions that addressed the problem in a sustainable way with an eye toward long-term implications), samples of which are in parts 1 and 2 of the book. As a result of the crisis-prompted innovations and research, we discovered new information about outcomes – both intentional and expected (i.e., part 3 of the book) and those that may have come as a surprise (i.e., part 4 of the book) in language learning, teacher training, and program design. The rationale for the book is to move forward with lessons learned from the crisis.

In selecting contributions to this volume, we were guided by four values. (1) Because the pandemic was experienced so differently in each context, we made a point of including chapters from around the globe. We used social media, professional organizations, and our networks to widely distribute the call for papers beyond North America. Initial proposals included proposals from every continent except Antarctica. The final product includes research studies conducted in Africa, Asia, Europe, and North America. (2) Due to the all-encompassing impact of the pandemic, we wanted to present diverse angles of the pandemic: different teaching contexts, different theoretical frameworks, different stakeholders, and different foci. The chapters present student, educator, and program level perspectives; discuss the interplay between the pandemic and other crises; and use qualitative as well as quantitative frameworks. Several of the chapters also present a longitudinal perspective showcasing the ever-evolving context of the pandemic. (3) In the wake of the pandemic, there were many reflective pieces and practitioner reports published. We, however, wanted to focus this book on original empirical research studies, ideally going beyond perception data, that can guide the field in evidence-based decision making. (4) The pandemic was a traumatic global historic event whose impact is still palpable. There is value in looking back and conducting trauma-informed research on the experiences. In this volume, however, our focus is on forward-thinking recommendations. Each chapter provides lessons learned from the pandemic and their implications for the future of language studies.

The book is structured in four parts. Each part has a longer lead chapter by invited authors and two to three shorter chapters by author teams who responded to our call for papers. The invited author teams were selected based on their existing prominent research on crisis-prompted language education. Initially we received almost 40 submissions in response to our open call for chapter proposals. After an editorial review, we invited the majority of authors to submit an expanded proposal. Expanded proposals were sent out for external review. Authors whose proposals received favorable reviews were invited to submit full chapters.

All chapters – invited lead chapters and solicited shorter chapters – underwent external and editorial review. The reviews were evaluated using the following criteria: (1) Systematic empirical investigation: the chapter is based on a systematic empirical investigation following reporting traditions in the discipline. (2) Contribution to the diversity of the volume: the chapter adds to the diversity of the edited volume. (3) Crisis-prompted relevance: the chapter contextualizes the study within the field of technology-mediated crisis response in language studies and builds upon existing research. (4)

Forward-thinking: the chapter has a forward-thinking perspective, making evidence-based suggestions and drawing implications for language education both generally and in the face of a variety of crises. (5) Formatting: the chapter follows formatting expectations and length requirements.

We would like to thank all authors who submitted proposals and our reviewers for all of their valuable feedback. For a full list of reviewers, please consult our book's website (https://sites.google.com/msu.edu/2024crisiscall/home). Furthermore, we would like to thank the editorial team from CALICO and Equinox, as well as our research assistants, for their support. Most importantly, we would like to extend our gratitude to all the research participants. The COVID-19 pandemic was an extraordinary and for many a traumatic event, and we acknowledge participating in or evaluating research on the pandemic can stir up many emotions. Furthermore, the burnout and fatigue that many experienced as a result of the health crisis, further took a toll on everyone's ability to do the extra (i.e., participating, writing, reviewing research). We are grateful for all who made this volume possible in small and big ways.

Book Preview

The book is guided by four broad questions: (1) What happened in language education during the COVID-19 pandemic? (2) What were the lived experiences of educators and students? (3) What were the impacts and outcomes for educators, students, and/or programs? (4) What can we learn from the COVID-19 crisis for language education in moments of crisis and the field more generally? The first two questions guide parts 1 and 2 of the book; the latter two guide parts 3 and 4 of the book. The book is divided into six parts. (0) Introduction; (1) Emergency response; (2) Problem solving; (3) Outcomes; (4) By-products; and (5) Lessons learned. Parts 0 and 5 are written by us as introduction and conclusion to the volume.

Part 1: Emergency Response

Part 1 of the book focuses on the emergency response and impact thereof guided by the following questions: What was done? What was missing? What training was offered for learners, educators, and/or support personnel? What changes were made initially and how were they improved upon as we moved through the pandemic? What were the unique challenges of language learning and teaching?

In chapter 2, Li Jin, Yi Xu, and Elizabeth Deifell discuss how college-level world language teachers' technology, pedagogy, and content knowledge (TPACK) and attitudes toward and practices with remote language instruction (RLT) changed once the emergency phase of ERTL had ended. Their chapter fills a much-needed gap in our understanding about what happened to teachers' technology use after the triage phase of the pandemic had ended. Among others, one major takeaway from this study was the flexibility of instructors and willingness to experiment with new instructional technologies (IT) during ERTL, as well as their continued creative uses of IT once language classes went back to their original F2F modality.

In chapter 3, Roshni Gokool and Shamila Naidoo give us insight into multiple ongoing crises in South Africa, such as the student-led movements starting in 2015 known as #FeesMustFall and #RhodesMustFall and later the pandemic, which required a change in course modality and by extension student engagement in a course on Basic isiZulu as an L2, one of many indigenous languages in South Africa, at the Howard College Campus of the University of KwaZulu-Natal. Their analysis of student engagement before the pandemic and during ERTL shows low student engagement with a slight improvement during 2021. One of the unique challenges in ERTL is the compounding factors of distance and life in a crisis, which may have contributed to the low engagement during both the student movement and the COVID-19 pandemic. Building incentives into courses may improve engagement.

Chapter 4 authors, Giovanni Zimotti and Alyssia Miller De Rutté, home in on a promising tech-mediated solution that emerged during ERTL, especially in applied/professional contexts: virtual reality (VR) immersion. Community-engaged language learning contexts were especially impacted by social distancing measures. To make up for the no longer available clinical settings, Zimotti and Miller examined two similar but distinct learning environments. They explored student perceptions of VR-mediated learning in the context of medical Spanish courses, finding that students experienced increased enjoyment and a reduction of anxiety. Given the increased stress often experienced during the pandemic, these were welcome additions which hold positive implications for continued VR use in L2 learning contexts post-pandemic. Nevertheless, the authors discuss how completely replacing real-world experiences with VR-mediated learning, as was required during ERTL, holds important implications which must be considered.

Part 2: Problem Solving

Part 2 of the book focuses on problem solving and is guided by the following questions: What infrastructures were created? What skills, strategies, and approaches did stakeholders develop? What was their process? What changes were made to curricula and their implementation? How were practices and policies changed? What do we want to/need to keep?

In chapter 5, Bernd Rüschoff reports on a large-scale survey project by the Council of Europe's European Center for Modern Languages. Through the insights of more than 1,700 teachers from 32 different European countries and 1,500 secondary school students from 10 European countries, we gain a comprehensive understanding of educator and learner perspectives on (post) pandemic teaching. For example, he reports that more than half of the teachers found the substitution of tests with other types of ongoing assessment helped to lower student stress. Students, on the other hand, reported negatives to the ERTL, such as feelings of loneliness, a lack of freedom (*unliberty* – a term coined by participants), and reduced or different types of interaction than they had been used to prior to pandemic learning. Both teachers and students felt that they had also experienced educational growth, developed an appreciation for flexible learning options and gained greater awareness and acceptance of digital learning. Participants acknowledged that simply going back to the way things were before was too simplistic as an option. Rüschoff provides a framework for the future, focusing on educational literacy and adaptability. Implied in his result is also a call for more agency for teachers and learners.

In chapter 6, Luca Giupponi, Bethany Zulick, and Emily Heidrich Uebel examine college-level language instructors' incorporation of technology through the lens of Diffusion of Innovation (DoI) Theory (Rogers, 2003). In particular, four DoI characteristics were found to influence teachers' decisions to innovate, including *Compatibility*, *Results Demonstrability*, *Relative Advantage*, and *Ease of Use*. The pandemic was transformative for the study participants, helping them refocus on learners' needs and engage with digital tools to innovate their teaching.

In chapter 7, Claudia Sánchez-Gutiérrez, Ana Ortega Pérez, Ana Ruiz-Alonso-Bartol, Paloma Fernández-Mira, Diane Querrien, and Shelley Dykstra offer a unique viewpoint from six teaching assistants on ERTL instruction during the pandemic as it compared to a return to the new normal post-pandemic. Unlike an abundance of research on ERTL which has pointed to elevated levels of stress and emotional labor, especially as experienced by educators, the authors explain how this was not the case in their particular context of a large lower-division Spanish program. The authors point to several key reasons, including their belonging to a close-knit community of practice, well-structured leadership that included lead TAs for each course level within the program, and a *pedagogization* of technology (Rapanta et al., 2021), which encouraged instructor flexibility and innovation. Similar to the findings from Rüschoff, as well as Guiponni and colleagues, this research points to educators' ability to adapt during a crisis – be it through their own reflection, the participation in professional development, or through local support.

The authors of chapter 8, Jill Landry and Marie-Josée Hamel, also showcase multiple language teachers' experiences with ERTL albeit from a different, more experienced cadre. The 10 teachers in their study were grouped along a continuum of willingness to implement change, with teachers on one end embracing it (finding solutions) and those at the other end experiencing a certain degree of resistance (facing challenges). The study is based on Hamel's (2017) model of teacher development. Like the previous chapters in this part of the book, their study shows the adaptability of teachers and their ability to use reflective and iterative teacher-researcher practices to adapt to new situations.

Part 3: Outcomes

Part 3 of the book focuses on outcomes and is guided by the following questions: How well did learners achieve the course goals? How well did educators teach? How well were educators and students supported? How well did language programs navigate the situation? What alternatives were found? How were programs, educators, and learners impacted in the short and long term?

In chapter 9, Jesse Gleason and Andrew Bartlett take a longitudinal approach to tracking learning outcomes in third semester Spanish. While changes made to the curriculum in the wake of the shift to ERTL were minimal, learning outcomes showed significant differences. Students who were forced to take online courses during the ERTL period outperformed students in forced face-to-face courses prior to the pandemic as well as students in online and face-to-face courses after ERTL. Their results suggest that there were differences in learner experiences and perhaps learner profiles that go beyond the delivery format before, during, and after ERTL. Like others, they found greater variation in learning outcomes in online courses. Both findings suggest the need for further investigation into student profiles to better assess optimal pairing between delivery format and student profiles. In addition to reporting on the impacts on the learners, this study also reports a programmatic impact, namely that the program was now empowered to offer online courses, which may be more suitable for the commuting and non-traditional students at this campus.

In chapter 10, Elizabeth Lavolette and Mayumi Asaba discuss how they used ERTL to create materials for asynchronous online delivery for the ERTL timeframe and possible use in flipped instruction thereafter. Using best practices for creating online lectures they developed materials for two content-based English courses in Japan. These materials addressed their immediate needs for asynchronous online teaching during the pandemic and served as the starting point for creating flipped classes once instruction resumed face-to-face. The flipped classroom was intended to provide more opportunities for peer interaction than is customary in English courses in Japan – thereby the need to address the COVID-19 remote teaching crisis provided a pathway to address the crisis in insufficient spontaneous oral interaction in English classes. Students enjoyed the online lectures – though they were perceived as more helpful if they included Japanese in addition to English. Students reached the learning goals – though improvements for the future to reach a deeper understanding of the materials were suggested. Lavolette and Asaba took advantage of the pandemic to create a delivery format that may be more suitable for the needs of their learners (i.e., more speaking time).

As the title suggests, in chapter 11 Kimberly Morris, Mikaela Robarge, and Pablo Robles-García report on how students confronted the crisis with craft across several language programs. As they transitioned through the pandemic, students had the opportunity to take language courses in different modalities, including online asynchronous, online synchronous, hybrid, and fully F2F. This mixed-method study of students' experiences in these modalities in Spring 2021 builds on Morris' prior research on teacher experiences. As in the other chapters of this section, Morris and her colleagues used the pandemic disruptions to explore students' perceptions of ERT practices in different modalities. In general, students perceived all modalities as effective and reported no significant differences in their workload, feedback, and time and effort between spring 2021 and pre-pandemic, regardless of modality. Students saw benefits and challenges in each format, although these differed by student profile and instructional practices. It is also clear that the continued life conditions of the pandemic influenced their experience with the modalities, specifically their comfort, ability to interact successfully, sense of community, and motivation.

Part 4: By-Products

Part 4 of the book focuses on the by-products of the pandemic and is guided by the following questions: How did remote work impact the emotions and emotional labor of learners, educators, and support personnel? What adjustments were made as a result of the pandemic to working and learning conditions? What were the program implications? What are the goals, needs, and lessons for the future?

In chapter 12, Chantelle Warner and Wenhao Diao use appraisal theory (Martin & White, 2007) to analyze affect and emotional attachment during remote teaching. Building on their previous research on emotion labor during the pandemic, they explore the connection between ubiquitous ERTL technologies and educators' emotions and emotional labor. Educators not only had to decide which tools to use and how to use them, but also navigate the emotions and the potential to conduct emotional labor in relation to the tools. No tool is emotionally neutral. Zoom, for example, both served as a vehicle to building connection, but also as a hindrance to connection. Similarly, communication apps typically used in private communication were implemented to build community, but may have been perceived as a blurring of the private and the public by students. Educators navigated the affordances and challenges of technology in terms of the pedagogical as well as the emotional decisions. Warner and Diao illustrate the complexities of ERTL and the adaptability of educators to constantly changing circumstances similar to the observations by Rüschoff in part 1 of the book.

In chapter 13, Marta Tecedor and Inmaculada Gómez Soler make recommendations for teacher training based on a global survey-based Latent Class Analysis of language educators' experience during the early days of ERTL. They classified participants into negative, neutral, and positive attitudes toward online education. Teachers with more experience tended to be more negative; teachers who received training during the pandemic tended to have a neutral rather than a negative attitude; and pre-K12 teachers were less positive than those teaching in higher education or language schools. The training that educators received was emergency training, that addressed mostly immediate needs and low-level skills and not the kind of deep understanding and reflection that is needed to change attitudes. As in other chapters (e.g., Gokool and Naidoo), educators reported challenges with motivation and designing engaging learning environments. Implied in Tecedor and Gómez Soler's study is that a by-product of ERTL was a shift in attitudes and that those attitudes were influenced by pre-pandemic and thereby pre-crisis conditions. This is similar to the observations made by Landry and Hamel in part 2 of the book.

In chapter 14, Elena Schmitt and Anastasia Sorokina analyze the evolution of their MS TESOL program during and after the pandemic. The forced ERTL opened the opportunity to explore flipped model online courses (similar to Lavolette and Asaba in part 3 of the book) and Schmitt and Sorokina designed a flipped curriculum in synchronous teacher training coursework that had been partially implemented before the pandemic. Across the iterations students were able to reach the course and program goals. Over time, students' attitudes toward online courses shifted to the more positive as they gained experience in the online format and could make a mindful choice of modality. While logistical reasons for opting for online courses still persisted, in the post-ERTL phase, learners also selected the online courses because of the increased focus on student-to-student interactions and community building opportunities. In the initial stages of ERTL, learners expressed concerns regarding the absence of a sense of community and challenges with interaction. However, this perception evolved as the program increasingly underscored the significance of fostering community and connections within their online courses. Being a commuter school in a state with a critical demand for ESL teachers, the pandemic presented the program with a path to further refine and enhance courses across delivery formats.

Part 5: Lessons Learned

Part 5 is the conclusion to the book and aims to answer the following questions: (1) What were the major lived experiences and lessons of the COVID-19 pandemic? (2) What are some recommendations for constructively, productively, and sustainably moving forward?

Guidance for Reading

For many people, the pandemic was a traumatic event (Husky et al., 2020) that continues to have emotional, financial, and educational ripple effects at the time of the writing of this book (The British Academy, 2021). Educators continue to be exhausted and burned out (Westphal et al., 2022) and many are disengaging – be it through leaving the profession, retiring early, or quiet quitting (Olen, 2022; Thokkechangarapatt, 2023). While the research in this book may trigger traumatic memories, we hope that – especially as time passes – this book becomes a resource for educators, researchers, and program directors to take agency in designing language learning and teaching environments for the "new normal" and for new crises. Ideally those designs will address the questions and inequities highlighted by the pandemic and will build on the innovations and experiences of those who lived through the challenges of the pandemic years. The intention of the book is to learn from the forced innovation as a catalyst for change, so that we can move forward constructively to be prepared for the future and address new and long-standing issues in language education.

Because we made an effort to showcase a variety of contexts and perspectives, you may want to seek out specific chapters in the book. The table below is intended to help you prioritize chapters to read.

Table 1 Overview of Chapters

Authors	Context	Language	Perspective
Li Jin, Yi Xu, & Elizabeth Deifell	US	All	Educators
Roshni Gokool & Shamila Naidoo	South Africa	isiZulu	Learners
Giovanni Zimotti & Alyssia Miller De Rutté	US	Spanish	Learners
Bernd Rüschoff	Europe	All	Educators & Learners
Luca Giupponi, Bethany Zulick, & Emily Heidrich Uebel	US	All	Educators
Claudia Sanchez-Gutierrez, Ana Ortega Perez, Ana Ruiz-Alonso-Bartol, Paloma Fernandez-Mira, Diane Querrien, & Shelley Dykstra	US	Spanish	Educators
Jill Landry & Marie-Josée Hamel	Canada & Brazil	English & French	Educators
Jesse Gleason & Andrew Bartlett	US	Spanish	Learners
Elizabeth Lavolette & Mayumi Asaba	Japan	English	Learners & Program
Kimberly Morris, Mikaela Robarge, & Pablo Robles-García	US	All	Learners
Chantelle Warner & Wenhao Diao	US	All	Educator
Marta Tecedor & Inmaculada Gómez Soler	Global	All	Educator
Elena Schmitt & Anastasia Sorokina	US	English	Learner & Program

To make a choice about the next chapter to read, you may also want to consult our book website (https://sites.google.com/msu.edu/2024crisiscall), which features chapter summaries written by the authors and hyperlinked video summaries of the chapters by the author teams. As you read through the book chapters, we encourage you to take notes on the lessons learned, the implications for the future, and the work that still needs to be done.

About the Authors

Senta Goertler (Ph.D., University of Arizona, Second Language Acquisition and Teaching) is Associate Professor of Second Language Studies and German at Michigan State University. Her research focuses on language program administration especially as it intersects with technology and/or education abroad.

Jesse Gleason (Ph.D.) is Associate Professor of Spanish and Applied Linguistics at Southern Connecticut State University in New Haven, CT, where she presently coordinates the Lower-Division Spanish program. Her teaching and research interests include world language education, pedagogy and curriculum, technology-enhanced language learning, and assessment.

References

Aldrich, R. S., & Moneypenny, D. B. (2019). Assessing Spanish proficiency of online language learners after year 1. *The EUROCALL Review*, *27*(2), 28–39. https://doi.org/10.4995/eurocall.2019.11500

Back, M., Zavala, V., & Franco, R. (2022). "Siempre adistanciados": Ideology, equity, and access in Peruvian emergency distance education for Spanish as a second language. *CALICO Journal*, *39*(1), 79–102. https://doi.org/10.1558/cj.19665

Blake, R., Wilson, N. L., Cetto, M., & Pardo-Ballester, C. (2008). Measuring oral proficiency in distance, face-to-face and blended classrooms. *Language Learning and Technology*, *12*(3), 114–127. http://dx.doi.org/10125/44158

British Academy. (2021). The COVID decade: Understanding the long-term societal impacts of COVID-19. Retrieved from: https://www.thebritishacademy.ac.uk/publications/covid-decade-understanding-the-long-term-societal-impacts-of-covid-19/

Gacs, A., Goertler, S., & Spasova, S. (2020). Planned online language education versus crisis prompted online language teaching: Lessons for the future. *Foreign Language Annals*, *53* (2), 380–392. https://doi.org/10.1111/flan.12460

Goertler, S. (2019). Normalizing online learning: Adapting to a changing world of language teaching. In N. Arnold & L. Ducate (Eds.), *Engaging language learners through CALL: From theory and research to informed practice* (pp. 51–92). Equinox.

Grgurović, M., Chapelle, C. A., & Shelley, M. C. (2013). A meta-analysis of effectiveness studies on computer technology-supported language learning. *ReCALL*, *25*, 165–198. https://doi.org/10.1017/S0958344013000013

Hamel, M.-J. (2017). Portraits d'enseignants de FLS, pédagogues de l'hybride. Vers une ébauche de modèle. *Alsic*, *20*(3). https://doi.org/10.4000/alsic.3138

Husky, M. M., Kovess-Masfety, V., & Swendsen, J. D. (2020). Stress and anxiety among university students in France during Covid-19 mandatory confinement. *Comprehensive Psychiatry*, *102*, 152–191. https://doi.org/10.1016/j.comppsych.2020.152191

MacIntyre, P. D., Gregersen, T., & Mercer, S. (2020). Language teachers' coping strategies during the COVID-19 conversion to online teaching: Correlations with stress wellbeing and negative emotions. *System*, *94*, 1–12. https://doi.org/10.1016/j.system.2020.102352

Martin, J. R., & White, P. R. R. (2007). *The language of evaluation: Appraisal in English.* Palgrave Macmillan.

Moser, K., Wei, T., & Brenner, D. (2021). Remote teaching during COVID-19: Implications from a national survey of language educators. *System, 97*, 1–15. https://doi.org/10.1016/j.system.2020.102431

Olen, H. (2022). How the pandemic ended America's bad romance with work. *Washington Post*. https://www.washingtonpost.com/opinions/2022/11/14/covid-pandemic-work-resignation-quitting-unionization/

Plonsky, L., & Ziegler, N. (2016). The CALL-SLA interface: Insights from a second-order synthesis. *Language Learning & Technology*, *20* (2), 17–37. http://dx.doi.org/10125/44459

Rapanta, C., Botturi, L., Goodyear, P., Guárdia, L., & Koole, M. (2021). Balancing technology, pedagogy and the new normal: Post-pandemic challenges for higher education. *Postdigital Science and Education*, *3*, 715–742. https://doi.org/10.1007/s42438-021-00249-1

Rogers, E. M. (2003). *Diffusion of innovations*. Free Press.

Tao, J., & Gao, X. (2022). Teaching and learning languages online: Challenges and responses. *System*, *107*, 1–9. https://doi.org/10.1016/j.system.2022.102819

Thekkechangarapatt, M. (2023). Quiet quitting in the education sector: Enumeration of three cases. *EPRA International Journal of Multidisciplinary Research*, *9*(5), 83–88. https://doi.org/10.36713/epra13159

Westphal, A., Kalinowski, E., Hoferichter, C. J., & Vock, M. (2022). K-12 teachers' stress and burnout during the COVID-19 pandemic: A systematic review. *Frontiers in Psychology*, *13*, 1–29. https://doi.org/10.3389/fpsyg.2022.920326

PART ONE

EMERGENCY RESPONSE

2 Remote Language Teaching and Changes in College-level World Language Educators' Knowledge and Attitudes Toward Online Language Teaching

Li Jin, Yi Xu, and Elizabeth Deifell

Administrative response to the COVID-19 pandemic required world language educators to adopt remote language teaching from the Spring of 2020 until 2021 or even until early 2022. Research has consistently reported inadequate preparation and training in language teaching with technology, including online language teaching even prior to the outbreak (e.g., Kessler, 2018; Paesani, 2020). In this sense, language educators participated in unprecedented and forced professional development in which many had to learn how to teach languages online amidst teaching online for the first time. Research on teacher cognition, which consists of teachers' knowledge, beliefs, and perceptions, stresses that learning how to teach is a long and complex process influenced by teachers' own prior learning and teaching experiences, as well as the contexts of these experiences (Borg, 2015; Paesani, 2020). Similarly, researchers of online language teaching also underscore that educators' prior experience with technology influences their technology use (e.g., Hubbard, 2019; Shelley et al., 2013). For a profession that has already been "in crisis" (e.g., enrollment decline) (Hiver & Dörnyei, 2017; MacIntyre et al., 2022), it is imperative to understand how this crisis-prompted remote language teaching experience has shaped world language educators' perceptions and attitudes toward online language teaching, a pedagogical approach that still induces doubts and even resistance from teachers (Goertler, 2019; Tarone, 2015; Winke et al., 2010).

In recent years, an increasing number of published empirical studies have shed light on the challenges and adaptations experienced by language educators as well as their perceptions of emergency remote language teaching in the initial phase, or the triage-mode of the COVID-19 pandemic (e.g., Jin et al., 2022; Moser et al., 2021). Less is known about how the experience of remote language teaching (RLT) for more than one year has impacted their knowledge and attitudes toward online language teaching, e.g., what changed and what remains to be changed after RLT. This chapter reports on an empirical study investigating college-level world language educators' self-reported changes in their knowledge about online language teaching through the framework of Technological Pedagogical and Content Knowledge (TPACK) (Mishra & Koehler, 2006) and self-reported attitudinal changes about online language teaching after more than one year of RLT. Considering the plethora and variety of online teaching resources (e.g., training sessions and workshops) provided throughout RLT and their potential influence on teacher cognition, how the pandemic-era online teaching training received by world language educators shaped these changes was also examined.

Literature Review

Technological Pedagogical and Content Knowledge (TPACK)

There exist many models describing the adoption of technology in education and especially in the language classroom (Hampel & Stickler, 2015). Technological, pedagogical, and content knowledge (TPACK) is a conceptual framework proposed by Mishra and Koehler (2006) to describe the interactive relationships among technology, pedagogy, and content when teachers are planning instruction. Built on the original work of Shulman (1986), Mishra and Koehler's TPACK framework consists of seven components:

1. teachers' technological knowledge (TK, i.e., their knowledge of how to use technological tools),
2. content knowledge (CK, i.e., knowledge of subject content),
3. pedagogical knowledge (PK, i.e., knowledge of instructional strategies),
4. pedagogical content knowledge (PCK, i.e., knowledge of how to use appropriate instructional strategies to teach subject content),
5. technological pedagogical knowledge (TPK, i.e., knowledge of applying technology to implement instructional strategies),
6. technological content knowledge (TCK, i.e., knowledge of representing subject content with technology), and finally

7. TPACK referring to knowledge of facilitating students' learning of a specific content through pedagogically sound technological adoption. The interaction between PCK, TPK, and TCK gives rise to TPACK, the core concept of the framework.

Since its introduction, the TPACK framework has been increasingly used to investigate language educators' knowledge about online language teaching (e.g., Tseng et al., 2011, 2020). TPACK has also been investigated as a significant predictor of language educators' intent to adopt web-based technologies in language teaching in both pre-pandemic times (e.g., Hsu, 2016; Mei et al., 2018) and online language teaching during the pandemic (e.g., Gao & Zhang, 2020; Sun & Zou, 2022). For example, Gao and Zhang's (2020) study found that the increased information technology literacy of three university instructors of English as a foreign language (EFL) in China during the shift to remote teaching soon after the outbreak of COVID-19 improved their teacher cognition about online language teaching, as reflected in a TPACK change. Based on both quantitative and qualitative data collected from 204 EFL pre-service teachers from three Chinese universities in October, 2020, Sun and Zou's (2022) study revealed that the participants were generally confident in their TPACK of online language teaching, which not only significantly shaped their perceived value and ease of use of online teaching, but also was a significant direct predictor of their acceptance of online teaching. In other words, this study indicated that pre-service teachers would be more amenable to online language teaching if their TPACK increases.

Attitudes toward Online Language Teaching in Pre-pandemic Times

Online language teaching has been increasingly adopted at the post-secondary-level in the U.S., mostly in Spanish language programs at lower-level proficiency levels (Klimanova et al., 2021; Murphy-Judy & Johnshoy, 2017). There are many types of fully and partially online courses. Goertler (2019) differentiates four types of language instructional delivery formats: traditional face to face (F2F) instruction that minimally adopts technology for instruction or practice in a course; technology-enhanced instruction that adopts technology to varying degrees for instruction and practice; blended or hybrid instruction that combines both F2F and online instruction and practice; and online or distance instruction that requires no F2F meeting between the instructor and students. During the pandemic, a new course delivery mode, HyFlex (Lederman, 2022), was created to accommodate diverse students' needs. A HyFlex course is delivered both in person and online simultaneously so students can choose to join a class meeting either in person or online.

Studies have consistently shown that online courses can be as effective as F2F courses in terms of language learning achievements, and there is even a slight advantage for online or hybrid/blended courses (e.g., Goertler & Gacs, 2018; Means et al., 2009). For instance, online courses are flexible and adaptive, thus can reach more students and enable more individualized instruction than F2F courses. However, language learning researchers have been calling for more evidence on learners' actual proficiency outcomes (e.g., Gleason & Bartlett, Chapter 9, this volume; Moneypenny & Aldrich, 2016; Tarone, 2015). On the part of language educators, there exists widespread doubt and even resistance to online language instruction (e.g., Blake & Guillén, 2020; Plonsky & Ziegler, 2016). Leading barriers related to teachers include time constraints (Arnold, 2008), lack of financial, administrative, and technical support (Lin et al., 2014), language teachers' limited TPACK (Hsu, 2016; Mei et al., 2018), and language teaching philosophy (Teo et al., 2017; Williams et al., 2014). Research also reveals certain language teachers' resistance to change in general as one persistent barrier (Blake, 2008).

Growth and Development During the Pandemic

Upon the pandemic outbreak, researchers on online language education warned the field of world language education that planned online language education is different from crisis-prompted online language teaching, and even experienced online language educators' need to adjust expectations and make substantial adaption when switching F2F instruction online with little preparation time (Gacs et al., 2020). Since then, many empirical studies have been published to help unpack how language educators and learners at various levels coped with emergency remote language teaching and learning (e.g., Jin et al., 2022; Klimanova et al., 2021; Moser et al., 2021). One line of research on remote language teaching focused on language educator development in terms of their acceptance of online language teaching in post-pandemic times.

Jin et al.'s (2021) study surveyed 662 US based college-level world language educators in Spring, 2020, less than one semester after the COVID-19 pandemic prompted the adoption of emergency remote teaching (ERT), focusing on language educators' intention to adopt online language teaching in post-pandemic times. The results showed that many language educators learned how to use new technologies to assist teaching in general and language teaching specifically. More importantly, the participants were moderately optimistic about adopting online language teaching in post-pandemic times. Educators' perceived values of online language teaching, their self-confidence in teaching online, and the stress felt in ERT were three significant factors shaping their acceptance of online teaching in post-pandemic times. However, through the emergency teaching experience, many participants also learned about limitations of 100% online language teaching. As a result, more participants preferred to integrate technologies they tried during ERT into their F2F classes or to attempt hybrid teaching instead of 100% online teaching in the future. The same sense of professional growth in terms of understanding how to conduct online teaching and facilitate students' online language learning has also been reported in a large survey study on language educators in Europe (Rüschoff, Chapter 5, this volume).

Drawing on concepts of teacher beliefs and teacher agency, Gao and Cui (2022) discovered how four EFL teacher participants in a Chinese university who adopted technologies during and after ERT were influenced by both their core beliefs, as reflected in their ideal teacher roles, and their teaching reality. Three out of the four participants decided to adopt blended teaching after resuming in-person teaching in Fall, 2020 because they believed blended teaching enabled them to fulfill their ideal teacher's role as a guide, a caring example, and a friend plus, respectively. Based on their survey of 574 US-based college-level second language (L2) instructors in March 2021, Waldvogel and Robayna (2022) showed that L2 educators thought their experience using virtual technologies during the pandemic positively changed their perceptions about technology use in language instruction and that the majority were ready to embrace more virtual technology in the classroom after the pandemic.

A few studies focused on changes in language teachers' emotions and well-being since early 2020 (MacIntyre et al., 2020, 2022; Warner & Diao, Chapter 12, this volume). Warner and Diao's study (Chapter 12, this volume) revealed that emotions mattered in remote language teaching and technologies used in remote language teaching deeply affected teachers' emotion labor. Despite the paramount stress and anxiety language teachers experienced in Spring, 2020, MacIntyre and his colleagues (2022) discovered that "language teachers appear[ed] to settle into a 'new normal'… the pandemic and associated changes to language pedagogy may have also been an opportunity for hope to exert its influence on well-being and even growth" (p. 22).

Training and Professional Development (PD) Opportunities During the Pandemic

It is worth noting that most of the aforementioned studies underscore language educators' growth in online language teaching through their remote teaching practice – in other words, trial-and-error and self-directed learning (e.g., Gao & Zhang, 2020). With the intent to provide support for and prepare language educators to teach online for the foreseeable future, researchers also offered suggestions for implementing coherent and sustainable professional development activities after the triage-mode teaching (e.g., Knight, 2020; Paesani, 2020). They stressed that effective and sustainable professional development opportunities should be goal-oriented, collaborative, experiential, scaffolded, and sustainable. Since Spring, 2020, more language teaching professional organizations such as the American Council for Teachers of Foreign Languages (ACTFL) and the Modern Language Association have provided resources including web-based guidelines, webinar series, hands-on workshops, as well as networking and socializing opportunities on social media to prepare language educators for potentially long-term remote language teaching. Workshops and training sessions were also provided by national language resource centers (e.g., National Foreign Language Resource Center, 2021), university technology centers and, in some universities, departments with computer-assisted language learning experts and experienced online language educators.

An increasing number of empirical studies have investigated language educators' perceptions of the effectiveness and impact of online teaching training provided to them during the pandemic, especially surrounding the chaotic transition in early 2020. Cheung's (2021) case study on an ESL teacher in a Hong Kong university showed that the teacher's pedagogical beliefs, school context, and PD opportunities collectively influenced their technology adoption during the pandemic. The study also highlighted how teachers may disengage from PD if PD activities are not hands-on and teachers are not provided time to take training. Al-Bargi's (2021) study investigated Saudi Arabian college-level English language teachers' perception of PD opportunities in Fall, 2020. The findings showed that the majority of the participants were satisfied with online PD opportunities provided by their institutions; however, many were concerned that the online training sessions were not tailored toward 100% online teaching. Rüschoff's study (Chapter 5, this volume) surveyed over 1,700 teaching professionals across 40 countries in Europe. Based on the findings, language teachers largely developed a positive attitude toward technology use in language teaching and believed there should be a fundamental change in the profession.

Xu et al.'s (2022) study surveyed 133 college-level Mandarin Chinese teachers in the U.S. after one term of ERT and discovered that the support the teachers received, such as workshops and virtual forums, statistically significantly correlated with their technology adoption during ERT. The teachers stressed their need for language- and topic-specific workshops, a resource-sharing community among peers, and long-term teacher community support. Drawing on data collected from U.S.-based college-level Spanish and Portuguese language educators, Walter and Schenker's (2022) study revealed that language teachers were generally satisfied with online teaching during the pandemic and their rating of training was positively correlated with feelings of satisfaction. However, only about half of the participants received training. Very few training sessions were mandatory and the majority of teachers did not receive any compensation for attending. In addition, the teachers perceived the training provided by professional organizations as helpful, whereas those provided by their universities were too general to be useful.

In spite of tremendous challenges encountered during the pandemic, the prolonged RLT provided an unprecedented opportunity for world language educators to have first-hand teaching experience online. The above review shows there is still a lack of understanding of the impact of world language educators' remote teaching experience from Spring, 2020 to Fall, 2021. In particular, how their knowledge and attitudes toward online language teaching have changed and how the remote teaching experience and training received during the pandemic affected their knowledge and attitudinal changes merit systematic investigation. To fill in the gap, the following research questions were addressed in the study:

> RQ1: How has college-level world language educators' Technological Pedagogical Content Knowledge (TPACK) changed since the COVID-19 outbreak?
> RQ2: What were the effects of both time and online teaching training on college-level world language educators' TPACK changes?
> RQ3: How have college-level world language educators' attitudes toward online language teaching changed since the COVID-19 outbreak?
> RQ4: How did training in online teaching affect world language educators' attitudinal changes toward online language teaching?

Methodology

As part of a larger research project conducted in Fall, 2021, the current study adopted an explanatory sequential mixed-methods design (Ivankova et al., 2006) to investigate college-level world language educators' changes in their knowledge about and attitudes toward online language teaching. In particular, the focus was on the effect of world language educators' remote teaching experience and online teaching training on these changes. Due to its limited scope, the study will investigate online pedagogy-oriented training instead of a broad range of PD opportunities as a factor. Both quantitative and qualitative data were collected in the study, with quantitative data collected through an online questionnaire (https://www.iris-database.org/details/QA-F6b-PuE13) and qualitative data from the online questionnaire and follow-up interviews. Quantitative data analysis preceded qualitative data analysis so the qualitative findings were used to illustrate and explain the quantitative ones obtained earlier. Eventually, both quantitative and qualitative findings were integrated to answer all research questions.

Participants

A total of 309 college-level world language educators located in the U.S. completed the online questionnaire. As shown in Table 1, the top ten languages taught by the survey respondents were Spanish, French, Mandarin Chinese, German, Italian, Japanese, Arabic, Russian, Portuguese, and Korean. A few participants taught two or more languages. A total of 77.0% of the participants self-reported that they had taught online synchronous courses since the pandemic outbreak, 30.7% online asynchronous courses, 39.8% online hybrid courses and 23.3% taught Flex/bimodal or HyFlex. Interestingly, only slightly more than half (54.4%) of the participants reported receiving training in online teaching during the pandemic. Those who received systematic training reported that they received training via webinars, online workshops, and online courses on technological tools, general online teaching methods, online curriculum design, logistics and equity issues in online teaching provided by their universities as well as language-focused online teaching pedagogy and online classroom management provided by world language professional organizations, academic conferences, in-house language labs, and vendors. A number of participants also reported on shadowing online courses of their more experienced colleagues. Many took training during Summer, 2020. The participants' expertise areas and other background information are reported in Table 1.

Table 1 Participant Background Information

Category	Level	N	% (N=309)
Target Language	American Sign Language	6	1.9%
	Arabic	15	4.9%
	French	67	21.7%
	German	28	9.1%
	Italian	23	7.4%
	Japanese	16	5.2%
	Korean	8	2.6%
	Latin	2	0.6%
	Mandarin Chinese	50	16.2%
	Polish	1	0.3%
	Portuguese	10	3.2%
	Russian	14	4.5%
	Spanish	77	24.9%
	Other	10	3.2%
Level taught in this academic term	1st-year language course	140	45.3%
	2nd-year language course	146	47.2%
	3rd-year language course	118	38.2%
	4th-year language course	65	21.0%
	Upper-division content course in the target language (e.g., film studies, linguistics, literature)	77	24.9%
	Professional language course (e.g., business, medical)	29	9.4%
	Other	16	5.2%
Age	20–29	29	9.4%
	30–39	91	29.4%
	40–49	93	30.1%
	50–59	62	20.1%
	≥ 60	34	11.0%
Gender	Male	84	27.2%
	Female	217	70.2%
	Prefer Not to Answer	7	2.3%
	Non-binary	1	0.3%

Academic Rank	Tenured Professor	89	28.8%
	Untenured Tenure-line Professor	33	10.7%
	Full-time Non-Tenure-line Faculty	136	44.0%
	Part-time Faculty	51	16.5%
Total Year of Language Teaching Experience	< 1	10	3.2%
	1–5	63	20.4%
	6–10	53	17.2%
	11–20	97	31.4%
	≥ 21	86	27.8%
Primary Areas(s) of Expertise	Literature	105	34.0%
	Culture studies (e.g., film studies, aesthetics)	68	22.0%
	Translation/Interpretation	38	12.3%
	Linguistics	83	26.9%
	Language, Language pedagogy, Second language acquisition	179	57.9%
	Other	6	1.9%
Type of Institution	Research-oriented public university	131	42.4%
	Teaching-oriented public university	77	24.9%
	Research-oriented private university	48	15.5%
	Teaching-oriented private university	37	12.0%
	Small liberal arts college	29	9.4%
	Community college/Technical school	19	6.1%
	Other	4	1.3%
Online Teaching Training Experience since the COVID-19 Outbreak	No	141	45.6%
	Yes	168	54.4%
Teaching Modalities since the COVID-19 Outbreak	Online synchronous courses	238	77.0%
	Online asynchronous courses	95	30.7%
	Online hybrid courses	123	39.8%
	Flex/bimodal courses	72	23.3%
	None of the Above	5	1.6%

*Some participants selected multiple options in some questions. Thus, the total % for each category may not be 100%.

Twenty survey respondents participated in the follow-up interviews. Among them, five taught Spanish (one taught both Portuguese and Spanish), three French, three Mandarin Chinese, three Japanese, two German, two Russian (one taught Polish, Russian, and Czech), one Portuguese, and one Italian. There were four tenured professors, 13 full-time non-tenure-line faculty members, and three part-time faculty members. In addition, since the pandemic outbreak, all had taught online synchronous courses, 11 online hybrid courses, two online asynchronous courses, and two HyFlex courses. Many had teaching experience with multiple modalities. During the pandemic, seven received no training related to online teaching where the other 13 received training from the department, the university, or their professional organizations.

Data Collection

As part of a larger project, two data collection instruments were employed in the study reported in this chapter: an online questionnaire and follow-up interviews. The online questionnaire was administered in October to December, 2021 through email or social media invitations. The online questionnaire contained two primary sections: 1) a background information section collecting information including participants' teaching experience and training received during the pandemic; 2) five Likert scales in which participants were asked to rate statements about their a) perceived value of online language teaching, b) self-confidence in online language teaching, c) TPACK, d) perceived student readiness for online language teaching, and e) perception of future teaching (i.e., attitude toward adopting online language teaching in the future). All five scales ended with open-ended questions asking participants to elaborate on their views. Data collected from two specific scales, TPACK and perception of future teaching were used in the present study. In these scales, participants were asked to respond on a scale of 1–5 (1=strongly disagree, 5=strongly agree) to all statements at two points of time: prior to the pre-pandemic times vs. Fall, 2021. The eight items in the TPACK scale were adapted from Cheng's (2017) study. Only the items related to TCK, TPK, and TPACK were included in the scale to meet this project's special interest. The three statements in the scale of perception of future teaching were adopted from the previous study (Jin et al., 2021). Each statement asks explicitly whether participants have become more willing to adopt 100% online language teaching, hybrid/blended teaching, or technology integration in F2F classes respectively in Fall, 2021, as compared to pre pandemic times

The follow-up interviews were conducted via Zoom from mid-December, 2021 to mid-January, 2022. Interviewees were selected among those who volunteered in the online questionnaire for a follow-up interview based on three criteria: 1) target language(s); 2) teaching modalities during the pandemic; and 3) online teaching training received since the pandemic outbreak. Each interview contained semi-structured open-ended questions prompting participants to provide more-detailed reflections on their experience since Spring, 2020. The study only focused on the answers to questions pertaining to two topics: faculty's perceived changes in their TPACK, and their attitudinal changes toward online language teaching. Example interview questions include: *What did you gain in terms of how to use technologies to teach languages online compared to your competence from pre-pandemic times? What are the new things you learned or realized you need to learn about online language teaching after this one year's remote teaching, compared to the pre-pandemic times and last spring? What do you think caused the changes? Do you believe online language teaching including both 100% online teaching and hybrid/blend teaching will be a norm in universities from now on? Please explain why.* All the interviews were recorded and later transcribed verbatim.

Data Analysis

Both quantitative and qualitative analyses were conducted, and quantitative analysis preceded qualitative analysis. The qualitative findings were used to illustrate and substantiate quantitative findings.

Quantitative Analysis. All quantitative analyses were conducted via SPSS Statistics Version 27 (IBM, 2020). For RQ1, first, descriptive statistics were calculated to show the participants' TCK, TPK, and TPACK means prior to the pandemic outbreak and in Fall, 2021. Then, three paired T-tests were conducted to identify significant differences between the pre-pandemic means and those in Fall, 2021. To answer RQ2, three two-way repeated ANOVA analyses were conducted after all assumptions were checked and met with the participants' TCK, TPK, and TPACK means as the dependent variable respectively. Time was considered as the within-subject factor with two categories, prior to the pandemic outbreak and in Fall, 2021; training status as the between-subject factor in two categories, yes and no. The training status refers to whether each participant received any training in online language teaching during the pandemic. Some participants had received online teaching training and were already experienced online language instructors upon the pandemic outbreak so they opted not to attend any training. Thus, the two-way repeated measures ANOVA was conducted to avoid directly comparing participants' TRACK changes before the pandemic outbreak vs. in Fall, 2021 regardless of their training status. Pairwise comparisons with Bonferroni adjustment were conducted as ad-hoc tests when significant interactions were found. To answer RQ3, first, the participants self-reported changes in terms of their willingness to teach 100% online courses, hybrid courses, and to adopt technologies in F2F courses respectively were calculated via tabulation. Then, the Spearman rank-order correlation analysis was conducted, which shows that answers to the three Likert-scale statements, willingness to adopt 100% online language teaching, willingness to adopt hybrid language teaching, and willingness to integrate technologies in F2F classes, were highly correlated (see Table 2). Therefore, the Friedman two-way ANOVA was conducted to analyze whether there were significant differences among the answers to the three questions. Upon significant findings, the Wilcoxon Ranks tests were conducted as a post-hoc to identify where the significant difference was located. To answer RQ4, three chi-square tests were employed to compare participants who received online teaching training and those who did not receive any training in terms of their respective answers to the aforementioned three Likert-scale questions.

Qualitative Analysis. To help further illustrate in what way the participants' TPACK and their attitudes toward online language teaching had changed since the pandemic outbreak and the effect from online teaching training during the pandemic on the changes, typological analysis (Hatch, 2002) was adopted to analyze qualitative data collected both from the open-ended questions in the online questionnaire and the follow-up interviews. Two

Table 2 Correlation Coefficients Between the Three Dependent Variables in Q3 (N=309)

	100% Online**	**Hybrid****	**Tech Integration****
100% Online	1.00		
Hybrid	.449*	1.00	
Tech Integration	.430*	.381*	1.00

* Correlation is significant at the .001 level (2-tailed).

** 100% Online = willingness to adopt 100% online language teaching; Hybrid = willingness to adopt hybrid language teaching; Tech Integration = willingness to integrate technologies in F2F classes.

typologies, changes in the participants' knowledge of teaching languages online and their attitudinal changes toward online language teaching, in connection with the participants' teaching practices and the training they received, were examined. Patterns and themes emerging from the data related to each typology were then identified, and examples were categorized and compared. Findings from both the open-ended questions and follow-up interviews were compared and verified. To ensure rater reliability in the qualitative analysis process, two primary researchers first reviewed the qualitative data and identified themes and patterns separately. They then met and compared their analysis results. Any discrepancy was discussed until an agreement was reached.

Findings

Changes in College-level World Language Educators' TPACK

As shown in Table 3 and Table 4, the paired sample tests results for TCK indicated that the participants' knowledge about how to use technologies to deal with the target language increased significantly in Fall, 2021 (M = 3.98, SD = .78), compared to prior to the pandemic outbreak (M = 3.67, SD = .81), t (308) = 7.24, p < .001. Their TPK, i.e., knowledge about how to use technologies for pedagogical purposes, also increased significantly in Fall, 2021 (M = 3.63, SD = .83), compared to prior to the pandemic outbreak (M = 3.26, SD = .86), t (308) = 7.95, p < .001. Their overall TPACK has also significantly improved from prior to the pandemic outbreak (M = 3.50, SD = .89) to Fall, 2021 (M = 3.96, SD = .84), t (308) = –9.25, p < .001.

Qualitative data analysis showed that many participants reported increased knowledge related to technology use, compared to pre-pandemic times. In terms of TCK, a part-time professor teaching French shared that "I

Table 3 Descriptive Statistics for the Participants' TPACK Prior to the Pandemic vs. Fall, 2021

		Min		Max		Mean		SD	
	N	Pre	Post	Pre	Post	Pre	Post	Pre	Post
TCK	309	1.00	1.67	5.00	5.00	3.6699	3.9827	.81317	.77784
TPK	309	1.00	1.00	5.00	5.00	3.2589	3.6332	.85567	.83179
TPACK	309	1.00	1.00	5.00	5.00	3.4951	3.9563	.88868	.84258

Table 4 Paired Sample T-Tests for the Participants' TPACK Prior to the Pandemic vs. Fall, 2021

	Mean	SD	SEM	95% Confidence Interval of the Difference		*t*	df	Significance	
				Lower	Upper			One-Sided *p*	Two-Sided *p*
TCK(Pre) – TCK(Post)	–.313	.76	.04	–.40	–.23	–7.24	308	<.001	<.001
TPK(Pre) – TPK(Post)	–.37	.83	.05	–.47	–.28	–7.95	308	<.001	<.001
TPACK(Pre) – TPACK(Post)	–.46	.88	.05	–.56	–.36	–9.25	308	<.001	<.001

have gained more knowledge and taught a workshop on how to learn French independently through various media, something I never would have been able to do before." As for TPK, participants reported that they not only were exposed to more technological tools that can be used for pedagogical purposes, but also gained more knowledge about additional pedagogical functions of tools they already knew and how to adopt certain technologies to effectively achieve specific pedagogical objectives. For instance, one part-time Mandarin Chinese instructor elaborated, "I definitely learned more tools to assist me in my teaching and assessment; I also learned how to assist students in connecting with and cooperating with one another." More participants specifically addressed their increased knowledge of using technologies to teach target languages. One full-time non-tenure-line professor in German agreed that their TPACK increased during the remote teaching experience:

> particularly in terms of collaboration and multimodality online (with tools like VoiceThread, where we comment on video content collaboratively or create a "children's book" of slides with narration together). I have a wider range of options and a better sense [sic] what they work well for.

Some participants already attended certain workshops on online teaching but never got a chance to teach an online course prior to the pandemic. Remote teaching during the pandemic offered a real-life experience that helped them develop deeper insights into language learning. For instance, a full-time non-tenure-line professor in Spanish reflected on the knowledge they gained during the pandemic:

> I sort of already knew this before pandemic, but, but remote and online teaching in the pandemic has really brought it home that as many assignments and activities as possible should be kind of brought into the social realm in some way… it's made me think about, you know, explore ideas of, of ways of, of course objectives that generate less stress rather than more…

Effect of Time and Online Teaching Training on Changes in TPACK

Table 5 shows the pre- and post-pandemic data based on participants' training status for TCK, TPK, and TPACK respectively. The two-way repeated measures ANOVA with the participants' TCK as the dependent variable reveals that there was a statistically significant interaction between the effects of time and training status, F (1, 307) = 25.632, $p < .001$. Its effect size is moderate ($\eta^2 = .077$). Ad-hoc pairwise comparisons show that prior to the pandemic, those who didn't receive training during the pandemic had significantly lower TCK than those with training, F (1, 307) = 6.107, $p = .014$, $\eta^2 = .020$). In Fall 2021, those without training also had significantly lower TCK than those with training, F (1, 307) = 32.423, $p < .001$, $\eta^2 = .174$. On the other hand, those with no training did not experience a significant increase in TCK between pre-pandemic time and Fall, 2021, F (1, 307) = 1.898, $p = .169$, $\eta^2 = .006$ whereas those with training significantly increased their TCK in Fall, 2021, F (1, 307) = 80.323, $p < .001$, $\eta^2 = .207$. As shown in Figure 1, training played a significant role in shaping language educators' TCK growth.

In terms of TPK, there was also a statistically significant interaction between the effects of time and training status, F (1, 307) = 29.136, $p < .001$, $\eta^2 = .087$. Ad-hoc pairwise comparisons show that prior to the pandemic, there was no significant difference in TPK between those without training and those with training, F (1, 307) = .014, $p = .914$, $\eta^2 = .000$. However, in Fall 2021, those having received training during the pandemic enjoyed

Table 5 Descriptive Statistics for Training*Time in TCK, TPK, and TPACK

Time	Training Status	Mean			SD			N
		TCK	TPK	TPACK	TCK	TPK	TPACK	
Pre	No	3.5469	3.2653	3.3592	.78031	.77950	.83234	142
	Yes	3.7745	3.2535	3.6108	.82811	.91778	.92065	167
Post	No	3.6315	3.3756	3.5915	.84933	.78787	.87035	142
	Yes	4.2814	3.8523	4.2665	.56086	.80710	.68059	167

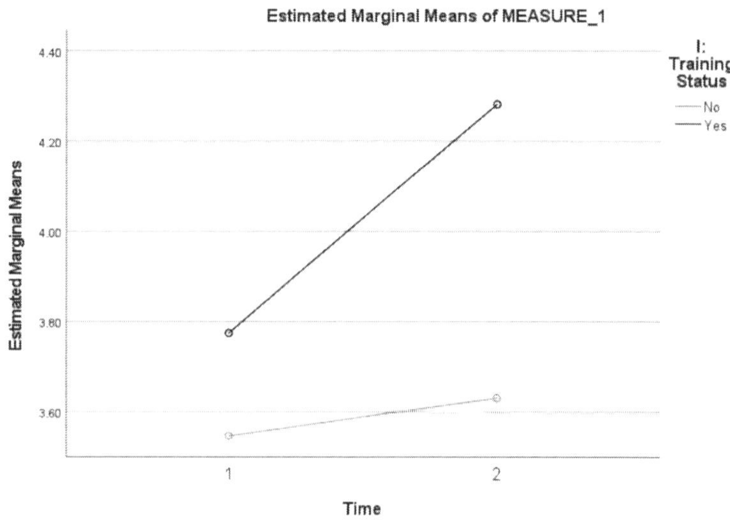

Figure 1 Time*Training Status for TCK

significantly higher TPK than those having received no training, F (1, 307) = 27.365, $p < .001$, $\eta^2 = .082$. On the other hand, those having received no training didn't show much change in TPK between pre-pandemic time and Fall, 2021, F (1, 307) = 2.750, $p = .098$, $\eta^2 = .009$ whereas those having received training significantly increased their TPK from pre-pandemic time to Fall, 2021, F (1, 307) = 95.276, $p < .001$, $\eta^2 = .237$. In other words, training also provided a significant role increasing language educators' TPK during the pandemic (see Figure 2).

Time and training status also had a significant interaction effect on the overall TPACK, F (1, 307) = 18.949, $p < .001$, $\eta^2 = .058$. Ad-hoc pairwise comparisons show that prior to the pandemic, those with no training had significantly lower TPACK than those with training, F (1, 307) = 6.258, $p = .013$, $\eta^2 = .020$. In Fall 2021, those without training also had significantly lower TPACK than those with training, F (1, 307) = 58.421, $p < .001$, $\eta^2 = .160$. However, both those with no training during the pandemic (F (1, 307) = 10.568, $p = .001$, $\eta^2 = .033$) and those with training (F (1, 307) = 98.939, $p < .001$, $\eta^2 = .244$) significantly increased their TPACK between pre-pandemic time and Fall, 2021. In other words, as illustrated in Figure 3, whether language educators received training or not, more than one year of RLT significantly increased their TPACK.

When discussing factors shaping their TPACK changes, many participants confirmed that both their teaching practice and training or technology

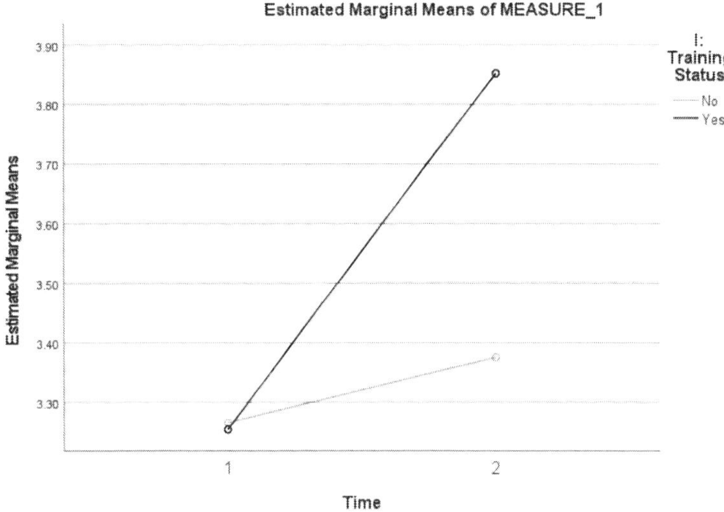

Figure 2 Time*Training Status for TPK

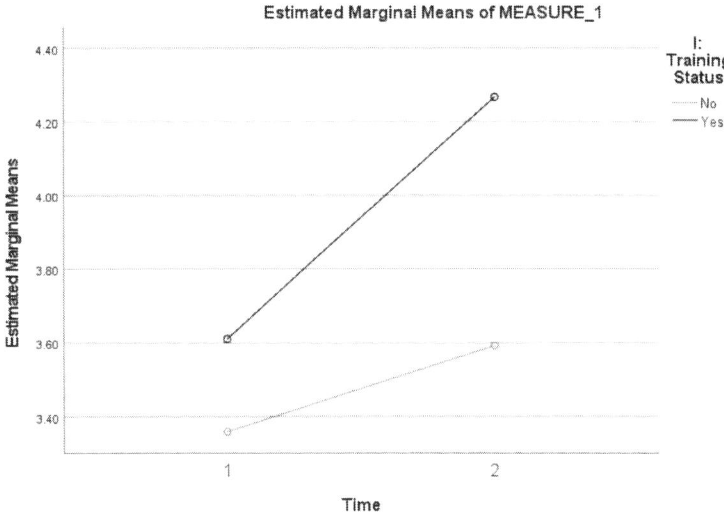

Figure 3 Time*Training Status for TPACK

support received during the pandemic were helpful in three main areas: 1) presenting content; 2) supporting student engagement; 3) online classroom management. For instance, one tenured professor in Spanish shared, "I learned how to use some platforms, such as Zoom, Teams, and Collaborate in Blackboard, in order to help my students. The areas that I feel more confident was [sic] the presentation of language content using these platforms. Again, I did workshops and webinars organized by the university and other institutions in order to gain some knowledge." Another full-time non-tenure-line Spanish professor who received systematic training in online language teaching before the pandemic shared how remote teaching experience helped them develop online classroom management skills such as how to allocate appropriate time in certain class activity, "that classroom management, right, is something that comes with experience. And classroom management online is very different from classroom management in face to face. And that is something that for sure I gained."

An untenured tenure-line professor teaching Urdu stressed the importance of actively seeking training and help to improve her TRACK, "Attending courses on LinkedIn Learning, listening to lectures on effective instructional techniques, reading new research papers; everything combined helped me in improving my overall TPACK knowledge." In contrast, some participants perceived only certain training as helpful, as illustrated in one full-time non-tenure-line Japanese professor's confession below:

> We had training in our department, but it was terrible… But we had one, like hour and a half session, the four of us with this one teacher, and that helped. But mostly you learn by doing. I, I don't have that much confidence in my university training sessions.

Despite different views about the effectiveness of online teaching training provided to language educators during the pandemic, not everyone received systemic training. Some didn't attend any training due to lack of institutional support or time constraint. For instance, a part-time Mandarin Chinese instructor shared, "My students recommended resources for me. My department on the other hand offered less support." Another instructor revealed that their busy teaching schedule prevented them from attending training during the pandemic. Other participants intentionally avoided training provided by their institutions. For instance, a senior lecturer in Spanish confessed that she had been avoiding online teaching training during the pandemic, citing bad prior experience with online teaching workshops, "I don't want any… like fancy bells and whistles. For example, a colleague once showed me how to use that special whiteboard on Google. It just was deeply confusing." She preferred to just "observe a couple of classes that work really well… as part of an integrated learning experience."

Attitudinal Changes toward Online Language Teaching

The descriptive statistics in Table 6 show that the participants' attitudinal changes toward 100% online teaching were similar to those toward hybrid teaching. About half (47.8%) of the participants either agreed or strongly agreed that they became more willing to adopt 100% online teaching in Fall, 2021, compared to prior to the pandemic outbreak, and 26.9% disagreed or strongly disagreed with the statement. 48.3% either agreed or strongly agreed about becoming more willing to adopt hybrid teaching and 27.5% disagreed or strongly disagreed. In contrast, 68.3% of the participants agreed or strongly agreed that they became more willing to integrate technologies to F2F courses in Fall, 2021 whereas only 11% disagreed or strongly disagreed with the statement.

The Friedman test result confirms that significant differences exist in terms of the participants' self-reported attitudinal changes toward 100% online teaching, hybrid teaching, and technology integration to F2F classes, $\chi^2(2) = 59.044$, $p < .001$. Post-hoc analysis with Wilcoxon signed-rank tests were conducted with a Bonferroni correction, resulting in a significant level set at $p < .017$. Median attitudinal changes for 100% online teaching, hybrid teaching, and tech integration to F2F courses were 3 (2 to 4), 3 (2 to 4), and 4 (3 to 5), respectively. There were no significant differences between attitudinal changes toward the 100% online teaching and hybrid teaching ($Z = -.021$, $p = .984$). But significant differences existed between the 100% online teaching and tech integration to F2F courses ($Z = -6.900$, $p < .001$) and between hybrid teaching and tech integration to F2F courses ($Z = -6.906$, $p < .001$). It indicates that significantly more participants became more willing to integrate technology in F2F courses compared to prior to the pandemic outbreak whereas the participants did not change much in terms of

Table 6 Attitudinal Changes toward Online Language Teaching

		Strongly Disagree	Disagree	Neutral	Agree	Strongly Agree	Total
100% Online	Count	30	53	78	93	55	309
	%	9.7%	17.2%	25.2%	30.1%	17.8%	100%
Hybrid Teaching	Count	26	59	75	96	53	309
	%	8.4%	19.1%	24.3%	31.1%	17.2%	100.0%
Tech Integration	Count	11	23	64	125	86	309
	%	3.6%	7.4%	20.7%	40.5%	27.8%	100.0%

willingness to adopt 100% online teaching or hybrid teaching after more than one year of remote teaching.

Qualitative data further shows that there are several reasons why the participants didn't become more willing to adopt 100% online teaching or hybrid teaching even after more than one year of remote teaching. For some participants, the reasons were not related to their perceived value of online language teaching. A few participants revealed that they were already aware of the benefits of 100% online teaching prior to the pandemic due to their prior training or experience with online teaching so their attitudes toward adopting 100% online teaching or hybrid teaching didn't change much. Some participants either were aware, or became aware, of the effectiveness of online language teaching but didn't become more willing to adopt it due to perceived lack of incentive and support from the university or school culture. One full-time Spanish professor shared:

> I sort of already knew this before the pandemic… Um, just that it can be very effective, and it can be done well… the part of the problem is that there are programs and universities that see online instruction as either an opportunity to teach more students with the same number of faculty, or to cut costs and some other sort of cost.

One tenured professor in Japanese pinpointed the school culture as a deciding factor:

> I think maybe [*sic*] depends on the type of school, right? I'm in a small liberal arts school, where that residential experience is… our brand… Students don't like it so much… Um, it's going to be harder for our kind of schools.

The vast majority of the participants tried 100% online teaching for the first time during the pandemic. Even after more than one year of remote teaching and recognizing the convenience and accessibility of online teaching, many still believed online teaching is not as effective as in-person teaching, citing both teacher-related and student-related factors: 1) preferred teaching style; and 2) student performance and engagement. In terms of preferred teaching style, one full-time non-tenure-line professor in Japanese shared, "It is far inferior to teaching in person… Because you can never, you can't see the people if you have more than four or five students… If you can't see him. It's always worse." Although some participants gained more knowledge and became more confident in online teaching, they became disappointed by students' performance and engagement during remote teaching, which affects their attitudes toward online language teaching. A full-time non-tenure-line professor in Spanish shared, "I did open my mind to other, you know, ways to use technology, and that we can be more creative in helping certain student groups, depending on how much effort they are willing to put into their online learning." She pointed out the biggest drawback of online teaching is lack of engagement from students, "I feel like online because they didn't have to share a lot, maybe it's harder for them to share that openly in front of their classmates.", which led to her view that 100% online teaching may be more suitable for highly motivated non-traditional students.

On the other hand, some participants cited fear for being replaced by online teaching as a factor preventing them from attitudinal changes. One senior lecturer in Spanish shared:

> I think that part of what held language faculty back from online teaching was the sense that they would be replaced. It would be language instruction delivered to the masses, and they would be replaced, there would be a need for fewer faculty members. Or sense of loss of control.

Despite the participants' hesitancy to adopt online teaching, especially 100% online teaching, overall, they demonstrated enthusiasm to integrate technologies they became familiar with during RLT into their F2F classes, thanks to their increased awareness of the advantages of online technologies in both language learning and intercultural learning. For instance, one part-time Russian instructor shared that she continued using VoiceThread in her F2F classrooms after resuming in-person teaching in Fall, 2021 and online teaching also inspired her to include more typing exercises and online essays in F2F classes, "So it's given me enough confidence and I've seen the value in it enough to utilize it even now that we're back in the classroom…"

Another veteran German professor resisted 100% online teaching, but highlighted the importance of computer-based intercultural communication in language learning:

> I think that was also very interesting, super interesting, just that you realize, oh, I can have a whole class just having nice students talk to someone I know in Germany. And it can't get more real. It can't get more motivational and very little preparation.

One tenured professor in Mandarin Chinese shared that she felt the need and even became enthusiastic to incorporate more technologies in traditional mode of teaching after RLT to meet students' learning needs:

> In the past, I would never think to incorporate anything in my beginning level courses, but now I'm open to all possibilities, and so I'm actually getting input from students. What works best for them. What are some of the apps they're using… So yeah, so if there are certain changes, I think it's maybe psychological. So I was hesitating before. I knew they are helpful, but I didn't think they are necessary. But right now, I think they are necessary and I need to learn every possible new technology that will benefit students.

Effect of Online Teaching Training on Attitudinal Changes

Table 7 shows the cross-tabulated data about the participants' attitudinal changes toward 100% online teaching, hybrid teaching, and technology integration to F2F courses with training status during the pandemic as a factor. Chi-square tests of independence indicate that there is a statistically significant relationship between training status and attitudinal changes toward hybrid language teaching. X^2 (4, $N = 309$) = 10.627, $p = .031$. Participants who received online teaching training during the pandemic were more likely than those who did not receive any training to claim that they became more willing to adopt hybrid language teaching since the pandemic outbreak. There is no significant relationship between training status and attitudinal changes toward 100% online teaching (X^2 (4, $N = 309$) = 5.713, $p = .222$) and technology integration to F2F courses (X^2 (4, $N = 309$) = 2.888, $p = .577$).

One part-time Russian instructor who received training before the pandemic stressed the negative impact of lack of training or inadequate training for language educators, especially those who did not have a positive remote teaching experience during the pandemic:

> I think that I had a unique experience with teaching and see value in it because my course was successful and many did not have that because they did not have the proper training. Instructors will participate if they have to, but if they had a bad experience before, I don't see why that would, why they would go out of their way now when there is an in-person option to just keep everything as it was before.

Some participants had more positive experiences with online teaching training during the pandemic. A tenured professor in Japanese Literature who also teaches Japanese language shared her positive experience with learning about online teaching from both ample resources on the American Association for Teachers of Japanese website and a Japanese language colleague who volun teered sharing her asynchronous teaching practices: "From everything I've seen of her, she is…, you know, she's just good at it… One of her training

Table 7 Cross-Tabulation on Attitudinal Changes Toward Online Language Teaching

	Training Status	Strongly Disagree	Disagree	Neutral	Agree	Strongly Agree	Total
100% Online Teaching	No	13	21	44	43	21	142
		9.2%	14.8%	31.0%	30.3%	14.8%	100.0%
	Yes	17	32	34	50	34	167
		10.2%	19.2%	20.4%	29.9%	20.4%	100.0%
Hybrid Teaching	No	12	35	38	41	16	142
		8.5%	24.6%	26.8%	28.9%	11.3%	100.0%
	Yes	14	24	37	55	37	167
		8.4%	14.4%	22.2%	32.9%	22.2%	100.0%
Tech Integration to F2F Courses	No	6	13	30	59	34	142
		4.2%	9.2%	21.1%	41.5%	23.9%	100.0%
	Yes	5	10	34	66	52	167
		3.0%	6.0%	20.4%	39.5%	31.1%	100.0%

seminars walked us through exactly how she does that. And many of the ideas I got were from watching that." She also shared that she has been actively seeking training on using technologies for teaching purposes, "I started using digital whiteboards. And then I started using Microsoft OneNote." In addition, she confessed that she wasn't aware of all the online language teaching resources until the pandemic as her field was not language teaching. However, when asked whether she was willing to adopt 100% online teaching, she hedged, citing their unique campus culture as a factor. In other words, although online teaching training opened the participant's eyes, she was not committed to 100% online teaching due to their particular school culture, i.e., a residential school. Therefore, adopting hybrid language teaching may be a compromised choice made by many participants who developed awareness of the value of online language teaching but had to be wary of realistic obstacles.

Discussion

Online language teaching experts have warned that RLT, especially crisis-prompted RLT, is not planned online language teaching (e.g., Gacs et al., 2020; Paesani, 2020). This view is echoed by language educators in earlier studies on ERT (e.g., Jin et al., 2021). However, RLT since Spring 2020 has undoubtedly provided an unprecedented opportunity for nearly every language educator to experience online teaching, which would not have been possible without the pandemic. Studies on language educators' emotions and wellbeing during the pandemic show that language teachers' stress caused by online teaching has eased and teachers even reported growth from the trauma as the pandemic proceeded (MacIntyre et al., 2020, 2022; Warner & Diao, Chapter 12, this volume). In other words, language educators seem to have psychologically adapted well to the remote teaching environment. Research on teacher cognition underscores the impact of teachers' prior learning experience and teaching practices on their knowledge, beliefs, and perceptions. Thus, it is unsurprising that the research findings in this study show college-level world language educators experienced significant growth in various aspects of online language teaching, as reflected in their self-reported TPK, TCK, and TPACK. For many participants, it was their first time experiencing teaching a target language in an online environment. Although not all college-level world language teachers were comfortable with online teaching, they reported increased knowledge about what and how to use technological tools and online materials available for language teaching, how to interact with students in class activities, and how to give online and offline feedback, etc. This is consistent with previous studies (e.g., Gao & Zhang, 2020; Sun & Zou, 2022) deploying a TPACK framework to analyze teacher learning during the pandemic.

Despite significantly increased knowledge in online language teaching, language educators investigated in this study only reported statistically significant changes in their attitude toward technology integration in F2F classes in Fall, 2021. Their overall attitudes toward online teaching and hybrid teaching did not shift significantly after more than one year of RLT experience, which is different from the findings in Sun and Zou's (2022) study that EFL pre-service teachers' strong TPACK significantly predicted their acceptance of online teaching. Although this study did not examine the participants' actual attitude toward online language teaching in pre-pandemic times and Fall, 2021, the findings of an earlier study (Jin et al., 2021) of a similar language educator population in Spring, 2020 revealed that language educators were only moderately positive about teaching online and the vast majority were enthusiastic about technology integration in F2F teaching instead. This finding resonates with those in Waldvogel and Robayna's (2022) study conducted about a year later. This indicates more than one year of RLT did not result in college-level world language educators' increased willingness to adopt 100% online teaching. In other words, hesitancy of or resistance to the adoption of 100% online language teaching still exists after the prolonged remote language teaching, not much different from pre-pandemic times (Blake & Guillén, 2020; Goertler, 2019; Plonsky & Ziegler, 2016). The qualitative data further illustrate that although many language educators gained tremendous knowledge about online teaching, there still exist a myriad of factors influencing language teachers' attitudes toward adopting online language teaching, such as student motivation and readiness, administrative support, school context, and personal beliefs, same as reported in Gao and Cui's (2022) study. Some perpetual myths about online language teaching, such as the view shared by some participants that online teaching is merely an administrative strategy to reduce cost and replace teachers with technology, apparently were not appropriately addressed during the crisis-prompted RLT.

A very interesting finding in this study is the intricate relationship between remote teaching practices and training received during the pandemic and language educators' knowledge and attitudinal changes toward online language teaching. It is worth mentioning that regardless of whether language educators received systematic training in online teaching during the pandemic, they significantly developed knowledge of how to teach languages online, which is consistent with findings in previous studies (e.g., Gao & Zhang, 2020; Jin et al., 2021; Sun & Zou, 2022). However, the findings also show that when training status was taken into consideration, experiencing remote language teaching alone did not significantly increase language educators' specific TCK (knowledge of representing the target language with technology) and TPK (knowledge of implementing instructional methods with technology). Only language educators who received training during the pandemic were able to significantly increase their TCK and TPK. This indicates that training provided since the pandemic outbreak played a positive role in shaping world language educators' knowledge about teaching with technologies in general, which corroborates the finding in Walter and Schenker's (2022) study. In addition, inspired by the training they received in RLT, some participants developed even more agency to actively seek additional professional development resources to meet their own needs. In other words, positive changes were made after Spring, 2020. Teaching experience and training received during the process may have helped address the prominent teacher training issue pointed out by Kessler (2018), which was the lack of appropriate pedagogical training in technology use. On the other hand, not all training was well planned and meeting language educators' needs; many language educators still weren't able to attend any training due to time constraint and lack of resources, even after Spring, 2020. This might be due to the fact that the COVID-19 pandemic had not ended when the data were collected in Fall, 2021.

Aside from its unique impact on language educators' TPACK growth, training also played an interesting role shaping their attitudinal changes toward online language teaching. The lack of impact of training on language educators' attitudinal changes toward technology integration in F2F teaching may be attributed to remote teaching practice through which language educators already learned the benefits of technology integration in F2F teaching. As for its lack of impact on attitudinal changes about 100% online teaching, the barriers preventing the changes may include inadequate training, lack of administrative support, teacher beliefs, and school context. Echoing findings in previous studies (e.g., Al-Bargi, 2021; Walter & Schenker, 2022), some training provided to language educators, especially those provided by the institution, may not be closely related to online language teaching, which failed to convince them to accept online language teaching. On the other hand, the fact that training significantly shaped language educators' attitudinal changes toward hybrid/blended teaching indicates that training was still helpful in general. However, language educators became more willing to only adopt hybrid teaching, as a compromise to address aforementioned barriers preventing them from adopting 100% online teaching. This reflects teachers' increased agency when making decisions about teaching modality, i.e., 100% online language teaching may not work in every class or school if certain infrastructure and support do not exist.

Conclusion

World language education in the U.S. has been considered a profession "in crisis" (Hiver & Dörnyei, 2017; MacIntyre et al., 2022). Many administrators and language educators have considered online education as a salvation to attract and serve diverse students. Despite the drastic difference between planned online language education and RLT during the pandemic, this study shows language teaching educators still developed knowledge about online language teaching and grew more open to technological integration in their F2F teaching. In other words, RLT contributed to the development of teacher cognition in online language teaching (Borg, 2003; Paesani, 2020). In addition, training provided during the pandemic, especially those that targeted language educators, were useful in terms of increasing language educators' knowledge in various aspects of online language teaching and shifted their views about hybrid teaching. On the other hand, the findings also shed light on issues world language educators still face. Most of the participants did not change their attitudes toward adopting 100% or hybrid online language teaching. Only about half of the participants in this study received training during more than one year of RLT. The quality of training was not consistent. This indicates there is still much work to be done if we expect to see more acceptance of online language teaching either to take advantage of the benefits of online language teaching or to prepare for future pandemics.

First and foremost, more systematic and sustainable training in post-pandemic times should be provided to help college-level world language educators develop appropriate knowledge, skills of and attitudes toward online language teaching. Some of the myths about why online education is necessary should be explicitly addressed to mitigate language educators' fear of, or resistance to, online language teaching or technology use. If possible, multiple training sessions with hands-on activities and teaching shadowing should be provided to address specific issues faced by language educators of similar languages. Some colleges or departments may not be able to afford expensive registration fees. Language professional organizations or national language resource centers should consider providing more resources free of charge and easily accessible to language educators who lack resources and time. In addition, developing language educators' knowledge and skills alone does not necessarily lead to their decision to adopt online language teaching. There needs to be appropriate university-wide infrastructure in existence, including sustainable training and technology support for online teaching, course release or other incentives for developing online courses, and consistent training for students. As participating in training is time-consuming, language teachers should be compensated for their time spent at workshops and webinars.

The findings of this study contribute to the growing research on world language educators' experience throughout the COVID-19 pandemic. Its unique focus on language educators' knowledge and attitudinal changes toward online language teaching will deepen the understanding of the impact of pandemic-era RLT. The findings about the influence from world language educators' remote teaching experience and training will help teacher educators and teacher PD professionals plan and implement more coherent and sustainable training activities and provide more targeted support that can tap into language teachers' increased knowledge and agency.

About the Authors

Li Jin is Professor in the Department of Modern Languages at DePaul University, Chicago, IL. Her research interests include the transdisciplinary approach to language teaching and learning, computer-assisted language learning, and Chinese as a second/foreign language pedagogy.

Yi Xu is Professor of Chinese Linguistics and Second Language Acquisition at the University of Pittsburgh, Pittsburgh, PA. She is interested in intersections of language acquisition theories and foreign language pedagogy, including orthographic learning, vocabulary acquisition, language processing, and technologies in language teaching.

Elizabeth Deifell is Senior Lecturer in the Department of Languages, Literatures and Cultures at Appalachian State University, Boone, NC. Her research interests include second language writing and vocabulary development.

References

Al-Bargi, A. (2021). ELT online teachers' professional development during the COVID-19 pandemic outbreak: Perceptions, implications, and adaptions. *Theory and Practice in Language Studies*, *11*(10), 1161–1170. https://doi.org/10.17507/tpls.1110.03

Arnold, N. (2008). Technology-mediated learning 10 years later: Emphasizing pedagogical or utilitarian applications? *Foreign Language Annals*, *40*, 161–181. https://doi.org/10.1111/j.1944-9720.2007.tb02859.x

Blake, R. (2008). New trends in using technology in the language curriculum. *Annual Review of Applied Linguistics*, *27*, 76–97. https://doi.org/10.1017/s0267190508070049

Blake, R., & Guillén, G. (2020). *Brave new digital classroom: Technology and foreign language learning* (3rd ed.). Georgetown University Press. https://doi.org/10.2307/j.ctv1nc6rkf

Borg, S. (2003). Teacher cognition in language teaching: A review of research on what language teachers think, know, believe, and do. *Language Teaching*, *36*(2), 81–109. https://doi.org/10.1017/s0261444803001903

Borg, S. (2015). *Teacher cognition and language education: Research and practice*. Bloomsbury. https://doi.org/10.5040/9781474219983.0008

Cheng, K. (2017). A survey of native language teachers' technological pedagogical and content knowledge (TPACK) in Taiwan. *Computer Assisted Language Learning, 30*(7), 692–708. https://doi.org/10.1080/09588221.2017.1349805

Cheung, A. (2021). Language teaching during a pandemic: A case study of Zoom use by a secondary ESL teacher in Hong Kong. *RELC Journal*, *54*(1), 55–70. https://doi.org/10.1177/0033688220981784

Gacs, A., Goertler, S., & Spasova, S. (2020). Planned online language education versus crisis-prompted online language teaching: Lessons for the future. *Foreign Language Annals, 53*, 380–392. https://doi.org/10.1111/flan.12460

Gao, Y., & Cui, Y. (2022). English as a foreign language teachers' pedagogical beliefs about teacher roles and their agentic actions amid and after COVID-19: A case study. *RELC Journal*, *0*(0). https://doi.org/10.1177/00336882221074110

Gao, L. X., & Zhang, L. J. (2020). Teacher learning in difficult times: Examining foreign language teachers' cognitions about online teaching to tide over COVID-19. *Frontiers in Psychology*, *11*. http://dx.doi.org/10.3389/fpsyg.2020.549653

Goertler, S. (2019). Normalizing online learning: Adapting to a changing world of language teaching. In L. Ducate & N. Arnold (Eds.), *From theory and research to new directions in language teaching* (pp. 51–92). Equinox Publishing.

Goertler, S., & Gacs, A. (2018). Assessment in online German: Assessment methods and results. *Die Unterrichtspraxis / Teaching German*, *51*(2), 156–174. https://www.jstor.org/stable/90026423

Hampel, R., & Stickler, U. (Eds.). (2015). *Developing online language teaching: Research-based pedagogies and reflective practices.* Palgrave Macmillan. https://doi.org/10.1057/9781137412263

Hatch, J. A. (2002). *Doing qualitative research in education settings*. State University of New York Press.

Hiver, P., & Dörnyei, Z. (2017). Language teacher immunity: A double-edged sword. *Applied Linguistics*, *38*(3), 405–423. https://doi.org/10.1093/applin/amv034

Hsu, L. (2016). Examining EFL teachers' technological pedagogical content knowledge and the adoption of mobile-assisted language learning: A partial least square approach. *Computer Assisted Language Learning*, *29*(1), 287–297. https://doi.org/10.1080/09588221.2016.1278024

Hubbard, P. (2019). Five keys from the past to the future of CALL. *International Journal of Computer-Assisted Language Learning and Teaching*, *9*(13), 1–13. https://doi.org/10.4018/IJCALLT.2019070101

IBM Corp. (2020). *IBM SPSS Statistics for Windows, Version 27.0.* Armonk, NY: IBM Corp. [Computer software]

Ivankova, N. V., Creswell, J. W., & Stick, S. L. (2006). Using mixed-methods sequential explanatory design: From theory to practice. *Field Methods*, *18*(1), 3–20. https://doi.org/10.1177/1525822x05282260

Jin, L., Deifell, E., & Angus, K. (2022). Emergency remote language teaching and learning in disruptive times. *CALICO Journal*, *39*(1), i–x. https://doi.org/10.1558/cj.20858

Jin, L., Xu, Y., Deifell, E., & Angus, K. (2021). Emergency remote language teaching and U.S.-based college-level world language educators' intentions to adopt online teaching in postpandemic times. *Modern Language Journal, 105*(2), 412–434. https://doi.org/10.1111/modl.12712

Kessler, G. (2018). Technology and the future of language teaching. *Foreign Language Annals, 51*(1), 205–218. https://doi.org/10.1111/flan.12318

Klimanova, L., Merrill, J., & Spasova, S. D. (2021). Introduction to the special issue: Emergency remote teaching, online instruction, and the community: Lessons from the COVID-19 crisis in language Education. *Russian Language Journal*, *71*(2), 1–22. https://doi.org/10.26067/FRVK-HA63

Knight, S. W. P. (2020). Establishing professional online communities for world language educators. *Foreign Language Annals*, *53*, 298–305. https://doi.org/10.1111/flan.12458

Lederman, D. (2022). HyFlex learning: Pros, cons, and the future. *Insider HigherEd*. https://www.insidehighered.com/quicktakes/2022/10/21/hyflex-learning-pros-cons-and-future

Lin, C., Huang, C., & Chen, C. (2014). Barriers to the adoption of ICT in teaching Chinese as a foreign language in US universities. *ReCALL*, *26*, 100–116. http://dx.doi.org/10.1017/s0958344013000268

MacIntyre, P. D., Gregersen, T., & Mercer, S. (2020). Language teachers' coping strategies during the COVID-19 conversion to online teaching: Correlations with stress, wellbeing and negative emotions. *System*, *94*, 102352. https://doi.org/10.1016/j.system.2020.102352

MacIntyre, P., Mercer, S., Gregersen, T., & Hay, A. (2022). The role of hope in language teachers' changing stress, coping, and well-being. *System*, *109*, 102882. https://doi.org/10.1016/j.system.2022.102881

Means, B., Toyama, Y., Murphy, R., Bakia, M., & Jones, K. (2009). *Evaluation of evidence-based practices in online learning: A meta-analysis and review of online learning studies.* US Department of Education, Office of Planning, Evaluation, and Policy Development, Policy and Program Studies Services. https://www2.ed.gov/rschstat/eval/tech/evidence-based-practices/finalreport.pdf

Mei, B., Brown, G. T. L., & Teo, T. (2018). Toward an understanding of preservice English as a foreign language teachers' acceptance of computer-assisted language learning 2.0 in the People's Republic of China. *Journal of Educational Computing*, *56*(1), 74–104. https://doi.org/10.1177/0735633117700144

Mishra, P., & Koehler, M. J. (2006). Technological pedagogical content knowledge: A framework for teacher knowledge. *Teachers College Record*, *108*(6), 1017–1054. https://doi.org/10.1111/j.1467-9620.2006.00684.x

Moneypenny, D. B., & Aldrich, R. S. (2016). Online and face-to-face language learning: A comparative analysis of oral proficiency in introductory Spanish. *Journal of Educators Online*, *13*(2), 105–133. https://doi.org/10.9743/jeo.2016.2.2

Moser, K. M., Wei, T., & Brenner, D. (2021). Remote teaching during COVID-19: Implications from a national survey of language educators. *System*, *97*, 102431. https://doi.org/10.1016/j.system.2020.102431

Murphy–Judy, K., & Johnshoy, M. (2017). Who's teaching which languages online? *IALLT Journal of Language Learning Technologies*, *47*, 137–167. https://doi.org/10.17161/iallt.v47i1.8570

National Foreign Language Resource Center. (2021). *2021 Online language pedagogy series: "Supporting students in online language learning: Voices of experience"*. https://nflrc.hawaii.edu/events/view/2021-online-language-pedagogy-series-supporting-students-in-online-language-learning-voices-of-experience/

Paesani, K. (2020). Teacher professional development and online instruction: Cultivating coherence and sustainability. *Foreign Language Annals*, *53*, 292–297. https://doi.org/10.1111/flan.12468

Plonsky, L., & Ziegler, N. (2016). The CALL–SLA interface: Insights from a second-order synthesis. *Language Learning & Technology*, *20*, 17–37. https://www.lltjournal.org/item/10125-44459/

Shelley, M., Murphy, L., & White, C. J. (2013). Language teacher development in a narrative frame: The transition from classroom to distance and blended settings. *System*, *41*, 560–574. https://doi.org/10.1016/j.system.2013.06.002

Shulman, L. S. (1986). Those who understand: Knowledge growth in teaching. *Educational Researcher*, *15*(2), 4–14. https://doi.org/10.3102/0013189X015002004

Sun, W., & Zou, B. (2022). A study of preservice EFL teachers' acceptance of online teaching and the influencing factors. *Language Learning & Teaching*, *26*(2), 38–49. https://doi.org/10125/73476

Tarone, E. (2015). Online foreign language education: What are the proficiency outcomes? *Modern Language Journal*, *99*, 392–393. https://www.lltjournal.org/item/10125-73476/

Teo, T., Huang, F., & Hoi, C. J. W. (2017). Explicating the influences that explain intention to use technology among English teachers in China. *Interactive Learning Environments*, *26*, 460–475. https://doi.org/10.1080/10494820.2017.1341940

Tseng, J. J., Cheng, Y. S., & Lin, C. C. (2011). Unraveling in-service EFL teachers' technological pedagogical content knowledge. *The Journal of Asia TEFL*, *8*(2), 45–72.

Tseng, J. J., Chai, C. S., Tan, L., & Park, M. (2020). A critical review of research on technological pedagogical and content knowledge (TPACK) in language teaching. *Computer Assisted Language Learning*, *35*(4), 948–971. https://doi.org/10.1080/09588221.2020.1868531

Waldvogel, D. A., & Robayna, T. (2022). Teaching languages virtually during a global pandemic: Perspectives from post-secondary language educators. *Dimension*, 57–79.

Walter, D., & Schenker, T. (2022). Surviving or thriving? Experiences and job satisfaction of language instructors in the USA during the COVID-19 pandemic. *Journal of Language Teaching*, *2*(11), 1–14. https://doi.org/10.54475/jlt.2022.014

Williams, L., Abraham, L. B., & Bostelmann, E. D. (2014). A discourse-based approach to CALL training and professional development. *Foreign Language Annals*, *47*, 614–629. https://doi.org/10.1111/flan.12119

Winke, P., Goertler, S., & Amuzie, G. L. (2010). Commonly-taught and less-commonly-taught language learners: Are they equally prepared for CALL and online language learning? *Computer Assisted Language Learning*, *23*, 199–219. https://doi.org/10.1080/09588221.2010.486576

Xu, Y., Jin, L., Deifell, E., & Angus, K. (2022). Facilitating technology-based character learning in emergency remote teaching. *Foreign Language Annals*, *55*(1), 72–97. https://doi.org/10.1111/flan.12541

3 An Examination of Online isiZulu Language Learning During COVID-19: A South African Perspective

Roshni Gokool and Shamila Naidoo

Introduction

The COVID-19 pandemic sent online pedagogies into a spiral worldwide, to the extent that emergency remote teaching (ERT) is often described as "Panicgogy" (Dhawan, 2020). While remote teaching and learning, in the form of online, blended and distance modes, were already in existence, ERT saw the face-to-face (F2F) modality make a sudden changeover (not necessarily a gentle transition) to the online modality. Crawford et al. (2020) describe the ERT experience as "transitioning content to an online environment without much contemplation of online pedagogy" (p.10), or as Hodges et al. (2020, p. 9) explain, a "temporary shift of instructional delivery to an alternate delivery mode due to crisis circumstances."

The South African higher education experience of ERT is unique in that the transition to the entirely online modality during the COVID-19 pandemic was preceded by bouts of ERT from 2015 onwards due to multiple ongoing social crises. In 2012, striking mine workers were massacred at Marikana (Cini, 2019). This act of violence by monopoly capitalists triggered rising discontent among the student population at various higher education institutions (Cini, 2019). On March 9 2015, the movement that came to be known as #RhodesMustFall began at the University of Cape Town and marked the beginning of a nationwide campaign led by students, calling for the decolonization of higher education (Cini, 2019). In October 2015, the #FeesMustFall movement gained impetus, calling for free higher education in South Africa. From 2015 to 2019, massive student protests led to the regular halting of F2F lectures and increased use of the online modality (Cini, 2019; Pillay, 2016).

However, like other contexts, South African society is characterized by unequal access to technology, making using the online modality a controversial decision (Ortega, 2017). Online learning has become a politicized issue in a society where "technology is anything but neutral" (Czerniewicz et al., 2019, p. 20). Potgieter et al. (2019) and Nkoala (2022) discuss the challenges of the online modality specific to South Africa, highlighting the issue of access to technology and the consequences for indigenous languages, respectively. These socio-political debates over online teaching and learning were paused with the arrival of COVID-19 in 2020, when there was a complete shutdown of South African universities, a transition to fully online instruction, and a rollout of data and devices for educators and students.

This chapter presents the crises-prompted experience of the Basic isiZulu module at the Howard College campus of the University of KwaZulu-Natal (UKZN). Using learning analytics data, this chapter examines the evolution of the Basic isiZulu module from 2017–2022, and presents an empirical evaluation on student engagement with online formative assessments.

ERT, South Africa, and Student Engagement

In most countries, the COVID-19 pandemic led to higher education institutions transitioning to ERT. The global adoption of ERT brought new perspectives to online teaching and learning pedagogies and technology-mediated learning. In the following discussion, we focus on research reporting on the global ERT experience and specifically on the African continent. Thereafter, the discussion proceeds to student engagement.

Emergency Remote Teaching in Global Contexts

Early in the pandemic, Crawford et al. (2020) documented the COVID-19 responses from institutions in twenty countries; six countries are classified as developed economies and fourteen as developing economies. The former were largely consistent in their pandemic response, with five of the six countries closing their higher education institutions and transitioning to ERT. Institutions in countries with developing economies had varied responses. Five of the fourteen opted for a semester break and thereafter closed. In two of the countries, selected institutions of higher education closed, but not all. Regarding the transition to ERT, in ten countries, only some institutions transitioned; one country did not adopt online teaching and institutions in the remaining three countries migrated to online. Crawford et al. (2020)

contextualize the global ERT scenario, with future studies also acknowledging the dichotomy between advantaged and less advantaged institutions and holds implications for the online teaching and learning modality.

As the pandemic progressed, ERT gained momentum. Tao and Gao's (2022) special issue of the journal *System* explored the challenges language educators and learners encountered during ERT and their responses. The 26 articles broadly address issues related to language learner perceptions of the online mode, educator readiness, competence and challenges experienced in using the online modality.

Harsch et al. (2021) report from a language center in Bremen, Germany, which teaches over 200 language modules and caters for 14 languages. Their research compares the online interaction challenges experienced by teachers and students. Among the challenges identified were netiquette, workload issues, technical issues, suitability of materials and course structure. Based on the findings, the researchers highlight the need for professional development for teachers; and for students, the development of skills and strategies for self-regulation.

Stewart (2021) conducted a review of 38 empirical studies reporting on the ERT experience. Echoing the observation of Crawford et al. (2020), studies reported by Stewart (2021) acknowledged the existence of digital and socio-economic disparity across the globe. Nevertheless, common challenges were identified, namely, embracing the modality change, evaluation, workload and mental health.

Bond et al. (2021) conducted a systematic mapping review of 282 empirical studies. The top three foci in these studies are student perception of online learning, the impact of change of modality and teacher perception of online learning. Two critical observations emanated from the Bond et al. (2021) review. Firstly, learning behavior and student performance are under-reported. Secondly, there is a lack of research from the Global South and Oceania regions.

Studies on the African ERT Experience

Among the few studies reported on the African ERT experience is that of Paschal and Mkulu (2020). They report on the challenges faced by educators and students at five institutions on the African continent, observing that "the majority of students and lecturers noted that online education is not effective in African universities... because of the inadequate computers, ... poor network, inadequate skills...." (p.18).

Upor (2021) reports from a university in Tanzania. The challenges identified resonate with that of Paschal and Mkulu (2020), namely data, F2F support and poor network issues. Moreover, there was unpreparedness for the shift to technology-based learning, which impacted autonomous learning. An interesting finding in the Upor (2021) study was the low acceptance of educational broadcasting and greater reliance on mobile learning.

Landa et al. (2021) present a qualitative case study, reporting on the challenges and intervention strategies used by two historically disadvantaged universities in South Africa. Teacher readiness to transition to the online modality and a lack of resources, digital literacy, and unconducive home learning environments were identified as challenges to both lecturers and students. The COVID-19 (and ERT) mental health challenge, which other studies report on, is also given prominence in the Landa et al. (2021) case study: "Given the ordinarily high emotional distress among university students in South Africa in the absence of a pandemic, a significant rise in unwellness due to COVID-19 is highly likely" (p.179).

Gumede and Badriparsad (2022) also used the qualitative research design in their study of student responses to ERT at the University of Johannesburg, a comparatively advantaged institution in South Africa. They report that students at this institution had similar experiences to those at less advantaged institutions. Many participants in the Gumede and Badriparsad (2022) study reported not having the necessary resources for online learning. Although students noted that support from lecturers was good, the change in teaching modality was challenging, with the majority preferring a F2F modality.

Assessment, Engagement and Self-Directed Learning

Whether in a F2F, blended, or fully online modality, formative assessment is a critical cog in the learning process, impacting teaching, student motivation and promoting engagement (Spector et al., 2016). Online Formative Assessment (OFA) has resulted from a convergence of formative assessment and computer-assisted assessment (Sudakova et al., 2022). Pre-pandemic research espouses the benefits of engagement with OFAs. Vonderwell and Boboc (2013) provide techniques to develop OFAs. Gikandi et al. (2011) and Vassiliou et al. (2023) provide comprehensive accounts of trends in online formative assessment in language teaching and learning.

The following empirical studies provide positive feedback on engagement with OFAs. Baleni (2015) reports that engagement with OFAs enabled students to identify gaps in their subject knowledge and revisit those topics.

Joyce (2018), from a study conducted with L1 speakers of Japanese, reports a statistically significant relationship between engagement with OFAs and summative scores. This is attributed to, inter alia, the immediate feedback associated with OFAs, and the ability to retake OFAs, resulting in improved learning. The inclusion of audio and video activities also enhances language learning. The absence of these benefits resulted in the group that used a paper-based formative assessment not achieving comparable summative scores to their OFA counterparts. The Palmer and Devitt (2014) study was conducted over two consecutive years with medical students. In Year 1, engagement with OFAs was voluntary. In Year 2, there was a change in strategy to incentivize engagement and elements from summative assessments were incorporated into OFAs. The result was a significant difference in the improvement scores between students in the two years. Nagandla et al. (2018), on the other hand, found no significant difference in the summative scores of students who engaged with OFAs versus those who did not engage with OFAs. However, students identified OFAs as tools to promote self-directed learning (SDL).

Engagement with LMS content requires a high degree of self-regulation; as Viberg et al. (2020) observe, "the ability to self-regulate learning becomes even more important in emerging online settings" (p.524). Self-regulation co-exists with the concept of SDL. Foung et al. (2022) provide a comprehensive discussion of the theoretical aspects of SDL and student engagement. Their study compared a pre-pandemic and a pandemic group of students and their engagement with online material. Using learning analytics data, the researchers analyzed data logs to examine student engagement and SDL patterns, finding that the pandemic cohort embraced SDL better and regularly interacted with the online material and accessed the material earlier. The pre-pandemic cohort, however, engaged with online material close to an assessment.

While not a replication of the Foung et al. (2022) study, this study also investigates student engagement with content placed on an online LMS. Naidoo and Naidoo (2021), reporting on one semester of the module in 2020, concluded that there were low levels of engagement with online formative assessments; 19% of the cohort did not attempt online formative assessments, and only 6% engaged with all the online formative assessments. This study extends the analysis of engagement with OFAs from 2017–2022 (timelines are selected on the basis that, in 2017, audio lectures were introduced, creating a more standardized e-environment).

Bond et al. (2021) identified two gaps in ERT research. Firstly, learning behavior and student performance are under-reported. Secondly, there is a paucity of research originating from the Global South. This chapter, which reports from the African continent and examines student engagement with OFAs, reduces the gaps identified by Bond et al. (2021). Hence, this chapter makes a unique contribution to the knowledge of teaching languages during ERT.

Research Questions

> RQ1: Was there a significant difference in students' engagement with OFAs pre-pandemic (2017–2019) and intra-pandemic (2020–2022)?
> RQ2: Did the intra-pandemic period (2020–2022) record a significant improvement in students' engagement with OFAs?

Methodology

Research Context

IsiZulu is an official language in South Africa and is the home language of 62% of the population of KwaZulu-Natal province (StatsSA, 2018). IsiZulu is a compulsory module for first-language (L1) speakers of English or other African languages. This 13-week, 39-hour module introduces basic isiZulu grammar, reading, writing, translation, history and culture of the Zulu people. It is taught using a communicative method to equip students with skills to interact in the L2. To achieve the learning outcomes, students must demonstrate reading, writing, speaking and understanding abilities in isiZulu at a foundational level. The assessment method comprised both formative and summative assessments. A 40:60 ratio was used to determine the assessment mark – 40% was obtained from oral/online/written summative assessments and 60% from a pen-and-paper formal examination. Pre-pandemic F2F sessions occurred for 180 minutes per week. The learning management system (LMS) Moodle was launched at UKZN in 2014, rendering the teaching modality for 2015–2019 blended/hybrid, whereas 2020 was the year of ERT, and the fully online modality continued until 2022, returning to blended/hybrid in 2023. Intra-pandemic contact time was reduced to 90 minutes of weekly online synchronous sessions. Asynchronous online activities were allocated for the remaining 90 minutes. The ZOOM platform was used for synchronous lectures and oral presentations, and Moodle for asynchronous learning and summative assessments.

Research Design

In this quantitative study, learning analytics were used to identify student engagement with the module across time in two different crisis conditions: 1) Pre-pandemic (country-wide protest actions) (2017–2019) and 2) Intra-pandemic (2020–2022)

Data Collection and Analysis

Tempelaar (2020) describes learning analytics as "the digital footprints of the learning process" (p. 580), and that footprint, extracted from the activity completion report from Moodle log files of 12 semesters, provided quantitative data to critique engagement with OFAs. The sample consists of five formative quiz activities. A one-way analysis of variance (ANOVA) was conducted to compare students' engagement with OFAs in the six-year period.

Results/Findings

The percentage of students who engaged with OFAs in semesters 1 and 2, between 2017–2022, are shown in Table 1.

Table 1 Percentage of Student Engagement with OFAs in Semesters 1 and 2

Semester	OFA1	OFA2	OFA3	OFA4	OFA5	Mean
2017 (2)	62	34	29	62	48	47
2018 (1)	36	60	57	47	60	52
2018 (2)	71	59	36	65	55	57.2
2019 (1)	65	48	37	57	51	51.6
2019 (2)	65	59	43	48	37	50.4
2020 (1)	56	47	37	58	35	46.4
2020 (2)	64	55	48	50	24	48.2
2021 (1)	77	50	48	42	33	50.2
2021 (2)	85	63	59	60	51	63.6
2022 (1)	81	43	38	40	34	47.2
2022 (2)	77	44	43	51	48	52.6

Table 2 Paired T-Test Inferential Statistics

	Pre	Intra
Mean	51.3333333	51.5
Variance	10.0666667	42.7
Observations	6	6
Pearson Correlation	0.7912361	
Hypothesized Mean Difference	0	
df	5	
t Stat	-0.0927677	
P(T<=t) one-tail	0.46484524	
t Critical one-tail	2.01504837	
P(T<=t) two-tail	0.92969047	
t Critical two-tail	2.57058184	

A one-way analysis of variance (ANOVA) was conducted to compare students' engagement (F 11,48) = 0.64, $p = 0.78$. $F = 0.64 < F_{crit} = 1.99$. With $p > 0.05$, the statistical analysis indicates that there is no significant difference in engagement across the six years.

To answer RQ1, a paired t-test was performed to compare the percentage of students who engaged with the OFAs pre- and intra-pandemic. The inferential statistics are shown in Table 2.

There was no significant difference in the scores for the pre-pandemic (M = 51.3, SD = 3.32) and intra-pandemic (M = 51.5, SD = 6.53) groups; t (5) = 2.57, $p = 0.92$. With $p > 0.05$, the results indicate that pre- and intra-pandemic, there is no significant difference in the percentage of students engaging with OFAs.

To answer RQ2, a visualization illustrated in Figure 1 was produced. Statistical analysis was not conducted to determine if engagement with OFAs improved during the pandemic years, as the learning analytics data does not include important factors like reasons for non-engagement per time period. This reduces the rigor of the analysis. Therefore, although rudimentary, a visualization provides descriptive statistics.

The visualization in Figure 1 illustrates that as the semesters progress, engagement with OFAs declines. This observation is applicable across the years.

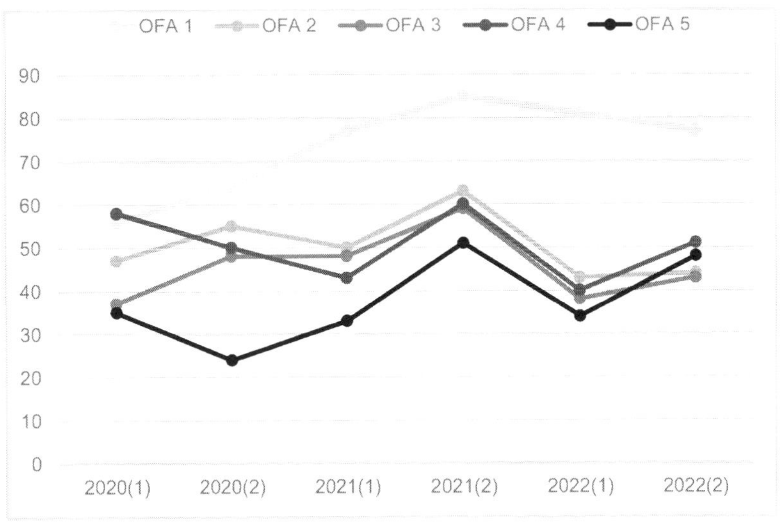

Figure 1 Engagement Trends

Discussion

When the blended format was introduced at the University of KwaZulu-Natal, pre-pandemic, the uptake for OFAs was suboptimal. However, during the pandemic, our assumption was that there would be greater engagement with OFAs as Basic IsiZulu was taught using the fully online modality. The latter presupposes greater SDL and, consequently, greater engagement. Unfortunately, "assumption is the mother of all mistakes." While research by Foung et al. (2022) reported that pandemic participants had better engagement practices than their pre-pandemic counterparts, that result was not replicated for Basic IsiZulu.

Research Question 1

In response to RQ1 – was there a significant difference in students' engagement with OFAs pre- and intra-pandemic – the finding is that there is no significant difference. The ANOVA and t-test results statistically verified this. Other empirical investigations reported on in the present study focus on the impact of engagement with OFAs. Joyce (2018), Nagandla et al. (2018) and Naidoo and Naidoo (2021) examine the impact of engagement with OFAs on summative performance. Foung et al. (2022) discuss the impact of self-directed learning. While Joyce (2018) and Foung et al. (2022) find positive consequences for engagement with OFAs, Nagandla et al. (2018) and Naidoo and Naidoo (2021) find no significant relationship. The present study differs from the aforementioned, reporting on a longitudinal engagement perspective with OFAs. Across the 12 semesters, 51.53% of students engaged with OFAs. Half the cohort did not engage with OFAs. An investigation by Naidoo and Naidoo (2021) identified low engagement levels in one semester of 2020. The present study, which tracks engagement levels from 2017–2022 across 12 semesters, finds unremitting low levels of engagement pre- and intra-pandemic.

Research Question 2

RQ2 investigated whether engagement with OFAs improved as the fully online modality progressed from 2020–2022. The visualization in Figure 1 illustrates engagement trends. OFA 1 had the highest percentage of student engagement; thereafter engagement declined. The highest average percentage of students who engaged in OFAs occurred in semester two of 2021, where 64% of the cohort engaged with OFAs. Here, the cohort was incentivized by being offered *mahhala* marks, which roughly translates to free marks. Students who completed the five selected activities were awarded ten marks towards their class mark.

The unsatisfactory results require reflection on how engagement with OFAs was dealt with and how it can be improved in the Basic IsiZulu module.

Contemplating the Statistics

Viberg et al. (2020) stressed the importance of self-regulation and engagement, particularly in “emerging online settings”. To aid self-regulation, the Basic IsiZulu module lecturers used the LMS online messaging to encourage students to engage with their online work to sustain their learning consistently. We remain unconvinced of the success of this tactic. However, grade incentivization appears to be a more successful tactic. The *mahhala* marks attempt was successful, as was the Palmer and Devitt (2014) inclusion of summative elements. In their study, participants were incentivized with the inclusion of summative elements in the formative assessments, suggesting that incentivization catalyzes engagement with OFAs. Thus, our study and previous research indicate that these options should be pursued.

Cognizant that engaging the students was challenging, the course coordinators sought to introduce e-tools. Kahoot, the game-based learning platform, was integrated to engage students and improve their vocabulary skills. Furthermore, H5P activities provided a platform for dictation and translation. YouTube videos were also included. Vassiliou et al. (2023, p.54) identify a variety of other technologies such as online peer feedback, e-journals, e-portfolios, e-artefacts that can be included in L2 formative assessment activities, most of which was not implemented in the Basic IsiZulu module. Given these findings, consideration must be given to including tools that stimulate engagement.

Gikandi et al. (2011) and Vonderwell and Boboc (2013) identify pedagogical strategies that support engagement and help to scaffold learning. An example thereof, in the isiZulu module was implemented for the weather theme. A YouTube video introduced the vocabulary, and a Kahoot quiz enabled revision of the vocabulary acquired from the YouTube video. Additionally, a listening comprehension activity required students to listen to the audio and drag and drop weather descriptions onto a map. Such a strategy, combined with incentivization, is likely to improve engagement with OFAs.

Contemplating the why question – why were engagement levels so low in the Basic isiZulu module – the researchers can only speculate. It is possible that the access to devices and data challenges that permeate higher education in South Africa contributed to low levels of engagement. It is also possible that students' attitudes to learning are governed by compensation and that compensation is marks contributing to a summative score. Poor pedagogical integration in the module might contribute to students' not realizing the value of formative engagement. Moreover, the e-tools may not be adequately enticing and engaging. Finally, South Africa has twelve official languages. With such linguistic diversity, we cannot ignore the possibility that many students may have no interest in learning a regional language. All these possibilities may be contributory factors to the low levels of engagement.

Conclusion

South Africa is a unique country. It transitioned peacefully, in 1994, to a democracy. It celebrated the linguistic diversity of the land and accorded official recognition to twelve languages, including sign language. However, socio-economic inequities persisted, and the effects thereof have been felt in the higher education sector resulting in the regular disruption of lectures from 2015.

This chapter chronicles student engagement with OFAs in the Basic Isi-Zulu module from 2017–2022. During these six years, student protest crises initiated the transition to intermittent online teaching and learning in 2017–2019, culminating entirely online during the COVID-19 pandemic. This created a unique higher education landscape that dabbled with the online modality before 2020 and continued with the fully online modality from 2020–2022. Consequently, the expectation is that students, being more familiar with the online modality, would record improving levels of engagement with OFAs. The findings in this study reveal that students' engagement with OFAs was consistent irrespective of a local or global crisis. Unfortunately, the level of engagement is low.

The results of this study have a few limitations. Firstly, the study focuses primarily on quantitative and statistical information. No pre- and intra-pandemic questionnaire was administered to students to probe the reasons for their engagement patterns with OFAs. Secondly, while the COVID-19 pandemic significantly contributed to the disruptions of online L2 isiZulu teaching and learning, other extenuating factors cannot be ignored. A series of unfortunate events have battered South Africa, mainly the KwaZulu-Natal province. These external factors, such as continuous power outages and the 2022 looting and flooding disaster, could have exacerbated the reduced student engagement with online activities. Thirdly, the lack of digital tools and the limited data provided by the University of KwaZulu-Natal to students can impact engagement.

Despite these limitations, the study has shown that lecturers actively responded to crises. Instructional design was adapted to suit the online modality. Various e-tools were incorporated into the course, learning was scaffolded, and OFAs were strategically situated, all done to support SDL. The critical discovery was that incentivization is a great motivator. As Basic isiZulu traverses into a blended modality post-pandemic, the module lecturers need to reflect on how the "construct" incentivization can be harnessed, not just for the sake of marks, but to achieve the aim of encouraging engagement and SDL.

Future research should focus on incorporating the learning analytics data with qualitative investigation into students' experiences of OFAs. In particular, the reasons for decreasing engagement as the semester progresses (and non-engagement) should be probed. This will have implications for instructional design and pedagogical practice.

About the Authors

Roshni Gokool is a lecturer in the Discipline of African Languages, College of Humanities at the University of KwaZulu Natal, South Africa. Her research interests are CALL, TBLT, and language for specific purposes, with particular interest in the teaching and learning of isiZulu in a health sciences context. Roshni has published several articles and a few book chapters. She is also the co-author for the prescribed manual *Asifunde isiZulu*.

Shamila Naidoo is a senior lecturer in the Discipline of African Languages, College of Humanities at the University of KwaZulu Natal, South Africa. Her research interests are in experimental Phonetics, Forensic Linguistics and CALL, with particular interest in Learning Analytics. Shamila has published several articles and a few book chapters.

References

Baleni, Z. G. (2015). Online formative assessment in higher education: Its pros and cons. *Electronic Journal of e-Learning*, *13*(4), 228–236. https://files.eric.ed.gov/fulltext/EJ1062122.pdf

Bond, M., Bedenlier, S., Marín, V. I., & Händel, M. (2021). Emergency remote teaching in higher education: Mapping the first global online semester. *International Journal of Educational Technology in Higher Education*, *18*(1), 1–24. https://doi.org/10.1186/s41239-021-00282-x

Cini, L. (2019). Disrupting the neoliberal university in South Africa: The #FeesMustFall movement in 2015. *Current Sociology*, *67*(7), 942–959. https://doi.org/10.1177/0011392119865766

Crawford, J., Butler-Henderson, K., Rudolph, J., Malkawi, B., Glowatz, M., Burton, R., & Lam, S. (2020). COVID-19: 20 countries' higher education intra-period digital pedagogy responses. *Journal of Applied Learning & Teaching*, *3*(1), 1–20. https://doi.org/10.37074/jalt.2020.3.1.7

Czerniewicz, L., Trotter, H., & Haupt, G. (2019). Online teaching in response to student protests and campus shutdowns: Academics' perspectives. *International Journal of Educational Technology in Higher Education*, *16*(1), 1–22. https://doi.org/10.1186/s41239-019-0170-1

Dhawan, S. (2020). Online learning: A panacea in the time of COVID-19 crisis. *Journal of Educational Technology Systems*, *49*(1), 5–22. https://doi.org/10.1177/0047239520934018

Foung, D., Chen, J., & Lin, L. (2022). When "blended" becomes "online": A data-driven study on the change of Self-Directed Engagement During COVID-19. *CALICO Journal*, *39*(1), 1–25. https://doi.org/10.1558/cj.19666

Gikandi, J. W., Morrow, D., & Davis, N. E. (2011). Online formative assessment in higher education: A review of the literature. *Computers & Education*, *57*(4), 2333–2351. https://doi.org/10.1016/j.compedu.2011.06.004

Gumede, L., & Badriparsad, N. (2022). Online teaching and learning through the students' eyes–Uncertainty through the COVID-19 lockdown: A qualitative case study in Gauteng province, South Africa. *Radiography*, *28*(1), 193–198. https://doi.org/10.1016/j.radi.2021.10.018

Harsch, C., Müller-Karabil, A., & Buchminskaia, E. (2021). Addressing the challenges of interaction in online language courses. *System*, 103, 102673. https://doi.org/10.1016/j.system.2021.102673

Hodges, C. B., Moore, S., Lockee, B. B., Trust, T., & Bond, M. A. (2020). The difference between emergency remote teaching and online learning. *EDUCAUSE Review*. https://er.educause.edu/articles/2020/3/the-difference-between-emergency-remote-teaching-and-online-learning

Joyce, P. (2018). The effectiveness of online and paper-based formative assessment in the learning of English as a second language. *PASAA: Journal of Language Teaching and Learning in Thailand*, *55*, 126–146. https://eric.ed.gov/?id=EJ1191739

Landa, N., Zhou, S., & Marongwe, N. (2021). Education in emergencies: Lessons from COVID-19 in South Africa. *International Review of Education*, *67*(1–2), 167–183. https://doi.org/10.1007/s11159-021-09903-z

Nagandla, K., Sulaiha, S., & Nalliah, S. (2018). Online formative assessments: Exploring their educational value. *Journal of Advances in Medical Education & Professionalism*, *6*(2), 51–57. https://pubmed.ncbi.nlm.nih.gov/29607332/

Naidoo, S., & Naidoo, K. (2021). Linking formative and summative performance in an online L2 module: Insights from learning analytics. In 2021 9th International Conference on Information and Education Technology (ICIET). Okayama, Japan, 227–231. https://doi.org/10.1109/ICIET51873.2021.9419626

Nkoala, S. (2022). Educators' experiences of using multilingual pedagogies during emergency remote teaching: A case study of South African universities. *International Journal of Multilingualism*, 1–14. https://doi.org/10.1080/14790718.2022.2074012

Ortega, L. (2017). New CALL-SLA research interfaces for the 21st century: Towards equitable multilingualism. *CALICO Journal*, *34*(3), 283–316. https://doi.org/10.1558/cj.33855

Palmer, E., & Devitt, P. (2014). The assessment of a structured online formative assessment program: A randomized controlled trial. *BMC Medical Education*, *14*, 1–10. https://doi.org/10.1186/1472-6920-14-8

Paschal, M. J., & Mkulu, D. G. (2020). Online classes during COVID-19 pandemic in higher learning institutions in Africa. *Global Research in Higher Education*, *3*(3). https://doi.org/10.22158/grhe.v3n3p1

Pillay, S. R. (2016). Silence is violence: (Critical) psychology in an era of Rhodes Must Fall and Fees Must Fall. *South African Journal of Psychology*, *46*(2), 155–159. https://doi.org/10.1177/0081246316636766

Potgieter, M., Pilcher, L. A., Tekane, R. R., Louw, I., & Fletcher, L. (2019). Lessons learnt from teaching and learning during disruptions. In M. Schultz, S. Schmid, & G. A. Lawrie (Eds.), *Research and Practice in Chemistry Education: Advances from the 25th IUPAC International Conference on Chemistry Education 2018* (pp. 89–107). Springer: Singapore. https://doi.org/10.1007/978-981-13-6998-8_6

Spector, J. M., Ifenthaler, D., Sampson, D., Yang, J. L., Mukama, E., Warusavitarana, A., Dona, K. L., Eichhorn, K., Fluck, A., Huang, R., Bridges, S., Lu, J., Ren, Y., Gui, X., Deneen, C. C., San Diego,J. & Gibson, D. C. (2016). Technology enhanced formative assessment for 21st century learning. *Educational Technology & Society*, *19*(3), 58–71. https://eric.ed.gov/?id=EJ1107417

StatsSA (Statistics South Africa). (2018). https://www.statssa.gov.za/?page_id=1021&id=ethekwini-municipality

Stewart, W. H. (2021). A global crash-course in teaching and learning online: A thematic review of empirical Emergency Remote Teaching (ERT) studies in higher education during Year 1 of COVID-19. *Open Praxis*, *13*(1), 89–102. https://doi.org/10.5944/openpraxis.13.1.1177

Sudakova, N. E., Savina, T. N., Masalimova, A. R., Mikhaylovsky, M. N., Karandeeva, L. G., & Zhdanov, S. P. (2022). Online formative assessment in higher education: Bibliometric analysis. *Education Sciences*, *12*(3), 209. http://dx.doi.org/10.3390/educsci12030209

Tao, J., & Gao, X. A. (2022). Teaching and learning languages online: Challenges and responses. *System*, *107*, 102819. https://doi.org/10.1016/j.system.2022.102819

Tempelaar, D. (2020). Supporting the less-adaptive student: The role of learning analytics, formative assessment and blended learning. *Assessment & Evaluation in Higher Education*, *45*(4), 579–593. https://doi.org/10.1080/02602938.2019.1677855

Upor, R. A. (2021). Rethinking teaching and learning language in the new era: Lessons from the Covid-19 pandemic in Tanzania. *LLT Journal: A Journal on Language and Language Teaching*, *24*(2), 574–596. https://doi.org/10.24071/llt.v24i2.3262

Vassiliou, S., Papadima-Sophocleous, S., & Giannikas, C. N. (2023). Technologies in second language formative assessment: A systematic review. *Language Teaching and Learning*, *13*(1), 50–63. https://doi.org/10.14705/rpnet.2022.60.9782383720133

Viberg, O., Khalil, M., & Baars, M. (2020). Self-regulated learning and learning analytics in online learning environments: A review of empirical research. In Proceedings of the Tenth International Conference on Learning Analytics & Knowledge (LAK '20). Association for Computing Machinery, New York, NY, USA, 524–533. https://doi.org/10.1145/3375462.3375483

Vonderwell, S. K., & Boboc, M. (2013). Promoting formative assessment in online teaching and learning. *TechTrends*, *57*, 22–27. https://doi.org/10.1007/s11528-013-0673-x

4 Developing and Implementing Virtual Reality Simulations for Medical Spanish as a Response to Emergency Teaching

Giovanni Zimotti and Alyssia Miller De Rutté

Introduction

Medical Spanish courses, also known as Spanish for the Health Professions, Spanish–English Medical Interpretation, etc., are growing in popularity, especially as, according to the 2020 U.S. Census, 19.1% of the U.S. population identifies as Hispanic or Latino (U.S. Census Bureau, n.d.). This number is expected to grow to 28% of the total U.S. population by 2060 (U.S. Census Bureau, 2018). In fact, over 41.7 million people speak Spanish at home in the U.S., and 39% of those who speak Spanish at home speak English less than very well (Dietrich & Hernandez, 2022).

While there is a large Hispanic population in the U.S., only 8.6% of healthcare practitioners and technical support are Hispanic or Latino (American Community Survey, 2018), and it is unknown how many healthcare practitioners speak Spanish. Healthcare professionals who do speak Spanish have found that they often lack appropriate medical Spanish language and cultural training (Lamas, 2015), and the complexities involved in patient-practitioner communication are compounded when there is no shared language (Ortega, 2018). Medical Spanish education lacks consensus and standardization (Morales et al., 2015) and, within medical interpretation, there is no federal requirement to be licensed or certified (Jacobs et al., 2018) even though federal mandates grant patients the right to receive medical care in the language of their choice (Affordable Care

Act, 2016; Exec. Order. No. 13166, 2000; Civil Rights Act of 1964). This information suggests a very clear need for multilingual healthcare practitioners who are trained to provide linguistically and culturally competent care in Spanish. It is equally necessary that future healthcare practitioners and interpreters be trained in medical Spanish and that they have the opportunity to interact with the Spanish-speaking population and be immersed in the language and culture.

Immersion has been referred to as language learning that is experienced in dual language or study abroad programs (Blyth, 2018) and has been shown to increase learners' listening, speaking, reading, and writing skills, vocabulary and grammar acquisition, and intercultural competence development (Goertler & Schenker, 2021; Schenker, 2018). In medical Spanish courses, immersion is a crucial training component that can improve language, cultural, and communicative outcomes with patients (Hardin, 2012; Reuland et al., 2012). Oftentimes, immersion opportunities for medical Spanish purposes are found in education abroad and experiential learning opportunities, where students volunteer or intern alongside medical professionals who work with Spanish-speaking patients, with some courses devoting high percentages of contact hours to these opportunities.

When the COVID-19 pandemic hit, these experiences were the first to be cut as the medical field was removing non-essential workers, and students did not have the same opportunity to train with medical professionals as they did prior to the pandemic. When forced to suddenly switch to online learning and teaching (i.e., Emergency Response Teaching and Learning – ERTL), instructors had to reevaluate their learning objectives and assignments and remove the course components that did not work in the new format (Gacs et al., 2020). Since students still needed these crucial opportunities of language exposure and immersion for their courses on medical Spanish, it was necessary to find a teaching and learning solution for these courses.

With the addition of emerging technology, immersion can now be done virtually through different means, such as videoconferencing, telecollaboration, open internet environments, global simulation, and augmented and virtual reality (Blyth, 2018). This chapter discusses how VR simulations were independently developed and implemented in two different medical Spanish courses as a solution during the COVID-19 pandemic to give students immersion practice when they were physically unable to enter medical facilities. This pedagogical change has remained in place even after the COVID-19 restrictions have been lifted.

Literature Review

Emergency Response Teaching and Learning in the Second Language Learning Context

ERTL describes the temporary and rapid shift in the modality of instruction that occurred in response to the COVID-19 pandemic when in-person, face-to-face classes shifted to online delivery (Hodges et al., 2020). While online language classes are common and can be beneficial, the sudden switch in the middle of a course yielded many challenges (Gacs et al., 2020), and educators worldwide were forced to adopt new digital tools, platforms, and techniques.

Research on ERTL in the second language (L2) learning contexts has found significant impact on emotions and emotion labor for both students and teachers (MacIntyre et al., 2020; Warner & Diao, 2022; Warner and Diao, Chapter 12, this volume; Wilson & Lengeling, 2021). Students reported experiencing both positive and negative emotions, including anxiety, motivation and resilience (Wilson & Lengeling, 2021), while teachers experienced high levels of stress and burnout (MacIntyre et al., 2020; Warner & Diao, 2022). In response, teachers used both approach and avoidance coping mechanisms in which there were correlations between positive psychological outcomes (e.g., wellbeing, health, happiness, resilience, growth during trauma) with approach coping, and negative outcomes (e.g., stress, anxiety, anger, sadness, loneliness) with avoidance coping (MacIntyre et al., 2020). The emotional labor required during the rapid switch to ERTL was often intense and mediated by the use of technology (Warner & Diao, 2022). Despite these challenges, teachers felt it was their job to foster a sense of connection and community, convey care and concern, and provide support to their students (Warner & Diao, 2022, Chapter 12, this volume).

Other studies found differences between Face-to-Face (F2F) and ERTL contexts (Czura & Baran-Łucarz, 2021; Katz, 2021; Moser et al., 2021). Students perceived online assessments more negatively and observed that student engagement, particularly participation, was lower in online classes (Czura & Baran-Łucarz, 2021). Teachers with no online teaching experience perceived lower outcomes due to the switch to ERTL, while teachers who had prior online teaching experience felt more confident about learning outcomes (Moser et al., 2021), and these perceptions can be complemented by actual proficiency outcomes (Gleason et al., in press; Gleason & Bartlett, Chapter 9, this volume). However, in terms of rapport-building, students and teachers have preferred the F2F modality (Katz, 2021; Jin et al., this volume).

ERTL has underscored the need for dedicated online teaching training (Fortova et al., 2021; Moser et al., 2021; Zainal & Zainuddin, 2021) especially since what is done in F2F contexts cannot always be directly translated to an online format, although technology can be leveraged in a way to facilitate that process (Fortova et al., 2021; Zainal & Zainuddin, 2021). Other factors also need to be considered in ERTL (and online teaching), such as access to internet, technology, and a private study space, and teacher support, as these can play a significant role in influencing student motivation and learning satisfaction (Echuari Galvan et al., 2021; Garcia Botero et al., 2021).

Virtual Reality and Language Learning

Although VR was in development and use in language learning contexts before COVID-19 (Dhimolea et al., 2022; Lin & Lan, 2015), several instructors and researchers implemented VR when the pandemic hit as an ERTL solution. Berns et al. (2020) developed a 360° language app for German students learning Spanish to explore Cádiz, Spain and practice their listening and reading skills; they found that participants perceived the VR experience to be helpful for learning vocabulary while fostering oral comprehension and pronunciation. Chao et al. (2021) created a VR-assisted Chinese writing course, which was found to foster autonomy and increase students' motivation and perception of competence in writing. Others, like Hein et al. (2021), developed and implemented social VR for learning and practicing English and found that there is potential for VR to positively influence the acquisition of inter- and transcultural competencies. Liu and Shirley (2021) conducted a VR redesign of a study abroad course and found that students engaged in active learning, and the redesign cultivated intercultural competence development.

VR may have been chosen as a tool in ERTL due to previous research on its immersive capabilities and its ability to provide an authentic, engaging, and safe environment to practice language (Berti, 2019; A. Cheng et al., 2017; Chien et al., 2020; Kaplan Rakowski & Gruber, 2021; York et al., 2021). High-immersion VR (HiVR) is "a computer-generated 360° virtual space that can be perceived as being spatially realistic, due to the high immersion afforded by a head-mounted device" (Kaplan-Rakowski & Gruber, 2019, p. 1). HiVR has been found to lead to a high degree of presence, which is the feeling of being physically present in the virtual environment even though it is simulated (Gruber & Kaplan-Rakowski, 2020; Zimotti, 2018). Studies on HiVR have reported increases in pronunciation, speaking, listening, and vocabulary learning and retention (Alfadil, 2020; Chen et al., 2021; Lee, 2019; Miller De Rutté, 2023; Tai et al., 2020; Xie, Chen et al., 2019; Xie, Ryder et al., 2019). Other studies have revealed that HiVR lowered language learners' levels of foreign language anxiety (Gruber & Kaplan-Rakowski, 2020, 2022; Liaw, 2019; Miller De Rutté, 2023; Thrasher, 2022; Xie, Ryder, et al., 2019; York et al., 2021) and influenced language learners' motivation (Chen & Hsu, 2020; Chien et al., 2020; Lan, 2020). It is important to note that none of the studies was using VR to fully replace a language course, but instead as a supplemental component. As mentioned by Jin et al. (Chapter 2, this volume), teachers do not want to see F2F instruction replaced by remote learning but rather integrate technology into F2F courses.

Research Question

The goal of the present study is to inform future use of VR technology in ERTL situations and beyond especially as there is a gap in the literature in using VR in combination with medical Spanish. This study investigates learners' perceptions regarding the use of an HiVR environment in their medical Spanish class. The VR experiences were developed at the beginning of the COVID-19 pandemic and were piloted the following semester. This study on students' perceptions was collected during Fall 2022 and Spring 2023 when students' access to clinic work was still restricted. The research question guiding this study is as follows: What were students' perceptions of their VR experience as implemented in their medical Spanish courses?

Methods

Study Design

This study followed a qualitative design that was guided by Constructivist Grounded Theory (Charmaz, 2014) and used open-ended survey questions to gauge students' perceptions of their VR experience. The utilization of qualitative research has gained prominence within the field of applied linguistics due to its capacity to capture the authentic perspectives of participants (Dewaele, 2019). By employing Constructivist Grounded Theory to analyze open-ended answers, researchers can gain insights into the process through which individuals and groups construct meaning and interpret their experiences within a specific context (Charmaz, 2014).

Participants

Participants included two cohorts of students (n=23) taking a Spanish for Healthcare course at Site 1 (a large western university) and one cohort of students (n=11) taking a Spanish–English medical interpreting course at Site 2 (a large mid-western university). Participants were recruited by the instructors of the course via email and completed the survey anonymously. The Spanish for Healthcare course was taught by one of the researchers of this chapter, while the interpreting course was taught by an experienced Spanish instructor. Thirty-four students from both sites agreed to participate in this study.

Participants' ages ranged from 18–30 years old, with the majority being within the age range of 18–21. Most of the participants did not belong to an underrepresented group while 32% indicated a minority group affiliation, with eight self-identifying as Hispanics/Latinos. Seven participants were first-generation students, and most participants were studying Spanish as a minor. Most participants were completing a major in a health-related field such as biology or neuroscience. One participant was studying Spanish as a major, and five participants were studying majors unrelated to health. With respect to their prior VR experience, three participants had used VR in an academic setting, while ten had used VR to play video games. Most participants had little to no experience using a VR headset.

Description of the Two VR Experiences

Experience 1: 3D Recreation of a Medical Office

The Spanish for Healthcare course was offered at Site 1 (Fall 2022 to Spring 2023). The objective of this course was to start training future healthcare practitioners to communicate directly to a Spanish-speaking patient without the use of an interpreter. A virtual world was created to simulate a medical clinic or doctor's office (Figure 1; see a detailed description of the design and task selection in Miller De Rutté, 2023). The virtual world consisted of a waiting room and an exam room. The waiting room had a list of tasks and instructions for students to complete. The exam room had a patient exam bed, a sink, cabinets, and medical equipment, such as a blood pressure cuff,

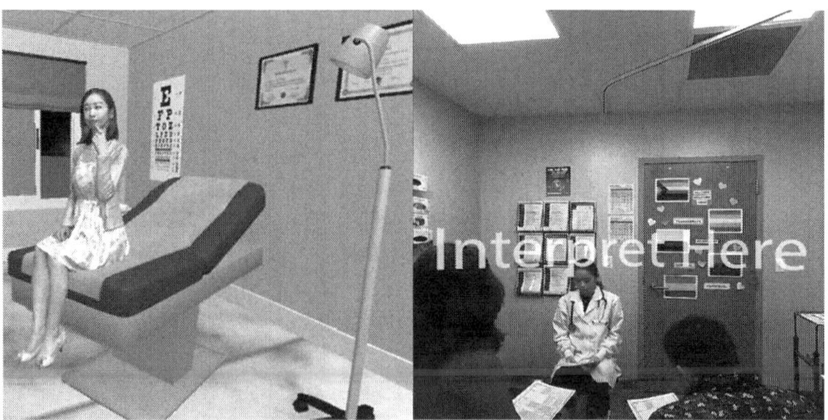

Figure 1 VR Experiences Side by Side

glucometer, pulse oximeter, thermometer, and height and weight scale. The purpose of this virtual creation was to simulate a modified medical interview in which participants gathered vital signs, which were visually displayed around the exam room, and asked their Spanish-speaking patient questions to elicit responses that participants could then synthesize into a diagnosis and culturally relevant treatment plan. Students used language (e.g., vocabulary, grammatical constructions, etc.) that they had learned in class, and patients answered questions using pre-recorded audios. Students practiced six VR scenarios throughout the semester before completing their final assessment of their Spanish medical interviewing skills using the same VR setup.

This experience was developed using Enduvo, which is a free software platform for educators. Enduvo provided a blank canvas for design, and the researcher designed and built the virtual simulations (Miller De Rutté, 2023). Since the platform was free, this experience was a low-cost solution, but it was time intensive, taking approximately 300 hours to develop 18 different scenarios. There were also technical limitations to the software itself. Enduvo does not have voice recognition capabilities meaning that patients could only answer questions with one pre-recorded response. The necessary hardware included a PC gaming laptop and the Oculus Quest 2 headset. Additionally, to run the Enduvo software with a headset, the headset needed to be connected to the computer through a Quest 2 link cable. The instructor provided two gaming laptops and two headsets, and students took turns using the equipment.

Experience 2: 360-degree Videos of a Medical Office

The Spanish–English Medical Interpretation course was offered at Site 2 (Spring 2023). The objective of this course was to start training future medical interpreters on the skills needed in medical interpretation. At Site 2, students used a series of prerecorded 360-degree videos (Figure 1) simulating a typical encounter between a patient and a medical provider communicating with the aid of an interpreter. Students used these videos to first develop interpreting skills in a simulated environment after having been introduced to the content in class. Each class started with group activities helping students develop a glossary for that week's video theme. For the second part of the class, students practiced interpreting at their own pace through immersion in the VR video. Additionally, similar videos were used at the end of the semester to assess the interpreting skills gained by the students. Students practiced interpreting individually using these videos every two weeks.

These 360-degree videos were recorded using a GoPro Max, a 360-degree camera, inside the offices of a public health clinic. Each video included three characters: a medical provider, a patient, and an interpreter. Health professionals and interpreters were used as actors to recreate common medical encounters. The actors loosely followed a prewritten script. This is a low-cost solution that can be accomplished with a small number of financial resources, as long as there are willing volunteers. Students watched the videos using an Oculus Quest 2 headset. Multiple students were able to practice interpreting at the same time and to pause or quickly rewind as needed. As with the VR experience from Site 1, there was no voice recognition in this experience. The videos used in this site are part of a project still in development by one of the authors (Zimotti & Jiménez, 2022).

Data Collection

Participants were asked to anonymously complete the same survey after a VR experience. The survey (https://sites.google.com/msu.edu/2024crisiscall/instruments-and-materials) collected both quantitative and qualitative data and asked questions about age, race/ethnicity, first generation status, previous VR experience, differences between in person clinical/interpreting experiences and VR ones, overall perceptions of using the VR as part of their course, benefits, and challenges to using the VR, and interest in taking more classes that used VR.

Data Analysis

Demographic questions were analyzed using descriptive statistics. Open-ended responses were imported into Consider.ly, an online tool for collaborative analysis of qualitative data. Both researchers coded responses independently using line-by-line coding. Then, the researchers met to review the codes, engaging in a discussion to address any discrepancies and reach an agreed upon consensus. The codes were then developed into categories and themes (Charmaz, 2014) and agreed upon by both of the researchers. This approach to qualitative data analysis prioritizes credibility, originality, resonance, and usefulness (Charmaz & Thornberg, 2021), and does not involve any quantification of codes or code frequencies. Instead, the themes encompass all individual codes and categories.

Findings and Discussion

This study was designed to understand students' perceptions of using VR in a medical Spanish course and not to compare the two VR experiences. Furthermore, the only difference between groups was found in challenges that arose due to the technology itself (which is discussed in a later section). Otherwise, there were no differences in responses between the two groups of participants. Therefore, the findings presented in this chapter represent the combined data collected from the two VR experiences.

Perceptions About Factors Affecting Language Learning

One major area that emerged from the data focused on participants' perceptions about factors related to language learning. Themes included enjoyment, alternative learning opportunities, immersion, opportunities for real world language usage, and reduced affective barriers (anxiety and pressure).

Enjoyment coupled with a different kind of learning opportunity was a theme throughout participants' responses. For example, one participant said, "I enjoyed [the VR] a lot. It was challenging but very fun at the same time. Really cool!" Another echoed these sentiments saying, "[The VR] was fun to do and it was nice to have a change… in the classroom;" while yet another indicated "I thought it was a cool part of the course. It was something interactive and different from what I had done in previous classes which I liked." Enjoyment and innovation with VR are areas that have been explored in other studies, which have found that VR significantly impacts both of these factors (Lan, 2020; Lee, 2019; York et al., 2021).

Participants also noted their enjoyment by using affective terms like "feel" alongside descriptors "immersive" and "immersed." One participant said, "I liked that it was immersive and felt more real than a simulation with classmates," while another participant said, "you feel more immersed in the environment compared to just watching a YouTube video." Other participants described the immersive experiences as "you feel more like you are in a healthcare setting and less like you are in a classroom" or "you feel like you are in a medical examination room" or there is "a 'feel' of being in a doctor's office." This feeling of being immersed in a healthcare setting confirms previous research that associated participating in HiVR with a high degree of presence (Gruber & Kaplan-Rakowski, 2020; Zimotti, 2018). The feeling of presence or the feeling of being in an environment without actually being there could have positive effects on language learning, especially as various studies have shown the benefits of immersion in various aspects of language learning (Goertler & Schenker, 2021; Schenker, 2018).

In conjunction with the theme of immersion, participants indicated that the VR experiences gave them real world practice. While the participants knew they were in a classroom learning environment, they nevertheless experienced real-world practice scenarios, connecting classroom skills to the medical context. One noted, "It was cool to feel like you are having a more real experience. It helps to get outside of a classroom mindset and more into a real-world situation." Another participant added that it was beneficial to have native Spanish speakers as part of the simulations, stating, "Overall I think [the VR] has helped create a more real-world feel to the conversation and allows us to hear responses from a fluent Spanish speaker rather than a classmate who is also learning as we go." This notion of real world practice is a feature of VR found in previous studies (Chien et al., 2020; Kaplan-Rakowski & Gruber, 2021; Miller De Rutté, 2023; York et al., 2021), and it could also be interpreted as enhanced role-play activities that are closer to a real-world experience than a commonly used conversation activity.

Additionally, participants noted that they had reduced anxiety and less pressure when using VR. One participant said, "I like [VR] because I don't feel as much pressure and can go through it as many times as I would like," and another participant said, "[VR] takes the anxiousness out of practicing a foreign language in front of other people." Previous research has also found that VR can help to lower foreign language anxiety and stress (Gruber & Kaplan-Rakowski, 2020, 2022; Liaw, 2019; Miller De Rutté, 2023; Thrasher, 2022; Xie, Ryder, et al., 2019; York et al., 2021), and the results from this study confirm that participants perceived that both of these areas were impacted.

Classroom vs. Real Life vs. VR

In their responses, participants compared traditional classrooms, VR experiences, and real-life interactions in a medical setting. These results reflect participants' responses to the question about comparing in-person interpretation or clinical work to the VR experience. Not all respondents had prior experience in the healthcare world, and so they were not able to provide a direct comparison. Some participants also compared the VR experience with a traditional classroom learning experience.

The participants described the VR experiences as similar to real life. For example, one respondent said that "the questions we ask during VR were somewhat comparable to the questions asked in the clinic," while another said that the experience "is actually very similar but a little easier than real life because you can replay the video." Others confirmed that the VR experiences felt like being in the real world saying "it was interesting and fun to feel like I was part of the real thing" and "it helps to get outside of a classroom mindset and more into a real world situation." However, a few noted that while VR is like real life, "it is not exactly the same."

The VR simulations were perceived as more structured and with fewer variables than found in a real healthcare encounter. While this could be considered a benefit for practice, it does not prepare students to deal with unforeseen circumstances. Additionally, some students felt the experience did not feel as real due to the limited conversational aspects (e.g., filler words and non-verbal cues). One participant noted that "real life medicine encounters are much more involved, and the medical professional is responsible for interacting with the patient much more than can be simulated using VR."

Despite these limitations, participants overwhelmingly saw the VR simulations as a tool to practice clinical interactions and were particularly useful for (1) learning to ask questions, (2) gathering important information from patients, (3) pausing and going back during a video to relisten to previous parts of the conversation, and (4) recording and replaying the video to review their performances.

In addition, these VR simulations proved to be valuable practice for participants who had never had the opportunity to work or volunteer in a healthcare setting. "The VR was a great experience because it showed us a glimpse of how medical interpreting really is." When comparing VR to a traditional classroom, participants found VR to be very realistic saying that "VR is the closest I can get to what a real life situation would look like" while staying in the physical classroom. It is important to note that, as of Spring 2023, many clinics were still not allowing students to volunteer, indicating that students could continue to benefit from this technology to prepare for a real-life encounter.

VR Use in Higher Education

The last survey question asked participants if they would be interested in taking future courses that incorporated VR. All participants, except one, supported the inclusion of VR in future courses, and they considered it an engaging, practical, and interactive learning experience.

Participants seemed excited by the possibility of taking more courses that integrated VR in their learning using words such as "most definitely" and "absolutely" to express their desire to keep learning in VR. Additionally, they described their current VR experience as a "fun way to practice" and "a great experience," which they found "engaging, rewarding, and useful!". Some expressed interest in continuing to use VR for learning outside the classroom saying, "I would honestly come in for fun if there were random practice conversations you could go through and just practice speaking." Previous research has found that "sitting down in one place (classroom) is confining for students and reflects the efficiency of an earlier era" (Alfadil, 2020, p. 9). VR gives students the freedom to explore and practice, and pairs learning with excitement and enthusiasm to help facilitate learning (Alfadil, 2020; Ebadi & Ebadijalal, 2022).

Participants believed that VR could be beneficial when used in classrooms that required students to practice in various scenarios which cannot be accessed due to different limitations. One participant said that VR is "great for courses where students cannot go into clinics or hospitals due to regulations." Similarly, most would like to see more VR use in classrooms that require students "to apply real life scenarios to the subject of study" indicating that nursing, biology, interpreting, and language courses would be the most fit areas for VR use.

Although participants expressed interest in having more courses using VR, they mentioned that their preference would be for VR to be an additional component of a traditional classroom, since this would be "better than just VR." Another participant mentioned that the combination of VR with traditional classes is important "to maximize the learning experience." While participants enjoyed VR and were "grateful to learn how to use this new technology," a few students would like to see technological improvements before fully committing to learning in VR. This notion of wanting VR to enhance the traditional classroom is important to note as VR cannot and should not replace human instruction and should instead be used as a tool to augment students' learning and class experiences.

Technology Challenges

While the previous sections highlighted the benefits and the affordances of using VR for certain aspects of language learning, this one presents the common challenges experienced by participants during their VR experiences. The two experiences analyzed in this chapter were designed with similar goals (e.g., to help the students practice medical interpreting or interviewing while being exposed to a medical setting), but as they were not created identically, they faced different challenges. Some of the participants at Site 1 experienced motion sickness, which was likely caused by the low frame rate and the fact that the 3D environment was not fully optimized. On the other hand, participants at Site 2 had difficulty hearing the audio "with multiple people in the room participating at the same time." A potential solution for this problem would be "a quieter or more private space" or to add a set of headphones to each VR headset to further immerse the students in the virtual environment. Other studies have also mentioned similar issues (Berti, 2019; A. Cheng et al., 2017), which will continue to improve as technology is enhanced.

There were other challenges that were common between sites and were related to technical difficulties, such as technology malfunctions and uncomfortable VR headsets. A few inexperienced participants also encountered usability issues like difficulty getting used to the controllers. Another challenge that emerged was the lack of interaction and "feeling awkward talking to an empty space." This last issue was caused by the limitations of both VR experiences to recreate real-time interactions and immediate feedback.

Pedagogical Implications

While the VR scenarios in this study were designed as a response to the COVID-19 pandemic, the use of VR as a teaching tool for medical Spanish has potential implications for the future. As Liu and Shirley (2021) discussed, VR offers a unique, immersive experience, making it an effective platform for engagement in educational contexts. This resonates with our findings suggesting that the interactive nature of VR can help add enjoyment and engagement to the language learning experience.

VR provides learners with unique opportunities that cannot be found in traditional classroom environments. In VR, students can be virtually transported to different settings, where they can apply their language skills in real-world scenarios, a potential noted also by Kaplan-Rakowski & Gruber (2019). However, it is important to note, as pointed out by Fowler (2015), that digital experiences should supplement rather than replace traditional classroom instruction, as also indicated by the results of this study. The immersive properties of VR can mimic the real-world, which has the potential to aid students in their linguistic and cultural competence development, but it does not fully replicate the complexity of real-world interactions as participants also noted in this study. Additionally, there is the potential of VR to lower affective barriers, such as anxiety (Thrasher, 2022), as VR acts as a safe environment for practice and can provide a space for students to make mistakes and learn from them.

While there are many perceived benefits of implementing VR, it is not without its challenges. Costs, particularly those associated with developing the software and obtaining the equipment, remain a concern. This is a common perception in technological adoption as indicated by Cheng and Annetta (2015). Other challenges include technological malfunctions and motion sickness. However, as technology develops, these concerns may be mitigated.

Conclusion

The purpose of this study was to present two VR experiences as a solution for the shift in teaching modality due to the COVID-19 pandemic. One of the VR experiences used a 3D recreation of a virtual clinic while the other used a 360-degree recording of a real clinic. Participants in this study perceived the VR simulations to be enjoyable and immersive while providing a new learning opportunity to practice real world language that lowered anxiety and pressure. Additionally, the participants saw that VR was a valuable tool to practice clinical interactions in a structured and safe environment. Results of this study provided evidence of the benefits of integrating VR simulations into language courses that require students to complete a certain amount of practical application and simulations. As participants expressed interest in this alternative approach to learning, educators should take this as a call to innovate and provide students with learning experiences that keep up with current technological innovations – innovations that, as with all those presented in this book, were the result of the COVID-19 pandemic abruptly disrupting the learning environment and most likely changing it forever. While some ERTL solutions were only temporary and were created as a patchwork to tackle the sudden changes in learning modalities, many have the potential to be used long term. In this case, the two VR simulations were designed as a response to ERTL, but they have since been implemented as regular classroom components, which is an example of how ERTL can inform non-emergency response teaching and learning.

While the lack of opportunities to practice in a healthcare setting during the COVID-19 pandemic was the impetus behind the development of these two VR experiences, the incorporation of immersive experiences should not be limited to the specific cases discussed in this chapter. Beyond the immediate scope of a pandemic, it is crucial to recognize the various circumstances in which using VR simulations can be beneficial for language learning. Certain financial limitations, emotional obstacles, or sociopolitical factors, such as areas made inaccessible due to safety concerns, are all compelling reasons to explore the adoption of this technology. VR experiences can provide a much-needed bridge to learning in these challenging contexts, thereby fortifying the case for their use across various crisis scenarios. Furthermore, implementation of VR experiences like the ones analyzed in this chapter can help train healthcare providers and medical interpreters on the linguistic and cultural competence needed to have successful interactions with Spanish-speaking patients, ergo addressing the needs of this growing population. VR is an innovative and transformative approach with proven potential to effectively respond to a wide range of situations, including crisis-prompted language learning and teaching, and is reshaping pedagogical possibilities.

This study is not without its limitations. First, there was no comparison of the two VR simulations, and while such a comparison was not the goal of this study, directly comparing the two experiences could provide additional information about the advantages and disadvantages of both experiences. This study also did not examine the impact that VR interventions had on students' grades, performance, or proficiency, and future research should address this limitation by analyzing the direct impact of practicing in VR, versus practicing in a classroom or in a real clinic.

About the Authors

Giovanni Zimotti, PhD, is the Director of Spanish Language Instruction at the University of Iowa. He is a champion of Open Educational Resources (OER), authoring three textbooks for Spanish learners. His research focuses on second language acquisition with a focus on technology such as Virtual Reality and Artificial Intelligence. His dedication to accessible education earned him awards such as the 2022 Educator Award for Open Education Excellence.

Alyssia Miller De Rutté, PhD, is an Assistant Professor of Spanish for Specific Purposes at Colorado State University (CSU). She is also the Director of Languages for Specific Purposes and the Graduate Teaching Coordinator at CSU and is the Vice President of the National Association of Medical Spanish. Additionally, Miller De Rutté is affiliate faculty at the University of Colorado School of Medicine's Fort Collins branch, where she is the Course Director of medical Spanish. Her research interests center on medical Spanish, technology for language learning, and the intersection of applied linguistics, culture, and health.

References

Affordable Care Act. (2016). *Federal Register*, *81*(96). Retrieved March 14, 2023, from https://www.govinfo.gov/app/details/FR-2016-05-18/2016-11458

Alfadil, M. (2020). Effectiveness of virtual reality game in foreign language vocabulary acquisition. *Computers & Education*, 153, 103893. https://doi.org/10.1016/j.compedu.2020.103893

American Community Survey. (2018). Detailed Occupations by Race and Hispanic Origin: 2018 ACS. Retrieved March 13, 2023, from https://www.census.gov/data/tables/2018/demo/industry-occupation/acs-2018.html

Berns, A., Reyes-Sanchez, S., & Ruiz-Rube, I. (2020). Virtual reality authoring tools for teachers to create novel and immersive learning scenarios. *TEEM'20: Eighth International Conference on Technological Ecosystems for Enhancing Multiculturality*, 896–900. https://doi.org/10.1145/3434780.3436668

Berti, M. (2019). Italian open education: virtual reality immersions for the language classroom. *New case studies of openness in and beyond the language classroom*, 37–47.

Blyth, C. (2018). Immersive technologies and language learning. *Foreign Language Annals*, *51*, 225–232. https://doi.org/https://onlinelibrary.wiley.com/doi/pdf/10.1111/flan.12327

Chao, G. C., Jong, M. S., & Luk, E. T. (2021). Work-in-Progress – Motivation in virtual reality Chinese language learning in the content of COVID-19. *2021 7th International Conference of the Immersive Learning Research Network (iLRN)*, Eureka, CA, USA, 2021 (pp. 1–3). http://doi.org/10.23919/iLRN52045.2021.9459245

Charmaz, K. (2014). *Constructing grounded theory*. Sage.

Charmaz, K., & Thornberg, R. (2021). The pursuit of quality in grounded theory. *Qualitative Research in Psychology*, *18*(3), 305–327. https://doi.org/10.1080/14780887.2020.1780357

Chen, Y. & Hsu, C. (2020). Self-regulated mobile game-based English learning in a virtual reality environment. *Computers and Education*, *154,* 1–26. https://doi.org/10.1016/j.compedu.2020.103910

Chen, C. H., Hung, H. T., & Yeh, H. C. (2021). Virtual reality in problem-based learning Contexts: Effects on the problem-solving performance, vocabulary acquisition and motivation of English language learners. *Journal of Computer Assisted Learning*, *37*(3), 851–860. https://doi.org/10.1111/jcal.12528

Cheng, L., & Annetta, L. (2015). Students' learning outcomes and learning experiences through playing a Serious Educational Game. *Journal of Biological Education*, *49*(4), 404–414. https://doi.org/10.1080/00219266.2012.688848

Cheng, A., Yang, L., & Andersen, E. (2017). Teaching language and culture with a virtual reality game. In *Proceedings of the 2017 CHI Conference on Human Factors in Computing Systems* (pp. 541–549). https://doi.org/10.1145/3025453.3025857

Chien, S., Hwang, G., & Jong, M. (2020). Effects of peer assessment within the context of spherical video-based virtual reality on EFL students' English-speaking performance and learning perceptions. *Computers and Education*, *146*, 1–20. https://doi.org/10.1016/j.compedu.2019.103751

Civil Rights Act of 1964 § 7, 42 U.S.C. § 2000e et seq (1964). https://www.justice.gov/crt/fcs/TitleVI-Overview

Czura, A., & Baran-Łucarz, M. (2021). "A stressful unknown" or "an oasis?": Undergraduate students' perceptions of assessment in an in-class and online English phonetics course. *Ikala, Revista de Lenguaje y Cultura*, *26*(3), 623–641. http://dx.doi.org/10.17533/udea.ikala.v26n3a09

Dewaele, J. (2019). The Vital Need for Ontological, Epistemological and Methodological Diversity in Applied Linguistics. In C. Wright, L. Harvey, & J. Simpson (Eds.), *Voices and Practices in Applied Linguistics: Diversifying a Discipline* (pp. 71–88). White Rose University Press. https://doi.org/10.22599/BAAL1.e

Dhimolea, T. K., Kaplan-Rakowski, R., & Lin, L. (2022). A Systematic Review of Research on High-Immersion Virtual Reality for Language Learning. *TechTrends*, *66*(5), 810–824. https://doi.org/10.1007/s11528-022-00717-w

Dietrich, S., & Hernandez, E. (2022). "Nearly 68 Million People Spoke a Language Other Than English at Home in 2019." Retrieved from https://www.census.gov/library/stories/2022/12/languages-we-speak-in-united-states.html

Ebadi, S., & Ebadijalal, M. (2022). The effect of Google Expeditions virtual reality on EFL learners' willingness to communicate and oral proficiency. *Computer Assisted Language Learning*, *35*(8), 1975–2000. https://doi.org/10.1080/09588221.2020.1854311

Echuari Galvan, B., Garcia Hernandez, S., & Fernandez-Gil, M. (2021). Enseñanza virtual de lengua inglesa durante el confinamiento domiciliario: Percepciones y reacciones del alumnado en una universidad española. *Ikala, Revista de Lenguaje y Cultura*, *26*(3), 603–621. http://dx.doi.org/10.17533/udea.ikala.v26n3a08

Exec. Order No. 13166, 3 C.F.R. (2000). https://www.justice.gov/crt/executive-order-13166

Fortova, N., Sedlackova, J., & Tuma, F. (2021). "And my screen wouldn't share…": EFL student-teachers' perceptions of ICT in online teaching practice and online teaching. *Ikala, Revista de Lenguaje y Cultura*, *26*(3), 513–529. http://www.scielo.org.co/pdf/ikala/v26n3/0123-3432-ikala-26-03-513.pdf

Fowler, C. (2015). Virtual reality and learning: Where is the pedagogy? *British Journal of Educational Technology*, *46*(2), 412–422. https://doi.org/10.1111/bjet.12135

Gacs, A., Goertler, S., & Spasova, S. (2020). Planned online language education versus crisis-prompted online language teaching: Lessons for the future. *Foreign Language Annals*, *53*(2), 380–392. https://doi.org/10.1111/flan.12460

Garcia Botero, J., Garcia Botero, G., & Botero Restrepo, M. A. (2021). Aspectos psicosociales y condiciones educativas de docentes de lengua en formación durante el confinamiento por la pandemia de Covid-19. *Ikala, Revista de Lenguaje y Cultura*, *26*(3), 553–569. http://dx.doi.org/10.17533/udea.ikala.v26n3a05

Gleason et al. (in press).

Goertler, S., & Schenker, T. (2021). *From study abroad to education abroad: Language proficiency, intercultural competence, and diversity.* Routledge. https://doi.org/10.4324/9780429290893

Gruber, A., & Kaplan-Rakowski, R. (2020). User experience of public speaking practice in virtual reality. In *Cognitive and affective perspectives on immersive technology in education* (pp. 235–249). IGI Global. https://doi.org/10.4018/978-1-7998-3250-8.ch012

Gruber, A., & Kaplan-Rakowski, R. (2022). The impact of high immersion virtual reality on foreign language anxiety. *SSRN*. https://ssrn.com/abstract=3882215

Hardin, K. (2012). Targeting oral and cultural proficiency for medical personnel: An examination of current medical Spanish textbooks. *Hispania*, *95*(4), 698–713. https://www.jstor.org/stable/41756421

Hein, R., Steinbock, J., Eisenmann, M., Latoschik, M. E., & Wienrich, C. (2021). Development of the InteractionSuitcase in virtual reality to support inter- and transcultural learning processes in English as Foreign Language education. In A. Kienle, A. Harrer, J.M. Haake, & A. Lingnau (Eds..), *Die 19. Fachtagung Bildungstechnologien (DELFI), Lecture Notes in Informatics (LNI), Gesellschaft für Informatik, Bonn 2021*(pp. 91–96). https://dl.gi.de/handle/20.500.12116/36994

Hodges, C., Moore, S., Lockee, B., Trust, T., & Bond, A. (2020). The difference between emergency remote teaching and online learning. [blog post] Educause Review. https://er.educause.edu/articles/2020/3/the-difference-between-emergency-remote-teaching-and-online-learning

Jacobs, B., Ryan, A., Henrichs, K., & Weiss, B. (2018). Medical interpreters in outpatient practice. *Annals of Family Medicine*, *16*(1), 70–76. https://www.annfammed.org/content/annalsfm/16/1/70.full.pdf

Kaplan-Rakowski, R., & Gruber, A. (2019). Low-immersion versus high-immersion virtual reality: Definitions, classification, and examples with a foreign language focus. In *Proceedings of the12th International Conference Innovation in Language Learning* (pp. 552–555). https://conference.pixel-online.net/files/ict4ll/ed0012/FP/6143-SLA4232-FP-ICT4LL12.pdf

Kaplan-Rakowski, R., & Gruber, A. (2021). One-on-one foreign language speaking practice in high-immersion virtual reality. In Y.J. Lan & S. Grant (Eds.), *Contextual Language Learning – Real Language Learning on the Continuum from Virtuality to Reality* (pp. 187–202). Springer.

Katz, S. (2021). Rapport in the foreign language classroom: From face-to-face to online in times of pandemic. *Ikala, Revista de Lenguaje y Cultura*, *26*(3), 485–511.

Lamas, D. J. (2015, November). The Danger of knowing 'Just enough' Spanish. *The New York Times*. https://well.blogs.nytimes.com/2015/11/12/the-danger-of-knowing-just-enough-spanish/

Lan, Y. (2020). Immersion into virtual reality for language learning. *Psychology of Learning and Motivation*, *72*, 1–26. https://doi.org/10.1016/bs.plm.2020.03.001

Lee, A. (2019). Using virtual reality to test academic listening proficiency. *Korean Journal of English Language and Linguistics*, *19*(4), 688–712. http://doi.org/10.15738/kjell.19.4.201912.6883

Liaw, M. (2019). EFL learners' intercultural communication in an open social virtual environment. *Educational Technology and Society*, *22*(2), 38–55. https://www.jstor.org/stable/26819616

Lin, T., & Lan, Y. (2015). Language Learning in Virtual Reality Environments: Past, Present, and Future. *Journal of Educational Technology & Society*, *18*(4), 486–497. https://www.jstor.org/stable/jeductechsoci.18.4.486

Liu, Y., & Shirley, T. (2021). Without crossing a border: Exploring the impact of shifting study abroad online on students' learning and intercultural competence development during the COVID-19 pandemic. *Online Learning*, *25*(1), 182–194. https://doi.org/10.24059/olj.v25i1.2471

MacIntyre, P., Gergersen, T., & Mercer, S. (2020). Language teachers' coping strategies during the Covid-19 conversion to online teaching: Correlations with stress, wellbeing and negative emotions. *System*, *94*, 1–13. https://doi.org/10.1016/j.system.2020.102352

Miller De Rutté (2023). The design and implementation of virtual reality simulations in Spanish for the Health Professions: What are learners' perceptions? Manuscript submitted for publication.

Morales, R., Rodriguez, L., Singh, A., Stratta, E., Mendoza, L., Valerio, M. A., & Vela, M. (2015). National survey of medical Spanish curriculum in US medical schools. *Journal of General Internal Medicine*, *30*, 1434–1439. https://doi.org/10.1007/s11606-015-3309-3

Moser, K., Wei, T., & Brenner, D. (2021). Remote teaching during COVID-19: Implications from a national survey of language educators. *System*, *97*, 1–15. https://doi.org/10.1016/j.system.2020.102431

Ortega, P. (2018). Spanish language concordance in U.S. medical care: A multifaceted challenge and call to action. *Academic Medicine*, *93*(9), 1276–1280. http://doi.org/10.1097/ACM.0000000000002307

Reuland, D., Slatt, S., Aleman, M., Fernandez, A., & DeWalt, D. (2012). Effect of Spanish language immersion rotations on medical student Spanish fluency. *Family Medicine*, *44*(2), 110–116. https://fammedarchives.blob.core.windows.net/imagesandpdfs/pdfs/FamilyMedicineVol44Issue2Reuland110.pdf

Schenker, T. (2018). Making short-term study abroad count: Effects on German language skills. *Foreign Language Annals*, *51*, 411–429. https://doi.org/10.1111/flan.12339

Tai, T., Chen, H., & Todd, G. (2020). The impact of a virtual reality app on adolescent EFL learners' vocabulary learning. *Computer Assisted Language Learning*, 1–26. https://doi.org/10.1080/09588221.2020.1752735

Thrasher, T. (2022). The impact of virtual reality on L2 French learners' language anxiety and oral comprehensibility: An exploratory study. *CALICO Journal*, *39*(2). https://doi.org/10.1558/cj.42198

U.S. Census Bureau. (n.d.). *Quick Facts: United States.* Retrieved March 13, 2023, from https://www.census.gov/quickfacts/fact/table/US/RHI725221#RHI725221

U.S. Census Bureau. (2018). *Hispanic Population to Reach 111 Million by 2060*. Retrieved March 13, 2023, from https://www.census.gov/library/visualizations/2018/comm/hispanic-projected-pop.html

Warner, C., & Diao, W. (2022). Caring is pedagogy: Foreign language teachers' emotion labor in crisis. *Linguistics and Education*, *71*, 1–12. https://doi.org/10.1016/j.linged.2022.101100

Wilson, A., & Lengeling, M. (2021). Language learning in the time of Covid-19: ELT students' narrated experiences in guided reflective journals. *Ikala, Revista de Lenguaje y Cultura*, *26*(3), 571–585. https://doi.org/10.17533/udea.ikala.v26n3a06

Xie, Y., Chen, Y., & Ryder, L. H. (2019). Effects of using mobile-based virtual reality on Chinese L2 students' oral proficiency. *Computer Assisted Language Learning*, 1–21. https://doi.org/10.1080/09588221.2019.1604551

Xie, Y., Ryder, L., & Chen, Y. (2019). Using interactive virtual reality tools in an advanced Chinese language class: A case study. *Tech Trends*, *63*(3), 251–259. https://doi.org/10.1007/s11528-019-00389-z

York, J., Shibata, K., Tokutake, H., & Nakayama, H. (2021). Effect of SCMC on foreign language anxiety and learning experience: A comparison of voice, video, and VR-based oral interaction. *ReCALL*, *33*(1), 49–70. http://doi.org/10.1017/S0958344020000154

Zainal, A., & Zainuddin, S. (2021). Malaysian English language teachers' agency in using digital technology during the pandemic: A narrative inquiry. *Ikala, Revista de Lenguaje y Cultura*, *26*(3), 587–602. https://doi.org/10.17533/udea.ikala.v26n3a07

Zimotti, G. (2018). *Virtual reality training: Reducing social distance abroad and facilitating Spanish second language acquisition. The University of Alabama.* https://www.proquest.com/docview/2189072178

Zimotti, G., & Jiménez, A. (2022). Virtual Reality Training for Language Medical Interpreting. *The FLTMAG*, (July). https://fltmag.com/virtual-reality-language-medical-interpreting/

PART TWO

PROBLEM SOLVING

5 The Future of Language Education in the Light of COVID: A European Survey Project on Lessons Learned and Ways Forward

Bernd Rüschoff[1]

Overview

The COVID-19 pandemic with its emergency lockdowns and alternating periods of emergency remote teaching (ERT), partial or full face-to-face (F2F) schooling with distance, blended, and hybrid language teaching has fundamentally impacted language education. "After the historic disruption of the COVID-19 pandemic, most schools are back open worldwide, but education is still in recovery assessing the damage done and lessons learned" (UNESCO, 2022, p.1). This chapter contributes to ongoing discussions about crisis-prompted problem-solving and lessons learned for language teaching and learning, as also reflected by the other contributions in this part of the publication. Concerning language education, the enforced switches to partial or complete modes of digital interaction resulted in significant challenges, considering its subject-inherent aims (i.e., communicative, interactional, and intercultural competence together with collaborative and social agency). Digital tools were key in this process, and already before the COVID-19 pandemic innovative uses of such tools had begun to lead to more flexibility in content and organization of learning. Thus, digital agency had already become recognized as an integral part of real-world communicative practice

[1] This text is based on the materials and reports collaboratively compiled by the team conducting the survey project discussed in this chapter, namely Peter Brown, Frank Heyworth, Richard Rossner, Bernd Rüschoff, Christine Lechner, and Pille Poiklik. All materials used with permission of the ECML and the project team.

that also needs to be addressed in the language classroom. The Common European Framework of Reference for Languages (CEFR) in its Companion Volume, launched in 2018 and published in print in 2020 (Council of Europe, 2020), has integrated descriptors identifying language competence levels that come to play in online interaction and transactions as well as covering mediation with and across media and digital tools. Yet, stakeholders and practitioners were concerned with the potential impact of social distancing and "remoteness" on language learners' linguistic and communicative mindsets in times when digitally enhanced learning became a necessity rather than an educationally planned option. This volume in general, and this part of the book in particular, investigates how the problems were solved and how we can move forward. As Hattie put it:

> Perhaps the greatest tragedy to come from COVID-related distance learning would be not learning from this experience to improve our teaching … . A robust discussion of the evidence of success during this pandemic school year could be a major boost to how we teach and learn (Hattie, 2021, p. 1).

The purpose of this chapter, however, is to report on a survey project conducted under the auspices of the Council of Europe's European Center for Modern Languages (ECML) and its Professional Network Forum (PNF). This Forum draws on the expertise of 16 international associations and institutions sharing common values and overlapping expertise in the field of language education and assessment.[2] The ECML is a Council of Europe institution with the mission "… to encourage excellence and innovation in language teaching and support its member states in the implementation of effective language education policies." Learning lessons from practice and experience to foster quality in language education is a key principle of the ECML, an institution situated at the interface between policy, research, teacher education, and practice. The survey project, conducted from 2020 to 2022, reflects the research-informed approach of the Center to identify key issues to provide relevant stimuli and resources for progress in language pedagogy and classroom practice.

---

[2] See: https://www.ecml.at/Aboutus/professionalnetworkforum/tabid/137/language/en-GB/Default.aspx

Literature Review: Learning from the Pandemic

The potential of digitally enhanced learning spaces and resources, including online remote and blended learning, has been the subject of reflection in language education ever since the advent of personal computers and the internet (cf. Davies et al., 2013). Yet, "[a]ffordances and constraints of ICT … gained greater significance due to the COVID-19 pandemic which forced schools, colleges, universities, and other educational institutions worldwide to stop face-to-face instructional practices and to continue their education in the form of remote teaching" (Akbana et al., 2021, p. 98). Thus, the main purpose of the survey was to explore how the COVID pandemic affected language education in Europe and to look at ways in which experiences may bring about beneficial changes in language education

Considering the relatively large number of works on the subject that became available as of 2020, such an initiative is in line with the fact that the language education community quickly recognized that the "involuntary field trial," as Elminger (2022, p. 18) put it, required responsible and robust analyses. Articles focusing on a review and analysis of publications on such initiatives identify between 45 publications (cf. Akbana et al., 2021) and 69 publications (cf. Erarslan, 2021) that appeared in 2020 until early 2021 as relevant. Ersalan points out in his analysis that most of the publications he discusses, 47 in total, focus on "the impact of Covid-19 on English language teaching and learning [in general]" and on the implementation and effectiveness of educational technologies, with only 22 addressing "perceptions and attitudes towards online language teaching and learning" on the part of teachers and learners, including "affective, cognitive, motivational, and … related aspects (Erarslan, 2021, p. 354). The ECML PNF project team provides a bibliography of publications since 2020 about language education during the pandemic, which is periodically updated and available online.[3] The potential of such an endeavor was supported by some of the literature as well as other studies that emerged at the time, containing a "breadth and depth of responses … and qualitative perspectives, [offering] a snapshot of the instances of, and attitudes to, hybrid learning among language teaching organizations in September–October 2020" (Kiddle et al., 2020, p. 26).

In general, the literature on COVID responses that emerged almost immediately, together with more detailed reflections and studies now available, confirm the observation that one of the things "that teachers do well [is to]

3 (https://www.ecml.at/Portals/1/6MTP/future-of-language-education/PNF%20bibliography_November%202022.pdf?ver=2022-11-08-092231-763)

respond imaginatively to a crisis," as noted by Stanley of the British Council in his foreword to their study on language teaching experiences during COVID-19, published in 2022. It shows that despite "the many challenges, … the pandemic has been an extraordinary time for learning and growth and … language teachers demonstrated remarkable determination, adaptability and resilience" (Mavridi, 2022, p. 9). Most literature is indicative of the equally rapid and reflected response of the research community concerned with education and language teaching, including the immediate framing and reflection of the characteristics of ERT (Hodges et al., 2020) or reflections on the differences between planned online language education as opposed to online language teaching prompted by the pandemic (Gacs et al., 2020). The role of technology in this context was an initial focus of attention. Some of the early texts pointed out that "the broader ranges of tools and platforms being incorporated and blending of asynchronous content with synchronous sessions" suggest the value of "[c]onsolidation and Future-proofing" and "considerations of what has worked well" leading to "new models combining online and face-to-face delivery, from blends to hybrids" (Kiddle et al., 2020, p. 2). Case studies on the use of particular tools for blended and remote learning in local contexts were put forward (cf. Acar & Kayaoglu, 2020), as were case studies discussing "students' perception of and attitudes to online foreign language learning in the COVID-19 pandemic" (Klimova, 2021, p. 1787). These informed the project as to its methodology, as collecting narratives and participant reflections afford valuable insights.

Several larger-scale studies researching how language education was affected by the pandemic and how teachers dealt with the challenges posed by ERT were initiated, such as a study by the Italian INDIRE project (e.g., Cinganotto et al., 2022), and the British Council (Mavridi, 2022). Cingatto and colleagues aimed to capture teachers' reactions during pandemic learning conditions, and Mavridi aimed "to inform language professionals' understandings … about the perceived impact of remote teaching on language teaching experiences during Covid-19" (Mavridi, 2022, p. 8). Mavridi concluded his study of the working conditions in 49 countries that the ERT may have a positive impact on CALL's prevalence. The pandemic might be an important catalyst to complete the evolution toward a normalized integration of digital tools into language education as put forth by Bax (2003). Bax (2003) offered a critical examination of the history of CALL and put forward the hypothesis that any medium or technology can only become a fully accepted and natural factor in language education once it is "so integrated into our lives that it becomes invisible – 'normalised'" (Bax, 2003, p. 25). Later he proclaimed that digital tools have the potential to foster "[p]articipation and interaction with others, which includes a social and even an emotional dimension, [considered to be] of value in education" (Bax, 2011, p. 10).

The pandemic has contributed to revised insights into the role of technology in language education. For example, a 2021 special issue of the quarterly journal *Íkala*, dedicated to the role of technology in language teaching due to the pandemic contains articles that "conclude that the participants normalize technology as a platform for teaching, and they use technology-specific language for teaching strategies and classroom events" (González-Lloret et al., 2021, p. 478). The issue presents articles with empirical studies and methodological papers "that explore how the authors coped with the teaching and learning situations that emerged from the covid-19 pandemic … and how their experiences inform their current and future practices" (González-Lloret et al., 2021, p. 478). Other publications also suggest that "… college-level … language educators were generally positive about adopting online language teaching in post pandemic times after the ERLT experience" (Jin et al., 2021, p. 412). Thus, there is "a clear need for models of best practice on the pedagogical side, and optimal solutions on the technological side, to be developed, tested and shared" (Kiddle et al., 2020, p. 27), leading us to pose the following questions in the effort to explore how the COVID pandemic affected language education in Europe. and identifying what lessons there might be for the future of language education in "normal" times: 1) What were the experiences and perceptions of language learners and language teachers during the exceptional events of the COVID-19 pandemic? 2) What suggestions for future practice were provided by learners and educators and what conclusions might be drawn for future policy and practice in language education? The distinct focus was on reflecting the sustainable impact on the future of language education in regular "post-pandemic" contexts.

Research Context, Participants, and Data Collection Methods

When considering the survey's research paradigm and design, it became clear that a simple quantitative collection of information would not provide the insights desired into the teaching and learning experiences, as such understandings cannot be adequately expressed through numbers alone. To gain a clearer and more profound understanding of how teachers and learners perceived and coped with the effects of the pandemic, a more qualitative paradigm suggested itself, which is often characterized in terms of its potential to elicit "… deeper insights … and exploring [participants'] behavior, perceptions, feelings, and understanding" (Rahman, 2016, p. 102). As far as research into using digital tools in language education is concerned, Stickler and Hampel (2015) also argue in favor of qualitative and mixed-method studies, as "… not only the richness of data gathered through qualitative and mixed studies but also the epistemological stance of hermeneutic 'understanding' of the learner and learning can add descriptive breadth and theoretical depth to research" (Stickler & Hampel, 2015, p. 380). The collection of participants' voices, particularly when involving learners, is often best done by providing space for expressing narratives. Concerning such approaches, Wilson & Lengeling in their paper discussing a case study of language learning in the time of COVID-19 convincingly argue the value of qualitative studies and narrative inquiry as a methodology that helps to understand how participants perceive and reflect on a particular experience in their language learning environment (Wilson & Lengeling, 2021, pp. 576–577). A major challenge in such endeavors is choosing suitable and appropriate options to gather open responses from participants. Another one is managing, analyzing, and interpreting the data collected to reach valid and representative conclusions.

Research Context and Participants

This survey project was conducted with language teachers and learners across Europe. The first phase included responses from 1,735 teachers from 32 European countries. Demographics showed that most were foreign language teachers in primary and secondary education, with some teaching in higher education and private institutions. Additional roles were identified as researchers, consultants, managers and owners of private language centers, testing experts, and policymakers. Over 82% had more than 10 years of professional experience, and only 3% had less than two years. In the second phase, learners were surveyed. The survey collected responses from some 1,500 secondary school students, i.e. age level 10+, from 10 European countries at CEFR levels B1 to B2+.

Instruments

The research period lasted from September 2020 until December 2022 and included two survey phases: initial teacher survey in early 2021 and the collection of learners' voices in the first half of 2022 through online as well as hybrid events. All activities conducted as part of the initiative were integral parts of the process of arriving at recommendations and guidelines

– summarized at the end of the chapter – to inform the ECML and stakeholders in language education. As a survey tool, the QuestionPro[4] survey software was used based on its track record as an easy-to-use tool with robust features to create and analyze surveys.

Teacher Survey

The teacher survey was launched in February 2021 and was open for a month. The invitation to participate in the survey was published by the ECML using its communication network while observing all data protection and data privacy regulations of the European Union (EU). All volunteering respondents were provided with access to the online survey, and all of these completed the survey in full. The basic research question of the teacher survey was to find out about the burning issues brought about by their COVID experiences as well as what pointers for the future teachers might have. Aspects to be looked at were the impact of remote or other forms of adapted (blended/hybrid) learning on classroom practice, the role of technology, the conditions teachers experienced concerning infrastructure, technical support, and teacher training, and the impact on learning outcome and assessment.[5]

The teachers' survey comprised a mixed-method design with a set of closed questions and several open-ended questions. The closed questions were intended to collect demographic data and statistical information on issues such as:

- Has remote learning affected teaching methods?
- Has there been adequate technical support?
- Have teachers received training for the new situation?
- What has been the effect of the pandemic on disadvantaged learners?
- What steps have been taken to cope with learner stress? And stress on teachers?

In addition, six open questions invited respondents to give their opinion on the lessons to be learned for language educators from the experience of teaching in the pandemic, positive and negative experiences to be reflected, positive aspects of such experience that might be integrated into future practice, and future challenges that need to be addressed. All responses to the

[4] https://www.questionpro.com/academic/

[5] In depth details available at https://www.ecml.at/ECML-Programme/Programme2020-2023/Thefutureoflanguageeducation/tabid/5491/language/en-GB/Default.aspx

open questions were compiled into a corpus. This body of text was analyzed and processed both by using corpus analyzers (see below) and by a critical reading of the complete discourses.

Learner Survey

The principal aim of the 2022 learner survey was to complement the teacher survey by allowing learners to contribute their views about their experiences of language learning during the pandemic and to collect their opinions about how these experiences might influence their future language learning. This focus was on:

- What helped or hindered learners' language learning?
- What worked well and should be maintained?
- What didn't work well and should be discarded in the view of the learners?
- What pointers for the future might learners have from their perspective?

In the survey of language learners, conducted in 2022 and focused on learners in the secondary school sector, an even more open approach to questioning was used. The central feature was the provision of a framework that allowed learners to openly write about their perceptions of and opinions on their experiences during the pandemic. Such an approach is also reflected in research designs used in some of the published case studies on learners' perceptions of online and remote learning during the pandemic. For example, Anwar and Wahid (2021) used a questionnaire consisting of open-ended and close-ended questions together with interviews in their study. Wilson and Lengeling (2021) invited 29 students to document and reflect on their language learning experiences through reflective journals. They also point out the importance and value "of creating activities that promote reflection" when attempting to appreciate the perceptions of learners in this context, continuing that the "use of narrative in a guided journal prompt gave students a space to reflect on their experiences during the … coronavirus pandemic" (Wilson & Lengeling, 2021, p. 582).

This led to the development of an action-research-informed package of classroom resources for volunteering teachers to use with their language classes. The design of a suitable framework for the learner survey was informed by the expertise of some team members and literature available on action research, a concept widely used in professional development of teachers. For example, Richardson's (2020) suggestions on how to support learners' collaborative creativity and critical thinking as well as on how to support teachers in the design and implementation of such activities provided some pointers. Further references on this are available on the website of the ECML documenting its project "Action research communities for language teachers"[6], including reports on "success stories" related to that project. The unit designed for the learner survey contained an adaptable task-based lesson plan, inviting learners to reflect, discuss and verbalize their experiences during the pandemic in an action-oriented learning mode. A detailed description and resources provided are available online.[7] The resources were designed to allow for the creation of a learning environment where the issues relating to language learning under COVID conditions could be debated by learners at class or group levels and compiled into a text. Members of the groups also had the option of submitting an additional second text to report additional alternative minority opinions they might have, and a large number of groups made use of this.

Once groups had discussed and prepared their written contributions, with a word limit of 1000, the learners uploaded these into our online survey. In addition to these texts, learners also completed another 11 questions to record further learner views. In this section, open-text questions with large word limits encouraged learners to write whatever they wanted concerning likes, dislikes, and what helped/did not help. The questions allowed for up to three entries, offering the learners the option to grade their suggestions. Responses were only required for the first level, but a large number of learners made use of all three levels. The outcomes of learners' deliberations in the open survey questionnaires and the narratives with group opinions and individual views were compiled into a second corpus. The corpus reflected the structure of the responses as entered into the survey by keeping answers to each question and the texts voicing opinions in separate strands, searchable in total or separately.

Think Tanks

In addition to the two surveys, a series of webinars, think tanks, and colloquia was organized. Participants were language professionals, members of

[6] http://www.actionresearch.ecml.at/

[7] Details of the activity are available online at https://www.ecml.at/Portals/1/6MTP/future-of-language-education/Lesson%20idea.pdf?ver=2022-10-07-121218-617

the PNF, selected volunteer respondents to the 2021 survey, and members of the ECML governing board. At these events, initial results from the surveys were presented with groups discussing what had been presented as well as contributing their perceptions. These activities were guided by the principle that the research team did not want to simply summarize the survey results, but rather to engage in an ongoing reflection process with the language education community on emerging results and conclusions as a form of member check.

Data Analysis

The closed questions in the teacher survey were processed using the range of statistical information provided by QuestionPro. The teacher and learner corpora from the open-ended items and the surveys were processed through corpus tools and also critical discourse reading of the open-text responses, supported through corpus tool analysis for confirmation or modification. As to suitable tools, e.g. for analyzing teachers' narratives to identify conveyed thoughts and feelings, a recent paper by Muchnik-Rozanov and Tsybulsky (2020) illustrates very practically how *AntConc* can be used effectively in the analysis of science teachers' narratives regarding their worldviews in the digital age and their views of technology. In addition to *AntConc*, a tool with a long tradition in data-driven language learning and discourse analysis (cf. Anthony, 2004, 2018), a second tool *Corpus Presenter* (cf. Hickey, 2003) was used. This tool in particular permitted an integrated in-depth analysis of the full corpus as well as focused searches of sub-corpora (strands) built from replies to separate questions. Both tools are freely available for download, and links are included in the references cited above. Replies to open questions, distinctly structured into addressing positive and negative perceptions and experiences, were kept in separate sub-files in the corpus. Thus, the team was able to weigh the representativeness of quotes selected from the respondents' comments when reflecting on the results. In addition to using frequency data to identify relevant aspects that concerned the teachers and the learners, the discussions at think-tank and webinar sessions were also used to further focus the "readings" and processing of the two corpora. Regularly, initial results were presented and discussed at these sessions (all documented online at the link provided above) to identify points of interest and "questions" to be considered when further processing survey responses.

Results

It goes beyond the scope of this chapter to report in detail all findings of the project. These are documented and available on the ECML website as well as in the report published by the ECML (cf. Rossner & Hayworth, 2023). This section will focus on an overview as well as on highlighting representative sample suggestions teachers and learners put forward with particular attention to issues related to technology. Not surprisingly, the data collected in the two surveys confirm that the pandemic has had an enormous impact on the organizational frameworks and contexts of language education, including the almost immediate implementation of a variety of digitally supported distance learning scenarios. Of focus first will be teacher perspectives followed by learner perspectives.

Teacher Perspectives

Infrastructure and Changes

The information collected in the closed questions showed that the majority of teachers felt their teaching had changed greatly. More than 90% referred in some way to the fact that teaching had been different due to the pandemic. About 27% said that planning had become more difficult, and 33.5% said the lessons have become more varied and more motivating, easier to plan, or at least been equally effective in developing learners' language competencies. As to infrastructures that were created, data show that in most contexts a system providing hybrid/blended learning arrangements alternating with fully remote distance learning scenarios was set up, depending on regulations established by the authorities. Regarding learning outcomes and learner achievements in hybrid and/or fully remote learning arrangements, a majority of teachers agreed or strongly agreed with the statement that they had been able to maintain the quality and variety of their students' learning experiences and achievements. Samples of practice described in open questions also suggest a very flexible use and integration of different learning spaces either in hybrid, blended, or full-distance ERT mode. Altogether, 38% of the teachers reported a switch to an alternating system, teaching both in fully remote and partially face-to-face modes. A further 30% switched to fully remote and hybrid distance learning arrangements, with a large majority working with their students in a synchronous mode.

Table 1 Impact on Future Teaching and Learning

Percentage	Theme
55	The replacement of tests and formal exams by continuous assessments has had a positive effect, especially in reducing stress on learners.
54	The challenge of teaching remotely has had a positive effect on lesson planning.
53	Learners have become more autonomous during the period of remote learning.
51	Hybrid models combining school learning and remote learning offer advantages which could be useful even after the pandemic.
46	The difficulties of including all learners in remote learning programs have increased awareness of problems of inclusion in face-to-face teaching.
44	Socially distanced classrooms pose problems for active methods which require reflection and creativity.
40	The experience of remote learning and teaching can cause us to reflect on the balance between face-to-face teaching and independent learning.
39	The technology used for remote learning can be used productively in "normal" schooling.

Impact on Skills and Approaches[8]

Teachers acknowledged that technology played a major role in – progressively – pedagogically empowering both teachers and learners. As one teacher put it: "*I think the fact that we were all forced to explore digital technologies in teaching has great potential to design useful asynchronous course activities between in-person classes and incorporate more useful digital tools into in-person sessions.*" Another teacher confirmed "*Greater flexibility in delivery methods; becoming familiar with online learning and the opportunities this creates for the future.*" A further statement to that effect addresses the potential of digital tools for language learning by proposing: "*Despite some difficulty in interacting with students ... the wide range of materials available has made teaching more varied and enticing.*" Caveats to be considered are also addressed, such as "*If we could train our students to take more responsibility for their language learning, hybrid teaching might prove to be more effective.*"

Amongst the key points that teachers see as having a significant (and potentially positive) impact on future teaching practices and learning arrangements, the following aspects were identified in Table 1 above.

The open questions in the survey elicited a total of 4,150 comments. A total of more than 1,200 teachers made relevant and valid contributions

[8] All quotes from teachers and learner responses are italicised

corroborating the above aspects concerned with lessons learned and/or challenges that need further reflection, potentially leading to improvements in language education. The general gist of these can be seen from the following two comments from different teachers: "*In future I would like to continue with the hybrid learning. I think that combining school learning and remote learning offer advantages which could be useful after the pandemic*" with the second one pointing out "*I really think that we cannot go back to traditional teaching after the end of pandemic. The future is only in front of us and it is based on blended learning.*"

The frequency list of the top 150 content words in the corpus identified variants of *student* and *learning* at the top of the list, closely followed by *teacher* and *teach/ing*. This, together with some of the other key terms (and variants of these) most frequently used either separately or in collocation and co-text in the open comments (e.g., *challenge/s*, *hybrid*, *remote*, *testing*, *technology*, *practice*, *method/s/ology*, *useful*, *experience*, *positive* etc.) is indicative of the fact that the teaching community contributing to the survey had extensively reflected their experiences from a classroom-practical perspective, also considering the impact of their practices imposed by the pandemic. Several statements also showed a tremendous amount of consideration for the concerns of their learners and the effects of changed learning arrangements and ERT on learners' achievements and well-being, as the following statement exemplifies:

> *Students have mentioned how much they prefer the flexibility of hybrid learning. It is easier to combine it with duties such as jobs, taking care of a family etc. Also, some students became a lot more active. However, others were overwhelmed by the choices they had to make – although we provided regular synchronous sessions in which teachers helped overcome tasks etc.*

The Impact on Future Flexibility of Integrated Learning Spaces

In the initial analysis of overall responses concerning this, 53% of respondents judged remote/hybrid learning as being less effective, 26% judged it as being more effective, and 22% thought it did not make a difference. Therefore, when the concordance lists of remote, distance, hybrid, and blended were considered further, finetuning the exact connotation of what teachers were referring to, it turned out that many were quite often commenting on some form of blended learning. As a result, a more differentiated perception of hybrid/blended learning emerged. Some responses pointed out the flexibility that is afforded when combining individual or group work online with face-to-face interaction. Many identified this as a welcome feature of post-pandemic language teaching, seeing this as allowing for the social contact missing in just remote teaching, while opening new options for learner collaboration as well as learner–teacher interaction, as exemplified here: "*Hybrid learning enables teachers to use innovative teaching methods, to engage students in the learning procedure more actively.*"

Other teachers, referring to hybrid in its defined understanding, found it a challenge to combine the two modes of teaching and thought that it was an additional workload without necessarily adding to efficiency. Some of the comments pointed out the potential benefits of blended learning, also highlighting the fact that the pandemic had positively impacted their awareness and understanding of such flexible learning arrangements, often perceived as offering "*advantages which could be useful after the pandemic.*"

Teachers also commented extensively on other aspects that need consideration when reflecting on the lessons that they have learned and that might need further deliberation when following up on the experiences during the pandemic. The range of topics and issues covered was broad and is documented in a report available online[9] that also contains a large number of representative teacher quotes on each of these. In general, the overall sentiment voiced by teachers was one that suggests that they have shown tremendous resilience and deeply reflected on the experience, with many identifying several points that lend themselves to contributing to sustainable changes in teaching and learning practice, as this comment shows:

> *Never back down. I have learned to adapt and have discovered a great number of resources for online teaching that I wouldn't have used if we hadn't been in lockdown. I have started to take part in social media groups of language teachers that give help, advice and exchange materials.*

Teachers also observed a positive impact of changed learning contexts on learner autonomy, when stating:

> *thanks to the remote learning students have started to be more independent in their learning process. ..., I believe that most of them have become more pragmatic and started to ask themselves what is necessary to learn in order to achieve a particular goal. They waste less time just because during remote learning there are less distractions.*

[9] https://www.ecml.at/Portals/1/documents/events/summary-of-ECML-PNF-survey-findings.pdf?ver=2021-04-27-190025-520

Comments such as this one as well as the following one showed that many believed the experience gained during the COVID emergency can and should be used to enrich language education in "normal" times. "*Language education has been more varied and required more creativity and those requirements can be maintained in face-to-face learning, as well.*" This is also a key sentiment voiced by numerous teachers, who – as quoted above – often refer to the fact that there should be no simple return to "*traditional teaching after the end of pandemic*", i.e. to a mere status-quo ante.

Overall, many teachers pointed out that "it is about time we joined the 21st century and adopted an approach more in keeping with the digital age and all the benefits and opportunities they afford going forward."

Learner Perceptions

Hybrid Learning Modes

Similar sentiments were also expressed by the learners in the 2022 survey, as exemplified by the following learner response: "We believe that in the future a mixture of learning both in class and remotely would be a perfect option. Students would … be provided with a bigger variety of tasks, which is perfect." In terms of key issues addressed, learner responses showed comments on their learning experiences (326) and perceptions of teaching (202) at the top of the list. These almost evenly balanced in terms of positive and negative responses. Responses addressing time, timetabling, and flexibility also ranked very high (181), and the majority of these mentioned positive aspects. Overall, a total of 384 learner responses specifically mentioned aspects that they had liked, enjoyed, and found helpful, with 249 identifying distinct activities and tasks. Responses also display a high level of reflection, as the number of very concrete references to specific language skills (141), to making use of digital resources, tools, and apps as well as to technology in general (205) show.

Learners also voiced many potentially useful reflections concerning online, hybrid/blended, and fully remote distance learning as well as motivational issues. It is interesting to note that the learners in their open comments on their experiences also frequently addressed issues concerned with how they perceived their role as learners and how the teachers acted. Based on the corpus structure, it was possible to distinguish clearly between responses to questions addressing negative and positive aspects and respective opinions. What came as a surprise was that the aspects that learners liked and enjoyed, based on the corpus data, outweighed the dislikes. Comments referring to helpful/not helpful aspects also provided more positive insights than

Table 2 Negative and Positive Aspects of Learning Experiences

Negatives	Positives
Motivation	Variety of online platforms, tools apps
Social Interaction & "Unliberty"	Individual attention
Social and practical experience	Quality & variety of tasks/activities
Assessment & Grades	Interactive & collaborative tasks
Spontaneous language production, lack of	Available Resources
Quality & variety of tasks/activities (lack of)	Personal growth
Quality of feedback	Technical skills
Boring	Information access
Stressful context	Visual aids
Distractions	Textbook & digital tools/activities combined

negatives. A very large number of responses addressed issues and sentiments concerned with remoteness and distance, as well as hybrid/blended learning as experienced by the learners. In summary, the negative and positive aspects of their learning experiences in remote and hybrid learning can be summarized as shown in Table 2.

Learners often commented on samples of successful practices in distance learning, referring to the potential of more flexible digitally enhanced modes of collaboration and interaction they would like to see more of in their regular learning, a point already exemplified by learner comments quoted above, but also underlined by the following comment: "*The fact that we had more time to organize our notes and that we could be more flexible in when we decided to learn. ... interactive exercises in the e-classrooms were great*". In principle, learners appear to have reflected on what they had experienced in terms of a challenge as well as something that led to new and useful skills and practices:

> *The way we learn is really important. We have learned to study in different environments. At first, when we unexpectedly had to start working online, both teachers and students encountered many problems. With time, everybody got used to this new way of teaching and learning and discovered its advantages.*

The Social Dimension of Language Learning in Digital Spaces

Amongst the top 50 most mentioned content words in the learners' comments were terms referring to the social context of learning or learning spaces, such as class, classroom, classmates, home (schooling), fellow students, etc. Learners often referred to the importance of interaction and social context, particularly in language learning. References to social contexts and interaction in hybrid and remote learning revealed a large number of learner responses that document a tremendous sense of feeling lonely and isolated in such learning arrangements. These were often directly related to comments on a perceived unimaginative use of digital tools in their learning. A phrase coined by a learner suggested that non-interactive and restricted "old school" online scenarios gave them a distinct "*feeling of unliberty* [sic]" and loneliness. Learners criticized the unimaginative use of break-out sessions in Zoom and similar platforms. They also often referred to useful exercises they worked with, and identified (collaborative) language games, a range of (language) learning specific apps, such as Kahoot etc., and access to online resources and video clips as examples, which they considered as key ingredients of more flexible teaching approaches. As one group of learners put it: "*We liked when teachers offered us active methods, like games, for learning new material, it made us feel more engaged in the lesson.*"

Educational Growth

Despite the challenges of coping with sudden isolation from classmates and other remote-schooling-related difficulties, a significant number of learner responses also identified some of the advantages of more flexible and digitally enhanced learning arrangements. Many learners agreed that technology positively impacted their learning, with some making a clear case for "*live lessons [to] stay, but integrating more technology into them.*" Further positive responses expressed an appreciation for having had the opportunity of being "*able to improve ... digital skills*" and "*acquiring new IT skills ... [and discovering] new websites ... and apps ... that we are still using today.*"

The surveys established that both teachers and learners appreciate that interaction in the target language among learners and between the teacher and learners is essential. The importance of "social participation," especially in remote language teaching, and making appropriate provisions for it in lessons, was referred to in numerous responses. The experiences during the pandemic led learners to reflect on language learning methodologies, for example by pointing out that "*language learning works much better in small groups. Such small group work activities can be done in face-to-face lessons as well as in remote learning.*" A significant number of teacher and learner responses also confirmed that the experience of remote learning and teaching had caused them to reflect on the balance between face-to-face teaching and independent learning.

Therefore, in the future language educators might try to achieve a more effective balance between whole-class work and activities in small groups and pairs. Such regular smaller group activities and tasks require an integrated approach to using the potential of digital tools to encourage socialization and peer language learning as a complement to whole-class learning. As to practices to be kept, tools that support collaborative learning and group work, affording greater flexibility in integrating different learning spaces and timeframes, and more integrated uses of in-class and home activities, were appreciated and enjoyed. Teaching with a broader scope of online learning arrangements, incorporating telecollaborative elements that included learning partners from outside their classes into their activities, was appreciated as motivating. Learners considered this helpful for their learning, as the following statement confirms: "*Meeting people from all over the world online in class, ... for example native speakers, ... [helped] to improve ... pronunciation*." A large number of learner responses commented favorably on the mix of teaching approaches and activities leading, in the learners' perceptions, to acquiring new and useful skills and becoming more autonomous. This was acknowledged by comments such as "*technology impacted ... learning in a positive way*" and "*we improved our technical skills ..., we learned how to manage our time, trying to take advantage of every single minute*." Both learners' and teachers' responses contained a significant number of constructive suggestions as to how the teaching and learning of languages might benefit from the experiences and insights gained during the pandemic. "*We became convinced that school systems should be updated and made more interactive*" was how learners put it.

Lessons for the Future

Based on the reflections discussed above, the survey team identified the following guidelines as key to rethinking some of the approaches and practices in language education, thus contributing to addressing some of the challenges the field is facing. The full text, only summarized here, is available in the final report (cf. Rossner & Hayworth, 2023).

Supporting Language Teaching and Learning

A representative share of teachers' responses suggests that changes in teaching and learning conditions imposed by the pandemic stimulated a lot of rethinking of teaching strategies, including the flexible integration of digital resources into learning practice. Teachers enjoyed "*having to use [their] wits and leaving [their] comfort zone*" and experimenting with new tools and scenarios. They also reported that the experience "*has given teachers a confidence boost*" in handling digitally enhanced teaching. Equally, learners commented that – while preferring the "real" classroom – online learning experiences allowed them to appreciate that "*different resources [can be] more interactive and the lessons ... more entertaining*" in such set-ups. There seems to be growing acceptance of approaches that offer greater flexibility in the use of classrooms, also integrating other learning spaces to foster varied and effective language learning. Such arrangements encourage a wide range of approaches, also allowing for the dedicated use of (online) resources.

This requires professional development that equips language teachers to align lesson objectives with different options for lesson design and integration of a variety of learning spaces, a point also addressed by Landry & Hamel (Chapter 8, this volume). Both teachers and learners remarked that this also leads to a growing need to respond effectively to mixed ability, heterogeneity, and individual needs among language learners, through different learning environments, remote or face-to-face. Educational versatility needs to be fostered both in initial and in-service teacher training. Survey responses suggest that teachers do welcome training and networking opportunities. "*Teachers worked together to find solutions to problems and attended seminars and free classes ... [on] ... adapting in-class teaching to distance teaching or in learning about new online teaching and learning environments.*" Though digital competence has grown dramatically, both for students and teachers, teachers did ask for more "*space for professional development for teachers*" and regarded a "*wide variety of webinars*" as one suitable option for future professionalization.

What is needed, as teachers remarked, is that a clear rationale for selecting distant, blended, or hybrid modes of learning is defined and that stakeholders ensure that language education can fully draw on experiences and expertise gained during the pandemic. Support is needed for developing and adapting a wider range of versatile language learning resources, including digital resources, and empowering teachers and learners in their use. Such frameworks will help teachers to quickly adapt or change resources and activities according to the context of learning, for example when changing from whole-class teaching to working in small groups or breakout rooms, and to cater to learners with mixed ability. Furthermore, professional networks are needed that support teachers in planning flexibility and variety into their teaching and taking account of real-world learner experiences in various learning environments. During the pandemic, even teachers mainly working in more traditional modes began to appreciate the affordances of project-based language learning options involving both interactions during the lesson and individual work or group activities in between sessions. Technology played a major part in this process, as the following response suggests:

> *Speaking from personal experience, after over 30 years of teaching face-to-face, the transfer to online teaching has forced me to re-evaluate a lot of what I do in class and provided an opportunity for creativity which has been beneficial to me and, I hope, to learners. I have developed a new set of skills and finally taken on board the enormous potential of the internet as a resource. This is also true for the majority of my colleagues.*

As a caveat, a fair share of learner comments suggest that when planning remote lessons, teachers might avoid selecting a single preferred technology or only one or two ways of doing collaborative work.

Adapting Assessment

"*We need more training on how assessment can work effectively within ... remote learning*" was a sentiment frequently expressed by teachers in the survey. This often came with the clear preference for a "*stronger focus on alternative forms of assessment ... [that keep] ... the students involved in their own learning*" and a complaint about "*the insistence on summative assessment as the only reported evaluation of performance.*" References to challenges in connection with assessment in remote settings were accompanied by the appreciation that "*it is really important to make sure that you record all progress and that each learner's progress is tracked, i.e. continual* [sic] *assessment is vital.*" While there already is a lot of research in this area (e.g., RELANG[10]) the language teaching community now appears to be well prepared for increasing the range of assessment practices by including continuous assessment techniques and assessment for learning to complement language exams and tests. Learners also appreciate such approaches; some learners commented on a lack of the work done in remote settings being reflected in their grades while others recognized that a lot of the project work

[10] See https://relang.ecml.at/

they did became part of the assessment procedures, which was seen as "*fun and motivating*."

Teachers' comments in the survey as well as current European post-COVID discourse in language education suggest that skills to use continuous assessment techniques effectively and to provide supportive feedback to learners now appear to have become more appreciated as key to successful language education. Due to the need to adapt assessment and grading during lockdown and hybrid learning, peer and self-assessment, also seen as a means of enhancing learner autonomy, are becoming appreciated as potential regular features of assessment in language learning. What is needed is further reflection as to assessment practices that enhance the validity and reliability of resources and techniques for alternative and continuous assessment of language learning.

Ensuring coherence between curricula, pedagogy, and assessment was often referred to among the concerns to be addressed when rethinking assessment and evaluation. For a representative proportion of teacher responses, effective assessment involves careful planning of teaching and classroom practice that encompasses assessment in various forms, necessitating an appropriate balance between formative and summative assessment and identifying suitable means of doing both. All this was seen as a way of shifting the balance from mere grading to assessment for learning, with some experiences during the pandemic hinting at how such approaches can be implemented effectively and justly. Teachers' responses suggest that they are ready for such a shift in assessment paradigm.

Supporting Language Learners

Learners' comments expressed their appreciation of being given the opportunity to expand their learning skills during the pandemic, as exemplified by the following response: "*I had to take responsibility for my work. Working with technology was fun. Online activities … are more fun than activity book exercises. Writing tasks are easier to do in a digital form.*" More than half of the teachers also confirmed their perception that learners have become more autonomous during the periods of remote learning. Regarding this, teachers and learners appreciated being introduced to new tasks, activities, and digital resources which they may not have previously encountered. More than one-third of the teachers reflected on the use of technologies in remote learning as being useful in "normal" schooling. However, steps need to be taken to carefully introduce these to the learners, explain their purpose, and demonstrate how they function as tools for learning. After all, "despite popular assumptions, digital literacies do not just refer to the skills for using computers but to new functional, sociocultural and transformational literacies that allow people to effectively navigate an increasingly multimodal and digital world" (Mavridi, 2022, p.50). Learners should be given opportunities from time to time to share their opinions on learning tasks and resources used during remote and other language learning contexts. Methodologies of action-research-oriented or other techniques of reflection on teaching and learning practice need to become an integral part of teacher professionalization. This survey shows learners respond well to being consulted as to their perceptions of a given learning arrangement and often offer enlightening insights into what works and what doesn't. Helping learners develop greater autonomy also requires foreign language curricula that highlight the importance of learners taking ownership of their learning and helping each other in peer learning.

Teachers also need to ensure that independent learning online and away from the screen or the classroom is built into their language courses both during and between regular sessions. Teacher training needs to support teachers in becoming skilled at preparing learners for independent practical language work alone or in groups between lessons and providing opportunities during whole class work for them to share their work and receive feedback on it. Again, as some learners perceived communicating via digital channels as "*getting more individual attention from [their] teachers*," the way digital tools support collaboration, communication, and interaction needs to be considered when reflecting on teaching and learning experiences during the pandemic. As some teachers put it: "*Things that are important in classroom teaching – establishing a relationship, communicating/discussing/agreeing on objectives, ensuring variation, giving effective feedback etc. are just as important or even more important in remote or hybrid teaching. Technology opens up new opportunities but must not be overused.*"

However, the responses to both surveys indicate that – while appreciating the potential afforded by technology for more learner-oriented and individualized learning arrangements – the inclusion of all students is an issue. Worries mentioned were concerned with maintaining access and equal opportunities, equitably supporting students with learning difficulties, creating safe and inclusive environments as well as providing suitable and sufficient digital infrastructures and training. Teachers did identify the creation of "*quality materials for students to devise inclusive lessons*" as key.

Supporting Language Teachers

During the COVID emergency teachers found themselves suddenly under greater pressure than their day-to-day experience had so far prepared them for. They were required quickly to adapt to teaching online, using technologies that many were unfamiliar with, and to prepare lessons and resources that were viable for this required mode of teaching. In addition, there was a need to develop means of dealing with the difficulties learners had in adjusting to the new learning environment. Many language teachers found the unfamiliarity of these pressures and the sense of being cut off from support stressful. Given the social nature of language learning, they were especially concerned that remote language learning would result in some learners falling behind. However, teachers also found that remote teaching opened up opportunities to experiment with a range of technological and organizational options that enriched their teaching and the language learning experience and decided to continue using these in their teaching after the COVID emergency. Teachers also seem to have begun to further reflect on their role, as represented by the following comment: "*I have rediscovered the limitations of my role and the importance of motivation and development of personal skills, autonomy, curiosity and self-teaching abilities*."

Teachers have had to cope with many difficulties – learning new skills, rethinking their teaching, working long hours at the computer, and so on. Therefore, teacher initial education as well as continuing and in-service training need to focus more than in the past on such issues, including teacher competencies in using relevant technologies. Enhancing formal teacher education and continuing professional development must include training in blended and socially distanced teaching. Teachers appreciated the benefits of networking and sharing during the pandemic. Therefore, educational authorities are well advised to provide support systems for change in language teaching through teacher communities of practice and peer-learning networks, including cross-pollination between language departments and between language teachers and teachers of other subjects. Such initiatives would provide adaptive professional learning opportunities, offering language teachers targeted opportunities for professionalization that address their specific needs in close cooperation with colleagues. For example, authorities could make provision for and encourage language teachers to set up self-run "communities of practice" at institutional, inter-institutional, or even international levels. During the pandemic, teacher training institutions and associations involved as well as educational publishers began to offer an increasing number of webinars, demonstrating how urgent individual teaching-related needs of teachers can be addressed beyond local levels, thus providing sustainable professional learning opportunities.

Developing Educational Adaptability, Flexibility, and Versatility

Views expressed by learners and teachers concerning broader aspects of learning and teaching, especially in the open questions of the survey project presented here, suggest that there might be the need for reflecting a general concept of "educational adaptability", which may help define strategies for language education in the future. On the part of both teachers and learners, a construct of "educational adaptability" might be categorized and reflected in the following main areas:

- the need to understand the educational processes and the competencies required to learn and teach successfully;
- the importance of digital skills and of being able to use a range of both general and specifically educational software and applications;
- the ability to redesign or adapt approaches to and means of education in an agile and imaginative way in response to unexpected environmental or other changes;
- the educational measures needed to safeguard and enhance the well-being of learners and teachers.

These concerns, which are implicit in many of the aspects discussed above, can be united in a general concept of "educational literacy" which may help define strategy for language education in the future. For the purposes of the guidelines derived from the survey project, "educational adaptability" means the ability of teachers to use effectively a very wide range of options in their teaching, and the ability of learners to take advantage of these richer and more varied opportunities in their language learning and in learning how to learn. This appears to have been taken on board by the language teaching community, as teachers' contributions to the survey indicate. In summary, such a literacy geared at fostering more flexibility in language education includes choosing methods that fit given learning spaces, deciding on how to use and combine a variety of learning spaces, including and also going beyond the traditional classroom, appropriately exploiting a variety of tools and resources, while competently managing the resulting diversity of learning spaces and interactions. The results and conclusions of the survey project to this effect do not stand alone, as a lot of the research referred to in the above literature review shows, suggesting that the pandemic has led to "new models combining online and face-to-face delivery, from blends to hybrids" (Kiddle, et al., 2020, p. 2). This applies to teachers as well as learners.

Conclusion

The survey project reported on in this chapter suggests that there are indeed lessons to be learned from the changes in teaching and learning practices enforced by the pandemic. For example, the survey project showed that – despite some negative aspects reported – language teachers and learners alike have begun to appreciate the sustainable benefits of digital tools and digitally enhanced learning spaces for creating more diverse and effective learning opportunities. Other chapters in this section also support the perception that, particularly when realigning the implementation of digitally enhanced, post-pandemic teaching scenarios, the pandemic was a deeply transformative experience, as discussed, for example, by Giupponi et al. (this volume). Similar to the way the professional world has taken on board the benefits of integrating the "home office" into working life, teachers also feel that "*[n]ow that we have gotten used to the hybrid way of learning, we see that both face-to-face and remote learning can be successfully combined*," as one teacher put it. Learner responses also suggest that, while in principle they want to learn in school, they do not want to learn in school or purely traditional settings only. As the data show, during the pandemic language education changed markedly as new ways had to be found to ensure that teaching and learning could continue. The field is still grappling with how to define the "return to normal" in language education, but it has already begun to reflect and learn from COVID experiences to potentially consolidate practices old and new into the future teaching and learning of languages. An important step might be to enable teachers through professional and peer learning to gain a broader perspective of the many options available in educational settings, to compare and reflect on these, to discuss relevant theories as well as practical implications, and to select wisely from a broader and deeper range of alternatives in their teaching and learning.

It is our understanding that such literacies would have educational adaptability, flexibility, and versatility as key ingredients, going beyond mere methodological skills. As the following survey response shows, teachers and learners alike have begun to appreciate that "*technology is an integral part of our daily lives and of education as well ... we ... now ... have a great tool in our hands. Teaching can be [more] motivating, interesting, pleasant, ...*"

The insights gained from the survey project discussed in this chapter, as well as the following chapters in this part, suggest a concerted effort in language education to reflect the true potential of the "pandemic experiences" and further flesh out the construct of educational adaptability while rethinking the necessary infrastructure as well as the theoretical and pedagogical mindset in language education at all levels.

About the Author

Bernd Rüschoff is Senior Professor (ret.) in Applied Linguistics, Anglophone Studies at University of Duisburg-Essen. Research focuses on digital resources in language education. Other research addresses language & culture, plurilingual education, and intercultural education. Former president of EUROCALL, of the German Association of Applied Linguistics, and of AILA, the International Association for Applied Linguistics.

References

Acar, A., & Kayaoglu, M. (2020). MOODLE as a potential tool for language education under the shadow of COVID 19*. *Eurasian Journal of Educational Research*, *90*, 67–82. https://doi.org/10.14689/ejer.2020.90.4

Akbana, Y. E., Rathert, S., & Ağçam, R. (2021). Emergency remote education in foreign and second language teaching. *Turkish Journal of Education*, *10*(2), 97–124. https://doi.org/10.19128/turje.865344

Anthony, L. (2004). AntConc: A learner and classroom friendly, multi-platform corpus analysis toolkit. *Proceedings of IWLeL*, 7–13. http://www.laurenceanthony.net/research/iwlel_2004_anthony_antconc.pdf

Anthony, L. (2018). Visualization in corpus-based discourse studies. In C. Taylor and A. Marchi (Eds.), *Corpus approaches to discourse: A critical review* (pp. 197–224). Routledge Press.

Anwar, I. W., & Wahid, J. H. J. (2021). Learners' perception on online learning implementation during covid-19 pandemic, *JOLLT Journal of Languages and Language Teaching*, *9*(2), 126–138. https://doi.org/10.33394/jollt.v%vi%i.3576

Bax, S. (2003). CALL – past, present and future. *System*, *31*(1), 13–28. https://doi.org/10.1016/s0346-251x(02)00071-4

Bax, S. (2011). Normalisation Revisited: The Effective Use of Technology in Language Education. *International Journal of Computer-Assisted Language Learning and Teaching, 1*(2), 1–15. https://doi.org/10.4018/ijcallt.2011040101

Cinganotto, L., Benedetti, F., Langé, G., & Lamb, T. (2022). A survey of language learning/teaching with an overview of activities in Italy during the COVID-19 pandemic. INDIRE. https://www.indire.it/wp-content/uploads/2022/02/Report-Survey-on-languages-13.02.2022.pdf

Council of Europe. (2020). *Common European Framework of Reference for Languages: Learning, Teaching, Assessment—Companion Volume*. Council of Europe Publishing. www.coe.int/lang-cefr

Davies, G., Otto, S. E. K., & Rüschoff, B. (2013). Historical perspectives on CALL. In M. Thomas, H. Reinders, & M. Warschauer (Eds.), *Contemporary computer-assisted language learning* (pp.19–38). Bloomsbury Academic.

Elminger, D. (2022). Le numérique dans l'enseignement/apprentissage des langues: Nouvelles promesse et anciens désenchantements. *Babylonia, tema2*, 18–24. https://babylonia.online/index.php/babylonia/article/view/179/157

Erarslan, A. (2021). English language teaching and learning during Covid-19: A global perspective on the first year. *Journal of Educational Technology & Online Learning*, *4*(2), 349–367. https://doi.org/10.31681/jetol.907757

Gacs, A., Goertler, S., & Spasova, S. (2020). Planned online language education versus crisis-prompted online language teaching: Lessons for the future. *Foreign Language Annals*, *53*(2), 380–392. https://doi.org/10.1111/flan.12460

González-Lloret, M., Canals, L., & Pineda, J. E. (2021). Role of technology in language teaching and learning amid the crisis generated by the COVID-19 Pandemic. *Íkala, Revista De Lenguaje y Cultura*, *26*(2), 477–482. http://dx.doi.org/10.17533/udea.ikala.v26n3a01

Hattie, J. (2021). What can we learn from COVID-era instruction? *Educational Leadership*, *78*(8). https://www.ascd.org/el/articles/what-can-we-learn-from-covid-era-instruction

Hickey, R. (2003). *Corpus Presenter: Software for language analysis*. John Benjamins Publishing Company. https://doi.org/10.1017/S0272263105220296

Hodges, C., Moore, S., Lockee, B., Trust, T., & Bond, A. (2020). The difference between emergency remote teaching and online learning. [blog post] Educause Review. https://er.educause.edu/articles/2020/3/the-difference-between-emergency-remote-teaching-and-online-learning

Jin, L., Xu, Y., Deifell, E., & Angus, K. (2021). Emergency remote language teaching and U.S.-based college-level world language educators' intention to adopt online teaching in postpandemic times. *The Modern Language Journal*, *105*(2), 412–434. https://doi.org/10.1111/modl.12712

Kiddle, T., Farrell, C., Glew-O'Leary, J., and Mavridi, S. (2020). *A survey of instances of, and attitudes to, hybrid learning in language teaching organisations around the world as a response to the Covid-19 pandemic.* Norwich Institute for Language Education (NILE). https://doi.org/10.5281/zenodo.4940034

Klimova, B. (2021). An insight into online foreign language learning and teaching in the era of COVID-19 Pandemic. *Procedia Computer Science*, *192*, 1787–1794. https://doi.org/10.1016/j.procs.2021.08.183

Mavridi, S. (2022). *Language Teaching Experiences During Covid-19*. British Council. https://www.teachingenglish.org.uk/sites/teacheng/files/2022-07/Language_teaching_experiences_Covid19_Final_web.pdf

Muchnik-Rozanov, Y., & Tsybulsky, D. (2020). Linguistic analysis of science teachers' narratives using AntConc software. In E. Kennedy, & Y. Qian (Eds.), *Advancing educational research with emerging technology* (pp. 211–230). IGI Global. https://doi.org/10.4018/978-1-7998-1173-2.ch010

Rahman, M. S. (2016). The advantages and disadvantages of using qualitative and quantitative approaches and methods in language "testing and assessment" research: A literature review. *Journal of Education and Learning*, *6*(1), 102–112. https://doi.org/10.5539/jel.v6n1p102

Richardson, C. (2020). Supporting collaborative creativity in education with the i5 Framework. *Educational Action Research*, *30*(2), 297–312. https://doi.org/10.1080/09650792.2020.1810731

Rossner, R., & Hayworth, F. (Eds). (2023). *Rethinking language education after the experience of COVID: Final report*. Council of Europe Publishing. https://www.ecml.at/Portals/1/documents/ECML-resources/Rethinking-language-education-after-the-experience-of-Covid-EN.pdf?ver=2023-04-06-132816-953

Stickler, U., & Hampel, R. (2015). Qualitative research in CALL. *The CALICO Journal*, *32*(3), 380–395. https://doi.org/10.1558/cj.v32i3.27737380–395

UNESCO. (2022). *UNESCO's education response to COVID-19.* https://www.unesco.org/en/covid-19/education-response/initiatives

Wilson, A., & Lengeling, M. M. (2021). Language learning in the time of COVID-19: ELT students' narrated experiences in guided reflective journals. *Íkala. Revista De Lenguaje y Cultura*, *26* (3). 571–585. https://doi.org/10.17533/udea.ikala.v26n3a06

6 Post-pandemic Language Teaching: Language Instructors' Technology Integration Practices

Luca Giupponi, Bethany Zulick, and Emily Heidrich Uebel

Introduction

Research in the last 20 years has continued to show the potential for various technologies to improve and augment language teaching and learning practices (Bikowski & Vithanage, 2016; García et al., 2020; Sato et al., 2020). However, language instructors can be hesitant to integrate technology in their teaching, resulting in a limited technological repertoire (Arnold & Ducate, 2015).

During Emergency Response Teaching (ERT), university faculty had to resort to using a variety of novel educational technology tools and approaches in order to deliver their courses remotely. For a considerable number of faculty, it is possible that had ERT not happened, they would have continued with the same teaching practices they were familiar with before the pandemic. While it is undeniable that ERT was a difficult, uncertain, and stressful period for faculty (MacIntyre et al., 2020), it is also possible that experimentation with new technologies and pedagogies could have resulted in a positive experience (Tao & Gao, 2022; Li et al., this volume). If so, there is a chance that this experience will impact faculty's practices moving forward.

The idea that positive experiences with technology are able to alter teachers' beliefs on the value of technology is not new (Kopcha et al., 2020; Shelley et al., 2013). Ertmer (2005), for example, reported that positive experiences with educational technology can increase the range of pedagogical and practical options faculty deem possible in their teaching contexts, while negative experiences tend to do the opposite. Other educational researchers (McQuiggan, 2012; Wargo, 2021) found that training faculty on online pedagogy led to positive change in pedagogical practices across all modalities.

Technology Integration and Language Pedagogy

Language Instructors' Technology Integration Practices

Research on technology integration in the language classroom paints a complex picture. Arnold and Ducate (2015) claimed that the technological repertoire of language teachers was severely limited when compared with the wealth of evidence-based options available to them. Even when instructors use technology in their courses, this is not always done appropriately. For example, in his review of the research on language teachers' use of Computer-Mediated Communication (CMC) activities, Troyan (2012) identified instances of poor task design and unsuccessful implementation of CMC practices. Kessler (2018), Cummings Hlas et al. (2017), and Arnold (2013) suggest that the quality and amount of CALL training in teacher preparation programs is partially to blame.

In addition to the limited training received, language educators also differ in the technology-oriented mindsets they bring to their profession. Tour (2015) brought to light the influence that assumptions about the affordances of teaching technologies had on teachers' use of technology in the classroom. Specifically, an underdeveloped digital mindset impeded participants from realizing the full potential of learning technologies even after they had been exposed to training.

The Pandemic Experience

The COVID-19 pandemic forced language instructors to abandon in-person teaching in favor of ERT, often with little to no time to prepare. Lederman (2020) found that faculty without previous online teaching experience were much more likely to report using new-to-them teaching methods during ERT than faculty with previous online teaching experience. It is worth noting that this shift happened in tandem with one of the most focused and intensive educational technology support efforts ever seen (Koraleski et al., 2020), so that instructional support was relatively available when needed, even if at times not adequate or appropriately focused, requiring instructors to supplement or make compromises (Gacs et al., 2020).

Language instructors responded to and coped with ERT in a variety of ways. Language instructors' ability to enjoy positive professional experiences and grow despite the stress brought on by the pandemic was partially determined by their ability to self-regulate and adopt approach strategies such as acceptance, seeking support, positive reframing, and planning (MacIntyre et al., 2020). Conversely, those who adopted avoidant strategies such as disengagement, denial, self-distraction, and venting were much more likely to experience negative outcomes such as anxiety, anger, and sadness.

ERT's impact on language instructors' attitudes towards online language teaching was equally complex. Jin et al. (2021) found three types of views among language faculty about online language teaching: willingness to embrace online language teaching in the future; resistance; and ambivalence. Perceived value, self-confidence, technological access, training and support, and student readiness were all significant predictive factors for faculty's intention to teach online in the future (see also Tecedor & Gómez Soler, Chapter 13, this volume).

Defining the Value of Technology Integration

While educational researchers usually study technology uses to promote a specific pedagogical agenda, such as student-centered or constructivist uses of technology (Harris, 2005), teachers themselves will adopt a more pragmatic stance, choosing technologies that are best for themselves, their students, or both (Kopcha et al., 2020). Exactly how "best" is defined varies from teacher to teacher, encompassing a range of considerations from pedagogical to administrative to practical (Heitink et al., 2016; Khan & Markauskaite, 2018; McCulloch et al., 2018). Ottenbreit-Leftwich et al. (2010) found that even teachers who were awarded for their exemplary use of technology regularly engaged in teacher-centered uses of technology because they contended it helped them meet their students' needs at that specific moment in time.

Rogers (2003) Diffusion of Innovation (DoI) theory has been used by educational researchers to investigate technology integration dynamics (Grgurović, 2014; Richardson et al., 2020; Straub, 2009). First proposed in 1962, DoI theory focuses on, as its unit of analysis, five different elements that play a role in the diffusion of innovation: the innovation itself, adopters, communication channels, time, and social systems. The element that is most relevant to the purpose of this study is the innovation itself; to describe and categorize innovations, Rogers' (2003) DoI theory provides a framework

Table 1 Rogers' (2003) Perceived Characteristics of Innovations

PCI	Degree to which an innovation
Relative Advantage	Is perceived to be better than what had been used previously, in terms of satisfaction, convenience, and economics
Image	Improves the user's reputation
Compatibility	Is consistent with the user's needs, values, and experiences
Ease of Use	Is difficult to learn, implement, and use over time
Visibility	Is visible or tangible
Results Demonstrability	Produces visible, tangible results as it is used
Trialability	Allows for practice, piloting, and experimentation
Voluntariness	Is considered voluntary

that defines eight Perceived Characteristics of Innovations (PCI), as shown in Table 1. The value in using Rogers' PCIs to analyze language instructors' technology integration practices lies in the fact that they can be used to describe practices independently of their purpose or theoretical underpinning.

The purpose of this study is to investigate the role of ERT in the technology integration practices of post-secondary language instructors after the pandemic. The research questions for this study are:

1. What innovations did post-secondary language instructors integrate into their practices during the pandemic?
2. Why did language instructors choose their specific innovations?
3. How did ERT impact these instructors' technology integration practices?

Methodology

Context and Participants

This study follows a Mixed-Methods Sequential Explanatory Design (Ivankova et al., 2006). Study participants were identified via purposeful sampling (Patton, 2015), that is, they were recruited among participants in a Summer 2021 professional development program called *Post-Pandemic Language Teaching* (PPLT). PPLT is a three-week online course (offered free of charge) that aims to create a space for post-secondary language instructors to process their remote teaching experiences during the pandemic, identify those technology-enabled practices having the most transformative potential, and design an intentional new normal for what language instruction might look like in the near future. The course was advertised via email and social media, and participants applied of their own accord. The course was led by the first author and mainly consisted of resource exploration, discussion, and task-oriented activities. The course culminated with participants delivering a Technology Integration Plan (TIP) that described in detail the innovative approaches that instructors intended to implement in their courses after the pandemic. It is important to note that the focus of this plan was largely a consequence of participants' own pandemic experience and was tailored to their own teaching context.

All 24 course participants were offered the opportunity to participate in this study; 18 participants chose to complete the survey and nine respondents elected to participate in the interviews as well. Using purposeful sampling means working with a self-selecting group of professionals who may possess a higher-than-average willingness to innovate using technology. We are aware and comfortable with this, as our goal is not to generalize to all instructors' experiences, but rather to learn more about innovators' experiences during the pandemic. Table 2 shows a demographic breakdown of the interview participants and their innovations. Pseudonyms have been used to protect participants' privacy and confidentiality.

Table 2 Demographic Information of Participants

Pseudonym	Age	Gender	Language	Years Teaching	Innovator Score
Julinha	40–49	Female	Portuguese	7 or more years	Early
Rick	30–39	Male	French	7 or more years	Early
Estela	60 +	Female	Portuguese	7 or more years	Early
Giulia	50–59	Female	Italian	7 or more years	Early
Hannah	60 +	Female	Spanish	7 or more years	Moderate
Rachel	30–39	Female	Yiddish	3–6 years	Moderate
Fernando	30–39	Male	Portuguese	7 or more years	Moderate
Olga	40–49	Female	Russian	7 or more years	Moderate
Duyên	30–39	Female	Vietnamese	3–6 years	Late

Data Collection

A survey to measure Rogers' (2003) PCIs was adapted from a validated instrument designed by Moore and Benbasat (1991). The survey used a 5-point Likert scale and consisted of eight sections (one for each PCI) for a total of 25 items. Items from the original validated instrument were reworded in order to reflect the implementations investigated in this study. In addition, three 5-point Likert-scale questions were used to assess participants' level of technology adoption, following Rogers' (2003) model. This score, referred to as innovation score, is calculated by averaging participants' self-rated level of adoption using digital technology, blended learning, and online learning, and is shown in Table 2.

To corroborate survey results and capture additional innovation dynamics, two semi-structured, 30-minute interviews were conducted. Both the survey and the first interview were conducted in early August 2021, immediately after the professional development course concluded, and before the beginning of the fall semester. The second interview was conducted in early December 2021, once the participants had a chance to implement their innovation for a semester. Data collection instruments are available on this volume's companion website (https://sites.google.com/msu.edu/2024crisiscall).

Data Analysis

All survey participants evaluated statements related to each PCI, the scoring of which was used to compute an influence rating for each of Rogers' (2003) PCIs (see Table 3). The influence ratings of each PCI question were then calculated into an overall influence score for each PCI.

All interviews were transcribed and analyzed utilizing thematic analysis (Braun & Clarke, 2006). Specifically, a first round of coding employed a deductive approach by using a set of eight codes corresponding to Rogers (2003) PCIs; in this first round, two raters coded the interview data independently and then came together to produce a consensus coding. Codes corresponding to each PCI were quantified to identify which characteristics were mentioned more frequently in the interviews.

Afterwards, one coder used open coding to allow additional codes and themes to emerge from the data. A second and third coder confirmed all the codes and, in case of disagreement, the three coders discussed the disagreement until a consensus was reached. This additional round of coding allowed the researchers to identify additional themes that may not have been captured by Rogers' (2003) PCIs.

Results

Research Question 1: What Innovations did Post-secondary Language Instructors Integrate into their Practices During the Pandemic?

Participants' innovations are summarized in Table 3. Data shows that all participants significantly altered their curriculum, course design, and/or routines in a significant way. Three instructors were motivated to make their program more affordable by replacing expensive textbooks with online materials that were developed in-house, with the added benefit of having more freedom to revise, add to, or update learning materials based on student needs. These instructors turned to a number of online platforms to find a vast selection of authentic, up-to-date, and relevant content. Two participants also did away with traditional exams, replacing them with alternative methods of assessment.

Table 3 Summary of Participants' Innovations

Pseudonym	Summary of Innovation
Julinha	Leverage the asynchronous modality to revitalize the Basic Portuguese curriculum. Goals include fostering authentic oral communication, pushing student output, and increasing cultural relevance.
Rick	Replace the textbook with online materials developed in-house. Implement tools such as Perusall, Anki, and Harmonize to asynchronously present material in an interactive way. Stop administering unit/module tests.
Estela	Launch a project-based course on the theme of travelling in Brazil. Students choose a state in Brazil and create a series of podcast episodes throughout the course.
Giulia	Replace the textbook with online materials developed in-house. Design a hybrid language course replacing some face-to-face class time with goal-driven online activities.
Hannah	Redesign an intermediate Spanish course around one main theme, three task-based projects, and e-portfolio assessment.
Rachel	Transition from traditional writing assignments to a series of scaffolded online writing assignments to be completed asynchronously and collaboratively on Google Docs.
Fernando	Adopt an open online textbook to reduce students' financial burden and implement a flipped-classroom model supported by online tools to enhance communication in class. Stop administering unit/module tests.
Olga	Design a Russian for STEM course incorporating a task-based approach with social annotation activities.
Duyên	Design a beginners' course under a blended learning model to allow students to work at the own pace and at their own language level.

Table 4 PCI Characteristics in Order of Influence Score

PCI	Influence Rating						
	Strongly Disagree (1)	Disagree (2)	Neutral (3)	Agree (4)	Strongly Agree (5)	Influence score (Scale: 1–5)	Frequency of Mention in Interviews
Compatibility	0%	2%	7.8%	45.1%	45.1%	4.33	28.4%
Results Demonstrability	0%	0%	16.2%	48.5%	35.3%	4.19	6.1%
Relative Advantage	1.2%	2.4%	22.4%	35.3%	38.8%	4.08	38.9%
Voluntariness	2.9%	14.7%	11.8%	32.4%	38.2%	3.89	4.4%
Ease of Use	0%	13.2%	14.7%	42.6%	29.4%	3.88	10.5%
Image	0%	3.9%	41.2%	37.3%	17.6%	3.69	6.6%
Visibility	5.9%	23.5%	14.7%	35.3%	20.6%	3.41	0.4%
Trialability	8.8%	23.5%	20.6%	32.4%	14.7%	3.21	4.4%

Research Question 2: Why did Language Instructors Choose their Specific Innovations?

Looking at responses through the lens of Rogers' (2003) PCIs can help shed light on participants' motivation behind their specific choices. Table 4 reports an influence score for each PCI as well as the frequency with which each PCI was mentioned in the qualitative data (frequency with which a particular quotation was coded with each PCI code among all interview quotations). We will discuss the PCI characteristics that were most influential for the survey participants, defined as having an influence score 4 and higher: Compatibility, Results Demonstrability, and Relative Advantage. Ease of Use will also be briefly discussed given its relatively high frequency of mentions in interviews.

Compatibility

Compatibility was the most influential PCI for survey takers and was the second most discussed characteristic during interviews. Most commonly, instructors discussed their innovation's compatibility with student pedagogical needs, schedule, and/or learning preferences. Hannah discussed the fact that her innovation was going to help students acquire the skills she thought they sought: "most of these students really want to be fluent and converse and be able to travel or talk to family in other countries or friends (Hannah, Interview 1)."

Instructors frequently mentioned being motivated by the fact that their innovation aligned with their own personality or personal need for change and exploration. Estela mentioned that continuing to innovate "is very important to me. It's validating; it means that I'm not just doing the same old. And for me, it gets boring if I do the same thing. What's in it for me? I want to be entertained, too (Estela, Interview 1)." Many others confirmed this sentiment as it related to pedagogical innovation: "I'm always looking for innovative types of assessment (Rick, Interview 1)."

Lastly, instructors found that their innovative experiences during the pandemic were more aligned with their own personal pedagogical beliefs and approach to teaching:

> I always believe that the students are the ones who should be doing the work in the sense that they're the ones there to learn…They need to practice to get there. So I give them more opportunities to own their own learning. (Fernando, Interview 1)

Results Demonstrability

Despite receiving an Influence Rating of 4.19, Results Demonstrability (an innovation's ability to produce visible, tangible results) was not often discussed by interviewees. Some instructors indicated that they hoped their innovations could spark measurable improvements in their students' language abilities. Giulia expressed this as a direct comparison between pre- and post-pandemic performance, saying, "I would like to see my students perform better, if not equally, but better than they were before the pandemic (Giulia, Interview 1)." Several others echoed this sentiment. Olga hoped that her innovation would help students develop "a more profound and more fluent vocabulary integration" than in prior years (Olga, Interview 1).

After implementing their innovations, several teachers noted improvements in their students' performance. Olga's hopes for her students' vocabulary proficiency were realized; she remarked that while she could not be certain whether it was a direct result of innovation, her students showed an increased awareness of word clusters and showed a stronger engagement with vocabulary. Estela noticed that students in her course showed a greater level of self-reflection and self-correction.

For other instructors, proficiency gains were less important than other kinds of results. For Hannah, the observable impacts of her innovation included increased engagement, enthusiasm, and motivation among students. She also indicated that inspiring students to connect their language learning with the real world (e.g., through studying abroad or finding a relevant internship) would be a valuable outcome.

Relative Advantage

Relative Advantage, a perception that the innovation is better than what had been used previously in terms of satisfaction, convenience, and economics, received an influence score of 4.08 and was by far the most discussed characteristic during interviews. Several instructors reported that the pandemic allowed them to discover tools and strategies that simplified the teaching and learning processes, cut down on administrative time, streamlined logistics, and increased accountability. Hannah reported that by implementing the strategies she adopted during the pandemic, "we have more teaching time, [so] the classes can be at a slightly slower pace, we're not cramming so much extra stuff in there every day (Hannah, Interview 1)."

Some instructors realized that some of the pedagogical strategies they were exposed to during the pandemic were more effective at helping students meet their learning goals or yielded unexpected pedagogical benefits. Rachel was positively surprised by the interaction she witnessed among students around her writing assignments: "rather than having the student write something and then bring it in, and then they get feedback a week later, it could be something that could happen in a more interactive, ongoing way (Rachel, Interview 1)." Along the same lines, Fernando discussed the value of enabling students to see his feedback as soon as he is done grading.

Ease of Use

With an influence score of 3.88 and 10.5% of mentions in the interviews, Ease of Use (whether an innovation is difficult to learn, implement, and use over time) was moderately important for study participants. Instructors discussed this topic in terms of their own workload in preparing aspects of their innovation, but also in terms of implementing the innovation and addressing anticipated difficulties that students might encounter. Hannah and Rachel both highlighted the fact that the tools they chose were very easy for the students to use, while both Estela and Fernando touched on how the preparation and routines that they created in implementing their innovation helped avoid anticipated difficulties that the students might have.

Less-Influential PCIs

Four PCIs were less influential for our participants: Voluntariness, Image, Visibility, and Trialability. All participants implemented their innovation of their own accord and were not motivated by considerations related to their professional standing or visibility at work. Whether an innovation could be trialed ahead of time also did not seem to influence participants' decisions.

Research Question 3: How did ERT Impact these Instructors' Technology Integration Practices?

To answer the third research question, additional codes from the interview data were grouped into four larger themes: technology-mediated life as normative, embracing asynchronous interaction, willingness to change, and focus on the student experience. These will now be discussed in turn.

Technology-mediated Life as Normative

A common theme discussed by participants in interviews was a closer alignment to current, everyday uses of technology, which was most apparent when looking at communication modalities. When forced to use technology to mediate the entirety of their communication with their students during the pandemic, instructors realized this was not too different from the way they already related with others outside of teaching:

> it feels like I'm accepting more of the ways that we actually communicate these days. So through discussion boards, through quick posts, memes, chats, things like that. Rather than having students think about writing a letter, which few people do at this point, we should really be prioritizing those forms of communication that we actually do on a daily basis. (Rick, Interview 1)

Instructors also realized that they could turn to a number of online platforms to find a vast selection of authentic, up-to-date, and relevant content. Doing so did not necessarily obviate the need for teacher-developed materials, but rather complemented and supplemented what was available through the already-existing curriculum to help students make the connection between the course content and the real world; it made language more real for students. Several participants underscored this experience: Hannah described students' excitement at discovering social media profiles of Spanish-speaking individuals that excelled at their passion, be it music, rock climbing, or photography; Julinha spoke of turning to media platforms as primary providers of content as a "value-rich environment (Julinha, Interview 2)." In short, technology-mediated spaces became essential components of the language classroom:

> Throughout this whole year, I've been learning new tools and thinking of [the] classroom as kind of a digital space that we create. It's a social space that we create. And I think that was my biggest takeaway from the class a year ago, that when we teach, even if we teach in person, there is this important component for social, cognitive, and emotional learning that we actually create on our [digital] class platform. (Olga, Interview 1)

Embracing Asynchronous Interaction

A number of participants reported realizing that the asynchronous modality was heavily underutilized. The pandemic forced participants to come to terms with the value of asynchronous work, and many cited the ability to free up class time and use it more intentionally as the main benefit:

> pandemic teaching allowed me to reconsider how I view asynchronous instructional time and how technology can improve the student learning experience…as a way to free up class time and to make sure students have as much relevant practice with their instructor as possible. (Fernando, Interview 2)

The asynchronous digital space becomes not only a destination for select activities previously relegated to the classroom, but also a central space students can use for reference work, interaction, and follow up. Fernando also highlighted the power of technology-supported follow-up:

> In the past, I might just write a [topic that comes up in class] on the board and that's it. Now I can follow up more without wasting a lot of classroom time. Or later I send a mass email or upload something onto Canvas so I can make better time and there's better follow up to what goes on in class. That's something I'm doing more because I know they're going to use Canvas no matter what, because their online resources are there. (Fernando, Interview 2)

Several other instructors found that embracing asynchronous work and interaction allowed them to make the most of what synchronous time they had. Rick's program had already been in the process of doing away with traditional exams and decided to fully switch to task-based assessment during the pandemic:

> while before the pandemic I was trying to figure out ways to move away from that kind of traditional paper exam, I felt like the pandemic kind of forced that change a little bit. Just because, when you're online, it just doesn't do quite the same things, students can have any number of resources around them, even if you're on screen watching them, it's kind of really hard to think about academic integrity. So, I've really refocused assessments on having students have real interactions on the spot with each other. (Rick, Interview 2)

Besides an increase in class time, the integration of new technologies brought positive changes at the logistical level. Grading procedures, for example, were positively impacted by transitioning to a digital workflow, as Fernando reported: "Oh my gosh, it's so much easier to grade. The one thing that I really liked, […] is how much faster things can be (Fernando, Interview 2)." Even instructors like Rachel, who might prefer a more traditional approach to grading, recognized the benefits of a digital workflow:

> I really prefer having the handheld materials and writing on them. I find the course management system very fussy; it takes me much longer. But it's all there. So the students can go back and refer to it and doesn't get lost or crumpled in the bottom of my bag or something like that. And that feels like more responsible teaching, even if it's much more time-consuming. So I do have hesitancy about it, but I think it will stay. (Rachel, Interview 2)

Willingness to Change

The challenges and opportunities presented by the pandemic pushed this group of instructors forward in a unique way. Participants discussed permanent changes in their use of technology as well as pedagogical approaches and were grateful for the opportunities for professional development that allowed them to be as ready as possible at the beginning of ERT. Olga discussed her resolve to rebuild her LMS course sites after the pandemic:

> I think just understanding the online class platform as a space that you create…has a lot of power. But that also requires a lot of work. So we had Canvas in the past, but it was kind of just an accumulation. Here's the reading. Here's the homework. And it just kind of went as we kind of progressed through the semester. Taking [a PD course on online teaching] two years ago has allowed me to see kind

> of the cognitive structure and the cognitive map that you create just by the way your models are set up, just by the way you welcome the students, explain the class goals, how you use visuals in the online pages. (Olga, Interview 2)

This mindset shift is apparent from all the innovations discussed above and is something that instructors intend to hold on to moving forward:

> the pandemic really has brought about a large interest in new ways and how we can [teach]. I'm never going to say that the pandemic was good. But one thing that came out of this is that we are looking for more innovation, for better ways of doing the things that we already do. (Fernando, Interview 2)

The pandemic also brought a heightened awareness of the need to evolve as educators, and an appreciation of the role of professional development communities and opportunities along the way. Study participants looked at their practice with a more critical eye and became more aware of opportunities that might be available to them:

> I think the pandemic was also, in a weird way, a better opportunity to connect to resources, to colleagues across the field, to online resource centers. So like, I've been exploring more, or looking at more websites that offer these kind of repositories of tools and pedagogical ideas. So I think, in the long run, it actually had a profound impact on my pedagogy and like, positive impact… I feel like this push to adjust to the new environment helped us all experiment more. (Olga, Interview 2)

Focus on the Student Experience

The pandemic, for some participants, brought a renewed focus on students' individual experiences. In some instances, this approach took a quite radical turn, with instructors redesigning entire courses to grant students more autonomy, Hannah, for example, redesigned her Spanish course from a traditional curriculum into a sequence of three smaller projects that would allow the students to choose the outcome format for each project and do more independent work; students then created an ePortfolio that included the three major assignment plus several smaller ones. This approach brought the added benefit of unifying the course content and activities under a single theme.

When in control of the focus of their own work, some students produced work that was dramatically different than expected. Estela, for example, "was astonished at [her students'] podcasts... Some were absolutely stunning (Estela, Interview 2)."

Barriers to Innovation

Instructors, by and large, spoke positively about experiences implementing their innovations, but the experiences were not always optimal. First of all, the need to change was at times welcomed with reluctance, as change is always demanding and time consuming. As Duyên pointed out, though, there was simply no choice. One had to adapt and innovate, or risk failing their students. This pressure to adapt was amplified when the technologies that were allowed by the institution were new to the instructors and the students; Duyên felt that she was "not a tech savvy person (Duyên, Interview 1)" and felt unsure when guiding her students through using the new-to-her technologies. Giulia stated that she used a lot of technology, "but nothing really well, because I just didn't have time to experiment with all of it (Giulia, Interview 1)." Some participants discussed the fear of digital materials quickly becoming outdated or locking them into a system or workflow for a long time. Given the time-consuming nature of developing these materials, the concern is certainly warranted.

Throughout the interviews, other more general implications of the pandemic on both faculty and students became apparent, including disengagement and fatigue, which weighed on several instructors' motivation to continue their efforts to develop new materials. Additionally, not all instructors had the freedom to do everything they deemed right or necessary, feeling at times constrained by their curriculum, department, or both. Examples of this ranged from delays in the integration of technological tools into the learning management system, to departmental decisions about proficiency testing that prevented adjustments to their curricular approach.

Discussion

For most of the language instructors that participated in this study, the pandemic was a deeply transformative experience. While some language educators have been innovating using technology for a long time, the pandemic seems to have accelerated a deeper integration of technologies in the language classroom and a closer alignment to current, everyday uses of technology involving the coordination of several platforms and modalities, or what Cappellini and Combe (2022) refer to as "orchestration of environments" (p.

2). From having video calls with native speakers to shopping using online portals, the pandemic finally made it okay to call online activities *real life*. Indeed, coming to terms with ERT brought about an epiphany: conducting class online opens a whole new definition of what it means to be engaged in authentic learning. In short, the language classroom became more aligned with the technology-mediated content engagement we all experience in the internet age: a hybrid space that allows individuals to effortlessly switch between modalities based on need.

The pandemic also brought a renewed focus on students' individual experiences, both within and outside the educational context. This focus came out of compassion for students' lived experiences during the pandemic, and also from a concern with how to best motivate students in the new modality, which has historically been perceived by many to be too impersonal (Tour, 2015). Several of the instructors we interviewed implemented curricular shifts to increase the amount of student autonomy and creativity, and this personalization allowed students to spend time doing activities and learning about topics they enjoyed. A common sub-theme was a shift towards alternative methods of assessment such as ePortfolios, containing artifacts produced by the students themselves. In general, instructors who previously felt stuck in a traditional curriculum realized during the pandemic that technology could make innovative teaching and learning possible.

An increase in class time was a common theme in many instructors' experiences, and it comes as a result of a variety of strategies that usually involve moving an instructional element to the asynchronous modality. Language instructors have a long history of favoring face-to-face, live interactions (Romeo et al., 2017), but this might have resulted in them missing exciting developments in asynchronous interaction that happened in recent years. The pandemic forced a lot of instructors to come to terms with the value of asynchronous work, and many cited the ability to free up class time and use it more intentionally as the main benefit.

For many participants, the pandemic represented an opportunity to discover new approaches and technologies. It is worth noting here that the lion's share of these innovations used the digital space as an integral part of the learning experience, which is in line with accepted models of digital pedagogies such as Reinhardt and Thorne's (2019) work on integrating digital literacies into the curriculum. For others, the fluid nature of ERT finally gave them permission to do away with legacy approaches and implement those innovations they had been aware of for a while but did not have the freedom, motivation, time, or energy to act upon. Among these innovations are the discontinuation of in-class testing (championed by several scholars such as VanPatten et al., 2015; see also Rüschoff, Chapter 5, this volume), the redesigning of curriculum around technology-mediated task-based methodologies (see Kaufmann et al., 2023, for one such model), and the adoption of in-house or open educational materials to supplement or replace traditional textbooks (Perifanou & Economides, 2022).

The primary implication of these findings is that these latent innovations may be more likely to be addressed by faculty in environments where experimentation is viewed in a positive light. While our lifetimes may not see another moment of such forced innovation as the COVID-19 pandemic, this time period highlighted how disruption of what is considered normal or typical can inspire and encourage innovative work. The perspectives quoted in this chapter provide a model for the ways in which other instructors can engage with the possibilities of innovation and make decisions that will serve them and their students well. One way to prepare for future crises, then, is to identify the instructors who will embrace innovation and encourage them so that they can guide the way for others.

Along the same lines, the study's findings highlight the importance of professional development in the areas of technology integration and online language teaching, as participants sought to improve themselves as professionals before, during, and after ERT. It is hard to discount the role of such mindset in the ways participants dealt with the challenges and opportunities of the pandemic; more than simply learning about a discrete topic, certain types of PD may have the potential to foster an innovative mindset across a larger percentage of the instructor population.

As discussed in the literature review, several studies have investigated the impact of extraordinary events such as the COVID-19 pandemic on language educators' technology integration approaches and ability to innovate more generally. Our data show that the recent pandemic, however difficult, gave these educators an opportunity to innovate and grow. The importance of this dynamic should not be discounted, and further investigation may deepen our understanding of what motivates language educators to innovate.

Conclusion

This study sought to illustrate how post-secondary language instructors' technology integration practices fundamentally shifted during and after the pandemic. As language instructors sought to ensure teaching continuity during ERT, they gravitated towards tools and approaches that were compatible with their student needs, had a demonstrably positive impact, and improved some aspect of teaching and learning compared to their pre-pandemic situation. Engaging in these innovative practices, over time, resulted in a renewed focus on the student experience, a realignment with present-day uses of digital communication and interaction, an embracing of asynchronous interactions, and overall professional advancement.

Acknowledgements

The author team would like to express gratitude to the Andrew W. Mellon Foundation's generous support of the LCTL and Indigenous Languages Partnership, through which the professional development course and this research project were funded. We also want to acknowledge the work of Keelyn O'Brien for her assistance in some of the data analysis.

About the Authors

Luca Giupponi Head of Technology, National LCTL Resource Center; Educational Technology Specialist, Center for Language Teaching Advancement, Michigan State University, East Lansing, MI. Luca's work focuses on online language teaching and learning, faculty development, technology integration, and program evaluation. He is a co-editor on a forthcoming volume on LCTL sharing.

Bethany Zulick International Systems Manager, the Mansfield Center at the University of Montana, Missoula, MT. Bethany's research interests include English Medium Instruction, language and identity, and language ideologies. In her current professional work, she has shifted her focus to public diplomacy programs and international exchanges that foster globally minded leadership and intercultural understanding.

Emily Heidrich Uebel Associate Executive Director, National LCTL Resource Center; Project Manager, Less Commonly Taught and Indigenous Languages Partnership, Center for Language Teaching Advancement, Michigan State University, East Lansing, MI. Emily is the lead co-editor on two forthcoming volumes on LCTL sharing and language enrollment. Her research interests include world language proficiency, educational technology and online instruction, curriculum design, LCTL education, and faculty development. More information can be found on her website: https://emilyheidrichuebel.com/

References

Arnold, N. (2013). The role of methods textbooks in providing early training for teaching with technology in the language classroom. *Foreign Language Annals*, *46*, 230–245. https://doi.org/10.1111/flan.12020

Arnold, N., & Ducate, L. (2015). Contextualized views of practices and competencies in CALL teacher education research. *Language Learning & Technology*, *19*(1), 1–9. http://llt.msu.edu/issues/february2015/commentary.pdf

Bikowski, D., & Vithanage, R. (2016). Effect of web-based collaborative writing on individual L2 writing development. *Language Learning & Technology*, *20*(1), 79–99. http://llt.msu.edu/issues/february2016/bikowskivithanage.pdf

Braun, V., & Clarke, V. (2006). Using thematic analysis in psychology. *Qualitative research in psychology*, *3*(2), 77–101. http://dx.doi.org/10.1191/1478088706qp063oa

Cappellini, M., & Combe, C. (2022). Multiple online environments as complex systems: Toward an orchestration of environments. *Language Learning & Technology, 26*(1), 1–20. https://hdl.handle.net/10125/73497

Cummings Hlas, A., Conroy, K., & Hildebrandt, S. A. (2017). Student teachers and CALL: Personal and pedagogical uses and beliefs. *CALICO Journal*, *34*(3), 336–354. https://doi.org/10.1558/cj.26968

Ertmer, P. A. (2005). Teacher pedagogical beliefs: The final frontier in our quest for technology. *Educational Technology Research and Development*, *53*(4), 25–39. https://doi.org/10.1007/BF02504683

Gacs, A., Goertler, S., & Spasova, S. (2020). Planned online language education versus crisis-prompted online language teaching: Lessons for the future. *Foreign Language Annals*, *53*(2), 380–392. https://doi.org/10.1111/flan.12460

García, C., Nickolai, D., & Jones, L. (2020). Traditional versus asr-based pronunciation instruction: An empirical study. *CALICO Journal*, *37*(3), 1–20. https://doi.org/10.1558/cj.40379

Grgurović, M. (2014). An application of the Diffusion of Innovations theory to the investigation of blended language learning. *Innovation in Language Learning and Teaching*, *8*(2), 155–170. https://doi.org/10.1080/17501229.2013.789031

Harris, J. (2005). Our agenda for technology integration: It's time to choose. *Contemporary Issues in Technology and Teacher Education*, *5*, 116–122. https://www.learntechlib.org/primary/p/21849/

Heitink, M., Voogt, J., Verplanken, L., Van Braak, J., & Fisser, P. (2016). Teachers' professional reasoning about their pedagogical use of technology. *Computers and Education*, *101*, 70–83. https://doi.org/10.1016/j.compedu.2016.05.009

Ivankova, N. V., Creswell, J. W., & Stick, S. L. (2006). Sequential explanatory design: From theory to practice. *Field Methods*, *18*(1), 3–20. https://doi.org/10.1177/1525822X05282260

Jin, L., Xu, Y., Deifell, E., & Angus, K. (2021). Emergency remote language teaching and U.S.-based college-level world language educators' intention to adopt online teaching in postpandemic times. *The Modern Language Journal*, *105*(2), 412–434. https://doi.org/10.1111/MODL.12712

Kaufmann, A., Gacs, A., Giupponi, L., & Van Gorp, K. (2023). A model for scaffolded technology-enhanced oral communicative tasks. In del Mar Suárez, M., & El-Henawy, W. M. (Eds.), *Optimizing Online English Language Learning and Teaching*. Springer. https://doi.org/10.1007/978-3-031-27825-9_7

Kessler, G. (2018). Technology and the future of language teaching. *Foreign Language Annals*, *51*, 205–218. https://doi.org/10.1111/flan.12318

Khan, Md. S. H., & Markauskaite, L. (2018). Technical and vocational teachers' conceptions of ICT in the workplace: bridging the gap between teaching and professional practice. *Journal of Educational Computing Research*, *56*(7), 1099–1128. https://doi.org/10.1177/0735633117740396

Kopcha, T. J., Neumann, K. L., Ottenbreit-Leftwich, A., & Pitman, E. (2020). Process over product: the next evolution of our quest for technology integration. *Educational Technology Research and Development*, *68*(2), 729–749. https://doi.org/10.1007/s11423-020-09735-y

Koraleski, B., Norin, M., Pitt, S., Seidl, D., & Dobbin, G. (2020, May 20). *A marathon sprint: How higher education is responding to COVID-19*. EDUCAUSE Review. https://er.educause.edu/articles/2020/5/a-marathon-sprint-how-higher-education-is-responding-to-covid-19

Lederman, D. (2020). *How teaching changed in the (forced) shift to remote learning*. Inside Higher Ed. https://www.insidehighered.com/digital-learning/article/2020/04/22/how-professors-changed-their-teaching-springs-shift-remote

MacIntyre, P. D., Gregersen, T., & Mercer, S. (2020). Language teachers' coping strategies during the Covid-19 conversion to online teaching: Correlations with stress, wellbeing and negative emotions. *System*, *94*. https://doi.org/10.1016/J.SYSTEM.2020.102352

McCulloch, A. W., Hollebrands, K., Lee, H., Harrison, T., & Mutlu, A. (2018). Factors that influence secondary mathematics teachers' integration of technology in mathematics lessons. *Computers and Education*, *123*(September 2017), 26–40. https://doi.org/10.1016/j.compedu.2018.04.008

McQuiggan, C. A. (2012). Faculty development for online teaching as a catalyst for change. *Journal of Asynchronous Learning Network*, *16*(2), 27–61. https://doi.org/10.24059/OLJ.V16I2.258

Moore, G. C., & Benbasat, I. (1991). Development of an instrument to measure the perceptions of adopting an information technology innovation. *Information Systems Research*, *2*(3), 192–222. https://doi.org/10.1287/isre.2.3.192

Ottenbreit-Leftwich, A. T., Glazewski, K. D., Newby, T. J., & Ertmer, P. A. (2010). Teacher value beliefs associated with using technology: Addressing professional and student needs. *Computers and Education*, *55*(3), 1321–1335. https://doi.org/10.1016/j.compedu.2010.06.002

Patton, M. Q. (2015). *Qualitative research and evaluation methods*. SAGE Publications, Inc.

Perifanou, M., & Economides, A. A. (2022). Discoverability of OER: The case of language OER. In Ó. Mealha, M. Dascalu, T. Di Mascio (Eds.), *Ludic, co-design and tools supporting smart learning ecosystems and smart education* (pp.55–66). Springer. https://doi.org/10.1007/978-981-16-3930-2_5

Reinhardt, J., & Thorne, S. L. (2019). Digital literacies as emergent multifarious literacies. In Arnold, N., & Ducate, L. (Eds.), *Engaging language learners through CALL* (pp. 208-239). London, U.K.: Equinox.

Richardson, J. W., Lingat, J. E. M., Hollis, E., College, R., & Pritchard, M. (2020). Shifting teaching and learning in online learning spaces: An investigation of a faculty online teaching and learning initiative. *Online Learning Journal*, *24*(1), 67–91. https://doi.org/10.24059/olj.v24i1.1629

Rogers, E. M. (2003). *Diffusion of innovations*. Free Press.

Romeo, K., Bernhardt, E. B., Miano, A., & Leffell, C. M. (2017). Exploring blended learning in a postsecondary Spanish language program: Observations, perceptions, and proficiency ratings. *Foreign Language Annals*, *50*(4), 681–696. https://doi.org/10.1111/flan.12295

Sato, T., Murase, F., & Burden, T. (2020). An empirical study on vocabulary recall and learner autonomy through mobile-assisted language learning in blended learning settings. *CALICO Journal*, *37*(3), 254–276. https://doi.org/10.1558/cj.40436

Shelley, M., Murphy, L., & White, C. J. (2013). Language teacher development in a narrative frame: The transition from classroom to distance and blended settings. *System*, *41*(3), 560–574. https://doi.org/10.1016/j.system.2013.06.002

Straub, E. T. (2009). Understanding technology adoption: Theory and future directions for informal learning. *Review of Educational Research*, *79*(2), 625–649. https://doi.org/10.3102/0034654308325896

Tao, J., & Gao, X. (2022). Teaching and learning languages online: Challenges and responses. *System*, *107*, 102819. https://doi.org/10.1016/j.system.2022.102819

Tour, E. (2015). Digital mindsets: Teachers' technology use in personal life and teaching. *Language Learning and Technology*, *19*(3), 124–139. http://llt.msu.edu/issues/october2015/tour.pdf

Troyan, F. J. (2012). Standards for foreign language learning: Defining the constructs and researching learner outcomes. *Foreign Language Annals*, *45*(s1), 118–141. https://doi.org/10.1111/j.1944-9720.2012.01182.x

VanPatten, B., Trego, D., & Hopkins, W. P. (2015). In-class vs. online testing in university-level language courses: A research report. *Foreign Language Annals*, *48*(4), 659–668. https://doi.org/10.1111/flan.12160

Wargo, K. (2021). Faculty development for online learning: catalysts for transforming practice across modalities. *Online Journal of Distance Learning Administration*, *24*(3). https://eric.ed.gov/?id=EJ1321266

7 Spanish Language Teachers' Experiences during the Pandemic: From In-person to Online Teaching and Back

Claudia Sánchez-Gutiérrez, Ana Ortega Pérez, Ana Ruiz-Alonso-Bartol, Paloma Fernández-Mira, Diane Querrien, and Shelley Dykstra

While online teaching was becoming more prominent in some countries such as the United States (Seaman et al., 2018), it was not the main format of instruction in most educational settings when the COVID-19 pandemic hit. The sudden shift to Emergency Remote Teaching and Learning (ERTL) caught educators worldwide by surprise, forcing them to teach online in stressful circumstances, often without prior training or experience (Zamborová et al., 2021). Several articles have documented teachers' experiences during the first few months of the pandemic, as they rapidly had to adjust to a new educational format in a global context of uncertainty and fear (Gao & Zhang, 2020; MacIntyre et al., 2020; Moser et al., 2021). Others also investigated teachers' uses of technologies post-ERTL (Giupponi et al., Chapter 6, this volume; Gruber et al., 2023).

Most of the literature has studied teachers' beliefs and practices either at the beginning of ERTL or in the "new-normal" era; we focus on the individual teachers' evolution throughout the period that connects the pre- and post-ERTL focusing on Graduate Teaching Assistants in a Spanish language program at a large public university in the United States. The purpose was to observe the common elements as well as individual differences in how these TAs navigated the changes that took place during the two years between the beginning of the pandemic and the moment when classes started being offered fully in person again.

Emergency Remote Teaching and Learning

Planned vs. Crisis-Prompted Online Teaching

Online teaching is an educational modality that can equal or surpass in-person teaching in student learning outcomes (Blake et al., 2008; Enkin & Mejías-Bikandi, 2017). Some student characteristics, such as self-motivation or technological skills, seem to positively impact their learning process in an online environment (Discenza et al., 2001). Additionally, several studies emphasize the role of the instructor in promoting learners' comfort in online courses (Levy et al., 2009; Hampel & Stickler, 2015).

Fostering a sense of community among learners and complications monitoring students' progress (Strambi & Bouvet, 2003) are typical challenges of online teaching. Some research-based resources, such as the *Quality Matters Course Design Rubric* (Quality Matters, n.d.), have established guidelines of what constitutes adequate online course design. Pre-ERTL, said design was often carried out by motivated teachers at institutions that supported online education and provided appropriate professional training (Castro & Tumibay, 2019).

In March 2020, when most teachers around the globe started teaching online, they did not have the time (and often the training) to take the above-mentioned guidelines into consideration. Instead, they engaged in a process that aimed "to provide temporary access to instruction and instructional support in a manner that is quick to set up and is reliably available during an emergency or crisis" (Hodges et al., 2020, p. 13). However, this shocking and rapid global educational shift also acted "as a source of productive tension prompting wider evaluation of a teacher's practice" (Ashton, 2022, p. 10).

Teachers' Reactions to ERTL

Teachers' initial reactions to this unexpected global emergency were documented in different countries and contexts (e.g., Ashton, 2022; Smith & Arnott, 2022). At the onset of the pandemic teachers across the globe displayed high levels of anxiety (MacIntyre et al., 2020; Smith & Arnott, 2022). Preoccupation about students' mental health was also pervasive (Ashton, 2022). While some teachers felt distressed by the lack of boundaries between work and home (Appel & Robbins, 2022), others saw ERTL as an opportunity to spend more time with their families (Kwee, 2022).

Learners' lack of engagement was repeatedly found to be a taxing aspect of ERTL (Leech et al., 2022; Walter & Schenker, 2022). Teachers identified the reduced opportunities for personal and non-verbal interactions (Gao & Zhang, 2020), as well as learners' tendency to turn off their cameras during synchronous sessions (Gruber et al., 2023; Walter & Schenker, 2022), as culprits of students' disengagement. Many instructors also worried about learning outcomes and cheating (Kwee, 2022; Walter & Schenker, 2022). In Walter and Schenker (2022) instead of transferring typical in-person assessments to an online setting, other types of assessments, such as projects, virtually eliminated cheating issues and promoted creativity (Link & Li, 2018).

As teachers attempted to provide more individualized attention to their students and to address cheating concerns, some felt overwhelmed by the resulting workload (Ashton, 2022; Leech et al., 2022). In Kwee (2022), however, instructors noticed that their workload had decreased during ERTL as they were already familiar with the technologies they needed and they felt they were making the most efficient use of them in this new context. Teachers in this study also reported having more control over their students' behavior, not less, thanks to some technological tools, such as Zoom recordings. In sum, teachers' familiarity with a variety of online learning tools significantly reduced their anxiety and workload in the ERTL context (Gao & Zhang, 2020; Moser et al., 2021).

Although technological readiness was necessary to feel less distressed during ERTL, it was not sufficient. In Lim (2022), teachers who had stronger pedagogical training (not specifically related to online teaching) were able to better respond to the challenges of ERTL. These data generally highlight the need for institutions to offer adequate pedagogical training to all teachers (Moser & Wei, 2023). As a complement to this institutional assistance, informal support groups and communities of practice were also useful resources for instructors during ERTL (Beardsley et al., 2021; Ulla & Perales, 2021).

Teachers' Perceptions of Online Teaching During and After ERTL

Teachers generally appreciated how online teaching pushed their students to be more autonomous (Gruber et al., 2023). Often, adaptations to ERTL followed a flipped classroom model (O'Flaherty & Phillips, 2015), where learners were exposed to specific contents through (self-paced) asynchronous activities prior to class. During synchronous classes, students then applied what they had learned asynchronously. After ERTL, many teachers and students wanted to maintain practices that favor students' autonomy, such as self-study asynchronous activities (Ashton, 2022; Lavolette & Asaba, Chapter 10, this volume).

Overall, many teachers held positive opinions about online education after ERTL (Gruber et al., 2023; Jin et al., 2021). In Gruber et al. (2023), most instructors enjoyed the flexibility in schedules and work settings, the sense of agency and self-efficacy that the selection of teaching materials and online tools allowed, or the collaborative problem-solving atmosphere that arose from addressing pedagogical challenges with colleagues. According to Jin et al. (2021), the best predictors of teachers' positive attitudes towards online teaching were the perceived value of the affordances of this educational format, their own self-confidence in teaching online and their stress levels during ERTL.

Most studies referenced above looked at instructors' challenges at the onset of ERTL or investigated their intentions to maintain pedagogical practices from ERTL in their post-ERTL courses. This study delves into the individual evolution of teachers', and specifically TAs', attitudes and challenges as they navigated the transition from in-person to online teaching and the second transition to a "new normal" in-person education. The present study documents the experiences of six L2 Spanish instructors from May 2020 to November 2021, using a multiple case study longitudinal approach. Concretely, our research questions were as follows: 1) Which factors contributed to increasing or reducing TAs' anxiety during and post- ERTL? 2) Which teaching practices did TAs maintain over time post-ERTL?

While the answers to RQ 1 can offer specific tips for Language Program Directors (LPD) on how to manage future crises and how to work with TAs in a way that reduces anxiety, answers to RQ2 could provide information on the lessons learned by TAs through the ERTL experience and how their individual characteristics and decision-making processes influenced said learning.

Methods

Research Context

This study took place in a lower-division first-year Spanish language program at a large public university in the Western United States. Each academic quarter (i.e., Fall, Winter, Spring), approximately 500 students enroll in the program. Courses are taught by graduate TAs. In addition to the in-person series of courses, two other series of blended and online introductory courses also existed pre-ERTL. However, no more than one section of these courses was offered each quarter before the pandemic, and the syllabus was different from that of the in-person courses. This study focuses on the in-person courses that transitioned to an online format.

At this institution, the transition to ERTL coincided with final exams' week during Winter 2020, which was followed by a week of Spring Break. This provided the LPD with two weeks to prepare the course modifications described hereunder. During these two weeks, she and a team of volunteering TAs adapted course contents and activities to an online environment. Before classes started in Spring 2020 (S20), the team organized an online teaching workshop for all TAs in the program. The department and university offered additional training. After the first quarter of ERTL, the same team improved the online version of the program over the summer, as the university announced that the 2020–2021 academic year would take place online. In Fall 2021 (F21) students and instructors came back to the classrooms.

During the 2021–2022 academic year, campus leadership insisted that the university was a "brick and mortar" institution, where classes should be taught in physical classrooms. Teachers who needed accommodations relative to COVID-19 could teach online only if their accommodation requests were granted. Additionally, the official process to get new online courses approved became more complicated than it was pre-pandemic, requiring detailed documentation on how the course would contribute to student learning to a greater extent than a similar in-person one. Given that the department where this study took place offered some online and blended courses pre-ERTL, it did not need to go through any administrative approval process to offer more sections of these courses post-ERTL or change their contents based on the lessons learned during ERTL. Online and blended courses now represent almost one third of the beginner language course offerings.

Before the pandemic, in-person courses were taught in five 50-minute sessions per week. Students had to complete homework in the online textbook *Contraseña* (Lord & Rossomondo, 2019) before each session, following a flipped classroom model. *Contraseña* had been adopted in September 2019. The year prior to its adoption, the LPD collaborated with a group of TAs to select the new textbook. This recent collaborative endeavor at the program level probably facilitated the efficient organization of the ERTL adaptation efforts, as many TAs had already worked closely with the LPD in the previous year.

Table 1 shows how the original in-person model (Pre-ERTL) was first modified in S20 so that asynchronous activities were completed in *Contraseña* and in the LMS on Mondays, Wednesdays and Fridays, while Tuesdays and Thursdays were reserved for small group conversation practice on Zoom. Instead of offering Zoom lectures, students signed up for shorter, 30-minute conversation sessions to promote students' participation (Ross & DiSalvo, 2020).

Table 1 Evolution of the Language Program from Pre-ERTL to Fall 2021

Weekday	Pre-ERTL	ERTL: S20	ERTL: F20–S21	Post-ERTL: F21–present
Monday	In-person	Asynchronous activities	Asynchronous activities	In-person
Tuesday	In-person	Zoom conversations	Zoom lecture	In-person
Wednesday	In-person	Asynchronous activities	Asynchronous activities	In-person
Thursday	In-person	Zoom conversations	Zoom conversations	In-person
Friday	In-person	Asynchronous activities	Asynchronous activities	In-person or online exam (biweekly)

While this new structure gave students opportunities for real conversational practice in Spanish, they missed discussing grammatical and lexical contents as a class (see Ruiz-Alonso-Bartol et al., 2022). As a result, during the 2020–2021 academic year, one session per week was devoted to a lecture-style Zoom session on Tuesdays and small group conversation sessions took place on Thursdays. Finally, starting in F21, in-person courses were again offered every day of the week for 50 minutes.

Participants

Six TAs participated in this study. In the text, they will be referred to using pseudonyms. None of them had experience teaching online, but all were involved in the above-mentioned ERTL adaptation efforts. As evidenced in Table 2, all were completing either an MA or a PhD in Linguistics or

Table 2 Participants' Teaching Experience and Training

	Specialization	Teaching experience at institution	Previous teaching experience
Ana	MA: Linguistics	Less than one year	None
Sonia	PhD: Linguistics	Less than a year	Several years
Lola	PhD: Linguistics	Two years	Several years
Clara	PhD: Literature	Less than a year	Several years
Daniel	PhD: Linguistics	Two years	None
Elena	MA: Linguistics	Two years	None

Literature, and had differing levels of teaching experience in the department and previous to their enrollment in the program.

Instruments and Data Collection Timeline

Participants completed three tasks (see: https://www.iris-database.org/details/twv2z-1MtCL) over a timespan of 18 months. In S20, they responded to a questionnaire that inquired about the issues they were finding in the process of adapting to this new teaching modality, and their overall perspective on said process. During F20, when they had already taught online for two quarters, they participated in a semi-structured Zoom interview that was audio-recorded and carried out by a member of the research team who did not personally know the participants. Finally, in F21, when classes were back in-person, they participated in a second interview where they reflected on the lessons learned as they had to repeatedly adapt to various teaching modalities in a matter of months. These interviews were again audio-recorded and carried out by the same interviewer as the first one.

Data Analysis

Interviews were transcribed and imported into MaxQDA (VERBI, 2022) alongside participants' responses to the open-ended questions in the initial questionnaire. Data were analyzed following an inductive open coding approach (Corbin & Strauss, 2014). First, an initial list of codes was established based on the themes that emerged from the data. Two researchers in the author team annotated 20% of the data using these codes. Inter-agreement scores were computed in MaxQDA and initially ranged between 85% and 98%. Discrepancies on codes with inter-agreement scores below 90% were discussed to adjust the list of codes (e.g., eliminate redundant codes). Based on this new list, both annotators coded the same 20% of the data again. Inter-agreement scores for all codes then surpassed 95%, and the two researchers each annotated half of the remaining data.

Description of the Research Team

The research team was composed of six co-authors, of whom two were also research participants, and another was the LPD of the program where the study was carried out. When the LPD originally started the project in collaboration with the co-Principal Investigator (PI), a professor from another university, they focused on students' perspectives of ERTL. Instructors' responses to the May 2020 survey and Fall 2020 interview were thus going to serve a triangulatory purpose. When two of the participants – graduate students in applied linguistics – joined the team, they played a central role in analyzing the student data. As the project further developed and aimed to document instructors' beliefs about online teaching over a longer time span, the two author-participants completed the second interview. To prevent them from analyzing their own data, two additional authors joined the team and carried out the coding of the data under the supervision of the co-PI. None of the participant-authors took part in the writing of this chapter but they did review it prior to submission.

Results

Results are presented as individual case studies divided into TA's initial reactions to ERTL and their views post-ERTL. Each TA's personal perspectives are illustrated with verbatim excerpts from their interviews and survey responses.

Daniel

Daniel expressed being nervous at the beginning of ERTL because he had not used Zoom, but the workshops offered before S20, as well as his familiarity with *Contraseña* made him feel more confident. Concerning the adaptations that were made for the synchronous Zoom activities, he appreciated having the opportunity to take part in those with the LPD and a group of peers and valued the sense of community that emanated from this experience. Daniel first worried about students not turning on their cameras and participating less. He also realized that even though pre-ERTL he liked having conversations with the whole class he had to accept that, on Zoom, students could only speak one at a time. This made him explore some apps, such as Nearpod, to enhance student engagement. Finally, he noticed that students were having better grades in the exams but was unsure if these grades reflected actual learning, since "it's easier to complete an exam online than in a class."

Post-ERTL Daniel was eager to teach in person again, as he felt that it was easier to "see in [the students'] face if they are paying attention." He liked that students were volunteering to talk more and that "everybody was talking with everybody." He also enjoyed "just walk[ing] in the class and see[ing] how all are doing." He noticed that, when teaching online, he "followed more activities in the book, and now sometimes [he] creat[ed] [his] own activities." He recognized, though, that some teaching practices from ERTL were useful even during in-person classes. For instance, "[he] started using the Google Doc as a tool to see that everybody was working in the activities, so, [he] implemented that also in the face-to-face." He generally felt that, although he preferred teaching in person, "[he] learned a lot during this experience."

Sonia

At the onset of ERTL, Sonia mentioned she was worried about the pandemic itself, but "teaching online, it was just the alternative, but it didn't make [her] anxious." The key for her was that she was already familiar with *Contraseña* and the LMS, and knew how to use some of their features, such as discussion boards, announcements, or peer-reviewing, to incentivize students' engagement. One of her challenges in those first steps of ERTL was making sure that students knew what they had to do during synchronous sessions. Initially, she did the conversation sessions without any visual support, such as a PowerPoint, but rapidly realized that students needed to visualize the instructions for each activity and be prepared for them. She, thus, "created a Google Doc where students could look at the agenda ahead of time."

When classes transitioned back to a fully in-person format, Sonia noticed that, since the asynchronous assignments on *Contraseña* were maintained while she also had to grade worksheets or other materials from the in-person classes, her workload had increased significantly post-ERTL. Additionally, when it came to the in-person activities, she wondered: "Are we coming to class for no reason? That's what we ask ourselves now. Could this have been done online, right?" This feeling that being in person was not automatically a better option, was particularly salient in her thoughts about interaction in the classroom. For instance, she mentioned that

> in-person I would walk into the class, and there would be students sitting there. And some days they weren't talking at all, right? And then if there were days where I got there earlier, and I would rearrange the desks into group formations [...] then they would start talking to each other, right?

She also appreciated that her and her students' comfort with online teaching made it possible to quickly switch to that teaching modality when needed. Overall, Sonia felt that after the experience of ERTL she was "a little more willing to try new things," took students' well-being more into consideration, and was more organized, more able to explicitly keep students informed "of things coming up."

Clara

Clara's vision of ERTL was essentially that "this is not ideal, and we can agree that it is not ideal, but within the realm of not ideal we can do a lot of things." She mentioned how her students missed "being in a room with other people" and how it was not easy to work from home and feel that everyone could see their rooms, living rooms, etc. Nonetheless, she was "blown away by some of [her] students and how they [became] friends and how it [spoke] volumes of the structure of the course", suggesting that the small conversation groups allowed students to develop relationships despite being remote. Concerning the aspects that lowered her stress levels at the onset of ERTL, "[she] was thankfully part of the conversation of how we're going to do it" and the workshops offered in the department and the university were an important source of support as well. Additionally, her network of fellow teachers became an important professional resource to exchange ideas and feel part of a community. However, she was still concerned about technologies being misused for cheating and plagiarism and was fearful that her teaching materials and Zoom recordings could be shared on social media.

Post-ERTL in F21, Clara noticed an increased level of interaction with students, since they could not "disappear or be absent from class" by turning off their cameras. Concretely, she stated that "being in the same room brings more energy." According to her, that collective energy made students more creative when working on their course projects. However, she observed that students who had to commute struggled to come to class every day and some even dropped the course. In general, she felt that she was "spend[ing] lots of time in dialogue with students, which [she] was missing from the online version." This enhanced investment in her students and in her classes increased her workload significantly, but she concluded that "all that takes time, but I think it's paying off."

Ana

At the beginning of the pandemic, Ana did not feel confident enough in her own pedagogical skills, but she still thought that ERTL was "an opportunity to try something different." She had only taught two full language courses prior to the pandemic and was still getting used to the typical in-person teaching when she had to suddenly switch to a completely new format. As an example of her insecurities, she avoided using break-out rooms on Zoom for many weeks because she did not feel comfortable using them. On a positive note, she noticed that "online classes didn't affect [students'] results, even it could be better", as students were "more focused on the activities, the steps, the instructions." Finally, Ana mentioned that she became stricter when it came to accepting late homework during ERTL, because "COVID was for everyone [...] so some [students] were working hard even though the situation and COVID and anxiety and everything but they did, and a couple of them didn't go to the class, didn't do their homework [...], so it was unfair."

For Ana, the transition to teaching in person again represented a significant increase in workload. While during ERTL she was using the lesson plans created during S20, she now had to prepare more activities and handouts for each class, which she then had to grade. She also declared being more creative in person, designing new activities and modifying others from the textbook to better respond to students' interests. Additionally, although she recognized that some specific online tools, such as Google Docs, kept students active during online synchronous sessions, she hesitated to incorporate those in face-to-face classes, since students "need to use computers or cell phones and [she doesn't] like that." Finally, Ana noticed that she was "more sensitive about all students' problems, more than in online classes."

Lola

At the beginning of ERTL, Lola mostly worried about Zoom, which she had not used in the past. She was specifically concerned about students' interactions, "how [she] would connect with them." Alternatively, "everything that was asynchronous, [she] wasn't really worried about it because we prepared it a lot, so it was already prepared, and [she] was involved in the preparation." Additionally, Lola had taught a blended course in the previous quarter, so she already knew "students could do a lot of things independently." Initially, she thought students would cheat a lot more than in person; but, after the first project that students completed, she "knew they weren't copying everything from the Internet, [she] could see that it was their work but still [the projects] were super, they were beautiful." An aspect that was still bothering her at the end of Spring 2020, was her own flexibility with deadlines as she had been accepting late assignments repeatedly and she eventually got frustrated with this dynamic.

Once classes were offered in person again, Lola felt that her workload reduced significantly. According to her, most students, but not all, interacted more, and "[communicative] activities worked much more organically in-person." She also noticed that students were staying to talk with her after class and were creating friendships among themselves. She generally felt that students were sharing more information about their mental health, which made her conclude that "maybe the pandemic made us learn more about each other's mental health or health in general" and that teachers "are people too, and [they] can understand. And we all went through the same stuff, so they can relate to us in that sense." This increased identification with the students also made her be "more flexible maybe, even more than before." However, she wondered "if that [was] good or bad." Looking back, she considered that she had become more productive, more organized, and that her explanations and instructions were clearer after going through ERTL.

Elena

Elena did not feel too overwhelmed by the onset of ERTL. She had taken a graduate seminar the year before that focused on L2 teaching with technologies, attended some of the training offered by the department and the university, and relied heavily on her community of teacher friends. She "would even practice with other colleagues, like [they]'d get on Zoom together and try out the whiteboard, try out all the little things you can do on Zoom, and make sure [they] knew how things would work before starting." Another factor that made it easier for her to adjust to the online environment was that the LPD "and everyone organized everything and made it so much less stressful." One of Elena's challenges during ERTL was making sure that students knew where and when assignments were due. She also noticed that some students were missing synchronous sessions or submitting assignments late and felt that, while some surely had good reasons to do so, she "didn't always just believe[d] them right off the bat because [she felt] like they were just tak[ing] advantage of [her]." Finally, she was concerned that students could complete their exams with the help of Spanish-speaking friends, or cheating in other ways.

As Elena went back to teaching face-to-face, "the first thing [she] decided was that [the students] could not use any electronics in class unless [she] [said] so." She did use more Google Slides or shared documents as part of assignments and replaced paper quizzes with online ones on the LMS. However, those technological tools were reserved for out-of-class activities, while she maintained the in-person sessions as technology-free as possible. By doing this, she felt that students were engaging more with her and with their peers. She particularly appreciated how she could "get to know them more." Finally, Elena felt she was struggling trying to keep track of students' absences and missed/late assignments, which she found more challenging in person. Overall, she thought that she "got more strict because of being online, that made [her] strict."

Discussion

This study aimed to document how six language instructors in an introductory Spanish language program navigated a first unexpected transition to crisis-prompted online teaching in S20 and a second one when they started teaching in person again in F21.

RQ1: Which Factors Contributed to Increasing or Reducing TAs' Anxiety During and Post-ERTL?

Overall, none of the TAs showed signs of excessive anxiety relative to their teaching, even at the onset of ERTL. This finding differs from studies where teachers tended to display high stress levels (MacIntyre et al., 2020; Smith & Arnott, 2022), but is consistent with others, such as Kwee (2022), where teachers were less anxious and felt more in control during ERTL despite the challenges they encountered. As evidenced in the present study, several factors seem to play a crucial role in reducing instructor's anxiety in crisis contexts.

First, Daniel, Clara, Lola and Elena mentioned that feeling part of a team at the beginning of the pandemic, as they all collaborated with the LPD and a team of peers to design activities and contents that were better adapted to the new online format, was key in making them feel less stressed during ERTL. These data mirror Gruber et al.'s (2023), who also found that teachers appreciated the opportunities for team work during ERTL. Given the sense of agency and community that arose from working together in adapting the program to ERTL, numerous collaborative pedagogical projects continued to flourish post-ERTL in the language program where the study took place. TAs are now encouraged to propose new ideas, work with peers and the LPD to try those ideas, and assess their impact on student learning outcomes. For instance, all courses in the program now include weekly reading workshops that are based on graded readers written and edited by a team of 13 TAs (see Dykstra et al., 2023). Similarly, four TAs developed materials for another sequence of workshops where students complete activities based on Spanish-speaking Netflix shows or Disney movies. Prior to the pandemic, TAs were not as engaged in the development of the program but, through the increased collaboration and creativity that started around ERTL, the TAs and LPD now feel more comfortable working together to make frequent changes to the program.

During ERTL, the department and the university also offered training opportunities, which were often seen as useful by the TAs. Daniel, Clara, and Elena specifically referred to these during their interviews. Elena also mentioned that taking a course on L2 teaching with technologies in previous years had greatly contributed to making her feel more comfortable during ERTL, showing that adequate pedagogical and technological training is necessary for instructors to adapt to sudden changes and new situations in online environments (Smith & Arnott, 2022; Tecedor & Gómez Soler, Chapter 13, this volume). In addition to this institutional type of support, Clara and Elena emphasized the importance of establishing networks of fellow teachers to feel supported and exchange creative ideas about teaching practices. These findings confirm that the establishment of communities of practice and professional support groups should be an integral part of teachers' professional development, beyond, or as part of, formal training (Beardsley et al., 2021; Moser & Wei, 2023; Ulla & Perales, 2021).

To continue encouraging peer-based support post-ERTL, the program now counts on a group of volunteer lead TAs, a role that did not exist in the department pre-ERTL. These lead TAs assist the LPD in creating the syllabi based on TAs' feedback that they collect informally through WhatsApp groups composed only of TAs. The LPD is thus not involved in the day-to-day conversations between TAs but rather receives the information through the lead TAs when designing the syllabi for the next quarter. This allows TAs to discuss pedagogical improvements among themselves, without the pressure of having a professor involved in the first stages of the discussion.

TAs' familiarity with the LMS and the online textbook were also seen as key in their overall efficient and positive handling of ERTL, as evidenced in Daniel, Sonia, and Lola's F20 interviews. Alternatively, Ana, who was still learning to use them when the pandemic started, felt more overwhelmed during ERTL. As was already found in Gao and Zhang (2020) or Smith and Arnott (2022), among others, awareness of the affordances and limitations of specific technological tools can ease teachers' response in crisis situations. It would thus be recommended to include opportunities to explore a large array of apps and technologies in the context of official teacher training courses and workshops but also in one-on-one discussions with TAs. For example, after visiting a TA's class and writing a report on the classroom observation, it would be useful that LPDs suggest specific tools that could be useful to address some of the issues observed or improve some aspects of the class.

RQ2: Which Teaching Practices did TAs Maintain over Time Post-ERTL?

In response to RQ2, two main themes emerged: TAs' use of technology post-ERTL and their flexibility with late assignments and other aspects of course management. Concerning the first theme, while Daniel and Sonia were open to incorporating technologies during in-person classes to enhance student participation post-ERTL, Ana and Elena were reluctant to do so out of fear that students would use their electronic devices for non-academic purposes or to cheat. All of them, though, acknowledged that using the LMS or the online textbook for asynchronous activities in preparation for in-person class saved some grading time and allowed students to study and work at their own pace in a more autonomous manner. Sonia, Clara and Lola also started using Google Docs to show students the agenda and plan for each synchronous session ahead of time, which helped them be more organized and clearer in their expectations. Overall, they tended to agree that the lack of in-person interaction during ERTL forced them to find new ways to communicate asynchronously through chats, shared documents, etc., and most continued using those post-ERTL outside of class.

As the context of ERTL forced us to rethink assessment methods, changes that were instituted during the pandemic, such as the focus on projects and formative rather than summative assessments have been maintained in the program. At the moment, unit exams are completed at home, considering them as opportunities to review contents from the unit rather than as evaluations per se, the final written exam was substituted for an oral exam which students train for over the course of the quarter, and a writing exercise that is completed in class in three parts: preparation, version 1 and version 2. Only the last version is given a grade using a rubric which students have access to in advance, while the first two steps of the writing process are graded with a Complete/Incomplete scheme. Overall, the program has adopted an assessment philosophy that values participation and work rather than grades, a change that was not even close to happening prior to the pandemic.

Going back to the use of technologies post-ERTL, as was mentioned by Sonia, effective teaching methods do not result from the technology used to teach but rather from establishing clear learning goals and using appropriate pedagogical resources (technological or not) to achieve them. This point is related to Rapanta et al.'s (2021) idea that what is needed is not a digitalization of education but rather a *pedagogization* of technology. The lessons of ERTL cannot simply be that we are now better acquainted with a larger range of technological tools but rather that, through them, we have solved pedagogical issues in productive and efficient ways. The discussions that started during ERTL on how specific technologies can be used to address the various needs and challenges of students and teachers in different contexts should continue as part of teacher training opportunities and discussions among LPDs and department chairs.

With respect to teachers' flexibility regarding late assignments or missed classes, during and after ERTL, TAs displayed very different profiles. For instance, Lola identified a lot with her students and, as a result, did not feel like she could say no to students' requests to submit assignments late. However, it was still unclear to her whether this attitude was productive or not post-ERTL. Daniel and Sonia also felt that they had become more flexible during ERTL. Ana and Elena, on the other hand, became stricter during ERTL. In Ana's case, she felt less connected to her students and had concerns related to fairness, which pushed her to not admit any late work. Once in-person teaching resumed, she became more accepting again, as she felt more attached to her students in that setting. Ana's pattern concurs with findings in Warner and Diao (Chapter 12, this volume) where teachers felt that Zoom did not allow them to connect properly with their students. In Elena's case, ERTL made her realize that she could be stricter as she had technological tools at her disposal to easily supervise her students' behavior and daily work. Post-ERTL, she maintained such stricter practices, since she felt they worked better for her. TAs' different reactions reveal that, in a time of crisis, when surrounded by uncertainty, some teachers may need to feel more in control and apply stricter rules, while others tend to identify and sympathize more with their students' struggles, resulting in enhanced flexibility. Our findings concur with Gülmez and Ordu (2022), where teachers also were divided into two groups post-ERTL: those who became more understanding and accepting to be closer to their students, and those who started exhibiting more authoritative behaviors to maintain a sense of control.

Conclusion

This study used a multiple case study approach to follow six TAs through 18 months between the onset of ERTL and the beginning of the first in-person academic year post-ERTL. Results indicate that each TA experienced ERTL and its aftermath in ways that were unique and were intimately related to their previous experiences with technology and pedagogy. Their personal sense of belonging to the language teaching profession, as well as their degree of connection with students during ERTL also shaped their practices and determined their level of flexibility even post-ERTL, in some cases.

What most of them shared was an impression that ERTL had made them learn about their own teaching practices and that they generally felt "way more flexible, way more light on [their] feet and ready to solve whatever problem." (Clara, F21).

About the Authors

Claudia Sánchez-Gutiérrez is an Associate Professor at the Department of Spanish and Portuguese at UC Davis. She specializes in second language acquisition and teaching, with a particular focus on vocabulary teaching/learning and the emotional aspects of learning a language as an adult. She is also the director of the First-Year Spanish program at UC Davis and, as such, she designs syllabi and teaching materials for the program while also training and supervising the TAs who teach them.

Ana Ortega Pérez is a PhD candidate in Spanish Linguistics at the University of California, Davis. She completed a BA in Journalism at the Universidad de Sevilla, an MA in International Relations at the Universidad Internacional de Andalucía and a PhD in Communication at the Universidad de Sevilla. Her research interests are heritage speakers, material development, Task-Based Language Teaching, and culture.

Ana Ruiz-Alonso-Bartol is a PhD student in Spanish Linguistics at the University of California, Davis, with an emphasis on second language acquisition. She completed her MA in Spanish with a Minor in TESOL at West Virginia University and a BA in Translation and Interpreting at the University of Salamanca (Spain). She is interested in SLA, L2 teaching methodologies and remote learning.

Paloma Fernández-Mira is a PhD candidate in Spanish Linguistics at the University of California, Davis. She completed her MA in Teaching Spanish as a Foreign Language at the University of Salamanca, Spain. Her research interests center around Spanish learner corpora, second language acquisition, and L2 Spanish teaching.

Diane Querrien is an Associate Professor at the Département d'études françaises at Concordia University (Montreal). Her research focuses on the teaching of French as a second/foreign language in higher education and second language teacher education. She is also an active participant and researcher in initiatives of the Québécois regional school communities to support the development of French among multilingual students.

Shelley Dykstra is a PhD candidate in Spanish Linguistics pursuing emphases in Second Language Acquisition and Writing, Rhetoric, and Composition Studies at the University of California, Davis. She completed her MA in Spanish Linguistics at University of Barcelona, Spain, and her BA in Linguistics Language Study from University of California, San Diego. Her current research interests are second language and heritage language reading and writing, online teaching and learning, and language learners' emotions.

References

Appel, C., & Robbins, J. (2022). Language teaching in times of COVID-19: The emotional rollercoaster of lockdown. In J. Chen (Ed.), *Emergency remote teaching and beyond: Voices from World Language teachers and researchers* (pp. 3–22). New York: Springer. https://doi.org/10.1007/978-3-030-84067-9_1

Ashton, K. (2022). Language teacher agency in emergency online teaching. *System*, *105*, 102713. https://doi.org/10.1016/j.system.2021.102713

Beardsley, M., Albó, L., Aragón, P., & Hernández-Leo, D. (2021). Emergency education effects on teacher abilities and motivation to use digital technologies. *British Journal of Educational Technology*, *52*(4), 1455–1477. https://doi.org/10.1111/bjet.13101

Blake, R., Wilson, N. L., Cetto, M., & Pardo-Ballester, C. (2008). Measuring oral proficiency in distance, face-to-face, and blended classrooms. *Language, Learning and Technology*, *12*(3), 114–127. https://www.lltjournal.org/item/10125-44158/

Castro, M., & Tumibay, G. (2019). A literature review: efficacy of online learning courses for higher education institutions using meta-analysis. *Education and Information Technologies*, *26,* 1367–1385. https://doi.org/10.1007/s10639-019-10027-z

Corbin, J., & Strauss, A. (2014). *Basics of Qualitative Research: Techniques and Procedures for Developing Grounded Theory* (4th edition). Thousand Oaks: SAGE. https://doi.org/10.1177/1094428108324514

Discenza, R., Howard, C., & Schenk, K. (2001). *The design and management of effective distance learning programs*. Hershey: IGI Global. https://doi.org/10.4018/978-1-930708-20-4

Dykstra, S., Sánchez-Gutiérrez, C., Marcos Miguel, N., & Alins Breda, D. (2023). Reading and affect: University Spanish learners' perceptions of a reading program. *Foreign Language Annals*, *56*(1), 191–213. http://dx.doi.org/10.1111/flan.12662

Enkin, E., & Mejías-Bikandi, E. (2017). The effectiveness of online teaching in an advanced Spanish language course. *International Journal of Applied Linguistics*, *27*(1), 176–197. https://doi.org/10.1111/ijal.12112

Gao, L., & Zhang, L. (2020). Teacher learning in difficult times: Examining foreign language teachers' cognitions about online teaching to tide over COVID-19. *Frontiers in Psychology*, *11*, 549653. https://doi.org/10.3389/fpsyg.2020.549653

Gruber, A., Matt, E., & Leier, V. (2023). Transforming foreign language education: Exploring educators' practices and perspectives in the (post-) pandemic era. *Education Sciences*, *13*(6), 601. https://doi.org/10.3390/educsci13060601

Gülmez, D., & Ordu, A. (2022). Back to the classroom: Teachers' views on classroom management after Covid-19. *International Journal of Modern Education Studies*, *6*(2), 257–286.

Hodges, C. B., Moore, S., Lockee, B. B., Trust, T., & Bond, M. A. (2020). The difference between emergency remote teaching and online learning. *Educause Review*, *27*, 1-12. https://doi.org/10.1007/978-981-15-7869-4_3

Jin, L., Xu, Y., Deifell, E., & Angus, K. (2021). Emergency remote language teaching and US-based college-level world language educators' intention to adopt online teaching in postpandemic times. *The Modern Language Journal*, *105*(2), 412-434. https://doi.org/10.1111/modl.12712

Kwee, C. (2022). To teach or not to teach: An international study of language teachers' experiences of online teaching during the COVID-19 pandemic. *SN Computer Science, 3,* 416. https://doi.org/10.1007/s42979-022-01323-6

Leech, N., Gullett, S., Cummings, M., & Haug, C. (2022). The challenges of remote K-12 education during the COVID-19 pandemic: Differences by grade level. *Online Learning, 26(1),* 245-267. https://doi.org/10.24059/olj.v26i1.2609

Levy, M., Wang, Y., & Chen, N. S. (2009). Developing the skills and techniques for online language teaching: A focus on the process. *International Journal of Innovation in Language Learning and Teaching, 3*(1), 17–34. https://doi.org/10.1080/17501220802655417

Link, S., & Li, J. (Eds.) (2018). *Assessment across online language education.* Bristol: Equinox.

Lim, J. (2022). Impact of instructors' online teaching readiness on satisfaction in the emergency online teaching context. *Education and Information Technologies*, 1–18. https://doi.org/10.1007/s10639-022-11241-y

Lord, G., & Rossomondo, A. (2019). *Contraseña: Your password to foundational Spanish 3.0*. Lingrolearning.

MacIntyre, P. D., Gregersen, T., & Mercer, S. (2020). Language teachers' coping strategies during the Covid-19 conversion to online teaching: Correlations with stress, wellbeing and negative emotions. *System, 94,* 102352. https://doi.org/10.1016/j.system.2020.102352

Moser, K., & Wei, T. (2023). Professional development in collaborative online spaces: Supporting rural language teachers in a post-pandemic era. *The New Educator*, *19*(1), 1–32. https://doi.org/10.1080/1547688x.2023.2174279

Moser, K., Wei, T., & Brenner, D. (2021). Remote teaching during COVID-19: Implications from a national survey of language educators. *System, 97,* 102431. https://doi.org/10.1016/j.system.2020.102431

O'Flaherty, J., & Phillips, C. (2015). The use of flipped classrooms in higher education: A scoping review. *The Internet and Higher Education*, *25*, 85–95. https://doi.org/10.1016/j.iheduc.2015.02.002

Quality Matters. (n.d.). *Course design rubric standards*. https://www.qualitymatters.org/qa-resources/rubric-standards/higher-ed-rubric

Querrien, D., Ruiz-Alonso-Bartol, S., Sánchez Gutiérrez, C., Ortega Pérez, A., & Fernández-Mira, P. (2023). Formation aux pratiques qualitatives à distance et en contexte de crise : le cas d'une équipe internationale féminine suite à la transition d'urgence en ligne 2020. In D. Demazière, J. Morrissette & M.-M. Dupont-Leclerc, *Former et se former en recherche qualitative: Pratiques et enjeux en tension.* Québec: Presses de l'Université Laval.

Rapanta, C., Botturi, L., Goodyear, P., Guárdia, L., & Koole, M. (2021). Balancing Technology, Pedagogy and the New Normal: Post-pandemic Challenges for Higher Education. *Postdigital science and Education. 3*, 715–742. https://doi.org/10.1007/s42438-021-00249-1

Ross, A. F., & DiSalvo, M. L. (2020). Negotiating displacement, regaining community: The Harvard Language Center's response to the COVID-19 crisis. *Foreign Language Annals*, *53*(2), 371–379.

Ruiz-Alonso-Bartol, A., Querrien, D., Dykstra, S., Fernández-Mira, P., & Sanchez-Gutierrez, C. (2022). Transitioning to emergency online teaching: The experience of Spanish language learners in a US university. *System*, *104*, 102684. https://doi.org/10.1016/j.system.2021.102684

Seaman, J. E., Allen, I. E., & Seaman, J. (2018). Grade increase: Tracking distance education in the United States. *Babson Survey Research Group.*

Smith, C., & Arnott, S. (2022). "French teachers can figure it out": Understanding French as a Second Language (FSL) teachers' work in the context of the COVID-19 pandemic. *Canadian Journal of Applied Linguistics*, *25*(1), 88–109. https://doi.org/10.37213/cjal.2022.32024

Strambi, A., & Bouvet, E. (2003). Flexibility and interaction at a distance: A mixed-model environment for language learning. *Language, Learning and Technology*, *7*(3), 81–102. https://www.lltjournal.org/item/10125-25215/

Ulla, M., & Perales, W. (2021). Emergency remote teaching during COVID19: The role of teachers' online community of practice (CoP) in times of crisis. *Journal of Interactive Media in Education*, *1*(9), 1–11. https://doi.org/10.5334/jime.617

VERBI Software. (2022). MAXQDA 2022 [latest version of computer software]. Berlin, Germany: VERBI Software. Available from http://maxqda.com/.

Walter, D., & Schenker, T. (2022). Surviving or thriving? Experiences and job satisfaction of language instructors in the USA during the COVID-19 pandemic. *Journal of Language Teaching*, *2*(11), 1–14. https://doi.org/10.54475/jlt.2022.014

Zamborová, K., Stefanutti, I., & Klimová, B. (2021). CercleS survey: impact of the COVID-19 pandemic on foreign language teaching in Higher Education. *Language Learning in Higher Education*, *11*(2), 269–283. https://doi.org/10.1515/cercles-2021-2032

8 Language Teachers as ERT Professionals During COVID: A Perspective from Professional Didactics

Jill Landry and Marie-Josée Hamel

Introduction

This chapter considers what was done by language teachers during Emergency Remote Teaching (ERT) (Jin et al., 2021; Moser et al., 2021) with a focus on their forced professionalization. It examines which digital competencies were missing, and how teachers identified and developed the digital skills required when classes moved online. This is considered from the viewpoint of professional didactics, which values what teachers did on their own and on the job through trial and error. We present a qualitative study of interviews conducted during the COVID-19 pandemic in which 10 higher education language teachers shared their experiences and digital practices in the first 18 months of ERT, and then we consider the initial changes and further refinements that teachers made from one semester to the next. From these accounts, we introduce three focal participants who illustrate the different experiences and transformations that occurred with ERT.

This research is in the tradition of professional didactics (Pastré, 1999; Piot, 2012), which values knowledge and professional development obtained on the job and approaches crises as opportunities for learning. This study refers to a model of language teachers' digital competencies to describe the ERT experience of the teachers interviewed (Hamel, 2017). Our qualitative analysis focuses on the tasks and activities language teachers did with their learners, why they made those choices, and how they acquired necessary digital skills to teach and reach their pedagogical objectives. We conclude with what lessons can be learned from the ERT experience, and how this study can inform stakeholders regarding language teachers' professional development going forward.

Language Teachers' Digital Practices Pre-COVID and Early COVID

Studies conducted prior to the pandemic provide insights into the digital competencies of educators and shed light on their initial interactions with digital tools. For instance, studies revealed language teachers actively utilized digital resources to access authentic audiovisual content (Germain-Rutherford & Ernest, 2015) and that they were acquainted with Learning Management Systems (LMSs), like Moodle and WebCT. Moreover, teachers made regular use of various digital tools, including word processing software, presentation slides, email communication, and authentic materials such as websites and recorded videos (Caws et al., 2021). In a survey from Francophone countries of nearly 2,500 language teachers, the majority reported giving students tasks to do on smartphones (Observatoire, 2018). Before the pandemic, language teachers also declared being generally interested in using digital tools for diagnostic and formative assessments, including writing, projects, oral productions, and providing feedback (Caws et al, 2021). In this particular study, teachers from Canada and France (n = 100) reported that they were "increasingly integrating digital technology into their language course," and almost half rated digital technology in the classroom as "important or very important" (Caws et al, 2021). However, half of these teachers also believed "online interactions promote little or no social or socio-emotional participation in their language lessons" (Caws et al, 2021). Pre-pandemic research in fact showed that language teachers had little or no experience with online synchronous teaching. For instance, in that same study by Caws et al. (2021), over half of the participants had "never taught in a remote or hybrid format." Prior to the pandemic, some researchers found that, rather than creating new practices, "many teachers still use the technology in predominantly 'old' ways, adapting new tools to their traditional teaching style rather than acquiring new skills to use the pedagogical affordances of the tools" (Hampel & Stickler, 2015, p. 65).

When classes shifted to ERT, many teachers reported they had just days to convert their courses (MacIntyre et al., 2020). Teachers who had "no prior online teaching experience were less confident" (Moser et al., 2021, p. 9), but even those teachers experienced with online teaching and course design were usually less able "to adhere to such principles" in the ERT context (Moser et al., 2021, p. 6). Some felt online ERT classes were a poor substitute for in-person classes, as well as "stressful, frustrating and impersonal" (ECML, 2021, p. 12).

Therefore, during ERT, teachers not only had to increase their knowledge of pedagogical technologies, but also their skills and understanding on how to effectively implement them in an online format during a global crisis. Not all teachers started ERT with the same level of digital competence (Hampel & Stickler, 2015; Delforge et al., 2022). For those teachers with lower levels of digital competencies, this "lack of digital expertise… resulted in an overwhelming workload" when their classes shifted into ERT (Werner & Küplüce, 2021, p. 300). As well, teachers discovered a lack of "quality resources for teaching and learning" online (Gao & Zhang, 2020, p. 7). The move to ERT provided a unique opportunity to see how pre-pandemic trends regarding the use of technology in the language classroom developed on an accelerated timeline. Before the pandemic, language teachers reported attending professional development course(s) on digital training and wanting more training (Germain-Rutherford & Ernest, 2015; Hampel & Stickler, 2015; Observatoire, 2018) to develop their digital skills. Early in the pandemic, teachers still attended formal professional development sessions. Yet, they also did "a lot of autonomous learning and exploration" along with online teaching practice (Gao & Zhang, 2020, p. 7) in order to develop needed competencies. In most cases, teachers felt they had not been trained in the necessary technological and pedagogical skills to integrate digital technology instruction (MacIntyre et al., 2020) such as "choosing the tool that met their own needs, including presence through the screen" (Delforge et al., 2022, par. 75, translated from French). Over time, teachers indicated that they had developed an "ability to integrate digital tools into language teaching" (Werner & Küplüce, 2021, p. 299). These pre- and early-pandemic studies left us wanting to know more about what effect teaching during the pandemic had on teachers' professional development; what they gained in terms of knowledge, experience, and expertise; and how they gained it; and how they perceived their digital competencies. These considerations led us to formulate the following research questions related to how language teachers (LT) developed professionally during the ERT context:

- RQ1: How have teachers transformed their pedagogical practice (their work situation) and constructed new learning activities concerning the specific dimensions of their "work" as online language pedagogues?
- RQ2: How did teachers envision their post-ERT practice and return to in-person teaching as LT professionals?

- RQ3: How did teachers perceive themselves as LT professionals in this ERT specific context?

Our focus on language teachers' transformation of their work situation was approached through the broader theoretical lens of CALL ergonomics and, more specifically, the field of professional didactics.

Theoretical Perspective

The present study is part of longitudinal research in CALL ergonomics (cf. Caws & Hamel, 2016) which considers technology as a vector of change and potential innovation in language education. It approaches language teachers' experiences and growth from their own perspective as professionals of their fields, in their specific "work" contexts. For the past ten years, the second author's research has focused on the digital usages of language teachers, including the proposal of a model of digital competencies in hybrid modalities (Hamel, 2017). This model, anchored in professional didactics (Pastré, 1999), was built to serve as "a tool for thinking" (Bertin, 2015, para. 13) to support teacher (self-)training.

Professional Didactics

Professional didactics is a theoretical formalization of adult learning (Piot, 2012) and focuses on analyzing professionals' activities in discipline-specific work situations in order to understand how skills and competences are developed through reflective and critical processes. It views and defines professional work as training and transformation opportunities (Mayen, 2012, p. 60), both within and outside of formal professional development training contexts. Professional didactics is conceived as an intersection of work, learning, and training. From this perspective, training or professional development are not seen as separate from the regular demands of professional work; rather as something integrated into both the routine and the exceptional demands of professional tasks, and combining formal professional development with on-the-job or "workplace learning" (Mayen, 2015, p. 201). This applies equally to novice and experienced professionals. Recognizing that work in all settings is dynamic, professional didactics analyzes "how competencies are constructed and developed in and for work" (Pastré, 1999, p. 109). It seeks to understand and promote learning related to work and the profession and to recycle this knowledge into opportunities for critical reflection, self-evaluation, and training. Professional didactics considers crisis contexts (e.g. economic, social) and moments of "ruptures" in the workplace as opportunities for learning (Piot, 2012).

A Model of Language Teachers' Digital Competencies in Hybrid Modalities

Bertin (2015), recalling Bertin et al. (2010 and 2013), suggests "a modeling approach as a means to structure an ever-evolving (teaching/learning) environment" (para. 10) and that a model can serve as a means to represent and explain the complexity of a work situation and be used with the purpose of: "understanding, designing, and training (teachers, tutors, learners, etc.)" (op. cit.). Hamel's (2017) model of digital competencies (see Figure 1) aligns with the aims of professional didactics and seeks to describe the specific tasks performed by language teachers in their technology-mediated professional "work" situations. This model stems from a qualitative research study aimed at documenting the digital practices of language teachers who were part of an initiative to transform their face-to-face language classes into hybrid ones and how they perceived themselves as professionals in this new context (see Nissen, 2019).

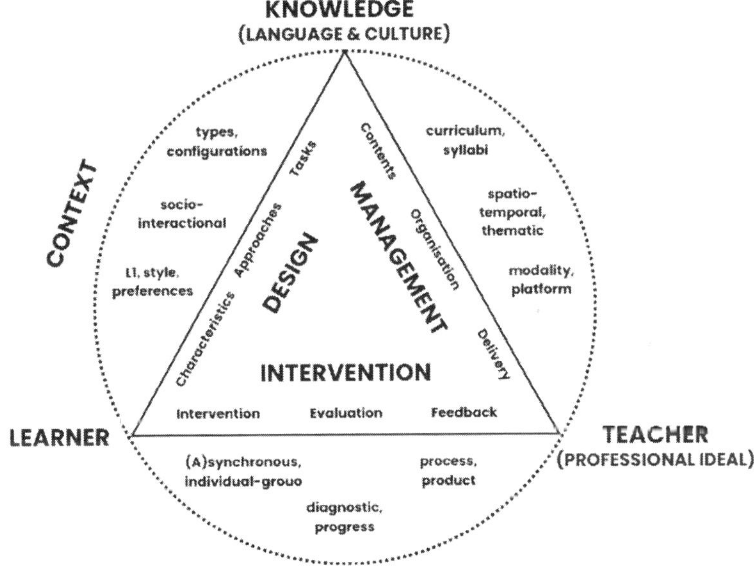

Figure 1 A model of Language Teachers' Digital Competencies in Hybrid Modalities (Hamel, 2017 Translated)

As illustrated in Figure 1, the model juxtaposes a *Contextual* dimension, represented as a dotted circle, and a *Pedagogical* dimension, depicted as a triangle recalling the "Houssaye triangle" (1988). The two dimensions intersect at the three axis points, which are named for the *Teacher*, the *Learner*, and *Knowledge*. Here, *Knowledge* encompasses language and culture, as well as the know-how (to do, to be, to interact) associated with the operationalization of such knowledge. Three main types of pedagogical competencies are emphasized which result from the relationship between teacher, learner and knowledge: *Management*, *Design*, and *Intervention*. Pedagogical *Design* competencies, the Learner-Knowledge relationship, concern the techno-pedagogical design, the consideration of learner characteristics, pedagogical approaches, learning objectives and results, as well as the types of tasks envisaged to reach these. Pedagogical *Management* competencies, the *Teacher-Knowledge* relationship, concern the management of contents, their organization, and presentation. These skills relate to the ability to orchestrate teaching–learning modalities. Pedagogical *Intervention* skills, the *Teacher–Learner* relationship, bring together skills related to interacting with the learner(s) in various contexts and modalities, evaluating their work and progress, and providing various forms and types of feedback. The model also importantly considers the *Professional Ideal* of the *Teacher*, which is linked to a teacher's perception of their own competencies, the expression of their values and beliefs, and their professional goals.

Methods

Participants

Ten participants who had previously answered a questionnaire about their digital practices participated in this qualitative interview-based study investigating educators' digital practices and learning. All participants were assigned pseudonyms (see Table 1). The participants were on average 50 years old – from 34 to 64. All of the participants were teaching languages (French or English as a second or additional language) at undergraduate level in major public universities; nine in Canadian universities (A, B and D were located in Ontario; C in Quebec) and the final participant was working in Brazil. All were experienced educators with an average of 24 years' experience. Of the 10 participants, all identified as female. To answer the research question, semi-directed qualitative interviews were conducted building on earlier studies by the second author and involving language teachers' digital

Table 1 Demographic Portrait of the 10 Participants

	University	Language(s) taught	Sex	Age	Experience in years
Béatrice	Canada A	ESL	F	49	25
Dina	Canada C	FLS	F	34	14
Élizon	Canada B	FLS	F	45	5
Éloise	Brazil	ESL / FLS	F	56	30
Laure	Canada A	FLS	F	64	30
Marie	Canada B	FLS	F	50	24
Marie-Anne	Canada A	FLS	F	54	20
Marielle	Canada D	FLS	F	40	20
Rosalie	Canada B	FLS	F	53	30
Shannon	Canada A	FLS/ESL	F	51	30

practices (Caws et al. 2021; Hamel, 2017). The semi-guided approach allowed for the exploration of subtopics as they arose (Gillham, 2005).

Data Collection

The one-hour interviews took place and were recorded on Microsoft Teams in October 2021 in English and/or French. They were a follow-up to a questionnaire on language teachers' digital practices distributed just prior to ERT in February 2020 (Hamel & Bibeau, 2021). The interviews were semi-guided (Gillham, 2005; Saldaña, 2021) and structured in two consecutive 30-minute parts: first, participants were asked to describe their teaching experiences from the initial eighteen months of ERT and second, focused specifically on their written-corrective feedback (WCF) practices during that period. The data analyzed here mostly concerns the first part of the interviews, but since language teachers revisited and expanded on responses from the first part in relation to our research questions in the second part, relevant pieces from both responses have been integrated here. The questions in the first part focused on the teachers' digital transformation: which new competencies they developed; how their self-perception as online teachers changed; and which digital practices they wanted to retain post-pandemic.

The interviews that were wholly or partly in English were transcribed automatically using the transcription feature of Microsoft Teams; the interviews or portions thereof in French were machine transcribed using Sonix.ai. In both cases, the transcripts were manually reviewed and corrected against the recordings. Both the recordings and the transcripts were uploaded into

NVIVO. The word frequency analysis feature was used to create word clouds, and the interviews were manually coded for keywords related to the research questions and then analyzed thematically (Miles et al., 2020; Saldaña, 2021); inter-rater reliability was verified by both research assistants and the supervisor. As the themes emerged, the interviews were revisited and codes were added.

After analyzing the themes from the interviews, we found that the 10 teachers could be placed somewhere along a continuum of three types according to their digital competencies at the beginning of ERT, and how that influenced their response and development throughout the pandemic until the time of the interviews: *Tech-inclined*, *On-the-move* and *Traditional* teacher types.

Results

Overall

Reviewing the qualitative corpus of interviews, our thematic data analysis revealed the 10 language teachers' display of digital competencies can be spread on a continuum from the challenged to the enthusiastic (cf. Figure 2). By analyzing their responses thematically, including the emotions, positive or negative, with which they describe their experiences with learning, using, adapting, or integrating digital tools and tasks into their language classrooms, we determined that the teachers ranged from those with less experience with technology and who were reluctant to make changes in their professional practice, to those with more experience and open to changes, to those who were already comfortable with technology and had a range of tools from which to choose, or competencies on which to build. The *Tech-inclined* sought solutions, whereas the *Traditional* struggled with challenges. The *On the move* teachers sought opportunities to introduce revisions in their professional practice. The *Traditional* teachers (Marielle, Shannon) expressed more rigidity and showed a higher level of stress and helplessness. The *Tech-inclined* teachers (Béatrice, Éloise, Rosalie) had more digital competencies at the start of the ERT, coped more easily with online teaching and adopted a critical distance vis-à-vis their techno-pedagogical decisions. In the middle group, the *On the move* teachers (Dina, Marie-Anne, Marie, Laure, and Élizon), we found flexible teachers, who, although they did not have a vast repertoire of online teaching strategies, were ready (to some extent) for challenges and embracing professional growth despite the stress brought by the ERT context.

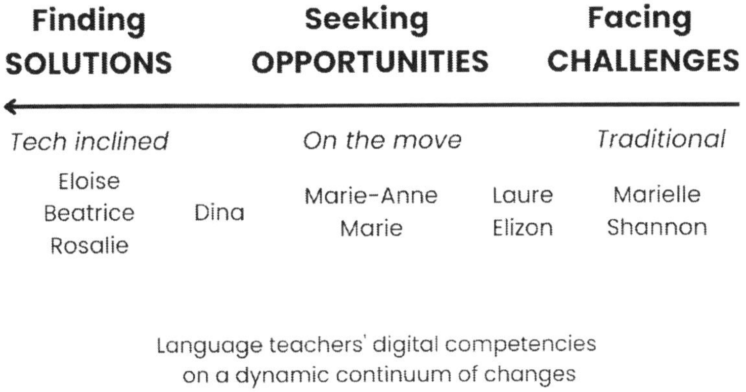

Figure 2 Teachers' Digital Competencies on a Dynamic Continuum of Changes

Figure 2 shows the 10 language teachers with regard to their stance/posture as "ERT professionals" during the COVID-19 pandemic; a posture on a dynamic continuum of changes as, to a diverse degree, they had to transform their professional practice in order to make it successful.

The following sections present descriptions of three focal participant teachers who were selected as representatives for each type: 1) Shannon, a traditional teacher, for whom the teaching experience was difficult and stressful; 2) Dina, an on-the-move teacher for whom ERT was emancipatory and transformative and, finally, 3) Éloise, a tech-inclined teacher for whom ERT consolidated her ways of teaching with technology. None of them had taught synchronously online before the pandemic.

Traditional Shannon: "I'm still very hesitant"

Shannon's university moved into ERT in late March 2020 near the end of her semester, so she found someone in her network to help adapt her final exams into a grammar-based, secure, multiple-choice format, a "very time-consuming" early success. During our interviews, Shannon still felt "very hesitant" with online teaching even after a year and a half. She used the LMS mainly as a repository, but was not comfortable using it to upload or share documents, nor to access Zoom. She tried breakout rooms, but after leaving students in a breakout room and ending the class, she goes "into breakout rooms with such dread and fear." Manipulating the LMS and the Zoom platform during a synchronous class left her feeling "deathly afraid."

Besides the technical challenges, Shannon found "the dynamic is different" and she was unable to "read the body language." This was compounded when students had their cameras off and might not have actually been present. Shannon feels calling on someone who is not there is "wasted time," and she "can't track the number of times students participate… [there's] just too much going on at the same time in the class." Shannon relied on people in her network to develop digital competencies: family, a close colleague, a TA, and her students. "The students have been very patient. They'll say, 'Madame, you have to click here, you have to do this'. I just have to put my pride in my pocket." After 18 months of teaching online, Shannon attended a formal presentation on using the LMS. She was aware that colleagues were using other digital affordances and her students experienced a variety of learning activities in other classes. "I've never created a Kahoot… I daren't go there. I don't have the confidence and if it fails I don't know how to fix it. And the last thing I want to do is waste students' time."

Shannon found marking assignments online "tedious" for health reasons and screen fatigue. The students scanned their assignments and uploaded them to the LMS, which she marked by inserting symbols of checkmarks, *x*es, and comment bubbles. Normally she enjoys providing feedback and feels "that's her role," but she did not feel "equipped" to record it orally. She felt the beginner students would not listen to it, and advanced students would prefer to read. Shannon's department provided a teaching assistant to help with the marking, but that meant Shannon missed seeing her students' patterns of errors and adding her own comments of correction and encouragement; it also led to inequitable support across educators. For oral presentations, Shannon took notes and emailed feedback because she "can't trust [the LMS] yet." She noticed more students attended one-on-one office hours on Zoom than pre-pandemic when those were in-person. One affordance Shannon identified is having all of the materials that she has developed over the years in the LMS. "It just became a really good repository," and it is now easy for her to copy everything over for future courses. However, she found doing all her work online, including class delivery, marking, individual meetings with students, and departmental meetings to be challenging. "I don't know that there's necessarily been an evolution," she said about her teaching practices overall throughout the pandemic. "I can kind of teach the way I taught before [ERT], but it's just all the buttons I have to press first in order to get there that can trip me up… I always go into class online with a knot in my stomach."

On the Move Dina: "I have completely changed"

Pre-pandemic, Dina was skeptical about teaching online and tried to avoid it. In March 2020, she was teaching graduate seminars and found the transition "mostly technical." However, she began teaching a French language class for beginners online in the Winter session of 2021.

When she started teaching the language class online, Dina questioned everything she had done in-person and found it did not work. She was concerned about "acquisition, learning, and motivation," so she "used technology to do a… remodel." She recreated exercises for grammar, vocabulary, and comprehension with self-correction or personalized correction along with assignments for oral production and reading exercises for pronunciation. Her class of 30 students had two sections, and she "used what the technology offered" to divide them into smaller groups, essentially creating three or four sections. She offered more synchronous sessions "using time the university had allocated" to her, which meant each learner had only three hours synchronously in a smaller group, rather than six hours synchronously as part of the whole group – "I told myself I'm taking a risk; we'll see what happens." The new arrangement meant more synchronous time per individual, and Dina perceived an improvement in students' speaking skills. The students "got very involved. They got motivated… I found [teaching language online] was much more positive than what I had been told." She found they did not have many technical problems and "the digital literacy of students helps enormously." Dina was aware some students faced challenges outside the classroom: "That's really what I found the most difficult. It's not the didactics [the teaching methodology]; it's not learning."

Pre-pandemic, Dina used aspects of her institution's LMS, but she wanted "to develop [her] knowledge of interactive tools… Sometimes we hear someone telling us to try a platform or a [tool] that is external to Moodle, and in fact when we dug ourselves, we realize there are many things that already exist." She discovered H5P, which she found easy and appealing. She developed skills "to refine the selection of a tool to meet a particular need." ERT forced Dina to do something she had previously avoided: teach language online; and, with the skills she subsequently developed, Dina found "the pandemic has empowered me to take some liberties that I've wanted to take for a long time." She created an integrative pedagogy project including activities plus an evaluation continuum for oral and written skills. "That was a change... that should have been done years ago." Beginners got two video projects with writing, which she later reduced to one "because the second project at the end of the semester is a lot." Other assignments were handwritten, photographed, uploaded to the LMS, and marked using annotation tools and rubrics with descriptions for each criterion and a comment box. Dina acknowledged "you need a certain ease with the annotation tool, and you also need to take the time." She recorded oral feedback to replace in-person comments ("Good job!"), and later, for targeted feedback. Dina felt the rubrics provided consistency when a TA did the marking, and the LMS submissions created a portfolio and a record of late assignments and communication, which she thought resulted in more detail than what she had provided in-person. In September 2021, Dina chose to continue teaching online. The pandemic "completely revolutionized our perception of teaching and learning… what we built during the past academic year will be used again." When she returns to in-person teaching, Dina will continue using asynchronous tasks for students to practice and get instant feedback on their own and free up synchronous sessions to "focus on acquisition and interaction practices." She plans to continue the video projects. "The pandemic has trained us, forced us to work a little more, but it's not lost work; we can reuse it… In my opinion, digital is the great transformation of the world of education for the 21st century."

Tech-inclined Éloise: "It's not that different from what I was doing before"

Pre-pandemic, Éloise had read extensively about technology in language teaching. In March 2020, the semester had just started and she had only given two weeks of in-person classes. Éloise's classes shifted from in-person to online from "one day to the next." She was teaching two groups of learners and meeting each group twice a week. She "tried to adapt" and decided, for each group, to switch to one synchronous session, for oral production, and one asynchronous session, for oral comprehension and reflection. However, for the following semester, she decided to have both sessions synchronously. "I realized that I was looking to have a course more similar to the in-person course, but with digital tools." The majority of her students were true beginners relying on internet translation. "I said to myself that, with a little more guidance twice a week with the teacher, [for them] it's not just learning the language, but it's [the teacher] showing the students how to learn." Éloise did not think her pedagogical practice changed. Pre-pandemic, interactions were an important part of her courses, with lessons co-constructed with her students, so she sought out digital tools to accomplish that. This led her to solutions she already knew of, such as collaborative writing and Padlet. "What I understand better [now is] how we can ensure [oral and written] online interactions." She shared Google slides or docs to write what the students said live: "it's not that different from what I was doing before with a blackboard in the classroom."

Pre-pandemic, Éloise's students submitted assignments on an LMS. She provided a variety of feedback on written assignments using track changes, with a coding legend and an error hit list for self-corrections and final copies with integrated corrections. In ERT, the students produced written and oral versions of each assignment, for which Éloise gave recorded oral feedback. This was time-consuming, so she adapted again and gave written feedback for both types of assignments, using phonetic transcriptions for pronunciation. This proved so beneficial that she increased the value of the assignments and dispensed with tests. Éloise realized she "learned to have alternatives," including mastering tools she had some familiarity with, and transferred what she did in-person to online: "I don't really see any difference between what I do now and what I was doing before, apart from the tools." For example, pre-pandemic she did collaborative writing tasks with voting and feedback on paper stuck to the walls of the classroom; during ERT she accomplished the same task on Padlet. "So it's not the idea that has changed, but it's the way of doing things." Besides these activities, Éloise wanted to keep having some classes online. Pre-pandemic, her students were often late or tired after commuting to campus. Looking ahead, she saw the benefits of continuing to teach online: "I don't know if we need to imagine that everything is always going to be in-person. We can really think about a teaching that combines both… I am not against a balance decided with the learners. When are we going to have lessons? When will the classes be online? When are the in-person sessions? I think it's something that can be adapted very well." During ERT, she realized the future benefits of keeping at least some classes online.

Discussion

All 10 teachers, in spite of their varying levels of digital competencies pre-pandemic (Delforge et al., 2022; Hampel & Stickler, 2015), rose to the professional challenge of ERT. This demonstrated their resilience and, above all, a high degree of professionalism and desire to succeed. None of them expressed a fear of losing their job, but rather an intention to help the students in the new environment. From Éloise, who saw no changes in her professional practice ("It's not that different from what I was doing before") to Shannon ("I can kind of teach the way I taught before"), all of the teachers took risks in using their platforms, LMSs, tools, and activities in different ways. This aligns with Delforge et al.'s (2022) study which also found that teachers, over time, developed some ability to choose tools to suit their pedagogical aims and needs; even if, for teachers with fewer digital competencies, it resulted in much more work (Werner & Küplüce, 2021).

We found that teachers indeed transformed their pedagogical practice (their "work situation") and constructed new activities within the three pedagogical dimensions (*Design*, *Management*, and *Intervention*) outlined in Hamel's 2017 model of digital competencies described above. More specifically for *Design*, with some variety according to their digital competencies, all the teachers made changes: with tools, such as H5P, Google Docs, Padlet, and breakout rooms; and the tasks and activities, such as for collaborative writing, and automated and engaging exercises. In pre-pandemic studies, for instance Caws et al. (2021), we notice that these tools and tasks, namely online collaborative ones, were not part of the pre-pandemic pedagogical portfolio.

For *Management*, modifications related to content *Organization* and *Delivery* modes, regardless of teachers' digital competencies. Between the initial shift to ERT and later semesters, Éloise, for instance, moved from teaching both (a)synchronously to synchronously only. Dina divided her class into smaller groups that met fewer hours per week. Shannon appreciated having all of her materials in an LMS repository to reuse them. Finally, creative *Intervention* solutions were sought to stay and remain connected with their students. Again, this varied with teachers' digital competencies, such as: adding synchronous sessions and collaboration, and co-constructing lessons. Evaluations were modified by including automation and video projects or eliminating tests.

We saw how teachers envisioned their post-ERT practice as language teaching professionals touched on all three pedagogical dimensions described in the model. For *Design*, there are automated activities and quizzes, as well as *Management* affordances such as online synchronous sessions and asynchronous activities. Dina for instance will continue using the LMS for feedback in F2F classes as part of *Intervention*. Teachers' self-perception as language teaching professionals in the ERT specific context relates to the concept of the *Professional Ideal* from the model (Section 3). We can see a spectrum of responses, even from teachers with mid- to high levels of digital competencies: Dina felt "completely changed," whereas Éloise felt she "didn't do anything different." However, in all cases, including from the corpus of 10 teachers, professional transformation and growth were evident.

Teachers grew quite reflective and critical about their teaching process over the pandemic period. Their approach to pedagogical design and intervention became very iterative as they went on to discover the affordances and limits of the tools at their disposal. From a professional didactics' standpoint (Pastré, 1999), in this ERT context, the dynamic of change was fast paced, and teachers had to react and adapt quickly to their new work environment. In essence, language teachers were pushed to "innovate," which itself is a transformative process (Hamel, 2017).

Finally, we also saw that, in the ERT context, teachers showed empathy and caring by being aware of students' challenges beyond the classroom. Teachers had to construct a "pedagogical presence online" (Guichon, 2017), which implies an important psycho-affective dimension: moments of revealing one's background and unveiling oneself.

Recommendations

Institutions and language programs are now positioned to build on the experience and expertise gained by teachers during the COVID-19 pandemic. Institutions should recall that teachers' starting points and trajectories with digital competencies during the ERT period varied, and so was teachers' means of furthering these competencies. Our 10 participants, for instance, mentioned attending workshops and webinars, doing their own research, self-testing tools, trial and error in their classrooms and, especially for *Traditional* teachers, asking a personal or professional contact for help. Hence, professional development needs to mirror this and be offered in a variety of ways, such as by providing formal, top-down opportunities; time and funding for personal exploration; and a digital resource person for colleagues to consult (Caws et al., 2021; Gao & Zhang, 2020; Mayen, 2015).

It is important to recognize each step, celebrate small successes, and build confidence as teachers continue to develop, feel empowered to use trial and error as they continue to learn, and refine and grow as language professionals. The changes to professional development and teaching practices from ERT directly impact the changes teachers bring to the language classroom. In terms of procedure and products, it is important for teachers to reflect and build on the ERT crisis period, both personally and professionally. In order to do so, language teachers should be encouraged to form and join (online) communities of language teaching professionals – institutional and beyond. The model detailed in Figure 1 (p. 159) could serve as a guide for such self-reflection, and help teachers to think critically about their work and professionalization, their strengths, and areas for further professional development. Considering the experiences of others can motivate teachers towards their own self-reflection, with the reassurance that there is no one "right" way to do things, and inspire teachers to try something new, whether that is a new tool, task, or activity, or the method of acquiring or developing it.

Finally, considering language teachers as people, they have developed professionally in a myriad of ways during ERT. They showed resilience and high levels of care for their students, professionalism, and effort; four features which are perhaps most characteristic of this ERT period. While this study highlights 10 language teachers in a crisis situation, the literature suggests their experiences hold lessons for other language teachers in non-pandemic contexts, for example in other ERT crises such as war or natural disasters (Berbyuk Lindstrom, 2022). There is evidence to suggest that these results can be generalized across other instructional contexts, including at the K-12 level, based on similar experiences of teachers and their professional development (Nguyen, 2022; Smith & Arnott, 2022).

Conclusion

This study looked at what was done during ERT by collecting and considering 10 French language teachers' experiences. It focused on their forced professionalization as well as their self-perception as online teachers, related to their *Professional Ideal* (see Figure 1, p. 159). We considered how teachers identified and then acquired the digital competencies they were missing. From the perspective of professional didactics, the time they spent developing and refining these skills outside of formal professional development opportunities is valued. We considered the changes to teachers' pedagogical practice, particularly to how they gave feedback and conducted their synchronous and asynchronous sessions. We considered what they would like to carry forward to F2F classes in light of the pedagogical dimensions of *Design*, *Management*, and *Intervention*. We saw how the teachers' responses aligned with the teachers' digital skills, which we spread along a continuum of three types named *Traditional*, *On the move*, and *Tech-inclined*. We identified some of the specific challenges of teaching online during ERT, from being aware of students' difficulties outside of the classroom, which affected their language learning, to teaching "the students how to learn" (Éloise). At the same time, some of these challenges were transformational opportunities to "have alternatives" (Éloise) or feel "empowered… to take some liberties that [teachers] wanted to take for a long time" (Dina). We recognize the limitations to this study as the following: the lack of focus on the students' side and the small number of participants (n=10).

In the near future, we wish to continue researching the themes that have emerged from this study by documenting language teachers' post-ERT digital practices, along with collaborative opportunities to further the digital competencies of language teachers, namely with specific skills such as written corrective feedback, how the skills needed to adapt nimbly to ERT can be taught, and what the TAs and teacher trainees of the ERT pandemic have learned and will pass down to future cohorts of language teachers.

Acknowledgements

We would like to thank the 10 language teachers who have agreed to participate in this study for their time and openness. The interpretation of their narrative remains ours. This research was in part funded by the Social Sciences and Research Council of Canada (grant #430-2020-00270).

About the Authors

Jill Landry is a recent graduate from the Master's in Bilingualism Studies at the University of Ottawa, with a research focus on CALL in ERT.

Marie-Josée Hamel is a Professor in second language didactics at the Institute of Official Languages and Bilingualism at the University of Ottawa. She has been actively involved in CALL teaching, research and development for over twenty-five years. Her background is in theoretical linguistics and language engineering. Dr. Hamel's research interests are in CALL design and ergonomics, language teachers' digital (corrective written feedback) practices, and teacher training. https://www.uottawa.ca/about-us/official-languages-bilingualism-institute/professors/marie-josee-hamel

References

Berbyuk Lindstrom, N. (2022). *ICALL for less commonly taught languages – what does the landscape look like* [Symposium case study presentation, August 17, 2022]. EuroCALL 2022, Reykjavik and online. https://whova.com/embedded/session/gICL1rhZvf1Gmk4cR321tedOBON4JVtnFWs%40c2S78mQ%3D/2537195/?widget=primary

Bertin, J.-C. (2015). "Modélisation en apprentissage des langues médiatisé: quelle utilité?". *Alsic*, *18*(2). https://doi.org/10.4000/alsic.2781

Bertin, J.-C., Gravé, P., & Narcy-Combes, J.-P. (2010). *Second-language distance learning and teaching: theoretical perspectives and didactic ergonomics*. IGI Global.

Bertin, J.-C., & Narcy-Combes, J.-P. (2013). Ordo Ab Chao: la modélisation pour gérer le chaos? Dispositifs d'enseignement/apprentissage en langues médiatisés et à distance". In M. Derivry, P. Faure & C. Brudermann (Eds.), *Apprendre les langues à l'université au 21e siècle* (pp. 113–130). Riveneuve.

Caws, C., & Hamel, M.-J. (2016). *Language-learner computer interactions: Theory, methodology and CALL applications.* John Benjamins. https://doi.org/10.1075/lsse.2

Caws, C., Hamel, M.-J., Jeanneau, C., & Ollivier, C. (2021). *Formation en langues et littératie numérique en contextes ouverts. Une approche socio-interactionnelle.* Éditions des archives contemporaines. https://doi.org/10.17184/eac.9782813003911

Delforge, C., Dachet, D., & Van de Vyver, J. (2022). Enseigner à distance en temps de confinement : enquête auprès des enseignants de langues en Belgique francophone, *Alsic*, *25*(2). https://doi.org/10.4000/alsic.5893

ECML (European Centre for Modern Languages of the Council of Europe). (2021). *The Future of language education in the light of Covid – Lessons learned and ways forward.* https://www.ecml.at/Portals/1/documents/events/summary-of-ECML-PNF-survey-findings.pdf?ver=2021-04-27-190025-520

Gao, L. X., & Zhang, L. J. (2020). Teacher learning in difficult times: Examining foreign language teachers' cognitions about online teaching to tide over COVID-19. *Frontiers in Psychology*, *11*, 549653. https://doi.org/10.3389/fpsyg.2020.549653

Germain-Rutherford, A. & Ernest, P. (2015). European language teachers and ICT: Experiences, expectations and training needs. In R. Hampel & U. Skickler (Eds.), *Developing online language teaching: research-based pedagogies and reflective practices* (pp. 12–27). Palgrave Macmillan.

Gillham, B. (2005). *Research interviewing: The range of techniques.* Open University Press.

Guichon, N. (2017). Se construire une présence pédagogique en ligne. In N. Guichon & M. Tellier (Eds.), *Enseigner l'oral en ligne – Une approche multimodale* (pp. 29–58). Editions Didier.

Hamel, M.-J. (2017). Portraits d'enseignants de FLS, pédagogues de l'hybride. Vers une ébauche de modèle. *Alsic*, *20*(3). https://doi.org/10.4000/alsic.3138

Hamel, M.-J., & Bibeau, L.-D. (2021) Pratiques (numériques) de rétroaction corrective des enseignants de langue et prototype d'outil numérique pour les optimiser. *Alsic*, *24*(2). https://doi.org/10.4000/alsic.5550

Hampel, R., & Stickler, U. (2015). *Developing online language teaching: Research-based pedagogies and reflective practices*. Palgrave Macmillan. https://doi.org/10.1057/9781137412263

Houssaye, J. (1988). *Le triangle pédagogique – Théorie et pratiques de l'éducation scolaire*. Peter Lang. DOI: 10.14375/NP.9782710126720

Jin, L., Deifell, E., & Angus, K. (2021). Emergency remote language teaching and learning in disruptive times. *CALICO Journal*, *39*(1), i–x. doi.org/10.1558/cj.20858

MacIntyre, P., Gregersen, T., & Mercer, S. (2020). Language teachers' coping strategies during the COVID-19 conversion to online teaching: Correlations with stress, wellbeing and negative emotions. *System*, *94*, 102352. https://doi.org/10.1016/j.system.2020.102352

Mayen, P. (2012). Les situations professionnelles: un point de vue de didactique professionnelle. *Phronesis*, *1*(1), 59–67. https://doi.org/10.7202/1006484ar Actions

Mayen, P. (2015). Vocational didactics: Work, learning, and conceptualization. In L. Filliettaz & S. Billett (Eds.), *Francophone perspectives of learning through work conceptions, traditions and practices* (pp. 201–219). Springer International Publishing. doi.org/10.1007/978-3-319-18669-6

Miles, M. B., Huberman, A. M., & Saldaña, J. (2020). *Qualitative data analysis: a methods sourcebook* (4th edition). Sage.

Moser, K., Wei, T., & Brenner, D. (2021). Remote teaching during COVID-19: Implications from a national survey of language educators. *System*, *97*, 102431. doi.org/10.1016/j.system.2020.102431

Nguyen, X. (2022). *Rising to the challenge: English language teachers developing digital literacy at Finnish universities*. [Conference presentation]. EuroCALL 2022, online. https://www.youtube.com/watch?v=SegsbRvGal8&t=708s

Nissen, E. (2019). *Formation hybride en langues: Articuler présentiel et distanciel.* Didier.

Observatoire de la langue française. (2018). *Rapport 2018 "La langue française dans le monde."* https://observatoire.francophonie.org/wp-content/uploads/2018/11/Apprentissage-Outils-Numeriques-Rapport-final.pdf

Pastré, P. (1999). Travail et compétences: un point de vue de didacticien. *Formation Emploi*, *67*, 109–125. doi.org/10.3406/forem.1999.2365

Piot, T. (2012). The role of professional didactics in skills development for training and education professionals. In V. Cohen-Scali (Ed.), *Competence and competence development* (pp. 53–72). Verlag Barbara Budrich. https://www.jstor.org/stable/j.ctvbkk2h9.7

Saldaña, J. (2021). *The Coding manual for qualitative researchers* (4 ed.). Sage, Kindle.

Smith, C., & Arnott, S. (2022). "French teachers can figure it out": Understanding French as a second language (FSL) teachers' work in the context of the COVID-19 pandemic. *Canadian Journal of Applied Linguistics / Revue canadienne de linguistique appliquée*, *25*(1), 88–109. doi.org/10.37213/cjal.2022.32024

Werner, S., & Küplüce, C. (2021). Digital language teaching after COVID-19: what can we learn from the crisis? In N. Zoghlami, C. Brudermann, C. Sarré, M. Grosbois, L. Bradley, & S. Thouësny (Eds.), *CALL and professionalisation – short papers from EUROCALL 2021* (pp. 296–301). Research-publishing.net. https://doi.org/10.14705/ rpnet.2021.54.1349

Appendix A: Semi-Guided Interview Questions

Part 1: Language teachers' digital practices in times of pandemic – an overview

Thinking from March 2020 when classes first went online until now:

- How did you as a [language] instructor cope?
- How has your online language teaching experience changed your pedagogical practice?
- How has your online language teaching experience changed your professional development?
- What digital competencies and literacies have you developed?
- How have you developed these? How did they evolve – teaching tasks, socialization, pedagogical preparation, management and intervention (inc. evaluation)?
- How have your day-to-day language teaching practices changed/evolved during the Covid pandemic? [Spring 2020, Fall 2020, Winter 2021]
- How do you perceive yourself as an online language teacher? – What is the perception of your successes and challenges?
- Once you have the option to safely return to an in-person class, what aspects of your digital practice are you going to retain?

Part 2: Language teachers' digital WCF practices in times of pandemic

- How has the pandemic affected the type of WCF you provide to your students? What about the amount of WCF? What about the modality?
- What changes have occurred in the writing tasks you ask of your students? (Do you ask for more, have you had to adjust the type of task, etc.?)
- How has your relationship with digital WCF tools changed? What tools have you been using since the start of the pandemic and how do they differ from those you used before?
- How do you envision your post-pandemic WCF practices in a face-to-face or hybrid setting? Which feedback practices (written or multi-modal) that you have developed would you like to keep and which would you prefer to abandon/modify?

PART THREE
OUTCOMES

9 The Impact of Technology-informed Crisis Response on Post-pandemic Spanish Proficiency

Jesse Gleason and Andrew Bartlett

The global pandemic of 2020 has added a layer of crisis to the field of language studies, which for decades has been grappling with multiple issues (Looney & Lusin, 2019; Murphy et al., 2022). While certain disciplines were well suited to the emergency remote teaching (ERT) brought on by the pandemic, second language (L2) learning contexts at many institutions found themselves in a challenging situation. With emphasis on key second language acquisition (SLA) principles such as *interaction* (Loewen & Sato, 2018; Long, 1981), *comprehensible input* (Krashen, 1985; Loschky, 1994), and *negotiation for meaning* (Long, 1996; Pica, 1994), the swift move to online language learning (now known as Emergency Remote Language Teaching or ERTL) (Gacs et al., 2020) found many language programs with solely face-to-face (F2F) course offerings ill-prepared.

While most university faculty and students rose to the occasion (Ross & DiSalvo, 2020), what ERTL and the "new normal" (Egbert, 2020, p. 314) post-pandemic classroom have ultimately meant for student language proficiency has yet to be fully understood. Proficiency is the ability for language learners to communicate in real world contexts across communicative modes (American Council on the Teaching of Foreign Languages [ACTFL], 2019) and is commonly measured using a battery of tests, including the ACTFL Assessment of Performance Toward Proficiency in Languages (AAPPL) (Cox & Malone, 2018), the ACTFL Oral Proficiency Interview (OPI) and Written Proficiency Test (WPT), and the STAndards-based Measurement of Proficiency (STAMP) (Santos, 2019). These norm-referenced instruments provide stakeholders with data for critical decision-making surrounding curricula, programming, recruitment, and more. The present study examined pre-, during- and post-pandemic STAMP data (Santos, 2022) in order to compare students' L2 proficiency outcomes across F2F and online course modalities in third-semester Spanish courses at one small regional public institution in the northeastern United States.

Technology-Mediated Change in Language Education

The global pandemic brought to light various other developments that had impacted language education and pressed the issue of technology in language education and delivery modalities for L2 courses. Rapid advancements in Web 2.0 technologies, which are now a typical aspect of our everyday lives (Zuboff, 2019), have meant that today's university students are being educated in a "hyper-novel" (Heying & Weinstein, 2021) environment, altogether different from that of their parents, professors, and even older siblings. The "digital divide" (Prensky, 2001), which was originally envisioned as a difference in lifestyle between generations of humans and later expanded to include differences in technology skills and access across a variety of factors (e.g., age, socioeconomic status, etc.), has become increasingly pronounced as technology is no longer a choice that one can make, but rather an essential element for one's participation in society (Ortega, 2017).

Equity and Access in Online Language Teaching and Assessment

Before the pandemic, the field of computer-assisted language learning (CALL) and language education more broadly was already focused on the complex yet critical role that technology plays in educational and social (in) equities (Gleason & Suvorov, 2019; Ortega, 2017; Piller, 2016). Over the past few years, we have seen an increasing amount of research related to the complex and multidimensional way that technology-mediated instruction impacts issues of access and equity (Britton et al., forthcoming; Castrillo & Sedano, 2021; van Dijk, 2020). An inequitable access to professional development in CALL, for example, has been brought to light especially during the pandemic due to the growing need for teacher expertise in online teaching and learning and inequitable distributions of resources in higher education contexts (Jin et al. 2021; Jin et al., Chapter 2, this volume). Another related area of focus has been an inequitable workload distribution during this moment of global change, of particular importance given students' increased need for emotional support and a clear lack of sustainability in terms of the increased emotion labor practices required of instructors of online courses (Warner & Dao, 2022; Warner & Dao, Chapter 12, this volume).

Another area with critical implications for equity and access, specifically with regards to gate-keeping and cybersecurity, is the area of online and technology-mediated assessment (Avant Assessment, 2022a; Goertler & Gacs, 2018; Link & Li, 2018). For example, in a pronounced effort to ameliorate disparate outcomes based on standardized testing practices, many colleges and universities have done away with their entrance exam requirements during the pandemic (Schultz & Backstrom, 2021). Contrastingly, online language proficiency testing has experienced a notable increase during the pandemic, as systems have been put in place to proctor and administer test-takers in secure and reliable environments (Hernández-Calderón et al., 2023). The impact (washback) and high costs of online assessments to students and institutions presents an important equity issue which must be considered, especially with the rising cost of higher education and technology more broadly (Hildebrandt & Swanson, 2019). On the other hand, online proficiency assessments may offer students the opportunity to earn college credit, potentially alleviating their student debt burden and encouraging them to continue language learning beyond the beginner/intermediate levels (Heineke & Davin, 2022).

Online, Blended/Hybrid and Face-to-Face Language Learning

One of the driving issues in the field of CALL has focused on how different technological interventions impact student outcomes (Blake et al., 2008; Chapelle, 2009; Larson & Sung, 2019; Tarone, 2015; Ushida, 2013). Not only has the internal landscape of this "brave new digital classroom" (Blake, 2008; Blake & Guillén, 2013) changed, but so too have the length and frequency of L2 lessons. While most language classes a decade ago met five times per week in their F2F physical classroom space, it is now not uncommon to see students in an F2F classroom only two or three times per week – if at all. Whereas the typical language class just a couple of decades ago occurred in a classroom with a teacher and minimal technology, today's classrooms in a U.S. university context often look very different: projection screen(s), individual hand-held devices (tablets, smart phones, smart watches etc.), few paper handouts, etc. In many contexts, hybrid and fully online modalities have replaced traditional F2F modality with the understanding that students will supplement reduced in-class time with significant amounts of independent online work outside of class (Chenoweth et al., 2006; Murday et al., 2008; Scida & Saury, 2006), often in the form of computer-mediated drills and vocabulary/grammar practice.

Similarly, the rationale for the flipped classroom (Lavolette & Asaba, this volume) is that students spend ample time outside of class completing autonomous tasks, and that this asynchronous language learning is equivalent to the time spent in a classroom with a teacher. However, different contexts and students will undoubtedly impact how traditional, hybrid, and online instruction is enacted, oftentimes producing unforeseen dilemmas or challenges (Gleason, 2013). Flipped and hybrid/online models may presuppose a certain type of self-directed learner who is able and willing to dedicate ample time to independent, self-directed work in online contexts (Martin et al., 2020). However, it is unreasonable to assume that all students are willing and able to engage in self-directed learning (SDL), nor that all are equally ready or prepared for blended and online learning (Gokol & Naidoo, Chapter 3, this volume). In fact, technological readiness has been found to be a major factor in predicting student success in blended and online courses (Geng et al., 2019) and factors such as motivation and stress undoubtedly play a role in college students' SDL and readiness for online classes (Heo & Han, 2018). Aspects such as required task engagement (Sun, 2014) and structured student-to-student interaction (Beyer et al., 2017) have been found to negatively and positively impact SDL, respectively, whereas Foung et al. (2022) found that student engagement and SDL increased during the pandemic in comparison to pre-pandemic.

Proficiency Outcomes Across Course Modality

Over the past decade, the field of language education has seen a marked uptake in the use of norm-referenced assessments of language proficiency (Gass et al., 2016; Lin & Warschauer, 2015; van Deusen-Scholl, 2015; Gass & Winke, 2019). While ongoing advancements in computer technology have led to an increase in commercialization and use of online proficiency assessment, it is now not uncommon to assess student language proficiency prior to, during and/or upon completion of university language courses (Isbell et al., 2018). The AAPPL test, for example, is currently being marketed to and used with language learners as young as 3rd grade (Language Testing International, 2023).

Although many pre-pandemic studies using student proficiency testing reveal similar language proficiency outcomes from students who take traditional, blended/hybrid and online courses (Aldrich & Moneypenny, 2019; Blake et al., 2008; Chenoweth et al., 2006; Grgurović et al., 2013; Larson & Sung, 2019; Moneypenny & Aldrich, 2016; Schmitt, 2014), recent research on student language proficiency outcomes during the pandemic (i.e., involving ERTL) have produced variable results. For example, data from Avant Assessment (2021, 2022b) revealed that university students' overall average

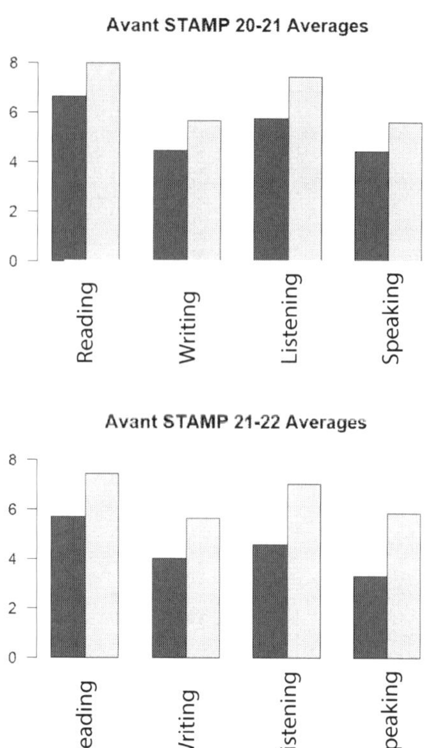

Figure 1 STAMP 4S Spanish Language Proficiency Averages (Avant Assessment, 2021, 2022b).

Spanish language proficiency at the 200-level as measured by the STAMP test dropped across all of the four skills. As shown in Figure 1, Reading scores dropped by 0.94 points (it was 6.64 and changed to 5.70), writing by 0.44 points (was 4.47, changed to 4.03), listening by 1.2 points (was 5.77, changed to 4.57) and speaking by 1.12 points (was 4.43, changed to 3.31).

While multiple possible reasons may exist for this observed decline in overall language proficiency (e.g., lockdown-related challenges, financial difficulties, health-related struggles, etc.), these national and international averages directly contradict those reported elsewhere. Gleason et al. (in press), for example, found a statistically significant increase in three out of the four language proficiency skills (reading, listening, and speaking) measured by the STAMP test for online Spanish courses offered during the pandemic compared to solely F2F courses offered pre-pandemic.

Given these contradictory findings, the present chapter investigates whether similar trends in proficiency across teaching modalities continued immediately post-pandemic, during which time both F2F and online modalities were offered simultaneously to students at a regional public institution. Specifically, we examined student STAMP scores within the 2021–22 AY, and then compared them to those collected in courses offered only F2F pre-pandemic, and those offered only in a synchronous online modality during the pandemic. Our research questions (RQs) were:

RQ1 Was there a significant difference in overall and skills-based Spanish language proficiency between F2F and online students taking third-semester Spanish courses post-pandemic (AY21–22)?

RQ2 Was there a significant difference in overall and skills-based Spanish language proficiency between students that chose F2F post-pandemic courses and those in required F2F courses pre-pandemic?

RQ3 Was there a significant difference in overall and skills-based Spanish language proficiency between students that chose the online modality post-pandemic and those in required online courses during ERTL?

Methods

Research Context

The context for the present study was a small, regional, public university in the northeastern United States. At the time of data collection, the university had a third-semester language requirement, which culminated in students taking the STAMP as their final exam in a Spanish course, and if passed successfully met their liberal education requirement. One of the major learning goals for students who were completing the course was to achieve a proficiency level of "Intermediate Low" on the ACTFL Scale (ACTFL, 2012). As explained in Gleason et al. (in press), the university decided halfway through the Spring 2020 semester to move all courses online in response to the global pandemic. As a result, all 11 sections of a third-semester F2F general Spanish course were converted into a fully online synchronous modality, which lasted for the remaining six weeks of the semester and constituted the "crisis phase" of the pandemic. In Fall semester 2020, despite the fact that many of the courses at this university and around the globe made the decision to hold classes F2F, the language department decided to continue with fully online instruction in all lower-division Spanish courses, which continued through Spring 2021.

With the significant changes experienced at all levels of university and societal life, it was the goal in the lower-division courses to minimize the curricular changes in the first three semesters of general Spanish as much as possible. As a result, very little innovation took place during this semester outside of the instructors and students adapting to ERTL. For example, the same textbook and online platform (Supersite) continued to be used across all three semesters of Spanish and all course-level grade allocations remained constant: Participation counted for 20% of the course grade, Online Homework for 15%, Lab Work for 10%, three Integrated Performance Assessments (IPAs), each worth 10% (30% total), and the STAMP test, which was administered as a final exam, and was worth 10%. The only significant change made to the lower-division Spanish curriculum was the switch from a F2F class and lab meeting to a fully online synchronous class and asynchronous lab meeting by using Zoom. The 50 minutes of lab time were reallocated to an asynchronous online modality, and instructors were advised to assign additional communicative activities from the class Supersite and/or to create other types of communicative activities for students to complete.

Participants

Participants consisted of students – completing a third-semester general Spanish course between Spring 2019 and Spring 2022 semesters – and their instructors. This included a total of 883 students across four semesters (Spring 2019, Spring 2021, Fall, 2021, and Spring 2022). In Spring 2019, a total of 269 students took the STAMP test; in Spring 2021, there were a total of 299, and in the 2021–22 AY, 315 students were tested. Specific information about the students is unavailable; however, the majority of students were undergraduates, between the ages of 18–21, taking a third-semester Spanish course to fulfill a general education requirement.

The 20 instructors of courses consisted primarily of part-time adjunct faculty (90%) and full-time tenured or tenure-track faculty (10%). They came from a wide array of age, cultural, and ethnic backgrounds and possessed a disparate range of experiences with technology and online language teaching. Every instructor except for one had taught the course F2F prior to ERTL and all had access to training workshops offered by the university and the department's lab director regarding best practices in online language instruction.

Data Collection

The data collected for this project included 883 students' Spanish STAMP 4S tests taken as a final exam over the course of the Spring 2019 and Spring 2021 semesters and the 2021–2022 AY, during which time students were taking a third-semester general Spanish course. The STAMP test was eliminated from the curriculum for 2019–2020 AY until the cost of online proctoring became more affordable in AY 2021–22. Prior to the pandemic, all students would take their STAMP test in the language lab on campus. Students in the online sections of the course during and post-pandemic took the test from their personal computer using a remote proctoring system, which included robust measures to ensure score security and reliability, (i.e., screen recording, artificial intelligence software, lockdown browser, trained human proctor).

The STAMP 4S test (Santos, 2019) measures students' reading, writing, speaking, and listening proficiency, producing a score between 1–9 on each of the receptive skills (i.e., reading and listening), and 1–8 on the productive skills (i.e., writing and speaking) which correspond to the level descriptors of the ACTFL proficiency scale (ACTFL, 2012), as shown in Table 1.

A composite score for all four skills was taken and used to represent the construct of overall language proficiency. To meet the university goal threshold of Intermediate Low (ACTFL, 2012), students were required to obtain a minimum level of 4 on each of the four skills, and a composite score of at least 16.

Table 1 STAMP Scores as Related to ACTFL Proficiency Scale

Reading and Listening Level Key			**Writing and Speaking Level Key**		
Novice	**Intermediate**	**Advanced**	**Novice**	**Intermediate**	**Advanced**
1 Novice Low	4 Intermediate Low	7 Advanced Low	1 Novice Low	4 Intermediate Low	7 Advanced Low
2 Novice Mid	5 Intermediate Mid	8 Advanced Mid	2 Novice Mid	5 Intermediate Mid	8 Advanced Mid
3 Novice High	6 Intermediate High	9 Advanced High	3 Novice High	6 Intermediate High	(beyond scoreable)

Data Analysis

In this study, the data collected were ordinal with categories such as "Novice Low," "Novice Mid", etc. While ACTFL assigns a numeric number to each level, it is important to note that numerical measures such as the mean and median are not meaningful. For this reason, the commonly used two-sample parametric *t*-test which assumes that the data is normal and continuous cannot be applied to detect differences between pre- and post-pandemic groups. Instead, a non-parametric test was performed, in which STAMP scores (reading, listening, speaking, and writing) were ranked from "Novice Low" to "Advanced High." Specifically, we used independent-sample Mann Whitney *U* tests in order to ascertain differences in STAMP proficiency scores obtained between (a) chosen F2F and online sections of third-semester Spanish post-pandemic (AY21–22), (b) forced F2F sections pre-pandemic (Spring 2019) and post-pandemic, and (c) forced online sections during the pandemic (Spring 2021) and post-pandemic.

Results

Descriptive statistics for the four semesters studied are provided in Table 2 below. In AY21–22, during which time students had a choice about which modality they could take (prior to the pandemic, it was the policy of the department not to offer any online language classes), F2F and online students outperformed the forced F2F students (Spring 2019) across all sub-skills, yet seemed to underperform compared to the forced online students (Spring 2021).

Post-Pandemic Proficiency Outcomes Across F2F and Online Modalities

To answer our first research question (Was there a significant difference in overall and skills-based Spanish language proficiency between F2F and online students taking third-semester Spanish courses post-pandemic (AY21–22)?), we first had to determine if semester was a confounding variable. Table 3 shows the descriptive statistics across Fall 2021 and Spring 2022 semesters, during which time we observed a higher average score and smaller variability for the F2F group compared to the online group across all sub-skills. A Mann-Whitney *U* test revealed that there were no significant differences between skills-based or overall proficiency across semesters.

Table 2 Descriptive Statistics for Sub-skill STAMP Results for Forced-F2F (Spring 2019), Forced-online (Spring 2021), and Choice Modality (AY21–22)

STAMP Skill	Choice Modality	Sample Size	Mean	Median	Standard Deviation
Overall	Forced (F2F)	269	13.33	13.00	3.38
	Forced (Online)	299	17.13	17.00	4.69
	Choice (FA21 – SP22)	315	15.74	16.00	4.11
Reading	Forced (F2F)	269	4.20	4.00	1.35
	Forced (Online)	299	5.79	6.00	1.42
	Choice (FA21 – SP22)	315	5.26	6.00	1.32
Writing	Forced (F2F)	269	3.68	4.00	0.79
	Forced (Online)	293	3.71	4.00	1.01
	Choice (FA21 – SP22)	307	3.69	4.00	1.06
Listening	Forced (F2F)	269	2.80	3.00	0.98
	Forced (Online)	294	4.80	5.00	1.61
	Choice (FA21 – SP22)	315	4.16	4.00	1.10
Speaking	Forced (F2F)	241	2.97	3.00	0.93
	Forced (Online)	272	3.28	3.00	1.29
	Choice (FA21 – SP22)	274	3.14	3.00	1.15

Table 3 Descriptive Statistics for AY 2021–2022 Courses Across F2F and Online Courses

STAMP Skill	Choice Modality	Sample Size	Mean	Median	Standard Deviation
Overall	Choice (F2F)	166	16.26	16.00	3.66
	Choice (Online)	149	15.17	15.00	4.50
Reading	Choice (F2F)	166	5.43	6.00	1.21
	Choice (Online)	149	5.07	5.00	1.41
Writing	Choice (F2F)	164	3.81	4.00	0.97
	Choice (Online)	143	3.56	4.00	1.14
Listening	Choice (F2F)	166	4.21	4.00	1.03
	Choice (Online)	149	4.11	4.00	1.18
Speaking	Choice (F2F)	146	3.26	3.00	1.08
	Choice (Online)	128	2.99	3.00	1.23

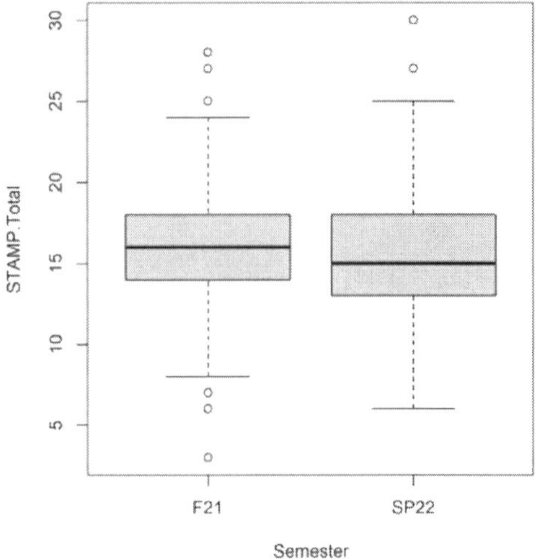

Figure 2 Boxplot Showing the STAMP Scores Across Fall 2021 and Spring 2022 Semesters

The boxplot in Figure 2 shows the parity in scores across semesters and the equivalency of student outcomes. Since there was no significant difference between semesters, we combined the data from both semesters and proceeded to test for difference between modalities.

As can be observed in Table 4, under the assumption that there was no difference between Fall and Spring semesters, the chances of observing the same test statistic (11,922 for writing) or one more extreme was 84%. Therefore, there was not a significant difference between semesters, because it was highly likely to observe this result. In addition, the effect size measured differences adjusting for sample size where a value greater than 0.5 is considered Large and significant, however, we observed a value less than 0.20 for all sub-skills. Therefore, there was no significant effect between semesters.

The Mann-Whitney *U* test results shown in Table 5 revealed significant differences between the total STAMP scores from F2F and online students in three out of the four skills (reading, writing and speaking) as well as in overall proficiency. Contrary to the earlier study (Gleason et al., in press), however, the F2F students during the 2021–22 AY this time significantly outperformed their online counterparts with a Medium effect size.

The boxplot in Figure 3 shows the distribution of overall STAMP scores across online and F2F modalities, with the F2F students performing significantly higher than online students. One can also observe a higher variability within the online sections.

Table 4 Mann-Whitney Test Results for Overall and Sub-skill STAMP Results Fall 2021 vs. Spring 2022

STAMP Test	Test Statistic	P-value	Effect Size*	Decision
Overall	W = 13,808	0.0797	0.1138 (Small)	Fail to Reject Null Hypothesis
Reading	W = 12,657	0.7378	0.0210 (Very Small)	Fail to Reject Null Hypothesis
Writing	W = 11,922	0.8388	0.0128 (Very Small)	Fail to Reject Null Hypothesis
Listening	W = 13,029	0.4076	0.0509 (Very Small)	Fail to Reject Null Hypothesis
Speaking	W = 10,529	0.1406	0.1987 (Small)	Fail to Reject Null Hypothesis

*Effect Size: r < 0.1 (Very Small), 0.1 < r < 0.3 (Small), 0.3 < r < 0.5 (Medium), r > 0.5 (Large)

Table 5 Mann-Whitney Test Results for AY 2021–22 Sub-skill STAMP Results for F2F vs. Online

STAMP Test	Test Statistic	P-value	Effect Size*	Decision
Overall	W = 10,063	0.0042	0.3726 (Medium)	Reject Null Hypothesis
Reading	W = 10,426	0.0122	0.3139 (Medium)	Reject Null Hypothesis
Writing	W = 10,088	0.0261	0.2794 (Medium)	Reject Null Hypothesis
Listening	W = 11,360	0.1867	0.1629 (Small)	Fail to Reject Null Hypothesis
Speaking	W = 7,759	0.0118	0.3393 (Medium)	Reject Null Hypothesis

*Effect Size: r < 0.1 (Very Small), 0.1 < r < 0.3 (Small), 0.3 < r < 0.5 (Medium), r > 0.5 (Large)

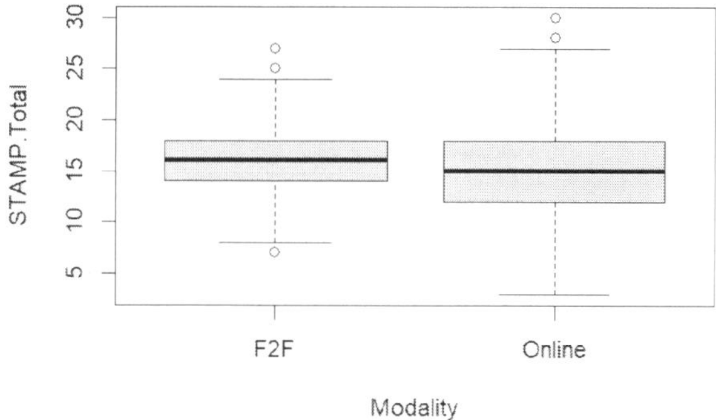

Figure 3 STAMP Scores Across F2F and Online Modalities in the 2021–22 AY

F2F Pre-Pandemic Outcomes vs. Online/F2F Post-Pandemic Outcomes

In addition to comparing students across modalities within the 2021–22 AY, our second research question inquired into the difference in proficiency scores between students who chose F2F and online classes during AY21–22 and those who were forced to take F2F classes prior to the pandemic. The results of the Mann-Whitney *U* test revealed that when given the choice of modality, students in post-pandemic F2F courses scored significantly higher both overall and across all four skills than their forced F2F counterparts pre-pandemic. As seen in Table 6, this occurred with a Large (overall, reading, listening) or Medium (writing, speaking) effect size. In particular, the effect size was 0.9281 for the overall scores indicating an extremely large significant difference between forced and choice F2F students.

The box plot graph in Figure 4 (left) revealed that only 25% of the students from the pre-pandemic forced F2F group (Spring 2019) scored above a 15 (overall score), thus achieving the Intermediate Low proficiency threshold. In contrast, approximately 75% of the students from the post-pandemic choice F2F group (AY21–22) scored above the same threshold (15). Furthermore, the Likert graph in Figure 4 (right) shows similar gaps in performance in Reading and Listening scores among the two groups. For example, within Listening scores, only 6% of the students from the forced F2F pre-pandemic group scored at or above an Intermediate Mid level, compared to 33% from the post-pandemic choice F2F group. Similarly, within the Reading scores, the percentage at or above the Intermediate Mid level was 16% compared to 58% respectively.

Table 6 Mann-Whitney Test Results for Sub-skill STAMP Results for Spring 2019 (Forced F2F) vs. AY 2021–22 (Choice F2F)

STAMP Test	Test Statistic	P-value	Effect Size*	Decision
Overall	W = 11,966	< 0.0001	0.9281 (Large)	Reject Null Hypothesis
Reading	W = 11,134	< 0.0001	0.5013 (Large)	Reject Null Hypothesis Ho
Writing	W = 20,127	0.0948	0.4555 (Medium)	Fail to Reject Null Hypothesis
Listening	W = 6,642	< 0.0001	0.7025 (Large)	Reject Null Hypothesis Ho
Speaking	W = 14,640	0.0036	0.3357 (Medium)	Reject Null Hypothesis Ho

*Effect Size: r < 0.1 (Very Small), 0.1 < r < 0.3 (Small), 0.3 < r < 0.5 (Medium), r > 0.5 (Large)

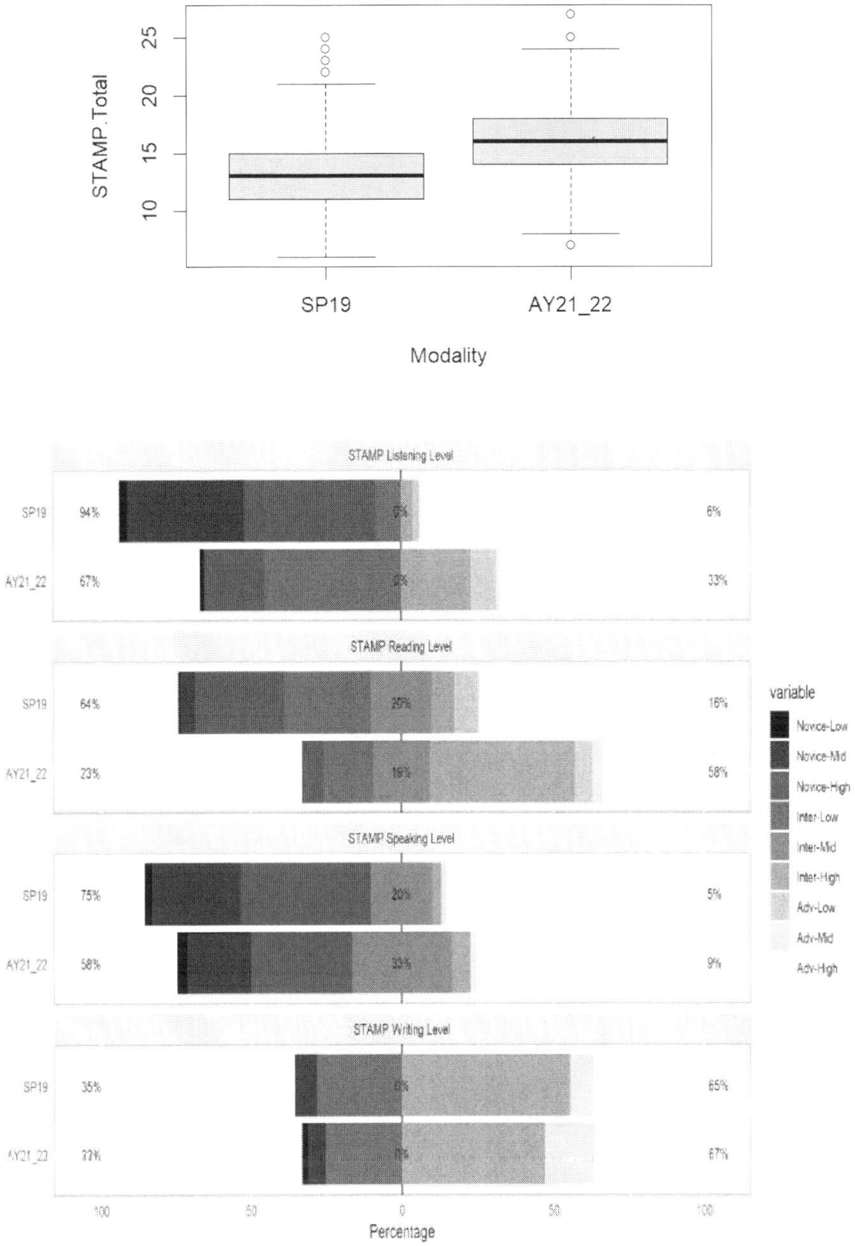

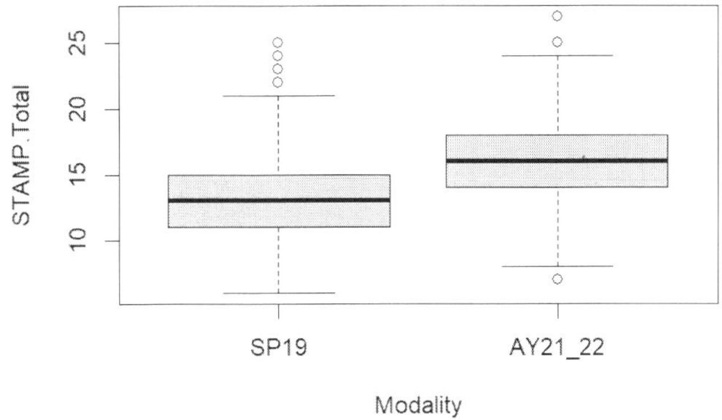

Figure 4 STAMP Scores Across Forced F2F Modality (Spring 2019) and Choice F2F Modality in the 2021–22 AY

Table 7 Mann-Whitney Test Results for Sub-skill STAMP Results for Spring 2019 (Forced F2F) vs. AY 2021-22 (Choice Online)

STAMP Test	Test Statistic	P-value	Effect Size*	Decision
Overall	W = 14,782	< 0.0001	0.5249 (Large)	Reject Null Hypothesis
Reading	W = 13,015	< 0.0001	0.7011 (Large)	Reject Null Hypothesis
Writing	W = 20,622	0.1928	0.0722 (Very Small)	Fail to Reject Null Hypothesis
Listening	W = 7,037	< 0.0001	0.6489 (Large)	Reject Null Hypothesis
Speaking	W = 15,767	0.7111	0.0222 (Very Small)	Fail to Reject Null Hypothesis

*Effect Size: r < 0.1 (Very Small), 0.1 < r < 0.3 (Small), 0.3 < r < 0.5 (Medium), r > 0.5 (Large)

Results of the Mann-Whitney *U* test results in Table 7 compare the STAMP results from students in pre-pandemic forced F2F courses with those in post-pandemic choice online courses. They reveal similar significant differences in both the overall STAMP scores and in the receptive skills of reading and listening, with students in online courses outperforming those in the pre-pandemic F2F courses. The effect size was Large, however, not as great as with the choice F2F group. Interestingly, there were no significant differences (effect size = 0.0722 and 0.0222) in scores on the productive skills of writing and speaking, respectively.

The box plot graph in Figure 5 (left) revealed 50% of the students in the post-pandemic choice online group (AY 21–22) scored above the threshold of Intermediate Low (15) compared to the 25% from the pre-pandemic forced F2F group (Spring 2019). Furthermore, the Likert graph in Figure 5 (right) shows similar gaps in performance of reading and listening skills among the two groups. For example, within the listening skills, only 6% of the students from the pre-pandemic forced F2F group scored at or above the Intermediate Mid level compared to 28% (5% drop from Figure 4) for the post-pandemic choice online group. Similarly, within the reading skills, the percentage at or above the Intermediate Mid level was 16% compared to 43% (a 15% drop from Figure 4) respectively.

Forced Online Outcomes During-Pandemic vs. Modality Choice Courses Post-Pandemic

To answer the third research question regarding whether there was a significant proficiency difference between students post-pandemic and those in forced online courses during the pandemic, a Mann-Whitney *U*

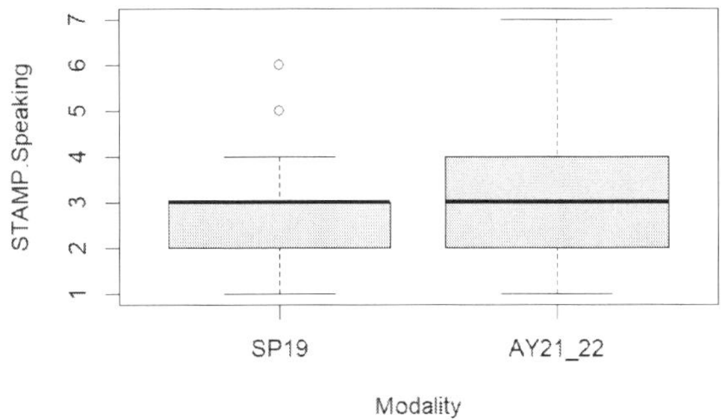

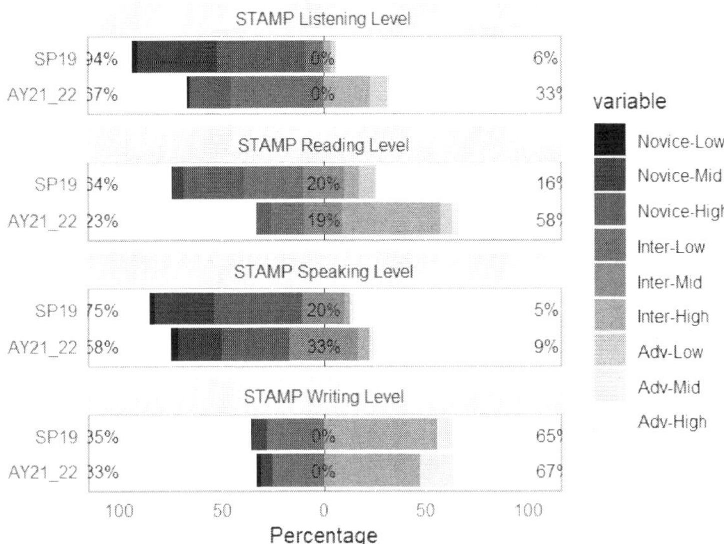

Figure 5 STAMP Scores Across Pre-pandemic Forced F2F Modality (Spring 2019) and the Post-pandemic Choice Online Modality (2021–22 AY)

Table 8 Mann-Whitney Test Results for Sub-skill STAMP Results for Spring 2021 (Forced Online) vs. AY 2021–22 (Choice F2F)

STAMP Test	Test Statistic	P-value	Effect Size	Decision
Overall	W = 27,661	0.0399	0.2292 (Small)	Reject Null Hypothesis
Reading	W = 28,937	0.0015	0.3320 (Medium)	Reject Null Hypothesis
Writing	W = 22,639	0.2772	0.1155 (Small)	Fail to Reject Null Hypothesis
Listening	W = 29,777	0.0005	0.4405 (Medium)	Reject Null Hypothesis
Speaking	W = 19,791	0.9544	0.0065 (Very Small)	Fail to Reject Null Hypothesis

*Effect Size: $r < 0.1$ (Very Small), $0.1 < r < 0.3$ (Small), $0.3 < r < 0.5$ (Medium), $r > 0.5$ (Large)

test revealed significant differences in the overall and receptive scores of Listening and Reading, with forced online students outperforming the choice F2F group, as shown in Table 8. A smaller effect size was observed, indicating less significance compared to the results comparing pre-pandemic forced F2F and post-pandemic choice groups (see Tables 6 and 7).

The box plot graph in Figure 6 (left) revealed higher scores on average along with a larger variation in the forced online group compared to the post-pandemic choice F2F students, as also reported in Goertler and Gacs (2018). While approximately 75% of the students from the forced online group (Spring 2021) scored above the threshold of Intermediate Low (a 15 overall score), the inter quartile range was three points higher compared to the post-pandemic choice F2F group (AY21–22). Furthermore, the Likert graph in Figure 6 (right) revealed that 54% of the students in the forced online group scored at or above the Intermediate Mid level, 21% higher than the post-pandemic choice F2F students. Within reading, the percentage at or above the Intermediate Mid level was 71% compared to 58% respectively. Within the productive skills (speaking and writing) similar percentages were found from Novice Low to Advanced High.

Finally, the results of the Mann-Whitney *U* test comparing STAMP scores for forced online courses during the pandemic and choice online courses post-pandemic also revealed significant differences, with students in online courses during the pandemic outperforming those in choice online courses post-pandemic, both in terms of overall scores as well as across three of the four skills (reading, listening, and speaking), as shown in Table 9. The effect size was Large (0.5242) for the overall score and in the receptive skills (reading and listening) and Medium for the speaking skills.

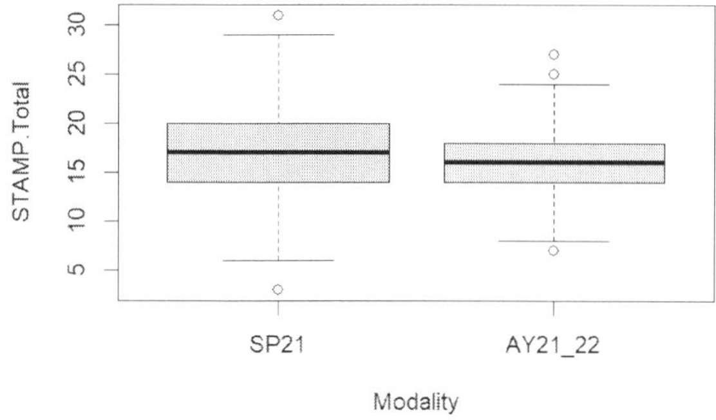

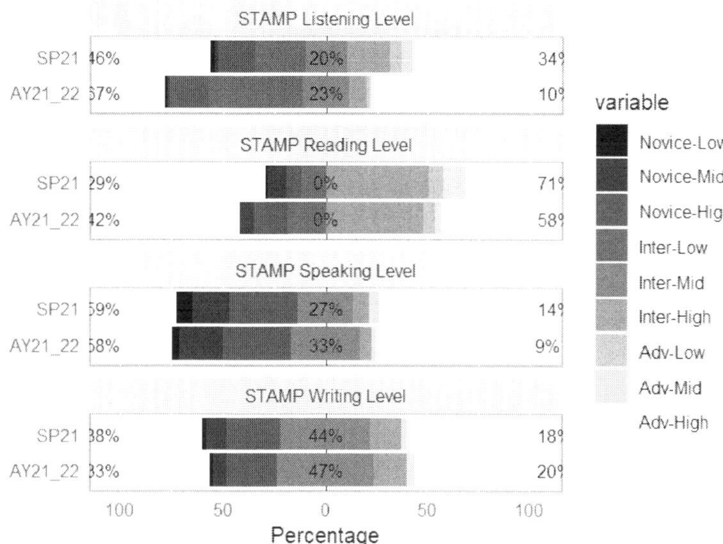

Figure 6 STAMP Scores Across Forced Online Modality (Spring 2021) and the Post-pandemic Choice F2F Modality in the 2021–22 AY

Table 9 Mann-Whitney Test Results for Sub-skill STAMP Results for Spring 2021 (Forced Online) vs. AY21–22 (Choice Online)

STAMP Test	Test Statistic	P-value	Effect Size	Decision
Overall	W = 28,114	< 0.0001	0.5242 (Large)	Reject Null Hypothesis
Reading	W = 28,720	< 0.0001	0.5786 (Large)	Reject Null Hypothesis
Writing	W = 22,702	0.1356	0.1673 (Small)	Fail to Reject Null Hypothesis
Listening	W = 27,758	< 0.0001	0.5346 (Large)	Reject Null Hypothesis
Speaking	W = 20,044	0.0115	0.3028 (Medium)	Reject Null Hypothesis

*Effect Size: $r < 0.1$ (Very Small), $0.1 < r < 0.3$ (Small), $0.3 < r < 0.5$ (Medium), $r > 0.5$ (Large)

The box plot graph in Figure 7 (left) revealed similar variation among the two groups of online students, with approximately 25% more students from the forced online group (Spring 2021) compared to the post-pandemic choice online group (AY 21–22) scoring above a level of Intermediate Low (15 overall score). Furthermore, the Likert graph in Figure 7 (right) revealed that 54% of the students in the forced online group scored at or above the Intermediate Mid level, compared to 27% from the post-pandemic choice online group. Within reading skills, the percentage at or above the Intermediate Mid level was 83% compared to 63% respectively. Within speaking skills, 13% more of the students from the forced online group scored at or above the Intermediate Mid level compared to the post-pandemic choice online group.

Discussion

In comparing student Spanish proficiency over a four-semester period (pre, during, post-pandemic), several interesting patterns emerged. Students across all skills performed the highest during the pandemic (i.e., during ERTL) when they were forced to take courses online. The next highest overall performance was post-pandemic, when students had the choice of modality, with students in the F2F courses outperforming their online counterparts. Perhaps surprisingly, the lowest observed student performance was pre-pandemic when students were forced to take all of their courses F2F, due to the fact that online courses were unavailable.

These patterns are most observable in the area of the receptive skills (listening and reading), with remarkable gains in receptive skill performance

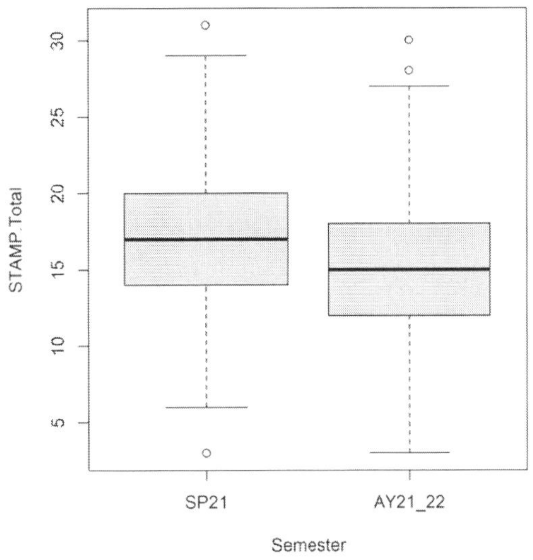

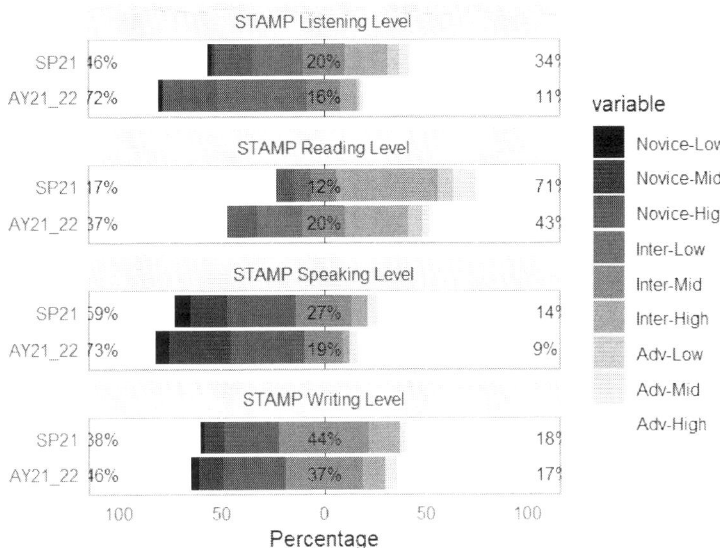

Figure 7 STAMP Scores Across Forced Online Modality (Spring 2021) and the Post-pandemic Choice Online Modality in the 2021–22 AY

– 1.59 points in Reading and a full 2.0 points in Listening – between the forced F2F and forced online semesters. We observed that these gains then leveled out slightly post-pandemic but were still higher (1.02 points in reading and 1.36 points in listening) than the forced F2F pre-pandemic outcomes. Receptive skills may be seen as a harbinger of overall and productive language development, and have consistently shown to appear before the productive skills (Richards, 2015; Swain & Lapkin, 1998).

In terms of the productive skills, a similar pattern held, but it was less dramatic, reflecting a general tendency of resistance to change, especially in Writing, whose scores were only 0.03 points higher when students were forced online during the pandemic compared to pre-pandemic forced F2F scores. Speaking scores only increased by 0.31 points online compared to pre-pandemic. Post-pandemic, when given a choice of course modality, productive skill scores decreased slightly compared to forced online scores during the pandemic (–0.02 Writing and –0.14 Speaking); however, they were still higher than students' pre-pandemic scores (0.01 Writing and 0.17 Speaking), when forced to take F2F classes.

After the pandemic, when students were for the first time given the choice of F2F or online sections, those who took a F2F section statistically outperformed those in online sections across all skills, with a Medium effect size for all skills, except Listening, which had a Small effect size. Variability was observed to be much higher in online sections, as has been found in other studies comparing online and F2F modalities (Goertler & Gacs, 2018).

In comparing forced pre-pandemic F2F student performance with choice post-pandemic F2F performance, we observed a remarkable difference. Students who chose the F2F modality significantly outperformed those who were forced F2F pre-pandemic across all four skills with a Large and Medium effect size (Large for the overall and receptive skills, Medium for the productive skills). This suggests at least three possibilities, which are not mutually exclusive: (a) the F2F modality may have been more effective post-pandemic for building student Spanish proficiency than it was pre-pandemic, (b) students who intentionally registered for F2F courses post-pandemic may have already had higher proficiency levels, or were perhaps stronger academically, than those who were forced to take F2F courses pre-pandemic, and (c) the quality of the post-pandemic courses improved, despite the minimal curricular changes that were made.

Given the lack of change or innovation in the courses across semesters (recall that the only modification made to the Spanish curriculum was the change of the synchronous F2F lab period to an asynchronous online modality), the second possibility seems likely, especially given the large number of historically underprepared students at this regional public institution. However, to investigate this hypothesis, we would need to use a logistic regression model to predict the probability of a student scoring above or below the Intermediate low (16) using student measures such as grade-point averages and/or course grades as explanatory variables (predictors).

An additional reason to support the possibility that students who chose the online courses post-pandemic were already lower in proficiency/academic preparedness is that when examining differences between forced F2F students pre-pandemic and those who chose the online courses post-pandemic, we see higher scores post-pandemic online, but not quite as remarkably high as between pre-pandemic F2F learners and those who chose the F2F courses post-pandemic. In the receptive skill scores (Reading and Listening) and overall proficiency, there was a statistically significant difference with a Large effect size between these groups, but not in the productive skill scores (Writing and Speaking). This suggests that failing to offer an online modality pre-pandemic, and thus forcing students to take F2F classes, does not ensure higher proficiency outcomes. Rather, by offering students choice of modality and enabling them to make decisions about which is best for them, overall proficiency outcomes improve, as learners take agency and make choices based on their overall life circumstances and needs.

However, students post-pandemic who chose the F2F courses not only outperformed those who were forced F2F pre-pandemic, but also those who chose the online modality post-pandemic. Effect sizes revealed that post-pandemic F2F students outperformed online students in the productive skill scores (Writing and Speaking) and the variability was 0.84 points higher amongst students who chose the online modality (Goertler & Gacs, 2018). This might be due to the fact that online learning puts everything in the hands of the student to decide when and how much to study, so staying motivated is a major factor to success. It could also mean that students who are in college have already proven that they can be successful in F2F environments – because if they had not been, they would not be there, but some students who chose the online modality may not have learned how to be successful in online learning contexts, while others may have been disadvantaged in F2F environments. We already saw that students who chose the post-pandemic online courses comprised a much greater range of abilities than those in the F2F courses, which suggests an equity issue (Ortega, 2017; van Dijk, 2020). In terms of receptive skills (a harbinger of overall language development), students who chose the online modality post-pandemic significantly outperformed forced F2F students pre-pandemic, but not by nearly as much as those who chose the F2F modality post-pandemic. The effect sizes were much greater between students who chose the F2F modality post-pandemic compared with students who were forced F2F pre-pandemic. Clearly, offering students an option was better than forcing them to take F2F classes; however, both online and F2F options produced equivalent results, with students in the online modality underperforming compared to those who chose the F2F courses.

When examining the differences between forced online students during the pandemic and those who chose the F2F modality post pandemic, we saw significantly lower performances overall (Small effect size) and in the receptive skill scores (Reading and Listening) among the F2F students. However, there were no differences in the productive skills and there was an even higher variability among the students forced online during the pandemic. This suggests that not offering a choice of modality – at least during the pandemic – seemed to have a positive impact on student proficiency; however, the extreme global conditions, such as lockdown measures, may also have been a factor and could not and should not be easily replicated, for other reasons. As reported in Gleason et al. (in press), one of the reasons for outstanding student proficiency and performance during online courses during the pandemic may have been the fact that the students at this particular regional public institution, many of whom had competing life responsibilities (e.g., working full-time outside of their college classes, taking care of family members, etc.) were advantaged by the lockdowns, in the sense that they had the benefit of being able to fully concentrate on their academic studies in ways that their normal non-pandemic lives would have never permitted.

Interestingly, while general university enrollments went down during the pandemic, Spanish enrollments increased, perhaps due to the fact that students hoped to take advantage of the online course offerings and were uncertain if the department would ever offer courses in an online modality once the pandemic was over. Furthermore, in comparing the proficiency outcomes between students who were forced online during the pandemic with those who chose online post-pandemic, we see that the forced online group significantly outperformed the choice online post-pandemic group, both overall and in three out of the four skills. This suggests that the gains in proficiency among students in forced-online courses during the pandemic cannot be expected to persist as we collectively move back into a new normal and normal life responsibilities resume. However, we should not underestimate the advantageous effect of pandemic working and learning conditions on student proficiency, as it may hold learning opportunities for future crisis preparedness.

The question of why students who chose the F2F courses statistically outperformed those who chose the online courses post-pandemic remains to be answered, and a possible confounding variable has yet to be identified. Perhaps, when given the choice, students with competing life interests and responsibilities (e.g., jobs, family, etc.) needed to choose the convenience of the online modality over the F2F modality post-pandemic. The F2F courses, which required students to be physically present in the classroom space often required them to make sacrifices, such as the time, energy, and resources it takes to commute significant distances to campus. Perhaps students who had sufficient time to devote to their academic experience chose the F2F modality not only because they had higher levels of self-awareness about how they themselves could learn and be successful (Heo & Han, 2018), but also because they had the resources (e.g., time, money, energy) to move out into the world and into the physical classroom space two or three times per week. The likelihood of greater community building in the physical F2F environment could have been an important factor in their proficiency gains, which would lend support to the importance of a residential college experience.

The purpose of our second research question was essentially to ascertain if a decision to force students to take F2F language classes by not offering online language classes could be supported with data and what we found was a resounding *no*. Pre-pandemic students who had no choice but to take F2F classes underperformed both overall and across all of the four sub-skills compared to those who voluntarily chose the F2F courses post-pandemic. Even the students who chose the online modality post-pandemic outperformed those forced to learn F2F pre-pandemic, and significantly so in the receptive skills. As mentioned, this latter group may have consisted of students who perhaps struggled academically. Students may have chosen online courses based on their convenience of modality rather than on the modality that best matched their learning styles and needs (Geng et al., 2019).

Of course, the question of whether or not we should force all students to take F2F courses by simply not offering online language courses may now be a moot point. Not only is online learning likely here to stay, it has also proven in most cases to be at least as successful for promoting language proficiency as F2F courses (Aldrich & Moneypenny, 2019; Goertler & Gacs, 2018; Grgurović et al., 2013), especially when well-planned and not ERTL (Gacs et al., 2020). Although online courses, due to their geographic and temporal flexibility, may increase access to language classes, which may seemingly serve to quell certain enrollment concerns, if there is a lack of community and/or student engagement in such courses, they may prove counterproductive for student retention. This has important implications for universities considering replacing courses or entire programs with online language learning apps or outsourced online lessons from other institutions (Quinn, 2023). While it may seem as if learners who belong to the "digital native" population (Prensky, 2001), and those with the resources to invest in their own technological literacies may be more adept at online learning (Ortega, 2017), this may not necessarily be the case. Learner preparedness and willingness to engage in online learning successfully may be more closely related to individual factors such as students' attitudes and motivations (Murday et al., 2008; Ushida, 2013), their ability to handle stress (Geng et al. 2019), their learning styles (i.e., level of self-directedness) (Heo & Han, 2018), and other critical life circumstances (Castrillo & Sedano, 2021).

Moreover, the data from this study reveal that, when given the choice of modality, both online and F2F language learners outperform those forced to learn F2F. Future research will need to examine if more self-determined and mature learners, who might otherwise do well in an online course, may actually prefer an F2F modality. While age may not play a role in learners' self-directed readiness for online learning, other life situations may (Heo & Han, 2018). For example, learners who come back to finish their degrees with full-time jobs and families may need the flexibility and convenience of online language courses in order to be able to meet other life responsibilities.

The implications of these findings for administrators and other university stakeholders should certainly be taken into account, especially when scheduling courses for reasons other than language proficiency. There may still be those who advocate for F2F-only language course offerings, but their numbers are likely dwindling, especially due to the forced innovation brought upon us by the pandemic (Rüschoff, Chapter 5, this volume). Logistically, since most universities are still brick-and-mortar institutions that depend on F2F student experiences to provide a traditional college experience, online-only language classes may threaten their economic livelihood in other ways. For example, a university model based on wrap-around services that have traditionally comprised the full college experience, such as housing, dining, athletics, and clubs, depends on students populating F2F classes to facilitate use of these other F2F services.

Alternatively, some stakeholders may prefer online-only language courses. There are a growing number of fully online universities which offer exclusively online courses, many of which occur in a fully asynchronous modality. Such asynchronous courses depend on online platforms and supports, such as those associated with the majority of educational language learning textbooks (e.g., the Supersite), as well as on video lectures, asynchronous discussion fora, and other technological tools that require zero live presence from students and instructors. The role of the instructor in fully asynchronous courses, however, looks very different from that of the traditional foreign language courses from years past and has been shown to produce students whose language proficiency differs qualitatively from that of their F2F counterparts (Lord, 2015). Online language courses, either synchronous or asynchronous – or a combination of the two – may be especially attractive for working students, older learners with families, courses that unite students from different time zones, and students with social anxiety; however, there are tradeoffs that are certainly at play when prioritizing their convenience.

Clearly, decisions about course offerings may be and are often made based on reasons other than student proficiency outcomes. However, it is our hope that administrators will take this study and other data driven studies into account, especially regarding the effectiveness of language classes for producing students with high levels of working language proficiency. From this and our prior study (Gleason et al., in press), we gain a clearer picture of how language course modality impacts proficiency. At least one plausible explanation for students' decreased performance in post-pandemic online courses as compared to their F2F counterparts is that students may tend to prefer online language classes for reasons other than their effectiveness and, in doing so, may end up compromising their own language proficiency development as a result. Further research will need to account for student course grades and grade-point averages in order to determine if academically challenged learners from different institutions and socioeconomic backgrounds end up choosing online courses to their detriment (Martin et al., 2020). Clearly, we need to better understand who benefits from online learning and who does not, as well as how we can support those who may struggle online but need the modality nonetheless.

Conclusion

There is certainly no shortage of change in today's educational settings – or world. But in the words of Heraclitus: change is the only constant (Graham, 2021). If one of our goals as educators is to educate a globally competent multilingual workforce (ACTFL, 2019), then we certainly need to provide options in terms of different learning modalities for students to effectively address their needs. One way to do so is for teachers and CALL practitioners to adapt our modalities and technology-enhanced pedagogies in traditional, hybrid/blended, and online courses in order to ensure that these modalities are producing comparable results. The present chapter has focused on one primary crisis – the pandemic – and its impact on student Spanish proficiency. We have illustrated how the crisis forced one particular institution (and other institutions) into experimenting with online education, which turned out to be beneficial for some students, and then fomented the continual offering of online courses, which increased learning outcomes overall compared to pre-pandemic, and gave students choices around which course modalities were most suitable for their lives. Thus, the crisis offered the kind of disruption which eventually led to an opportunity. As authors, we hope to see a greater emphasis and additional research in the area of proficiency development vis-a-vis online language instruction more broadly (Goertler et al., 2016). Perhaps in this way we will be able to better understand and address the challenges and inequities of our times in ways that bring together the best of both tradition and innovation.

About the Authors

Jesse Gleason, PhD is Associate Professor of Spanish and Applied Linguistics at Southern Connecticut State University in New Haven, CT, where she presently coordinates the Lower-Division Spanish program. Her teaching and research interests include world language education, pedagogy and curriculum, technology-enhanced language learning, and assessment.

Andy Bartlett, PhD is Assistant Professor of Statistics and Mathematics at Southern Connecticut State University in New Haven, CT, where he is presently the Data Science Coordinator. His teaching interests include Bayesian Statistics, Non-Parametric Statistics, and Data Science models, while his research interests include Extreme Value Theory and Time Series.

References

Aldrich, R. S., & Moneypenny, D. B. (2019). Assessing Spanish proficiency of online language learners after year 1. *The EUROCALL Review, 27*(2), 28–39. https://doi.org/10.4995/eurocall.2019.11500

American Council on the Teaching of Foreign Languages (ACTFL). (2012). *ACTFL Proficiency Guidelines*. Alexandria, VA: ACTFL. https://www.actfl.org/uploads/files/general/ACTFLProficiencyGuidelines2012.pdf

American Council on the Teaching of Foreign Languages (ACTFL). (2019). *Making languages our business: Addressing foreign language demand among U.S. employers.* https://www.leadwithlanguages.org/wpcontent/uploads/MakingLanguagesOurBusiness_FullReport.pdf

Avant Assessment. (2021). Avant STAMP Annual Averages 2020. Avant Assessment, LLC. Retrieved from: https://avantassessment.com/research

Avant Assessment. (2022a, March 11). Avant STAMP language proficiency tests approved for college credit–Increasing access and equity. https://avantassessment.com/press/avant-stamp-language-proficiency-tests-approved-for-college-credit-increasing-access-and-equity

Avant Assessment. (2022b). Avant STAMP Annual Averages 2021. Avant Assessment, LLC. Retrieved from: https://avantassessment.com/research

Beyer, C. K., Brownson, S., & Evans, S. (2017). Enhancing interactivity in online classes: A framework for enhancing instructor-student, student-student, and student-content engagement. *International Journal of Learning, Teaching and Educational Research, 16*(5), 53–71.

Bivens-Tatum (2010, Nov. 5). The crisis in the humanities. *Academic Librarian*. Retrieved from: https://blogs.princeton.edu/librarian/2010/11/the_crisis_in_the_humanities/

Blake, R. (2008). *Brave new digital classroom: Technology and foreign language learning*. Georgetown University Press. https://doi.org/10.1353/book13058

Blake, R., & Guillén, G. (2013). *Brave new digital classroom: Technology and foreign language learning* (2nd Ed.). Georgetown University Press. https://doi.org/10.2307/j.ctv1nc6rkf

Blake, R., Wilson, N. L., Cetto, M., & Pardo-Ballester, C. (2008). Measuring oral proficiency in distance, face-to-face and blended classrooms. *Language Learning and Technology, 12*(3), 114–127. http://dx.doi.org/10125/44158

Britton et al. (Eds). (forthcoming). TBA.

Castrillo, M. D., & Sedano, B. (2021). Joining forces toward social inclusion: Language MOOC design for refugees and migrants through the lens of maker culture. *CALICO Journal, 38*(1), 79–102. https://doi.org/10.1558/cj.40900

Chenoweth, N. A., Ushida, E., & Murday, K. (2006). Students learning in hybrid French and Spanish courses: An overview of language online. *CALICO Journal, 24*(1), 115–145.

Cox, T. L., & Malone, M. E. (2018). A validity argument to support the ACTFL Assessment of Performance toward proficiency. *Foreign Language Annals, 51*(3), 548–574. https://doi.org/10.1111/flan.12353

Egbert, J. (2020). The new normal?: A pandemic of task engagement in language learning. *Foreign Language Annals, 53*, 314–319. https://doi.org/10.1111/flan.12452

Foung, D., Chen, J., & Lin, L. (2022). When "blended" becomes "online": A data-driven study on the change of Self-Directed Engagement During COVID-19. *CALICO Journal*, *39*(1), 1-25. https://doi.org/10.1558/cj.19666

Gacs, A., Goertler, S., & Spasova, S. (2020). Planned online language education versus crisis-prompted online language teaching: Lessons for the future. *Foreign Language Annals, 53*, 380–392. https://doi.org/10.1111/flan.12460

Gass, S. M., & Winke, P. (2019). Proficiency testing in the US context. In P. Winke & S. M. Gass (Eds.), *Foreign language proficiency in higher education,* (pp. 1–14). Springer. https://doi.org/10.1007/978-3-030-01006-5_1

Gass, S., Winke, P., & van Gorp, K. (2016). The language flagship proficiency initiative. *Language Teaching, 49*(4), 592–595. https://doi.org/10.1017/s0261444816000215

Geng, S., Law, K. M. Y., & Niu, B. (2019). Investigating self-directed learning and technology readiness in blending learning environment. *International Educational Technology in Higher Education 16*, . https://doi.org/10.1186/s41239-019-0147-0

Gleason, J. (2013). Dilemmas of blended language learning. *CALICO Journal, 30*(3), 323—341. https://doi.org/10.11139/cj.30.3.323-341

Gleason, J., Cardone, R., & Bartlett, A. (2024). The impact of the pandemic on student Spanish language proficiency. *Language Learning and Technology*. https://osf.io/preprints/edarxiv/g4qd8

Gleason, J., & Suvorov, R. (Eds.) (2019). Moving forward with CALL to promote Social Justice. *CALICO Journal, 36*(1). https://doi.org/10.1558/cj.37162

Goertler, S., & Gacs, A. (2018). Assessment in online German: Assessment methods and results. *Die Unterrichtspraxis / Teaching German, 51*(2), 156-174. https://www.jstor.org/stable/90026423

Goertler, S., Kraemer, A., & Schenker, T. (2016). Setting evidence-based language goals. *Foreign Language Annals, 49*(3), 434–454. https://doi.org/10.1111/flan.12214

Graham, D. W. (2021). Heraclitus. *The Stanford Encyclopedia of Philosophy.* https://plato.stanford.edu/archives/sum2021/entries/heraclitus/

Grgurović, M., Chapelle, C. A., & Shelley, M. C. (2013). A meta-analysis of effectiveness studies on computer technology-supported language learning. *ReCALL*, 25(2), 165–198. https://doi.org/10.1017/S0958344013000013

Heineke, A., & Davin, K. (2022). *Promoting multilingualism in schools: A framework for implementing the Seal of Biliteracy*. ACTFL. https://doi.org/10.1002/tesj.451

Heo, J., & Han, S. (2018). Effects of motivation, academic stress and age in predicting self-directed learning readiness (SDLR): Focused on online college students. *Education and Information Technologies, 23*, 61–71. https://doi.org/10.1007/s10639-017-9585-2

Hernández-Calderón, J.-G., Soto-Mendoza, V., Montané-Jiménez, L.-G., Meunier Colula, M. A., & Tello-Carrillo, J. (2023). Information visualization dashboard to proctor test-takers during an online language proficiency test. *Interacting with Computers, iwac043*, https://doi.org/10.1093/iwc/iwac043

Heying, H., & Weinstein, B. (2021). *A hunter-gatherer's guide to the 21st century: Evolution and the challenges of modern life*. New York, NY: Penguin Random House.

Hildebrandt, S. A., & Swanson, P. (2019). The control, content, and consequences of edTPA: World language teacher educators' perceptions. *Foreign Language Annals, 52*(3), 670–686. https://doi-org.scsu.idm.oclc.org/10.1111/flan.12415

Isbell, D. R., Winke, P., & Gass, S. M. (2018). Using the ACTFL OPIc to assess proficiency and monitor progress in a tertiary foreign languages program. *Language Testing, 36*(3), 439–465. https://doi.org/10.1177/0265532218798139

Jin, L., Xu, Y., Deifell, E., & Angus, K. (2021). Emergency remote language teaching and U.S.-based college-level world language educators' intentions to adopt online teaching in postpandemic times. *Modern Language Journal, 105*(2), 412–434. https://doi.org/10.1111/modl.12712

Krashen, S. D. (1985). *The Input Hypothesis: Issues and implications*. New York, NY: Longman.

Language Testing International. (2023). AAPPL – K-12 Testing. Retrieved from: https://www.languagetesting.com/lti-for-organizations/k-12-aappl

Larson, D. K., & Sung, C.-H. (2019). Comparing student performance: Online versus blended versus face to face. *Journal of Asynchronous Learning Networks*, *13*(1), 75–87. https://doi.org/10.24059/olj.v13i1.1675

Lin, C., & Warschauer, M. (2015). Online foreign language education: What are the proficiency outcomes? *The Modern Language Journal, 99*, 394–397. https://doi.org/10.1111/modl.12234_1

Link, S., & Li, J. (Eds.) (2018). *Assessment of online education.* San Marco, TX: CALICO.

Loewen, S., & Sato, M. (2018). Interaction and instructed second language acquisition. *Language Teaching, 51*(3), 285-329. https://doi.org/10.1017/s0261444818000125

Long, M. H. (1981). Input, interaction and second language acquisition. In H. Winitz (Ed.), *Native language and foreign language acquisition* (p. 379). New York, NY: Annals of the New York Academy of Sciences. https://doi.org/10.1111/j.1749-6632.1981.tb42014.x

Long, M. H. (1996). The role of the linguistic environment in second language acquisition. In W. C. Ritchie & T. K. Bhatia (Eds.), *Handbook of research on language acquisition* (vol. 2) (pp. 413-468). New York: Academic Press. https://doi.org/10.1016/b978-012589042-7/50015-3

Looney, D., & Lusin, N. (2019). *Enrollments in languages other than English in United States institutions of higher education, summer 2016 and fall 2016: Final report. Modern Language Association.* www.mla.org/content/download/110154/2406932/2016-Enrollments-Final-Report.pdf

Lord, G. (2015). "I don't know how to use words in Spanish:" Rosetta Stone and learner proficiency outcomes. *The Modern Language Journal, 99*(2), 401-405. https://doi.org/10.1111/modl.12234_3

Loschky, L. (1994). Comprehensible input and second language acquisition: What is the relationship? *Studies in Second Language Acquisition, 16*(3), 303-323. https://doi.org/10.1017/s0272263100013103

Martin, F., Stamper, B., & Flowers, C. (2020). Examining student perception of their readiness for online learning: Importance and confidence. *Online Learning*, *24*(2), 38–58. https://doi.org/10.24059/olj.v24i2.2053

Moneypenny, D., & Aldrich, R. (2016). Online and face-to-face language learning: A comparative analysis of oral proficiency in introductory Spanish. *Journal of Educators Online*, *13*(2), 105–174. https://doi.org/10.9743/JEO.2016.2.2

Murday, K., Ushida, E., & Chenoweth, N. A. (2008). Learners and teacher perspectives on language online. *Computer-Assisted Language Learning*, *21*(2), 125–142. https://doi.org/10.1080/09588220801943718

Murphy, D., Sarac, M., & Sedivy, S. (2022). Why U.S. undergraduate students are (not) studying languages other than English. *Second Language Research & Practice*, *3*(1), 1–33. https://doi.org/10125/69866

Ortega, L. (2017). New CALL-SLA research interfaces for the 21st century: Towards equitable multilingualism. *CALICO Journal*, *34*(3), 285–316. https://doi.org/10.1558/cj.33855

Pica, T. (1994). Research on negotiation: What does it reveal about second language learning conditions, processes, and outcomes? *Language Learning*, *44*(3), 493–527. https://doi.org/10.1111/j.1467-1770.1994.tb01115.x

Piller, I. (2016). *Linguistic diversity and social justice: An introduction to applied sociolinguistics*. New York: Oxford University Press. http://dx.doi.org/10.1093/acprof:oso/9780199937240.003.0008

Prensky, M. (2001). Digital natives, digital immigrants, part 1: *On the Horizon*, *9*(5), 1–6. http://doi10.1108/10748120110424816

Quinn, R. (2023, August 11). West Virginia's unprecedented proposed cuts become clear. Inside Higher Ed. Retrieved from: https://www.insidehighered.com/news/faculty-issues/tenure/2023/08/11/west-virginia-universitys-unprecedented-proposed-cuts-become

Richards, J. (2015, August 26). *Moving beyond the plateau: From intermediate to advanced levels in language learning*. Cambridge ELT Blog: World of Better Learning. https://www.cambridge.org/elt/blog/2015/08/26/moving-beyond-plateau-lower-upper-intermediate/

Ross, A. F., DiSalvo, M. L. (2020). Negotiating displacement, regaining community: The Harvard Language Center's response to the COVID-19 crisis. *Foreign Language Annals*, *53*, 371–379. https://doi.org/10.1111/flan.12463

Santos, V. (2019, November 5). The development of a STAMP test: Support for test validity. Avant Assessment, LLC. Retrieved from: https://avantassessment.com/research

Santos, V. (2022). *Psychometric evidence for the validity of STAMP 4S assessments*. Avant Assessment, LLC. Retrieved from: https://avantassessment.com/research

Schmitt, E. (2014). Seat time versus proficiency: Assessment of language development in undergraduate students. In J. Norris & N. Mills (Eds.), *Innovation and accountability in language program evaluation* (pp. 110 –130). Cengage.

Schultz, L., & Backstrom, M. (2021). Test-optional admissions policies: Evidence from implementations pre- and post-COVID-19. *Policy Brief: Nelson A. Rockefeller Institute of Government*. https://rockinst.org/

Scida, E. E., & Saury, E. R. (2006). Hybrid courses and their impact on student and classroom performance: A case study at the University of Virginia. *CALICO Journal*, *23*(3), 517–531. https://doi.org/10.1558/cj.v23i3.517-531

Sun, S. Y. H. (2014). Learning perspectives on fully online language learning. *Distance Education*, *35*(1), 18–42. https://doi.org/10.1080/01587919.2014.891428

Swain, M., & Lapkin, S. (1998). Interaction and second language learning: Two adolescent French immersion students working together. *Modern Language Journal*, *82*(3), 320–337. https://doi.org/10.1111/j.1540-4781.1998.tb01209.x

Tarone, E. (2015). Online foreign language education: What are the proficiency outcomes? *The Modern Language Journal*, *99*(2), 392–393. https://www.jstor.org/stable/43650033

Ushida, E. (2013). The role of students' attitudes and motivation in second language learning in online language courses. *CALICO Journal*, *23*(1), 49–78.

Van Deusen-Scholl, N. (2015). Assessing outcomes in online foreign language education: What are key measures for success? *The Modern Language Journal*, *99*(2), 398–400. https://www.jstor.org/stable/43650035

Van Dijk, J. (2020). *The digital divide.* John Wiley & Sons.

Warner, C., & Dao, W. (2022). Caring is pedagogy: Foreign language teachers' emotion labor in crisis. *Linguistics and Education*, *71*. https://doi.org/10.1016/j.linged.2022.101100

Zuboff, S. (2019). *The age of surveillance Capitalism: The fight for a human future at the new frontier of power.* New York, NY: Hachette Book Group.

10 Exploring Flipped English-medium Content Courses in Japanese Higher Education

Elizabeth Lavolette and Mayumi Asaba

Introduction

Universities around the world have taken different approaches to educational continuity during the COVID-19 pandemic and have drawn different conclusions on how to move forward, as is discussed in many chapters of this volume. In this chapter, the authors discuss how they used the move to emergency remote teaching (ERT) as an opportunity for curricular innovation. At the authors' institution in western Japan, the administration designated which classes would be delivered asynchronously online, as opposed to synchronously online or face-to-face, during the first two years of the pandemic. Specifically, in the 2021 academic year, World Englishes (WE, taught by the first author) and Introduction to Intercultural Understanding (IIU, taught by the second author)—the classes in focus for this study, henceforth referred to as focal classes—were designated for asynchronous online delivery. Without knowing if and when the designation would be changed back to face-to-face (FTF) delivery, the authors took this challenge as an opportunity to create materials that could both be used for asynchronous delivery and later be repurposed for flipped delivery.

In accordance with university policy, the authors taught the focal classes fully asynchronously during the academic year 2021 (Table 1). *Asynchronous* was not formally defined at the university. Therefore, the authors decided to teach the asynchronous courses using instructor-made videos and follow-up assignments (for justification and details, see Asaba & Lavolette, 2022). The asynchronous learning materials (instructor-made videos, readings, quizzes, etc.) were provided via a course management system, which

Table 1 Modality and Teaching Methods of World Englishes and Introduction to Intercultural Understanding

Semester	World Englishes and Introduction to Intercultural Understanding
2021 Fall	Online asynchronous
2022 Fall (data collection)	Face-to-face flipped

allowed students to access the materials on their own schedule, with deadlines set by the instructors. As is often the case with new curricular initiatives, the implementation was a process of constant adjustments in response to evaluation of the lessons and the students' responses.

In the academic year 2022, the focal classes returned to synchronous FTF classroom delivery per university policy. As required by the Ministry of Education of Japan (Daigaku setchi kijun [Basis for establishing universities], 2019) for all university classes, 90-minute FTF class meetings were held once per week.

The aforementioned constant adjustments during the ERT asynchronous teaching provided the authors with an opportunity to reexamine how to best help students achieve course objectives while recycling materials created during asynchronous teaching. Consequently, in the academic year 2022, they decided to implement flipped learning as a teaching method that incorporates both synchronous and asynchronous teaching. The university did not have a formal definition of flipped learning, so the authors followed that of Lage et al. (2000): Flipped learning refers to learning where the asynchronous classwork provides explanations and instruction to prepare students for applied and engaged student-centered work during the synchronous portions of the class. In the focal flipped classes, students watched video lectures and completed homework between FTF class meetings. In the classroom, they participated in activities such as discussions and mini projects. During academic years 2020 and 2021, the authors gradually prepared materials for a flipped learning format by first creating the homework portions of the flipped instruction as the asynchronous course, then in academic year 2022, adding the in-class activities.

Because flipped classes are relatively rare in Japan, understanding how students would perceive and interact with the homework and in-class elements of a flipped class was important to determine students' acceptance of flipped classes and to find ways to improve the class materials and delivery for students in this context. To judge the effectiveness of the flipped classroom, the authors also asked the students to report their perceived learning outcomes.

Flipped Learning in University Education

Post-Pandemic Contexts

Pandemic contexts for flipped learning have been studied in EFL contexts (e.g., Al-Naabi et al., 2022; L. Hung, 2022; Roarty, 2021). In the post-pandemic return to FTF teaching, the authors are not alone in taking advantage of the online pandemic teaching requirements to plan for improved learning. A design feature of the flipped classroom is that lectures are moved to asynchronous online time. In relation to lectures, academics in the UK were surveyed on how they predicted lectures would be conducted post-pandemic, and around 30% predicted a change, with the flipped classroom model mentioned in some cases (Robson et al., 2022). Similarly, university educators, mainly based in Germany, mentioned the flipped classroom as a desirable change in the post-pandemic era (Gruber et al., 2023), and Rapanta et al. (2021) predicted that the flipped learning approach would be used more frequently in higher education than purely FTF learning. Valentine (2022) explained how she flipped her classroom using materials that she created during the pandemic.

Students, too, have noticed that circumstances favor a change from traditional lectures to flipped classrooms; a Harvard student opinion piece called for the replacement of lectures with flipped classrooms, referring to the fact that lecture recordings already exist from pandemic-era online teaching (Berman, 2023). This literature suggests that for both instructors and students, the pandemic cast a new light on the desirability of flipped learning.

Advantages of Flipped Learning

Flipped learning has been shown to have advantages over traditional lecture classes in improving areas such as language skills, student satisfaction, achievement of course goals, student engagement, and time for practice (Bener, 2021; H. Hung, 2015; Obari & Lambacher, 2015; Okuda et al., 2015; Shahnama et al., 2021; Vitta & Al-Hoorie, 2020). Moreover, flipped classes provide students with more opportunities to learn through scaffolding each other's understanding of the in-class work (e.g., John-Steiner & Mahn,

1996; Lantolf et al., 2015) and interacting in the target language (e.g., Ellis et al., 1994; Loewen & Sato, 2018). Another advantage to creating flipped courses is that they are flexible in the face of future crises: they can quickly be converted to fully asynchronous courses or adapted for a synchronous online flip.

Japanese University Contexts

The Ministry of Education, Culture, Sports, Science, and Technology of Japan (MEXT) found that approximately 36% of university students had no or almost no opportunities to engage in group activities or discussions (MEXT, 2021), and flipped learning may ameliorate this issue (e.g., Mehring, 2015; Roarty, 2021). Hence, implementing flipped learning in Japanese university contexts in particular may be beneficial to increase interaction among students. Even though previous research points to positive effects of flipped learning, limited research on this model of teaching has been conducted in Japanese university contexts, suggesting that few flipped classes are taught in Japan.

This chapter reports on a study of students' perceptions of two English-medium content-based courses taught FTF at a large private university in western Japan during the fall semester of 2022. While the university designated these courses as lectures, the authors could teach them as they saw fit (with the restriction that FTF contact hours could not be reduced), which allowed the change to flipped delivery. Each instructor implemented flipped learning in their own way, so comparing students' perceptions of the classes can provide further pedagogical implications on which approach to flipped learning is seen as more effective.

To date, no studies have investigated students' perceptions of either their learning experiences or learning outcomes in the context of flipped English-medium lecture classes at Japanese universities. To understand how flipped classes can be effectively implemented in this context, the authors posed the following questions:

1. How do students perceive and interact with the homework elements (videos and quizzes) of a flipped class?
2. How do students perceive in-class elements?
3. What learning outcomes did students report in their reflections?

Methods

Data Collection

A total of 57 students were enrolled in the two FTF English-medium content courses, and 42 students consented to participate in the research (WE: 25 students; IIU: 17 students). The students were L1 speakers of Japanese, except for one L1 Russian speaker in IIU. While more than half of the students in WE majored in English (52%), nearly all students in IIU majored in Asian languages. Most of the students reported no previous experience with flipped learning. See Table 2 for more details about the participants.

The instructors created instructional materials for flipped learning, including videos, described in Table 3. The first author used English only in instructional materials. The second author followed recommendations from other researchers who have argued that the use of the L1 in content-based classes allows learners to improve not only linguistic but also thinking abilities (Lin, 2019; Turnbull et al., 2011) because of her concerns for her students who were mostly non-English majors.

To answer the research questions, the authors conducted questionnaire surveys and focus group interviews.

During the first class session of both classes, the authors explained how the flipped classroom is different from traditional lecture classes and how students would be expected to prepare for the synchronous in-person class and participate during class. Students completed online questionnaires at three

Table 2 Participant Demographics

		WE	IIU
Enrollment		30	20
Consent to research		25	17
Mean age (in years)		19.1	20.3
Gender	Female	11	11
	Male	13	5
Major	English	13	1
	European language (other than English)	9	0
	Asian language	2	15
Flipped class experience		0	2

Note: One participant in each class did not complete the initial survey.

Table 3 Instructional Materials and Procedures

	WE	IIU
Textbook	NA	Students were required to read a textbook in Japanese before watching videos
Video length range (average)	0:35–4:49 (2:24)	1:18–5:06 (2:43)
Number of videos per week	3–9	2–4
Average total video time per week	13:39	6:54
Language(s) used	English	English and Japanese
Other homework activities	Each instructional video was usually followed by a quiz; 5 quizzes per week on average.	Each instructional video was followed by a quiz and reflections on the textbook and video materials reviewed in response to question prompts.
In-class activities	• Students wrote a reflection on the homework. • Instructor presented good examples of mini projects submitted by students the previous week, reviewed homework, answered questions, and conducted a review game. • Students completed a mini project in a group of two or three.	• Students took a quiz based on the reading and videos. • Students discussed issues with a partner. • Students completed a mini project in a group of three or four.
Class activity example	Students created comic strips that explained a word or phrase used in Japanese English and took a position on whether they wanted to celebrate the usefulness of Japanese English or promote learning another variety of English.	Each group examined a case study demonstrating a problematic situation resulting from differing values. Then they developed a solution based on what they had learned in their homework. Finally, they discussed possible causes of the conflict and proposed a solution through a role-play.

Table 4 Timing of Questionnaires

Week	Questionnaire
Week 1	Pre-semester
Weeks 2–14	Pre-class Post-class
Week 15	Post-semester

stages: pre-semester, weekly, and post-semester (Table 4). All questionnaires were written in English and Japanese and are available on the book website (https://sites.google.com/msu.edu/2024crisiscall/instruments-and-materials). The pre-semester questionnaire included demographic questions. In the pre-class questionnaires, students were asked about their interactions with the homework (WE: 13 weeks; IIU: 11 weeks), and in the post-class questionnaires, they were asked about perceptions of the in-class work (WE: 14 weeks; IIU: 12 weeks). Students also reported what they had learned (WE only). The post-semester questionnaire was used to investigate students' overall perceptions of the flipped learning experience and learning outcomes.

Focus Group Interviews

To help explain and clarify the questionnaire results by exploring individual students' experiences, the authors conducted a focus group interview after the semester ended in Japanese with four students from the IIU class. The second author explained the focus group interview in class, and students who indicated their interest and could meet on the same day were chosen. All focus-group students majored in Asian languages; three participants were second-year and one participant was a third-year student. Focus groups were chosen over individual interviews because they are used to explore "participants' attitudes and opinions on a researcher's topic of interest" (Morgan, 1997, p. 20) and to obtain data that can be produced in dynamic group interaction among group members as they compare their experiences with each other. The students were prompted to discuss their experience with the flipped class, such as what they liked and disliked about it and what they learned. The questions are available on the book website (https://sites.google.com/msu.edu/2024crisiscall/instruments-and-materials). No focus group was conducted for the WE class because of incompatible student schedules.

The researchers were the instructors of the classes reported in this chapter, so their positionality affected data collection. A potential negative effect is that the participants, their students, may have felt that they needed to provide positive responses about the teaching in their presence.

Analysis

The researchers followed explanatory design (Ivankova & Creswell, 2009) to answer the first two research questions regarding how students perceived and interacted with the homework elements and how they perceived the in-class elements of the flipped classes. In this design, qualitative findings are used to understand quantitative findings. Therefore, the authors first analyzed the closed-response findings and then the open-ended items in the questionnaires and focus group data. To answer the third research question, concerning learning outcomes reported in students' reflections, the researchers analyzed qualitative data from the open-ended items in the pre-class questionnaires (WE only) and end-of-the semester questionnaire and focus group data.

Descriptive statistics were calculated for each closed-response questionnaire item. For the open-ended items, the second author organized the data into themes. She used a deductive approach, in which she relied on themes indicated in the research questions. Themes included design principles (Asaba & Lavolette, 2022), such as video length, and students' perceptions about learning outcomes. Then, she coded the data by focusing on each word indicating students' opinions and feelings about each theme. Finally, both researchers examined and refined the codings together.

Focus Group Interviews

The second author obtained a machine-generated transcript, which she revised as she listened to the recording multiple times. Three cycles of coding were conducted. The first cycle involved structural coding. According to Saldaña (2013), structural coding can be used to categorize data for research that involves multiple participants and semi-structured interviews. In this cycle of coding, the second author segmented the data based on the research questions into five categories: class activities, videos, homework, perceptions about the flipped class, and self-assessed learning outcomes. The second cycle of coding was descriptive coding (Saldaña, 2013), in which she summarized excerpts into a word or short phrases to identify the topic. The third cycle involved pattern coding, a process of identifying themes (Miles & Huberman, 1984). Based on the results of the descriptive coding, the second author identified patterns that holistically captured segments of data in each category and created themes for each pattern. The second author conducted the initial coding for each cycle, then both researchers modified it together.

Results

How Do Students Perceive and Interact With the Homework Elements (Videos and Quizzes) of a Flipped Class?

Perceptions

Students' perceptions of the homework elements are summarized in Table 5. The average video length in the two classes was similar (WE: 2:24; IIU: 2:43), and the students similarly perceived the video length as good (WE: 90%; IIU: 100%). On average, they reported that the ideal video length was approximately 2 minutes (WE) or 4 minutes (IIU). This discrepancy may have resulted from the L1 use in the IIU class videos. That is, students may have been willing to watch longer videos if they included L1 support.

The students in each class differed somewhat in their perceptions of how easy the video content was to understand. Three-quarters of the students in WE thought that the video content was "very easy" or "easy" to understand, while 5 (25%) thought that it was difficult to understand. All 17 students in IIU reported that the video content was "very easy" or "easy" to understand.

The students who thought that the videos were easy to understand were asked to choose or write reasons, with multiple selections possible. In WE, the greatest numbers of students chose "Instructor spoke slowly" (80%) and "Instructor used easy words" (67%). The greatest numbers of IIU students chose "Instructor used some Japanese" (94%), and "Instructor used easy words" (71%). The 5 students in WE who thought the videos were difficult to understand chose the reasons "Instructor used difficult words" (2), "Words on PowerPoint slides" (1), and "Instructor used only English" (1).

The reasons that students selected for the video difficulty indicate that the instructor's language choice was a major difference between the classes. Students' comments in the focus group further exemplified the importance of the use of Japanese in the IIU class. The use of Japanese played two main roles: making the content comprehensible and allowing students to take a risk to use English in class. Emma (all names are pseudonyms) explained that reading the textbook in Japanese first helped her not only understand the videos but also learn new English words. Furthermore, students felt safe to use English. Kodai explained that he felt safe to use English because he knew he could switch to Japanese if he got stuck explaining his ideas in

Table 5 Students' Perceptions of the Homework Elements (Post-semester Questionnaires)

		WE		IIU	
		Count	*Percentage*	*Count*	*Percentage*
Responses to final questionnaire		20		17	
Ease of understanding video content	Very easy	2	10%	5	29%
	Easy	13	65%	12	71%
	Difficult	5	25%	0	0%
	Very difficult	0	0%	0	0%
What made videos easy to understand? (WE: 15 responses; IIU: 17 responses)	Images on PowerPoint slides	7	47%	11	65%
	Words on PowerPoint slides	7	47%	8	47%
	Instructor used easy words	10	67%	12	71%
	Instructor spoke slowly	12	80%	7	41%
	Instructor used some Japanese	0	0%	16	94%
	Instructor used only English	1	7%	1	6%
What made videos difficult to understand? (WE: 5 responses; IIU: 0 responses)	Words on PowerPoint slides	1	20%	0	0%
	Instructor used difficult words	2	40%	0	0%
	Instructor used only English	1	20%	0	0%

English. These comments illustrate how students' first language can be effectively used in a flipped class. Given the students' positive reactions to the use of Japanese in the IIU class, the use of Japanese in the WE videos is worth considering to make the content more easily comprehensible to students.

All of the IIU students thought that the amount of work assigned was good, while only 45% of WE students thought the same. Fully 50% of them thought the workload was too much. This difference can be explained by the time students reported spending on the homework in each class, detailed in the next section.

Interactions

In WE, 95% of the time, students responded that they spent 75 minutes or less working on the homework. Students in IIU reported spending 45 minutes or less in 96% of cases. In both classes, students generally reported that they completed all parts of the homework (WE: 92%; IIU: 95%).

Students in the WE class may have spent more time on the homework for several reasons. First, the average weekly video time for WE was nearly twice that of IIU (WE: 13:39; IIU: 6:54). While the average video time for WE was less than 14 minutes, the videos were completely in English, so students may have taken extra time to understand them as compared to the IIU videos, which included some explanations in Japanese. Although most students watched each instructional video only once (WE: 80%; IIU: 59%), the students in the WE class may have occasionally paused the videos or watched them at reduced speeds because of language difficulties. Second, WE students may have checked unknown words when completing the quizzes, which required additional time.

Some students reported watching videos multiple times, especially in IIU, where 40% of students reported watching the videos twice or more. One reason IIU students may have watched the videos multiple times is that they needed to type responses to an assignment after watching the video, so they needed to watch it again to find the answers. On the other hand, the WE students were provided with the correct answers to each quiz after completing it, so to improve their scores, they could simply repeat the quiz without watching the video again.

How Do Students Perceive In-Class Elements?

Turning to the in-class work, students most commonly reported that they liked talking to classmates (WE: 100%; IIU: 76%), which was further reflected in their weekly questionnaires (mean rating of 4.9 on a 5-point scale for how much they enjoyed working with their classmates). They also reported that they liked the chance to learn new ideas (WE: 35%; IIU: 71%), being able to use English (WE: 30%; IIU: 59%), and the chance to understand the content better (WE: 25%; IIU: 65%). While small numbers of students reported disliking various aspects of the class activities, the most commonly reported dislike was "Nothing" (WE: 65%; IIU: 71%). The qualitative data aligns with the quantitative results. On the post-semester questionnaires, the majority of responses to the question about what students enjoyed the most in class concerned working with their classmates. Students' responses included

"(My favorite activity was) pairwork because I did not have to work alone and instead I could enjoy it by talking with my friend" (WE) and "It was fun to check with each other what we individually learned through homework by communicating in class" (IIU). In the focus group interview, Kako explained her experience in this class as, "You deepen your thinking by listening to other peoples' opinions and thinking about them." Pairwork may have helped to initiate a process for some students to deeply engage with the content and their own ideas.

Interaction with others also had a positive effect on using English. Students in the IIU class were encouraged to use as much English as possible in their discussions. Comments from the post-semester questionnaire support this point, such as "It is not easy to speak in English, but I feel I should try even if I make mistakes" and "I learned how to use English in this class, you know, English to communicate with others." For non-English major students, the majority of students in this class, it may have been their first time to use English as a tool of communication.

What Learning Outcomes Were Reported in Students' Reflections?

Students reported what they had learned at the beginning of each class session (WE) and in the post-semester questionnaire (both classes). They tended to report topics that they learned about, rather than facts or ideas. For example, in the WE post-semester questionnaire, one student wrote "English history, technology, inner circle" without any further details of what they learned about each topic.

Based on the results of the post-semester questionnaire, the authors identified five themes related to what students reported that they learned in the WE (Table 6) and IIU (Table 7) classes. The most commonly mentioned theme in WE was *history,* which included both factual information, such as when modern English began, and the importance of learning English language history. This topic was probably most frequently mentioned because it was the final topic covered in the course. Next most frequent was *varieties of English*, which the majority of the class encompassed. Although fewer comments were related to the themes of *social aspects* and *technology*, some students saw the value of flipped class activities to learn to work with others and respond to projects with creativity. The university recently introduced a policy in which students are required to bring laptops to class, so some students also saw the value of increasing their proficiency in using their laptops.

Table 6 Themes in Learning Outcomes Reported in Students' Reflections (World Englishes)

Ranking	Theme (count)	Example comments
1	History (25)	• It is important for English learners to have knowledge about English history. • The importance of English in the world.
2	Varieties of English (19)	• Inner circle • Pidgin • Singlish
3	Social aspects (4)	• I was able to learn to be creative by doing pair activities.
3	Pronunciation (4)	• It is important for English learners to have knowledge about IPA.
5	Technology (3)	• Learning how to use a laptop computer.

In the IIU class, five themes were identified (Table 7). The most commonly mentioned themes were *new perspectives* and *definitions of different cultures*.

The results of the IIU focus group align with the themes reported above. That is, in addition to learning factual information related to intercultural understanding, students' attitudes and perspectives were also influenced by what they learned in the class, indicating that students were able to connect what they learned in class with their own lives. Students in the focus group attributed their learning of new concepts and ideas to in-class activities, such as a guest lecture and discussions with international students. For example, Yota reflected on a class in which international students shared their experiences in Japan: "I had opportunities to learn… what people from different countries struggled with." Similarly, Kodai discussed the guest lecture about LGBTQ issues in Japan: "I hadn't had a chance to learn about these topics." These comments indicate that they have gained experiences unique to flipped learning. The instructor was able to allocate one lesson to having a guest speaker in class because the lecture content for the lesson had been already provided in videos in this flipped model. Students in the focus group also discussed the change in their attitudes toward those who belong to a different culture, which was defined in the class as anyone other than oneself. For example, Kodai said he became "more generous" towards people, and Yota said he "thinks more when talking" with others. However, Kako said that communicating with others is still a struggle for her as "the balance between saying what I think and accepting what others say is difficult to maintain."

Table 7 Themes in Learning Outcomes Reported in Students' Reflections (Introduction to Intercultural Understanding)

Ranking	Theme (count)	Example comments
1	• New perspectives (14)	
	• Themselves (4)	• My perspectives are still narrow • I learned the importance of trying to do things that I lack confidence in.
	• Intercultural understanding (10)	• My common sense is not common sense in other areas of the world • In order to understand people from different cultures, it is necessary to think from different perspectives.
1	• Definition of different cultures (14)	• It is important to understand different cultures rather than judging if one is better or the other • Different cultures are not negative.
3	• Concepts related to understanding different cultures (8)	
	• Prejudice, discrimination, stereotypes (4)	• Discrimination is new information • Lack of understanding of different cultures we experience in our daily lives such as stereotypes harms people's minds.
	• Assertive communication (4)	• When I almost let my emotions control me and say hurtful things, I can tell myself to use assertive communication and make sure that we can all improve (the situation) without feeling uncomfortable.
4	• Positive aspects of communication (5)	• The joy of communication • You have a wider perspective by inputting and outputting ideas and opinions.
5	• Linguistic aspects (3)	• The joy in speaking in English • Even if my English is not good, I can manage with gestures, pictures, and simple words.

Interestingly, even though it was not the main objective of the class, students also mentioned learning how to communicate with others and how to use English as a tool through in-class activities. When asked what they learned in class, Emma said the following: "I learned how to communicate with older students… I learned I could initiate a conversation with them and how to communicate." Emma entered the university during the COVID-19 restrictions and had limited opportunities to meet people in person in 2020–2021, so working on tasks with people of different class years and majors gave her an opportunity to gain confidence in her social skills.

Summary

Three research questions were asked in the current study, starting with how students perceive and interact with the homework elements (videos and quizzes) of a flipped class. The results showed that students found that the video lengths in the two classes (average: WE, 2:24; IIU, 2:43) were appropriate and that the video content was "very easy" or "easy" to understand (WE: 75%; IIU: 100%). The use of the students' L1 in the IIU videos is one reason that they were perceived as easier to understand than the WE videos, which did not include the L1. The required homework time (WE: less than 75 minutes; IIU: less than 45 minutes) was perceived as appropriate by all of the IIU students, but only 45% of WE students.

The second research question was, "How do students perceive in-class elements?" Students reported that they liked talking to classmates (WE: 100%; IIU: 76%) and gave high ratings to their in-class partners in their weekly questionnaires (mean rating of 4.9 on a 5-point scale in both classes). The most commonly reported dislike was "Nothing" (WE: 65%; IIU: 71%).

The third research question was, "What learning outcomes did students report in their reflections?" In the questionnaires, students tended to report topics that they learned about, rather than facts or ideas. However, the focus group interview revealed examples of how students were able to connect what they learned in class with their own lives and improve their communication skills, which can be attributed to experiences that were only possible due to the flipped class format.

Discussion

The pandemic restrictions on how to teach classes provided the impetus for flipping the focal classes. While both authors initially felt constricted by the requirement to teach asynchronously, they decided to flip both their classes and their mindsets. That is, the authors took the situation as an opportunity to create teaching materials that would meet the criteria that they were presented with, improve teaching and learning in the future when the classes could go back to a FTF format, and be further adaptable to teaching synchronously or asynchronously, online or offline, as future conditions demanded. This is similar to the approach taken by colleagues such as Gleason and Bartlett (Chapter 9, this volume).

While the authors predicted that the flipped teaching materials would be an improvement over traditional lecture materials (e.g., John-Steiner & Mahn, 1996; Loewen & Sato, 2018), they wanted to find out how such materials would be perceived and used by students in Japan, prompting them to conduct the current study. The results indicated that students generally had positive attitudes toward the homework materials, perhaps because of the design principles that were followed regarding video length (under 6 minutes), technical quality (clear audio and video), instructor presence (instructor's face should appear in videos), and content (Asaba & Lavolette, 2022).

The students' perceptions of the workload for the classes correspond to their reported time spent on the homework, which may be more for flipped classes than for traditional classes (Gillis-Furutaka, 2020; Leis et al., 2015). Students in IIU generally spent 45 minutes or less per week, and they were satisfied with this workload. In contrast, many of the WE students thought the workload was too heavy, and they reported spending more time: 75 minutes or less in most cases. According to university policy, which is in turn based on Japanese law (Daigaku setchi kijun [Basis for establishing universities], 2019), students should expect to spend 4 hours per week doing homework for classes like the two-credit classes in the current study. However, in practice, students expect to do much less, with most students (approximately 60%) spending 0 to 5 hours total per week studying for all classes that they take (MEXT, 2021). This may explain why students felt the homework load in the WE class was too heavy.

Conclusion

In both classes, students reported generally positive perceptions of the quizzes at the beginning of class, other class activities, and their interactions with their classmates. As the instructors of the classes, the authors observed students enjoying working together in class, which has also been seen in previous work (e.g., Lee & Wallace, 2018; Zhong & Rohaya, 2023). Students also seemed engaged while participating in activities. Because flipping the classes freed up in-class time that would have otherwise been used for lecturing, the instructors were able to maximize class time for activities such as discussions, creating comic strips, role-plays, and interactions with guest speakers. Similarly, in previous research, students in flipped classes reported higher class engagement because they spent more class time doing activities than listening to lectures (e.g., Elmaadaway, 2018; Merlin-Knoblich et al., 2019).

Before the pandemic, the first author had taught the WE class as a traditional lecture, and students rarely voluntarily responded to questions or asked questions during class. In comparison, the first author observed that the flipped version of the class had a much more relaxed atmosphere, with students interacting in a friendly manner and frequently asking the instructor questions as they arose.

Pedagogical Implications and Future Directions

As Harvard undergraduate student Julien Berman pointed out (Berman, 2023), the raw materials for flipping classes already exist in some cases, thanks to the pandemic. That is, many instructors have lecture videos available or, in other cases, have developed the skills to create instructional videos that can be used to flip the classroom. Flipping the classroom is certainly more complicated than simply assigning these videos as homework, but the pandemic has provided a starting point.

While flipped classes are still uncommon in Japan, the results of the current study show that students appreciated flipped learning. On the other hand, despite previous studies that have shown that students can achieve deeper information processing in the flipped classroom (e.g., Kim et al., 2017; Zhong & Rohaya, 2023), many of the reported learning outcomes were relatively shallow in both focal classes. In the WE class, an important learning objective is the idea that all Englishes, including Japanese English, are equally valid, but this idea was not mentioned by any student. It could be further emphasized in the course, although with care taken to allow students to form their own opinions and interpretations. Given that students are immersed in a context in which the superiority of the "native speaker" of English is unquestioned, more than a few lessons focused on the validity of all varieties of English may be needed to overcome students' preconceptions. The flipped classroom is suitable for achieving this goal because examples of the communicative effectiveness of various Englishes can be shown in homework videos, and students can discuss their opinions with each other and the instructor during FTF classroom time.

A major difference between the two focal courses in this study was in the instructors' use of the students' first language. The results suggest that judicious use of the first language is beneficial to students' confidence to speak in English and increases their understanding of related content provided in English (Nguyen, 2022). Similarly, Aoyama (2020), who examined the use of L1 in translanguaging among Japanese high school students in an EFL classroom, reported a similar finding that the reasons that the participants used the L1 were mainly related to students' attempts to communicate with each other to understand and complete the task.

The school's requirement for asynchronous courses during the first two years of the pandemic, coupled with the requirement for FTF class time later in the pandemic, created an opportunity to introduce the flipped classroom. The flipped classroom in this context was hypothesized to be especially helpful given the educational practices common in the Japanese context that limit peer interaction in English. This move to more peer interaction was appreciated by students, resulted in some learning, and anecdotally also resulted in a more enjoyable experience for the educators.

Given the positive results of this study, both authors intend to continue teaching these classes in a flipped format. The first author also added another flipped class to her roster, starting in the spring semester of 2023. While no new disasters have yet arisen necessitating a return to online teaching, the materials created during the pandemic have again proved their value when classes needed to be canceled, and these materials could be used to hold asynchronous make-up classes. Through trial and error, the authors hope to spread the benefits of flipped learning to more students.

About the Authors

Elizabeth (Betsy) Lavolette is Associate Professor, Department of English, Kyoto Sangyo University, Kyoto, Japan. Her research focuses on language learning and teaching with technology, professional development, and language learning spaces.

Mayumi Asaba is Associate Professor of English, Faculty of Foreign Studies, Kyoto Sangyo University, Kyoto, Japan. Her research interest is expertise in L2 teaching and teacher development.

References

Al-Naabi, I., Al-Badi, A., & Kelder, J. A. (2022). Implementing flipped learning during Covid-19 in Omani higher education: EFL teachers' perspectives. *Issues in Educational Research*, *32*(2), 413–433.

Aoyama, R. (2020). Exploring Japanese high school students' L1 use in translanguaging in the communicative EFL classroom. *TESL-EJ*, *23*(4), 1–18.

Asaba, M., & Lavolette, E. (2022). Design principles for asynchronous classes. *JAALT in JACET Proceedings*, *4*, 1–7.

Bener, E. (2021). Flipping EFL classes in higher education: A systematic review. *Language Education and Technology*, *1*(2), 90–109. https://langedutech.com/letjournal/index.php/let/article/view/25

Berman, J. (2023). Are lectures obsolete? *The Crimson*, January 24, 2023. https://www.thecrimson.com/column/toward-a-higher-higher-education/article/2023/1/24/julien-are-lectures-obsolete/

Daigaku setchi kijun [Basis for establishing universities]. (2019). https://elaws.e-gov.go.jp/document?lawid=331M50000080028

Ellis, R., Tanaka, Y., & Yamazaki, A. (1994). Classroom interaction, comprehension, and the acquisition of L2 word meanings. *Language Learning*, *44*(3), 449–491. https://doi.org/10.1111/j.1467-1770.1994.tb01114.x

Elmaadaway, M. A. N. (2018). The effects of a flipped classroom approach on class engagement and skill performance in a blackboard course. *British Journal of Educational Technology*, *49*(3), 479–491. https://doi.org/10.1111/bjet.12553

Gillis-Furutaka, A. (2020). Making a lecture course student centered: Steps and issues. In P. Clements, A. Krause, & R. Gentry (Eds.), *Teacher efficacy, learner agency* (pp. 18–26). JALT. https://doi.org/10.37546/JALTPCP2019-xx

Gruber, A., Matt, E., & Leier, V. (2023). Transforming foreign language education: Exploring educators' practices and perspectives in the (post-)pandemic era. *Education Sciences*, *13*. https://doi.org/10.3390/educsci13060601

Hung, H. T. (2015). Flipping the classroom for English language learners to foster active learning. *Computer Assisted Language Learning*, *28*(1), 81–96. https://doi.org/10.1080/09588221.2014.967701

Hung, L. N. Q. (2022). EFL students' perceptions of online flipped classrooms during the Covid-19 pandemic and beyond. *International Journal of Learning, Teaching and Educational Research*, *21*(9), 460–476. https://doi.org/10.26803/ijlter.21.9.25

Ivankova, N. V., & Creswell, J. W. (2009). Mixed methods. In J. Heigham & R. A. Croker, (Eds.), *Qualitative Research in Applied Linguistics: A practical introduction* (pp. 135–161). Palgrave Macmillan.

John-Steiner, V., & Mahn, H. (1996). Sociocultural approaches to learning and development: A Vygotskian framework. *Educational Psychologist*, *31*(3/4), 191–206. https://doi.org/10.1080/00461520.1996.9653266

Kim, J. E., Park, H., Jang, M., & Nam, H. (2017). Exploring flipped classroom effects on second language learners' cognitive processing. *Foreign Language Annals*, *50*(2), 260–284. https://doi.org/10.1111/flan.12260

Lage, M. J., Platt, G. J., & Treglia, M. (2000). Inverting the classroom: A gateway to creating an inclusive learning environment. *Journal of Economic Education*, *31*(1), 30–43. https://doi.org/10.1080/00220480009596759

Lantolf, J., Thorne, S. L., & Poehner, M. (2015). Sociocultural theory and second language development. In B. van Patten (Ed.), *Theories in second language acquisition* (pp. 207–226). Routledge. https://doi.org/10.2495/SDP

Lee, G., & Wallace, A. (2018). Flipped learning in the English as a foreign language classroom: Outcomes and perceptions. *TESOL Quarterly*, *52*(1), 62–84. https://doi.org/10.1002/tesq.372

Leis, A., Cooke, S., & Tohei, A. (2015). The effects of flipped classrooms on English composition writing in an EFL environment. *International Journal of Computer-Assisted Language Learning and Teaching*, *5*(4), 37–51. https://doi.org/10.4018/ijcallt.2015100103

Lin, A. M. (2019). Theories of trans/languaging and trans-semiotizing: Implications for content-based education classrooms. Interna*tional Journal of Bilingual Education and Bilingualism*, *22*(1), 5–16. https://doi.org/10.1080/13670050.2018.1515175

Loewen, S., & Sato, M. (2018). Interaction and instructed second language acquisition. *Language Teaching*, *51*(3), 285–329. https://doi.org/10.1017/S0261444818000125

Mehring, J. G. (2015). *An exploratory study of the lived experiences of Japanese undergraduate EFL students in the flipped classroom* (Unpublished doctoral dissertation). Pepperdine University, Malibu, CA.

Merlin-Knoblich, C., Harris, P. N., & McCarty Mason, E. C. (2019). Examining student classroom engagement in flipped and non-flipped counselor education courses. *Professional Counselor*, *9*(2), 109–125. https://eric.ed.gov/?id=EJ1221519

Miles, M. B., & Huberman, A. M. (1984). Drawing valid meaning from qualitative data: Toward a shared craft. *Educational Researcher*, *13*(5), 20–30. https://doi.org/10.3102/0013189X0130050

Ministry of Education, Culture, Sports, Science and Technology (MEXT). (2021). *Zenkoku gakusei chosa* [National student survey]. https://www.mext.go.jp/a_menu/koutou/chousa/1421136.htm

Morgan, D. L. (1997). *Focus groups as qualitative research* (2nd ed.). Sage. https://doi.org/10.4135/9781412984287

Nguyen, T. N. T. (2022). A review of studies on EFL teachers' and students' perceptions of translanguaging as a pedagogical approach. *International Journal of TESOL & Education*, *2*(3), 324–331. https://doi.org/10.54855/ijte.222322

Obari, H., & Lambacher, S. (2015). Successful EFL teaching using mobile technologies in a flipped classroom. In F. Helm, L. Bradley, M. Guarda, & S. Thouësny (Eds), *Critical CALL – Proceedings of the 2015 EUROCALL Conference, Padova, Italy* (pp. 433–438). Research-publishing.net. https://doi.org/10.14705/rpnet.2015.000371

Okuda, A., Miho, N., Mori, T., & Mizokami, S. (2015). Effects of the flipped learning model on academic English classes at a Japanese university: A case study of Nagasaki University. *Kyoto University Higher Education Research, 21*, 41–52. http://hdl.handle.net/2433/210136

Rapanta, C., Botturi, L., Goodyear, P., Guàrdia, L., & Koole, M. (2021). Balancing technology, pedagogy and the new normal: Post-pandemic challenges for higher education. *Postdigital Science and Education*, *3*, 715–742. https://doi.org/10.1007/s42438-021-00249-1

Roarty, A. (2021). Japanese EFL university student attitudes and engagement in a flipped learning course in combination with synchronous online classes. *Journal of Foreign Language Education and Research*, *2*, 3–21. https://rikkyo.repo.nii.ac.jp/?action=pages_view_main&active_action=repository_view_main_item_detail&item_id=21359&item_no=1&page_id=13&block_id=49

Robson, L., Gardner, B., & Dommett, E. J. (2022). The post-pandemic lecture: Views from academic staff across the UK. Education Sciences, *12*(123), 1–16. https://doi.org/10.3390/educsci12020123

Saldaña, J. (2013). *The coding manual for qualitative researchers* (2nd ed.). Sage.

Shahnama, M., Ghonsooly, B., & Shirvan, M. E. (2021). A meta-analysis of relative effectiveness of flipped learning in English as second/foreign language research. *Educational Technology Research and Development*, *69*(3), 1355–1386. https://doi.org/10.1007/s11423-021-09996-1

Turnbull, M., Cormier, M., & Bourque, J. (2011). The first language in science class: A quasi-experimental study in late French immersion. *The Modern Language Journal*, *95*, 182–198. https://doi.org/10.1111/j.1540-4781.2011.01275.x

Valentine, S. (2022). *Taking pandemic online learning into a flipped classroom for in-class teaching.* Paper presented at Festival of Teaching and Learning, Alberta, Canada, May 3–5, 2022. https://www.ualberta.ca/centre-for-teaching-and-learning/events/festival-of-teaching/2022/schedule.html

Vitta, J. P., & Al-Hoorie, A. H. (2020). The flipped classroom in second language learning: A meta-analysis. *Language Teaching Research*. Epub ahead of print 24 December 2020. https://doi.org/10.1177/1362168820981403

Zhong, L., & Rohaya, A. (2023). The Impact of COVID-19 pandemic on flipped classroom for EFL courses: A systematic literature review. *SAGE Open*, *13*(1), 1–13. https://doi.org/10.1177/21582440221148149

11 Confronting Crisis with Craft: Students' Perceptions of Language Teaching During the COVID-19 Pandemic

Kimberly Morris, Mikaela Robarge, and Pablo Robles-García

The onset of COVID-19 crept upon our world with little warning, wreaking havoc on the education system (LeLoup & Swanson, 2022). The repercussions from the pandemic took a heavy toll on second language (L2) classrooms due to the disruptions of face-to-face (F2F) opportunities for interaction and negotiation of meaning in the target language (TL), essential facets of second language acquisition (Lantolf & Thorne, 2006; Long, 1996). Although computer-assisted language learning (CALL) had been implemented successfully prior to the pandemic, the abrupt transition to emergency remote teaching (ERT) was, in most academic contexts, a mandatory yet unanticipated alternative to F2F instruction. According to Gacs et al. (2020), "What teaching staff were being asked to do was not typical online teaching but online triage" (p. 381). In turn, it became necessary to reconceptualize L2 learning in an online environment on the fly. As new technologies spread into every corner of the education system, language teachers and students alike faced the challenge of remaining well-informed about new tools and the different affordances they provide, oftentimes with little training (Morris, 2022).

From an educator's perspective, the transition to ERT was neither smooth nor straightforward (MacIntyre et al., 2020; see Part 1, this volume). In fact, many educators felt they were "building the plane while flying it" (Trust & Whalen, 2020, p. 193). In addition to educators' experiences, it is crucial to examine students' experiences and perceptions of L2 learning during the pandemic to evaluate the practices that were considered effective and ineffective so that these can be enhanced for the future (Jansem, 2021). Because students' perceptions and attitudes of teaching practices can directly impact their L2 development and success in the classroom (Kern, 1995), analyzing their experiences during this disruptive time allows educators, institutions, and even the wider field to take action to ensure the success of L2 learning in the future, even in crisis situations.

A Review of CALL in Crisis and Beyond

As conceptualized from sociocultural and interactionist perspectives (Lantolf & Thorne, 2006; Long, 1996), L2 learning is fostered through social interactions in the TL, thereby promoting the gradual internalization of new knowledge and skills. Language teachers can scaffold students' L2 development by creating guided opportunities for social interaction, allowing them to process the strategies needed to be successful L2 users and notice and negotiate mistakes or confusions that arise during their interactions. In previous decades, a growing body of research has confirmed the benefits of interaction on L2 learning outcomes across various learner ages, contexts, and learning modalities (e.g., Mackey, 2020; Ziegler, 2016).

Nevertheless, since the onset of COVID-19, numerous safety measures limited the nature of F2F interactions among students and educators, as traditional classrooms were forced to shift to ERT through various modalities such as asynchronous (not in real time), synchronous (in real time), or hybrid (a blend of F2F and online). Although social interaction can be carried out effectively in carefully planned online language environments (Ziegler et al., 2022), the swift transition to ERT required teaching and learning to be conducted behind a screen with little-to-no training.

For educators who lacked prior experience with CALL practices, the transition to ERT was especially difficult (Bader, 2021). With minimal training, educators were forced to shift students to more "informal, self-directed learning" as opposed to traditional F2F methods (Trust & Whalen, 2020, p. 191). Results from a survey distributed to over 300 K-12 teachers during spring 2020 confirmed that educators did not feel prepared to teach online, and if they had received prior training, it would have ensured a more successful transition (Trust & Whalen, 2020). Morris (2022) found similar results through interviews with K-16 language teachers yet concluded that the demands of the transition to ERT pushed educators to expand their instructional repertoire (see also Landry & Hamel, Chapter 8, this volume). The challenge to adapt instruction while also supporting students (and themselves) through a significant life change provided room for both pedagogical and personal growth that had remained otherwise unexplored.

Before COVID-19, much previous research supported the successful implementation of CALL practices, with different tools having distinct affordances in particular contexts (see Arnold & Ducate, 2019). While F2F and online L2 instruction share the same objective of advancing learners' proficiency, Goertler and Gacs (2018) highlight that effective online teaching requires that teachers are both technologically competent and capable of making assessment accommodations. During COVID-19, these requirements were likely neglected due to the lack of necessary training to transition curricula to online formats effectively. Nevertheless, CALL methods can be effective when carried out properly, as demonstrated by the comparison of F2F and virtual-learning assessment scores (Blake et al., 2008; Goertler & Gacs, 2018; Moneypenny & Aldrich, 2016). Therefore, successful online L2 instruction is possible if it is focused on implementing virtual learning practices rather than F2F methods.

Even when educators effectively integrate CALL practices into their curriculum, in the end, students' learning depends largely on their preferences (Klimova, 2021). Such perception data, including learning preferences, provides specific insights detailing what and how students *felt* about their learning and why those feelings occurred. Considering the impact that students' perceptions can have on their learning and motivation, it is critical to collect their feedback to identify improvements that can enhance their development (Harvey, 2011; Humphrey & Wiles, 2021). Student perceptions provide first-hand accounts of the success of their own learning, allowing instructors to conceptualize how their teaching was (or was not) received. In theory, learning outcome data should illustrate the effectiveness of instruction, yet educators can be left guessing about *how* and *why* their lessons fostered positive comprehension. In this sense, student feedback allows educators to revise current and future online instruction with an aim to enhance learning (Humphrey & Wiles, 2021).

Several studies have explored L2 students' experiences and preferences regarding different instructional modes and their perceived impact on L2 learning. Prior to the pandemic, Wright (2017) and Yördem (2015) found that EFL students preferred the F2F modality over online classes because it was familiar and afforded more seamless interactions between peers and the instructor. Nonetheless, both modalities were considered effective by EFL students in Montiel-Chamorro's (2018) study. A recent study conducted by Adelson and Simonnet Keen (2023) examined students' perceptions of the transition from F2F to ERT in spring 2020, revealing a general preference for the F2F modality for engagement, participation, peer interaction, and practicing L2 skills. While these findings shed light on the immediate impact of COVID-19 on language classes, it is no surprise that the online modality was overwhelmingly considered less satisfactory than traditional F2F classes, considering the many instructional changes that needed to be made on the fly. Thus, it is important to explore students' perceptions beyond the immediate onset of COVID-19 to learn more about the sustained impact of the pandemic on L2 learning (see Schmitt & Sorokina, Chapter 14, this volume).

As such, this study is guided by the following research questions: 1) How do students believe L2 teaching and learning has been impacted by the transition to ERT due to COVID-19? and, 2) What practices do students perceive as most effective in remote L2 teaching and learning?

Methods

Research Context

This study was conducted at a mid-sized public university in the U.S. in spring 2021, precisely two semesters following the onset of COVID-19 in March 2020. Prior to the pandemic, the language courses at this institution were offered largely in person apart from occasional Spanish courses held online in the summer. Additionally, the department offers some courses in Chinese, German, French, and Russian through a system-wide program to local students on campus who are joined virtually by students from other institutions statewide.

At the beginning of the spring 2020 semester, the language programs that held their traditional F2F courses were forced to shift to an online format (with a mix of synchronous and asynchronous tasks) as of mid-March through the end of the semester. In this initial stage, instructors were given one week to transition their courses online (with no training) and encouraged to accommodate students' extenuating circumstances. As the pandemic continued to evolve, so too did restrictions related to quarantine, social distancing, and mandatory masking, thus rendering it impossible for a vast majority of classes to be offered on campus. Hence, as of fall 2020, language classes were offered through a blend of online and hybrid modalities with minimal F2F sessions to limit the spread of the virus. As the lengthy reality of COVID-19 set in, additional measures were taken in spring 2021 based on public health recommendations, including a one-week delay of classes and the elimination of spring break. As such, language courses continued to be offered in a mix of modalities, with online and hybrid classes dominating the scene along with a handful of F2F offerings. While the pandemic had become more normalized, the spring 2021 semester was still one of crisis due to the prolonged impact of related restrictions and their consequences on both academic and personal functioning.

Table 1 Number of Participants by Level, Language, and Modality

LEVEL		LANGUAGE		MODALITY			
Lower Division	*Upper Division*	*Spanish*	*Other*	*Synch.*	*Hybrid*	*F2F*	*Multiple (Including Async.)*
31	91	103	19	43	44	17	18

Participants

A total of 122 undergraduate students from the aforementioned university participated in this study. Of these students, 103 were L2 Spanish learners, while 19 were L2 learners of other languages including nine in French, five in German, three in Chinese, and two in Russian. The study was conducted with students from all language courses in all modalities at this university, including lower-division courses typically taken during the first and second years of language study as well as upper-division courses taken toward the latter half of the program. Considering that most participants were enrolled in upper-division courses, it is presumed that they had taken prior language classes in college or high school, allowing them to compare their experiences with pre-pandemic times. Table 1 represents the participants by level, language studied, and modality.

Instrument

A survey developed by the researchers was administered to students online via Qualtrics (Schmith, 2002) at the end of the spring 2021 semester (visit the book's website https://sites.google.com/msu.edu/2024crisiscall/instruments--and-materials for the instrument). The survey aimed to explore students' experiences and perceptions of language teaching and learning during the pandemic. Initially, students were asked to evaluate the effectiveness of different instructional modes, including asynchronous online, synchronous online, hybrid (a blend of F2F and online), and fully F2F, using a three-point scale of effectiveness: 1 = Not effective; 2 = Somewhat effective, 3 = Very effective. Next, they were provided with space to articulate their reasoning behind their evaluations. Additionally, the survey inquired about changes in students' workload and participation in language courses, feedback received, and potential modifications made to the time and effort they allocated to language courses, compared to a pre-COVID traditional semester. Finally, students were invited to identify their most significant language learning challenge during the pandemic and describe their overall experience in one word.

Data Analysis

A series of both quantitative and qualitative analyses were conducted depending on the type of question in the survey. Numeric scale questions were analyzed in SPSS using one-way ANOVAs to identify statistical differences between the independent variables of instructional mode (asynchronous, synchronous, hybrid, and F2F) and the dependent variables pertaining to effectiveness, workload, feedback, time and effort, and participation. Students' perceptions of their experiences were thematically analyzed (Braun & Clarke, 2006) in two stages. Initially, the researchers used the open-ended questions from the survey as the main themes. Next, they proposed an additional set of codes that emerged from an independent reading of all the students' responses, focusing on salient concepts that were shared among participants to explain their perceptions. The previous two sets of codes were discussed among the researchers to establish the final themes, which are described in detail in the next section.

Results

Quantitative Results

To compare students' perceived effectiveness of the different modalities of language classes offered during spring 2021 (asynchronous online, synchronous online, hybrid, and fully F2F), a one-way ANOVA was conducted to determine if these groups differed significantly. The results showed no significant differences between instructional mode and perceived effectiveness ($F = 1.593$, $p = .209$). As demonstrated in Figure 1, students largely found all modalities to be very or somewhat effective. In fact, nearly all students in the F2F modality considered it very effective. However, over 75% of the students surveyed for this study were enrolled in synchronous or hybrid courses at the time, which were perceived to be effective (very or somewhat) in 95% of those cases.

Additionally, students were asked to compare their workload, feedback received, overall time and effort put forth, and participation during spring 2021 with a traditional semester pre-COVID. To determine if there were statistical differences between instructional delivery mode and students' perceptions, a series of one-way ANOVAs were conducted. The results revealed no significant differences between the instructional modes and self-reported workload ($F = .148$, $p = .931$), feedback ($F = 2.173$, $p = .095$), and time and

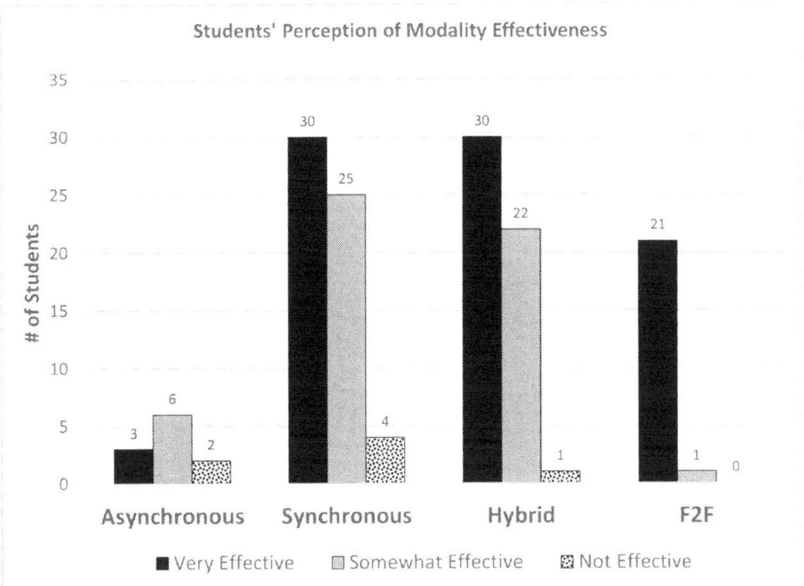

Figure 1 Students' Perception of Modality Effectiveness

effort (F = 1.415, p = .242). As outlined in Table 2, over half of the students surveyed from all instructional modalities considered these factors to be largely the same, thus suggesting a relatively successful transition to ERT during this disruptive time.

Nevertheless, there was a statistically significant difference in perceived participation between students enrolled in synchronous and hybrid courses (F = 3.098, p = .03). Specifically, students found hybrid courses significantly less conducive for participation than synchronous courses, as illustrated in Table 3. In fact, 40% of students in synchronous classes reported participating more frequently than in traditional classes pre-COVID, whereas only 4% of those in hybrid classes reported the same. (For further discussion on

Table 2 Students' Reported L2 Learning Factors During the Pandemic Compared to a Pre-COVID Semester

	Workload	Feedback	Time & Effort
More (+)	35%	13%	22%
Same (=)	60%	71%	52%
Less (-)	5%	16%	26%

Table 3 Students' Reported Participation Compared to a Pre-COVID Semester

	Participation in Synchronous	Participation in Hybrid
More (+)	40%	4%
Same (=)	39%	69%
Less (-)	21%	27%

students' perceptions of flipped classes, see Lavolette & Asaba, Chapter 10, this volume; Schmitt & Sorokina, Chapter 14, this volume).

Qualitative Results

Perceived Effectiveness of Instructional Modes

Although students generally found all instructional modes to be very or somewhat effective, their justifications varied based on the delivery mode. In this section, student comments will be introduced from modalities that had an online component, as no participants commented on the perceived effectiveness of fully F2F courses.

Synchronous Instruction. Students perceived online synchronous instruction as highly effective due to the engagement it afforded despite the remote context. For instance, one student noted, "Although online, having synchronized Zoom meetings kept me engaged in class and I was able to learn directly from my professor." For some, synchronous classes helped with time management and accountability: "I liked synchronous because we had dedicated meeting times and we were taught live by our professor. Although it was online, he was still right there to answer any questions." Many students in synchronous classes considered group and peer interactions as effective strategies to support their learning without sacrificing their health. For example, a student pointed out that synchronous classes were most effective because, "We still got to talk and interact but did it at home safely." Nevertheless, roughly 40% of those in synchronous language classes found them only somewhat effective because they posed challenges in carrying out L2 interactions: "Overall, I like the flexibility of the course, and synchronous online sounds like a good idea in theory, but I noticed that participation is much lower during our Zoom classes." Another student insisted, "It was much more effective than asynchronous, but you cannot replace the in-person element of learning a language." From these comments, it appears that students valued the engagement, flexibility, and accountability that synchronous classes afforded them during times of crisis, yet they deemed F2F interactions as most beneficial in supporting their L2 development.

Hybrid Instruction. The most notable feature of the hybrid modality was the flexibility afforded by having a "split schedule," allowing for both engaging in-person communication and time for self-directed learning in a virtual format. The benefits of a hybrid method were recognized by some students who appreciated the convenience it offered: "I liked the hybrid method because the thing that takes the most time out of my day isn't homework, it is going to class. So having class from my room on some days just was easy to go right back to working on other stuff." Nevertheless, students' perceptions were influenced by the way their teachers structured the frequency and content of the F2F and virtual components of the classes. For instance, one student declared, "The hybrid mode was very effective because of how the professor taught the course. In-person days allowed us to converse with one another and practice our speaking skills. During online days, we had to complete assignments that practiced our listening, reading, and writing skills. The combination of all of these was very effective in teaching me." While some hybrid courses met F2F weekly, others met only a few times throughout the semester, depending on the content and objectives of the course. A student enrolled in two hybrid French courses highlighted the importance of meeting F2F weekly for their pronunciation class, whereas a course focused on science and technology only met F2F once for presentations, which, according to the student, "was okay because there really wasn't a need for the class to be in-person every week."

The limitations of online learning did not go unnoticed: "We had synchronous online class one day a week and in person the other day. Class didn't work as well online due to internet issues and also, it's harder to pay attention to online class." Due to these limitations, one student even added, "The [online] class felt off sometimes." Thus, while the hybrid modality appears to provide the best of both worlds, it is not inherently better than fully online or fully in-person classes. Rather, students' perceptions of their own learning are linked to what teachers actually *do* in their classes to keep learners engaged.

Asynchronous Instruction. Students in asynchronous courses also found flexibility to be a significant advantage, as it allowed them to effectively manage their time and work at their own pace: "We were able to work on our individual skills using our own time, which was very helpful." Another student added, "I was able to work at my own pace, and as a student who works almost full time, it was easier for me to manage." Additionally, some students found asynchronous instruction beneficial for classes that involved extensive reading and analysis, as it provided them with extra time during the week to engage with the assigned materials. However, concerns were raised regarding limitations such as assignments feeling like busywork, lacking guidance, and feeling overwhelmed by the speed and difficulty of certain listening tasks. Lastly, while overall satisfaction was observed with the asynchronous modality, some students expressed a preference for in-person learning, emphasizing the importance of interactive engagement and guidance from the professor.

Workload

Students' comments provided valuable insights into workload. More than half of students reported that their workload was the same compared to a traditional semester. The effective workload distribution, with different activities planned for F2F and online sessions, was appreciated by students. Specifically, one hybrid course student noted, "The workload was spread out effectively, having different activities depending on whether we were face-to-face or online." However, workload varied across different classes, suggesting that delivery mode did not significantly impact workload, but rather the expectations and content introduced by individual language instructors. One student in multiple courses expressed, "It varied class to class. For one class that was synchronous online, I found I was assigned a lot of work in addition to still attending the classes for the full time. The other two Spanish classes I was given a more manageable workload."

It is worth noting that 35% of students reported that their workload increased during COVID-19, which is not surprising due to the sharp pivots that had to be made by both teachers and students throughout the pandemic. One student stated, "I think in general everything feels like it takes longer to do in a pandemic (especially when you have to do classes online and don't have the separation of school and home, it is easy for it all to feel like homework)." This comment suggests that the increased time on task coupled with the lack of boundaries between schoolwork and personal life may have contributed to the perceived increase in workload during the pandemic. However, because these issues existed in hybrid and online courses prior to the pandemic, the comment may simply speak to the fact that pandemic life was hard. Additionally, concerns were raised about assignments, which some students perceived as busywork that did not contribute significantly to their L2 development. One asynchronous student expressed their frustration, stating, "Sometimes I felt like the assignments were just busy work and didn't help develop my language skills. When we were given listening assignments, like videos to watch, I felt overwhelmed about the speed and difficulty, and I felt like I wasn't learning." Students also highlighted the need for dedicated time and effective work management to keep up with coursework: "I had to dedicate a lot of time to my language course in order to stay up to date with the homework and quizzes." This additional time undoubtedly contributed to students' perceived workload.

Feedback

In general, students found their online learning management system (Canvas) very effective for the provision of organized and individualized feedback. Furthermore, students also commented on the benefits of synchronous meetings, since they allowed instructors to effectively provide immediate feedback. For example, one student highlighted that meeting online "allowed us to work together despite being in many different living places. It allowed us to learn from one another and practice oral pronunciation live with real-time feedback." Nevertheless, one student pointed out having received feedback in an untimely manner: "Turned-in assignments took over a month to get feedback on. Especially towards the end of the semester, work that was turned in at the beginning of April was not returned until the day of the final." As this was an isolated case, it may relate to the many pandemic challenges experienced by the instructor that went far beyond teaching remotely, such as establishing a healthy work–life balance and attending to their own and students' mental health (see Morris, 2022).

Time and Effort

Although students largely perceived investing the same amount of time and effort on tasks compared to a pre-pandemic semester, the transition to ERT may have impacted how students prepared for their coursework and assessments. For instance, one hybrid student admitted, "I ended up doing more leisure studying (reading, watching TV, listening to music in TL, etc.) but I didn't study as much for my classes because tests were online." This comment highlights the potential shift in study habits and the allocation of time for studying for online classes, as students may have felt less direct pressure to prepare for online assessments because they had access to external support such as textbooks, notes, translators, etc. Furthermore, another hybrid student expressed, "It was definitely easier to slack off in class and let my mind wander because I wasn't being engaged in the same way that I am during face-to-face." These varied experiences and perspectives shed light on the potential impact of the online learning environment on students' study habits and the need to adapt time management strategies in response to the challenges posed by remote teaching.

Participation

Like the data in Table 3, students' comments reflected that those in synchronous courses participated significantly more when compared to those in hybrid classes. For example, one synchronous student stated, "I participated more than a traditional face-to-face [class] because I felt less pressure when I was not in a classroom setting. I was comfortable in my own home and felt that talking in Spanish was an easier task than in the classroom. The online experience in a foreign language was much easier for me to comprehend and understand because no one is wearing masks and I read people's lips in daily conversations." However, students with different personalities, such as those who are highly conscientious, have been found to be more successful in online L2 classes (Arispe & Blake, 2012).

For students taking hybrid courses, participation seemed to be lower for the online component: "It was harder to participate because most people did not have their cameras on, and we spent a lot of time in breakout rooms, but some students did not unmute themselves or participate." Lower participation in the online portion of hybrid courses could be attributed to a combination of factors, including the complexity of the delivery mode, student individual differences, and the need for teacher training. When blended modalities are not effectively managed, the transition between in-person and online classes can disrupt the development of a consistent rhythm, making it challenging for students to fully engage in learning. Sequencing that is not systematic or purposeful can hinder the development of classroom community and impact learning dynamics. As one student expressed, "While we still met as a class [synchronously], there was not as much participation as in face-to-face classes." This lack of continuity in the online learning environment coupled with the need to adapt to different settings may have created a sense of disconnection, hindering students' ability to actively participate.

These comments suggest that the migration to ERT may have impacted not only the way students participated in class but also how instructors fostered participation due to a lack of experience teaching in online or blended formats. It also highlights that online courses help some people focus and feel more comfortable and others be more easily distracted and fearful. Furthermore, it speaks to the need for instructors to adapt their teaching strategies and create supportive online learning environments that promote active engagement and community building among students (see Schmitt & Sorokina, Chapter 14, this volume).

Key Challenges

The main challenges experienced by students in language classes during COVID-19 corresponded to four interrelated themes: motivation, interaction, technology, and distance. Specifically, students' motivation decreased due to limited interactions, whereas issues with technology and social distancing further impeded students' success. The most common challenge mentioned by students was motivation to stay engaged in their language classes during COVID-19: "Being online made me feel disconnected from my class and made it hard to stay motivated in my class. Not being able to see people made me hesitant to answer questions." A second challenge that was salient in the survey data was limited interactions during the pandemic: "I felt like class discussion time was lost. I like to be able to turn to a partner and chat about the content. Breakout rooms just aren't the same." The third challenge that was shared by many was that of issues with technology during language classes. One student reported "having technology issues with wifi connection or not being able to hear anything." Finally, the challenge of social distance was expressed by many students: "Social distancing is the worst in language classes. It's hard to hear and understand people when they're so far away and have a mask on."

Despite these challenges, many participants described their experience taking a language class during the pandemic as unique, effective, and even fun. To conclude the survey, students were asked to describe their experience learning a language during COVID-19 in one word. The words most frequently used are represented in Figure 2, including: challenging (14), difficult (9), fun (7), different (5), interesting (5) and, even, effective (4), among others.

Figure 2 Students' Description of Language Learning During the Pandemic in One Word

Table 4 Classification of Students' Descriptors According to Instructional Mode*

	F2F (n=17)	Hybrid (n=44)	Synchronous (n=43)
Positive	29%	59%	63%
Neutral	24%	14%	11%
Negative	47%	27%	26%

* Those who selected more than one delivery mode were excluded (n = 18), including all asynchronous students.

Furthermore, students' reactions were categorized by instructional mode, revealing the classification of positive, neutral, and negative descriptors. As shown in Table 4, the students in hybrid and synchronous courses provided more positive responses than those in fully F2F classes. Interestingly, even though all F2F students found the modality to be effective, nearly half of them expressed a negative overall experience learning a language during the pandemic possibly due to masking mandates and social distancing restrictions. These descriptors highlight the duality of language learning and teaching during the pandemic and the many lessons learned about new ways to engage in the L2 that go beyond traditional classroom walls.

Considering these findings, the L2 classroom represents an exceptional space due to the meaningful interactions that are prioritized, even during times of crisis. Results suggest that language classes brought students together in a time when social distancing was the norm, even when learning was conducted remotely or in a hybrid format. In fact, one student stated that synchronous Zoom classes, "allowed us to work together despite being in different places," a common limitation posed by the pandemic. Another student added, "We all became friends, and the culture of the class was great and supportive." Thus, the human connection and collaboration that form the foundation of language classes appeared to have played a positive role in these students' lives during this disruptive time.

Discussion and Implications

The findings from this exploratory study conducted during COVID-19 highlight the importance of collecting feedback from students regarding their own learning experiences to better understand and support their future development. Results confirmed that participants believed that the transition to ERT during COVID-19 impacted L2 teaching and learning by introducing a new set of challenges that required many adjustments to be made both by teachers and students. Despite these challenges, students were able to craftily identify practices that sustained effective L2 learning, even during disruptive times. In this section, we answer the questions that guided this study and provide a discussion of their importance, highlighting the pedagogical implications for future language classrooms.

Challenges and Opportunities

It is no surprise that the students in this study perceived the adverse impact posed by COVID-19 in their university L2 classes, considering that it "radically and rapidly, and perhaps forever, changed the K-20 educational landscape" (LeLoup & Swanson, 2022, p. xxiii). The most salient challenge observed in the data is that of peer interaction, which lies at the heart of L2 development (Lantolf & Thorne, 2006). This is likely why the fully F2F modality was considered very effective by nearly all students who had F2F courses, aligning with findings from Yang and Lin (2020). Specifically, the abrupt shift to ERT forced both students and teachers to reimagine how L2 interactions could be maintained during a time when social distancing was encouraged and masking was required. Suddenly, many of the ways in which language teachers mediated student learning were either impossible or required a careful redesign of tasks for students to complete them successfully given the constraints. This created additional labor for both teachers and students, adding to the already taxing emotional stress experienced by most during this time of crisis (Moser et al., 2021; see Warner & Diao, Chapter 12, this volume).

With the pandemic limiting many opportunities for F2F instruction, interaction was facilitated mainly through synchronous Zoom classes and small group discussions during breakout sessions. Participants in this study expressed mixed feelings about breakout rooms, aligning with the positive and negative experiences faced by students across the globe during the pandemic (Bamidele, 2021; Wong, 2020; Yoon, 2021). On the one hand, small-group synchronous activities not only foster L2 proficiency by improving listening skills (Yoon, 2021), but also create a sense of community in which students can be "more relaxed, excited to interact with each other, and provide peer-to-peer support both during and after time in breakout rooms" (Bamidele, 2021, p. 7). On the other hand, participants in this study became aware of the limitations of online group work, highlighting issues with technology and motivation to actively participate. This aligns with Wong's (2020) study, in which students conveyed their discomfort by pointing out, "the camera places some sort of barrier for starting conversation and it makes it awkward to initialise any discussion" (p. 90). Thus, even when connected synchronously, the social distance felt by some learners highlights the need to promote engagement and buy-in among all students, regardless of the modality.

While virtual platforms such as Zoom have the potential to foster effective communication, utilizing techniques to overcome lack of student engagement and "screen fatigue" is key to successful Zoom sessions (Kohnke & Moorhouse, 2022). If educators lack the knowledge to integrate successful strategies, students are likely to perceive synchronous sessions as ineffective. The issue of minimal training expressed by educators at the beginning of the pandemic (Morris, 2022; Trust & Whalen, 2020) may explain why some students perceived synchronous classes (particularly breakout rooms) as less engaging. Even though educators gained some experience utilizing Zoom during the pandemic, various strategies and recommendations have been shared to support future instruction. Primarily, smaller groups are key for successful interactions (Payne, 2020). With turn-based discussion necessary to foster meaningful discussion, four to six students or less is optimal. Shorter sessions are also beneficial to counteract fatigue and avoid losing focus (Kohnke & Moorhouse, 2022). Finally, Bamidele (2021) stresses the need to provide students with opportunities to explore and build their technological literacy, and the importance of flexibility between educators and students when working within breakout rooms.

The key challenges mentioned by students regarding motivation, interaction, technology, and distance all relate to the basic human condition of seeking out social interaction and the tools that are used to satisfy that need. The main question for L2 classrooms in moving forward is the following: How can language educators best harness technologies that foster interaction and engagement, thereby supporting student motivation and minimizing the feeling of isolation? While COVID-19 certainly introduced new challenges to L2 classrooms, it also highlighted a long list of innovative solutions to such challenges. Based on students' responses from this study, along with the lessons learned by teachers in the respective programs (see Morris, 2022), we suggest the following essential practices be implemented in moving forward.

Reflect, Revise, Repeat. The COVID-19 pandemic has exposed the need for educators to be flexible, try new things, and modify, as needed. Reflective practice empowers teachers to question "moral, ethical, and other types of normative criteria related directly and indirectly to the classroom" (Glynn et al., 2018, p. 94). As such, educators who think critically about their practice and its effects on learners align with a social justice orientation, which is sorely needed during such disruptive moments in history.

In moving forward, language teachers need not revert to pre-COVID methods nor reinvent the wheel. Instead, revisiting the main learning objectives for specific programs, courses, units, and even lessons can help remedy the challenges mentioned earlier with respect to engagement, workload, and feedback, among others. By more carefully aligning all tasks and assessments with specific learning objectives, teachers can essentially "cut the fluff" (Morris, 2022, p. 13), thereby boosting student engagement in meaningful activities, alleviating issues related to busywork, and lessening the load of instructor feedback. When integrating technology, language teachers must think beyond the tool itself and focus more on if and how the tool can facilitate the accomplishment of the learning objective(s) at hand. Additionally, because the theme of interaction surfaced frequently throughout this study, it is crucial to create opportunities for interactions that help build community. By creating a dynamic and interactive classroom community, whether in the confines of a traditional classroom or behind a screen, students will be more motivated to engage in the lesson, regardless of the modality (see Dörnyei & Muir, 2019; González-Lloret, 2020).

While the COVID-19 pandemic pushed students into new and unfamiliar territory, participants in this study were still able to see these experiences with a positive outlook. Exploring new modes of learning imparted challenges that prompted students to discover innovative ways to connect to both academic content and their peers. The diversity of experiences displayed by students through their one-word responses provides insight on the full spectrum of possibilities into L2 ERT. Overall, students were able to take a difficult period in their learning and flip it to see the light in the darkness, much like the language teachers studied in Morris (2022). Even when distanced, the L2 students in this study were able to build bridges between screens to participate in online classroom communities that they considered as highly effective for their learning. Building relationships is critical to student success in the classroom (Dörnyei & Muir, 2019), especially when interaction is integral to L2 development (Lantolf & Thorne, 2006). In fact, the L2 classroom helped foster social interactions in a time when both social and physical distancing was necessary. Such interactions can help students cultivate real interpersonal relationships that extend beyond the confines of the classroom, whether online or in-person (Bamidele, 2021; Chandler, 2016).

Conclusion

Despite the many challenges posed by the pandemic, the students in this study perceived their L2 learning experiences as largely effective, aligning with previous research supporting CALL (Arnold & Ducate, 2019). Although COVID-19 forced all language teachers to make sharp pedagogical shifts to accommodate the evolving needs of their learners throughout the many peaks and valleys of the pandemic, this expanded repertoire will likely impact how languages are taught and learned as we move beyond the pandemic. Consequently, language teachers should not simply revert to pre-pandemic methods. Instead, we must advocate for continued professional development and harness this opportunity to normalize CALL (Giupponi et al., Chapter 6, this volume; Goertler, 2019), accounting for the perceived benefits and challenges highlighted by students in this study. This normalization should occur not only during a time of crisis, but rather as an essential part of the curriculum.

About the Authors

Kimberly Morris is Associate Professor of Spanish at the University of Wisconsin, La Crosse, where she currently directs the World Language Education program. Her recent research explores the teaching and learning of second language pragmatics in various contexts, including during study abroad, in computer-assisted settings, and through a task-based approach. Her other professional interests include computer-assisted language learning, curriculum design, and language teacher preparation.

Mikaela Robarge is an undergraduate student in the Department of Global Cultures and Languages at the University of Wisconsin, La Crosse. Her research interests include sociolinguistics and language pedagogy.

Pablo Robles-García is Assistant Professor of Spanish at the University of Toronto, Mississauga, and the Ontario Institute of Studies in Education. His primary research interest focuses on vocabulary acquisition, with an emphasis on the role of high-frequency words in the vocabulary development of L2 learners. His research also extends to instructional strategies and practices for L2 Spanish vocabulary acquisition, with an aim to enhance vocabulary learning experiences and outcomes for L2 learners.

References

Adelson, L., & Simonnet Keen, G. (2023). F2F versus online: Student perceptions of foreign language learning in the time of COVID-19. *Journal of Educators Online*, *20*(1), 1–18. http://dx.doi.org/10.9743/jeo.2023.20.2.1

Arispe, K., & Blake, R. (2012). Individual factors and successful language learning in a hybrid course. *System*, *40*(4), 449–465. https://doi-org.libweb.uwlax.edu/10.1016/j.system.2012.10.013

Arnold, N., & Ducate, L. (Eds.) (2019). *Engaging language learners through CALL: From theory and research to informed practice* (pp. 51–92). Equinox Publishing. https://www.equinoxpub.com/home/engaging-language/

Bader, S. A. (2021). The impact of instructors' perceptions of e-learning on the quality of online teaching: A case study of the French language instructors at the University of Bahrain during COVID-19 pandemic. *International Education Studies*, *14*(12), 152–162. https://doi.org/10.5539/ies.v14n12p152

Bamidele, A. (2021). Student-centered interactions within an ESL classroom using online breakout room. *Proceedings of the AUBH E-Learning Conference 2021: Innovative Learning & Teaching – Lessons from COVID-19*. 1–9. http://dx.doi.org/10.2139/ssrn.3878774

Blake, R. J., Wilson, N. L., Cetto, M., & Pardo–Ballester, C. (2008). Measuring oral proficiency in distance, face-to-face, and blended classrooms. *Language Learning & Technology*, *12*(3), 114–127. http://dx.doi.org/10125/44158

Braun, V., & Clarke, V. (2006). Using thematic analysis in psychology. *Qualitative Research in Psychology*, *3* (2), 77–101. http://doi.org/10.1191/1478088706qp063oa

Chandler, K. (2016). Using breakout rooms in synchronous online tutorials. *Journal of Perspectives in Applied Academic Practice*, *4*(3), 16–23. https://doi.org/10.14297/jpaap.v4i3.216

Dörnyei, Z., & Muir, C. (2019). Creating a motivating classroom environment. In X. Gao (Ed.), *Second Handbook of English Language Teaching* (pp. 719–736). Springer International Handbooks of Education. https://doi.org/10.1007/978-3-030-02899-2_36

Gacs, A., Goertler, S., & Spasova, S. (2020). Planned online language education versus crisis prompted online language teaching: Lessons for the future. *Foreign Language Annals*, *53*, 380–392. https://doi.org/10.1111/flan.12460

Glynn, C., Wesley, P., & Wassel, B. (2018). *Words and actions: Teaching languages through the lens of social justice* (2nd ed.). Alexandria, VA: ACTFL. https://www.ipgbook.com/words---actions-products-9781942544630.php

Goertler, S. (2019). Normalizing online learning: Adapting to a changing world of language teaching. In N. Arnold & L. Ducate (Eds.), *Engaging language learners through CALL: From theory and research to informed practice* (pp. 51–92). Equinox Publishing. https://www.equinoxpub.com/home/engaging-language/

Goertler, S., & Gacs, A. (2018). Assessment in online German: Assessment methods and results. *Die Unterrichtspraxis/Teaching German*, *51*(2), 156–174. https://doi.org/10.1111/tger.12071

González-Lloret, M. (2020). Collaborative tasks for online language teaching. *Foreign Language Annals*, *53,* 260–269. https://doi.org/10.1111/flan.12466

Harvey, L. (2011). The nexus of feedback and improvement. In C. S. Nair & P. Mertova (Eds.), *Student Feedback: The Cornerstone of Effective Quality Assurance System in Higher Education* (pp. 3–26). Chandos Publishing. https://www.amazon.com/Student-Feedback-Cornerstone-Effective-Assurance/dp/1843345730#detailBullets_feature_div

Humphrey, E. A., & Wiles, J. R. (2021). Lessons learned through listening to biology students during a transition to online learning in the wake of the COVID-19 pandemic. *Academic Practice in Ecology and Evolution*, *11*(3), 3450–3458. https://doi.org/10.1002/ece3.7303

Jansem, A. (2021). The feasibility of foreign language online instruction during the Covid-19 pandemic: A qualitative case study of instructors' and students' reflections. *International Education Studies*, *14(*4), 93–102. https://doi.org/10.5539/ies.v14n4p93

Kern, R. G. (1995). Students' and Teachers' Beliefs about Language Learning. *Foreign Language Annals*, *28*(1), 71–92. https://doi.org/10.1111/j.1944-9720.1995.tb00770.x

Klimova, B. (2021). An insight into online foreign language learning and teaching in the era of COVID-19 pandemic. *Procedia Computer Science*, *192.* 1787–1794. https://doi.org/10.1016/j.procs.2021.08.183

Kohnke, L., & Moorhouse, B. L. (2022). Facilitating synchronous online language learning through Zoom. *RELC Journal*, *53*(1), 296–301. https://doi.org/10.1177/0033688220937235

Lantolf, J. P., & Thorne, S. (2006). *Sociocultural theory and the genesis of second language development*. Oxford University Press. https://www.amazon.com/Sociocultural-Theory-Genesis-Language-Development/dp/0194421813

LeLoup, J. W., & Swanson, P. (2022). Preface. In J. LeLoup & P. Swanson (Eds.), *Handbook of research on effective online language teaching in a disruptive environment* (pp. xxiii–xxviii). IGI Global. http://doi.org/10.4018/978-1-7998-7720-2

Long, M. H. (1996). The role of the linguistic environment in second language acquisition. In W. C. Ritchie & T. K. Bahtia (Eds.), *Handbook of second language acquisition* (pp. 413–468). New York: Academic Press. https://doi.org/10.1016/B978-012589042-7/50015-3

MacIntyre, P. D., Gregersen, T., & Mercer, S. (2020). Language teachers' coping strategies during the Covid-19 conversion to online teaching: Correlations with stress, wellbeing and negative emotions. *System*, 94, 102352. http://doi.org/10.1016/j.system.2020.102352

Mackey, A. (2020). *Interaction, feedback and task research in second language learning: Methods and design.* Cambridge University Press. https://doi.org/10.1017/9781108589284

Moneypenny, D., & Aldrich, R. (2016). Online and face-to-face language learning: A comparative analysis of oral proficiency in introductory Spanish. *Journal of Educators Online*, 13, 105–174. http://doi.org/10.9743/JEO.2016.2.2

Montiel-Chamorro, M. L. (2018). *Comparing online English language learning and face-to-face English language learning at El Bosque University in Colombia* (Publication No. 10815517) [Doctoral dissertation, Virginia Commonwealth University]. ProQuest Dissertations Publishing.

Morris, K. (2022). Language teaching in the time of COVID-19: Insights from experienced and pre-service teachers. In J. LeLoup & P. Swanson (Eds.), *Handbook of research on effective online language teaching in a disruptive environment* (pp. 1–23). IGI Global. http://doi.org/10.4018/978-1-7998-7720-2

Moser, K. M., Wei, T., & Brenner, D. (2021). Remote teaching during COVID-19: Implications from a national survey of language educators. *System*, *97*, 1–15. http://doi.org/10.1016/j.system.2020.102431

Payne, S. J. (2020). Developing L2 productive language skills online and the strategic use of instructional tools. *Foreign Language Annals*, *53*, 243–249. https://doi.org/10.1111/flan.12457

Schmith, R. (2002). Qualtrics [survey software]. https://www.qualtrics.com

Trust, T., & Whalen, J. (2020). Should teachers be trained in emergency remote teaching? Lessons learned from the COVID-19 pandemic. *Journal of Technology and Teacher Education*, *28(*2), 189–199. https://www.learntechlib.org/primary/p/215995/

Wong, J. O. (2020). A pandemic in 2020, and the arrival of the online educator. *International Journal of TESOL Studies*, *2*(3), 82–99. https://doi.org/10.46451/ijts.2020.09.19

Wright, B. M. (2017). Blended learning: Student perception of face-to-face and online EFL lessons. *Indonesian Journal of Applied Linguistics*, *7*(1). 64–71. http://dx.doi.org/10.17509/ijal.v7i1.6859

Yang, L., & Lin, J. (2020). The impact of online teaching on interaction during the pandemic: An exploratory study in CFL Classes. *International Journal of Chinese Language Teaching*, *1*(2), 37–50. https://doi.org/10.46451/ijclt.2020.09.03

Yördem, A. (2015). Vocational college students' perceptions of a newly implemented online course of teaching English as a foreign language. *International Journal of Languages' Education and Teaching*, *3*(2), 1–9. http://dx.doi.org/10.18298/ijlet.428

Yoon, J. (2021). Students' perceptions of blended asynchronous and synchronous learning in an advanced Spanish conversation class. *European Journal of Foreign Language Teaching*, *5*(6), 32– 66. http://dx.doi.org/10.46827/ejfl.v5i6.4065

Ziegler, N. (2016). Synchronous computer-mediated communication and interaction: A meta-analysis. *Studies in Second Language Acquisition*, *38*(3), 553–586. https://doi.org/10.1017/S027226311500025X

Ziegler, N., Parlak, O., & Phung, H. (2022). Interactionist perspectives and the role of computer-mediated communication in SLA. In N. Ziegler & M. González-Lloret (Eds.), *The Routledge Handbook of Second Language Acquisition and Technology* (pp. 50–64). Routledge. https://www.routledge.com/The-Routledge-Handbook-of-Second-Language-Acquisition-and-Technology/Ziegler-Gonzalez-Lloret/p/book/9780815360773

PART FOUR

BY-PRODUCTS

12 Feeling Through Technology: Affect and Emotional Attachments During Remote Teaching

Chantelle Warner and Wenhao Diao

Introduction

When the COVID-19 pandemic hit in spring 2020 it triggered a public health crisis that was simultaneously an educational crisis. As teachers across all levels of education were asked to move to emergency remote teaching, they were also compelled to create new digital classroom spaces, working with the technologies at hand. While the experience of teaching online was new to many teachers, both digitally mediated learning and the technological tools used to facilitate were not unknown to most teachers or students; however, these took on new associations and emotional attachments as they became part of the phenomenological texture of pandemic life.

In this contribution we expand upon early studies that have drawn attention to the affective dimensions of emergency remote teaching (e.g., Moser, et al., 2021; Li et al., 2021) by focusing on language educators' discourses around the technologies that were prevalent in emergency remote language teaching, specifically the video-conferencing platform Zoom and digital communications apps such as GroupMe and Slack. Previous studies have pointed to the centrality of affect in language teachers' experiences during the pandemic. For example, educators reported feeling stressed and anxious about online teaching (Li et al., 2021). At the same time, the pandemic exacerbated an already mounting mental health crisis among university students. Teachers thus often not only felt called to adapt their pedagogical methods to the virtual classroom but also engaged in nuanced forms of emotion labor, adopting new practices of care as they supported the social and emotional well-being of their students in a collective moment of crisis.

Teaching is in many keyways an emotional profession (see Liu, et al., 2021), and this reality was heightened during the early phases of the COVID pandemic. Building on our own research examining the kinds of emotion labor described by language educators in their recounts of teaching during the pandemic (see Warner & Diao, 2022), the current study considers the affective relationships with types of technology that became ubiquitous in emergency remote teaching and how these intersected with teachers' educational values, including both pedagogical principles and emotional expectations that guide their work:

1. How did participants discuss their own and their students' emotional relationships with Zoom and digital communications apps in the context of remote language teaching/learning?
2. How did participants describe the affordances and constraints of these technologies for realizing emotion labor?

In the spirit of this special volume, our motivation for investigating the unique situation of emergency remote teaching arises from a concern with the ways in which the extraordinary can help highlight underexamined aspects of the ordinary. This study thus seeks not simply to document and make sense of the experience of teaching during the early phases of the pandemic in spring and fall of 2020, but to better understand the complex relations between affect and technology-enhanced language teaching and the implications thereof for working and learning conditions going forward.

Affect in (Emergency Remote) Language Teaching: A Review of the Research

In this section, we begin with the context of emergency remote language teaching in the early months of the COVID-19 pandemic, emphasizing the centrality of affect in this experience for both teachers and students. We then focus in on research on emotion labor, which connects these affective dimensions directly to the work of being a *good* language teacher. This sets up the questions about the role of technology in pedagogical emotion labor and the regulation of emotions, which are discussed in the final sub-section of this literature review.

Affective Dimensions of Technology and Language Teaching in the COVID Pandemic

In the just over three years since the widespread campus closures of spring 2020, a plethora of scholarship has appeared examining the situation of teaching during the pandemic, including a significant body of work focusing on the particularities of second language education. Many of these publications consider the sudden, unanticipated need to adopt educational technologies, with which many instructors and students were previously unfamiliar. In addition to issues with access and bandwidth (e.g., Hakim, 2020), teacher readiness and preparation is heavily thematized in these publications (e.g., Back et al., 2021; Lee & Ogawa, 2021; Meirovitz et al., 2022; Tafazoli & Meihami, 2022). Echoed across these studies is the technostress and uncertainty teachers faced. While one possible implication drawn by scholars is that educators need more training so that they can "become lifelong independent digital learners" (Meirovitz et al., 2022, p. 6), there is also often a recognition that an emphasis on professional development alone ignores the particularities of emergency remote teaching in the midst of a crisis. Based on the findings of a national survey conducted by Moser et al. (2021), even world language teachers with experience teaching online felt unprepared to face the particular challenges of the pandemic response. In this context, pedagogy sometimes even became sidelined, as demonstrated by the autoethnographic reflections of the student teacher/researchers in Back et al. (2021), who reported an overall feeling of disconnect between their beliefs about language teaching and learning, administrator guidance, and student participation which intersected with a sense of diminished expectations.

The very nature of emergency remote teaching is that it is not methodologically designed or planned (see Hodges et al., 2020; Krsmanovic, 2022). Thus, while the need for language educators to be more familiar with digital tools and online modalities is one possible lesson of the pandemic, the lived reality of teaching in spring and fall 2020 was, for many, more like being thrown into a "painful, natural experiment" (Jones & Kessler, 2020, p. 1) with limited resources, multiple external stressors, and a heightened sense of precarity. Online teaching, especially in the first six months of the pandemic, was not only pedagogically complex but also emotionally intense (Appel & Robbins, 2021; Jones & Kessler, 2020; Liu et al., 2021; McAlinden & Dobinson, 2022; Pham & Phan, 2023). Technologies involved in remote teaching often created additional emotional stress for language teachers. The stress associated with emergency remote language teaching could be so detrimental that some language teachers felt they had no or little confidence in adopting online teaching at all in their post-pandemic future (Li et al., 2021). MacIntyre et al. (2022) similarly found that teachers' feelings of well-being decreased in those early months of the pandemic, but also that a significant number of educators reported a sense of growth that they associated with hope – defined by the authors as a positive orientation towards the future.

Maican and Cocorada's (2021) survey shows that new technologies adopted in online foreign language teaching, combined with the reduced interaction with peers and teachers during remote learning, were likewise major stressors for many students. Language teachers had to therefore up the additional affective responsibility to "stimulate positive activating emotions" among students and "increase their wellbeing" (p. 17). Students were likewise navigating pandemic-induced disruptions to their everyday realities, for example the closures of campus housing, as they adapted to their new lives as online learners. The isolation of lockdown meant that synchronous online lessons were often a primary source of social interaction, and students reported a greater need for interpersonal engagement and feelings of belongingness (e.g., Alger & Eyckmans, 2022; Besser et al., 2022; Resnik & Dewaele, 2023). Thus, even though learning technologies were acting as a major source of stress and anxiety, they were also the primary means through which communities, including those of the classroom, were able to sustain meaningful forms of interaction.

Emotion Labor and Caring as Pedagogy (in Language Teaching)

As many of the scholars cited in the previous section note, the stress and emotional impact of the COVID pandemic on teachers was both specific to the social and psychological circumstances of living through a public health crisis and rapidly shifting teaching modalities, but also was bound up in the broader context of education, including the emotional dimensions of this work. There is a tendency in these discussions to place the responsibility for regulating both their own affect and that of their students on teachers (see also Warner & Diao, 2022). Emotions are not just part of the experience of teaching, but part of the work. Hochschild (1979, 2012[1983]) coined the term emotion(al) labor to capture the institutionalized expectations of emotional management associated with specific professional roles. Although Hochschild's early research on emotion(al) labor focused on service industry jobs, such as flight attendants, a more recent body of work has considered the emotion(al) labor of teachers (e.g., Hargreaves, 2000; Nias, 1996) and a smaller subset examines the specific context of language teaching (Gkonou & Miller, 2019, 2021; Miller & Gkonou, 2018, 2020).

Emotional labor is not only institutionalized in job descriptions and expectations, but often internalized as part of teachers' professional identities. Education, Noddings (2013) argued, in contemporary US society is understood as inextricable from an ethic of care; in caring for and about their students, teachers impart moral ideals to their students and enact their ideal of a *good teacher*. Inspired by Noddings' work, Gkonou and Miller (2019) have argued that this same ethics of care motivates language educators to work to mitigate negative emotions such as language anxiety; however, emotion labor for teachers can also involve the suppression of any negative emotions, including their own, potentially leading to psychological fatigue and even burnout. Studies from the broader field of education have shown that emotion labor can have both negative (e.g., King, 2016; Yuan & Liu, 2021) and positive effects (e.g., Benesch, 2018; Cowie, 2011; Zembylas, 2005) for teachers, in terms of immediate performance and longer-term feelings of professional satisfaction and general well-being.

Recognizing the ambivalent potential effects of emotion labor for language teachers, Miller and Gkonou (2018) have advocated that reflexivity is key. Concluding their study of language teachers in tertiary settings in the UK and US, they write that "[d]eveloping teachers' awareness of their potential for exercising agency relationally can enable them to reflect on, respond to, and sometimes challenge the feeling rules active in their teaching contexts in their ongoing efforts to become better teachers" (p. 57). In their autoethnographic study of an English-as-a-foreign-language instructor teaching in Wuhan during the COVID-19 pandemic, Liu et al. (2021) echo this finding, arguing that teacher emotion is an integral functional component of professional practice and development. Writing in the first-person, Liu, who is both the first author and the instructor, describes the ways in which new technologies, pedagogy of care, and emotion labor intersected during emergency remote teaching:

> Different from my previous beliefs, my relationship with students and colleagues actually strengthened, and my attitude towards technology improved, as I learned to acknowledge, analyse and regulate my emotions in the online English classroom. (p. 17)

Liu, et al.'s (2021) research shows that emotional relations to technology and emotion labor can be quite ambivalent, nuanced, and dynamic.

In our own research on university-level language teachers' emotion labor during the early months of remote teaching (Warner & Diao, 2022), we found that an ethic of care was foregrounded in participants' discussions of their experiences teaching during the pandemic. Based on our analysis of participant interviews, we identified three overarching feeling rules that guided the teachers' decisions at the start of the pandemic:

1. Language teachers must establish/maintain personal connections to students;
2. Language teachers must create/maintain a sense of classroom community between students;
3. Language teachers should offer/express emotional support beyond the course.

This research suggests that emotions were central to teachers' understanding of their teaching practice during the pandemic in ways that go beyond the stress of having to implement new technologies. At the same time, it raises the question: how do teachers manage emotions and emotion labor given the particularities of technology-mediated language teaching and learning, which were instigated by the pandemic?

Emotions and Technology

Gilmore and Warren (2007) are among the early researchers who studied the specificities of teacher emotions in online settings. Their study examines the authors' own experiences leading two seminar groups over the course of a 12-week undergraduate module on virtual society, using chat rooms, and considers how the virtuality of the class transformed emotions of both the teachers and students. Their analysis focuses on three emotional categories that emerge from their interview data: intimacy, play, and pride/shame. Gilmore and Warren show how the absence of the body and removal of physical socio-spatial indicators compelled teachers and students to renegotiate feeling rules. The lack of familiar ways of enacting social-emotional cues heightened the emotional dimension, and this in turn had a "re-humanizing" effect on their professional work as teachers (p. 604). Their claim is not that only positive emotions were evoked during the online seminar, but rather that relationships and forms of interaction afforded through the digital media shifted in ways that re-centered the place of emotions in the classroom.

Gilmore and Warren's research serves as a reminder that while feeling rules are rooted in specific cultures, including cultures of (language) education, they are also shaped by the circumstances within which they are enacted. Writing about language teaching during the pandemic, Guillén, et al. (2020) note that "Language teachers are often masters of using the physical space in their language classrooms, rearranging furniture, groups, and artifacts to facilitate meaningful encounters with and among learners" (p. 320), and consequently many educators experienced the virtual nature of remote teaching as a loss. And yet "technology also affords human connections which are broader than what is possible within a traditional classroom's four walls" (p. 320). Pham and Phan's (2023) study of the emotional orientations of Vietnamese language teachers during emergency remote teaching, also found that the pedagogically and technologically distinctive features of online teaching aroused unique emotional responses – ranging from readiness and confusion at the start of remote teaching to frustration and fear as the situation dragged on and, in some cases, reports of improved pedagogy and increased closeness with students. These studies point to the need for further research into virtuality, emotion and teaching; in an online environment, the technology may foreground the operation, but to quote Pham and Phan (2023), "teachers and teachers' emotions still act as the fuel that keeps the machine running" (p. 8).

Technologies enter the virtual classroom already imbued with certain emotional valences. In her critical approach to emotions in English language teaching, Benesch (2019) draws on Ahmed's (2004, 2010) critical affect theory to examine the ways in which certain emotions become *stuck* on objects. For Ahmed, affect is not just about internal experiences of human beings but is far more about feelings that accumulate around certain objects, including things, people, practices, and events. Benesch extends this concept to classroom objects, including cell phones as one of her focal examples. Based on a survey and interview data, Benesch shows how cell phones in the classroom are sticky with unhappy emotions; both teachers and learners of English as a foreign language associated distraction, disruption, and disrespect with in-class cell phone use. The word "hate" appeared in multiple of the teacher responses. For teachers, the emotional toll of having to police students to enforce their own classroom policies was a significant part of their affective relationship with cell phones. Emotions are sticky not only because they attach to certain objects, but also because they can get us stuck (Ahmed, 2004). In the case of this example, the potential of cell phones to connect students with the world outside of the classroom gets stuck on feelings of resentment, even as language educators try to make these real-world connections in their teaching (Benesch, 2019, p. 74).

Methods

To understand university-level language educators' discourses about their experiences with emergency remote teaching at the start of the COVID-19 pandemic, we designed an interview-based study – the details of which are described in this section. For this chapter, where we focus on the participants' affective stances in relation to the technologies they used for teaching, we rely on qualitative methods of analysis concerned with human relationships and ways of making meaning. Our goal is to contribute to existing studies on affect and (language) education by providing a snapshot of the complex emotions these participants attached to technologies and their use during this moment of crisis.

Participants

The 19 participants for this study were recruited using a digital survey, which was broadly distributed through the email listservs of professional organizations and through the authors' own networks of US-based educators. The survey asked potential participants to provide their contact information and to answer several demographic questions (see Warner & Diao, 2022 for the complete survey). We then contacted respondents via email to arrange a time for digital interviews, which were conducted and recorded using Zoom – a technology that had become ubiquitous in the initial weeks of the pandemic. Of the 21 individuals who met with us for first interviews in spring or early summer of 2020 after emergency remote teaching policies had been put in place on most campuses, 19 also agreed to do a follow-up interview in fall 2020. These 19 are the focal participants for this study.

Participants included teachers at US institutions of higher education working in six different languages: Chinese, French, German, Italian, Japanese, and Spanish (see Table 1). Although these are among the most typically offered languages on US college campuses, according to data collected by the Modern Language Association (Looney & Lusin, 2019), they were not represented proportionately, e.g., only one person taught Spanish, which ranks #1 in the number of US student enrollments among all languages, and there were six instructors of German, which ranks #4. All participants were in-service instructors at the time of the study. Only one participant had returned to in-person teaching at the start of fall 2020; the remainder were still teaching remotely. They held a wide variety of different positions at a range

Table 1 Distribution of Languages, Institutions, and Positions Among the Participants

Languages	Institutions	Positions
Chinese = 2	Large State = 12	TT = 8
French = 5	Small Public = 1	NTT = 8
German = 6	Private = 4	Visiting = 1
Italian = 4	Community College = 1	Grad = 5
Japanese = 1	Private Religious = 2	LPD/Coord. = 7
Spanish = 1		

of different institution types across the US (see Table 1). There was a balance between tenure-track (TT) and non-tenure track (NTT) faculty (eight of each), and seven of these faculty were serving as language program director (LPD) or level coordinator at the time of the interviews. There was also one whose title was visiting lecturer. Five participants were PhD students, and two of them (Nedda and Ying) had extensive teaching experience prior to enrolling in their graduate programs.

Table 2 provides an overview of the participants, as well as the languages they teach and their positions at the time of the interviews. To ensure that the participants remain anonymous, we will use pseudonyms throughout this chapter, and will otherwise minimize the inclusion of identifying information. This is particularly important in the context of this work because university language educators in the US are often closely connected through professional networks, leaving it more likely that the mention of a location, institution type, and position would make it too easy to identify a set of potential individuals.

Data Generation and Selection

This interview-based study was conducted between spring 2020 and fall 2020, as most university and college campuses in the US – and much of the rest of the world – shifted to emergency remote teaching out of public health concerns. We conducted two rounds of semi-structured interviews; the first round, conducted in late spring and summer, lasted an average of about an hour and the second round, conducted in early fall, lasted an average just over half an hour. The first interviews focused on participants' backgrounds and experience with online and otherwise computer-mediated language teaching prior to the COVID pandemic, their experiences teaching and, in some cases, supporting other instructors as teaching went remote in

Table 2 Participants' Teaching Profiles

Pseudonym	Language	Position
Alejandra	Spanish	Faculty (TT)
Alice	French	Faculty – Admin
Annetta	Italian	Faculty – Grad
Claudia	German	Faculty (TT) – LPD/Coord.
Edmondo	Italian	Faculty
Erika	German	Faculty (TT) – LPD/Coord.
Holly	French	Faculty (TT) – LPD/Coord.
Kai	Chinese	Faculty (Visiting)
Lily	French	Grad
Linda	French	Faculty (TT) – LPD/Coord.
Nathaniel	Italian	Grad
Nedda	Italian	Faculty – Grad
Rachel	German	Faculty (TT)
Regina	German	Faculty (TT) – LPD/Coord.
Ruth	Japanese	Faculty
Tyler	German	Faculty (TT)
Violet	German	Faculty
Ying	Chinese	Faculty – Grad – LPD/Coord.
Yvonne	French	Faculty – LPD/Coord

spring 2020, and their expectations for the coming fall semester. The second round of interviews was intended as a follow-up, capturing an additional moment in the ongoing experience of emergency teaching circumstances rather than as a point of comparison. We conducted, recorded, and preliminarily transcribed the interviews using Zoom – which had become a ubiquitous means of communication in spring 2020. English was the primary language used in the interviews; however, both we and the interviewees did engage in codeswitching when another language (i.e., German or Mandarin Chinese) was shared and one first interview was almost exclusively in Mandarin. In such instances, the relevant author completed the transcription and, where needed, translation of the interview text.

For the purposes of this study, we were primarily interested in how the feelings and feeling rules we had previously analyzed (Warner & Diao, 2022) were associated with the forms of technology that were commonly used by university language educators during the COVID-19 pandemic. Our first step in the analysis was thus to identify which forms of digital technology were most often discussed in the interviews. Overwhelmingly, the most ubiquitous of all the forms of communications technology referenced in the transcripts was Zoom. Zoom was mentioned directly by all 19 participants in this study, and all but one of the participants indicated that they had used Zoom for teaching. (That one individual had used Google Meet, a similar platform, instead.) In addition to more explicit references to Zoom, it was often clear within the context of an interview that this particular technology became synonymous with synchronous remote teaching. This is perhaps unsurprising, given that Zoom was the most widely adopted technology tool during the pandemic in education and many other sectors, which gave rise to the pervasiveness of phrases like "Zoom school" and "Zoom fatigue" in everyday discourse (see also Cheung, 2021; Kohnke & Moorhouse, 2022). In addition to Zoom, participants reported using a variety of other forms of technology, including several that are primarily used in educational settings (e.g., Flipgrid, Perusall, and Padlet); however, it was freely available digital communications apps such as GroupMe, Slack, and WhatsApp that were most often discussed as key tools for staying in contact with students during remote teaching. It is thus these two types of digital technologies – video conferencing (i.e., Zoom) and digital communications apps – that we will focus on in this chapter.

Analyzing Affective Attachments vis-a-vis Technology

After identifying which forms of technology would be most relevant, we analyzed moments in the transcripts where these were directly discussed in terms of the emotions expressed by the instructors. This qualitative emotion coding (see Saldaña, 2016) focused on both references to their own emotional states and associations and any emotions they attributed to others, typically the students in their classes. As a metalanguage for analyzing feelings in language, we drew from appraisal theory (Martin & White, 2007), a framework conceptualized within Systemic Functional Linguistics (SFL). Appraisal theory is most concerned with the aspects of what Halliday, in his original modeling of SFL, dubbed the *interpersonal* metafunction, the lexicogrammatical resources through which language users enact relationships between the speaker and any addressees as well as the speaker and their message. More specifically, appraisal theory is based on a notion of discursive stance, which maintains that "whenever speakers (or writers) say anything, they encode their point of view towards it" (Martin & White, 2005, p. 92). Educators' emotional attachments to technologies and their use in the language classroom during emergency remote teaching fall under a category of appraisal that Martin and White (2005) identified as *attitude*, the expression of value.

In Martin and White's framework, affect is one of three domains of attitude, and it relates closely to the other two – judgment and appreciation. The former has to do with evaluations of behavior with respect to social norms (including, in the context of this study, the norms governing language classrooms), and the latter the evaluation of products and practices, including those involved in teaching and learning activities (Martin & White, 2005, pp. 35 & 45). Judgment and appreciation can be understood as institutionalized forms of affect (Martin & White, 2005, p. 45). Attitude, as expressed in these three domains, provided a means for attending closely to the affective dimensions of participants' accounts.

For the purposes of this study, we used all three sub-categories of attitude to analyze the interview extracts where the use of Zoom and digital communications media in emergency remote teaching were discussed. We then interpreted these within the broader context of emergency remote language teaching at the start of the COVID-19 pandemic. We deliberately avoided categorizing the emotions in a binary way – as either positive or negative – or quantifying the frequencies of different emotional codes. This allowed us to pay attention to the reality that the educators' relationship with the technologies they used in emergency remote teaching were nuanced and sometimes even contradictory, and it was the complexities of these emotions – rather than the magnitude or frequency that a quantitatively oriented method of counting would convey (Creswell, 2013) – that best addressed our research questions. In the subsequent section, we present the findings of this analysis, before returning to our guiding questions as to how these emotional orientations and responses intersected with the enactment and negotiation of feeling rules through the affordances of the digital communication technologies.

Findings: Affective Attitudes toward Technologies for Remote Teaching

Zoom

As already indicated, Zoom was the most frequently mentioned technological tool used during emergency remote teaching, and in the context of our study and in education more broadly was effectively synonymous with synchronous remote teaching in 2020. While Zoom was ubiquitous, it was not universally embraced. The decision of whether and to what extent to adopt synchronous versus asynchronous teaching featured prominently in several of the interviews, where it was often affectively shaded.

For example, Rachel expressed that her first inclination was to teach synchronously with Zoom, because that felt more familiar. Describing her reaction when it was announced that courses would need to be moved online, she said:

> Immediately, I was like, oh, we're gonna be fine. We're just gonna, we're going to put this all, you know, it'll - most of my stuff the texts and everything are all, they don't have a copyright. So, I have PDFs of them. They're all in Canvas already. I was like, yeah, we'll use Zoom and we'll just have like synchronous class on Zoom and I did not… like I toyed with… there was a lot of people talking about the advantages of asynchronous learning, especially in terms of being more flexible for students who are, you know, having to deal with switching remote as well. […] But I was overwhelmed with the thought of how that would look and kind of overwhelmed by the world around me and all the implications, my job. And so I was like, No, I'm not doing that.

For Rachel, during the first weeks of the pandemic, Zoom was associated with an affective stance of doing "fine", with making the best out of the technologies already in place and creating a sense of security. This stood in contrast to the affective evaluation of being "overwhelmed" in a moment where both professional work and everything else around it was in flux. Thus, although despite the judgment and appreciation she heard from colleagues in the field in relation to certain technologies and how they could be used, she decided to use Zoom. She then went on to describe the efforts she made to poll students on their technological capabilities and communicate the plan going forward, so that she could make this work.

For some participants, namely Regina and Erika, Zoom was first and foremost a medium for staying connected with students as campuses closed down. Regina, who was a language program director overseeing graduate student instructors of German at the time, Zoom was one means among many for checking in on students. Recounting what she told the instructors whom she supervised, she said,

> Right, now I just want you to check in with people and check on people's mental health, like if their German is not the best at the end of the semester they will survive and you will survive. And we're

> going to be okay. So that was, that was basically my constant email to all of them was like, "So, are you okay? Are you feeling okay or your students? Okay, how do you checked in with them emotionally, you know, and if Zooming makes you happier then do that, but if you can't do it, don't do it.

Like the word "fine" in Rachel's excerpt, the repeated word "okay" here is indexical of an affective stance vis-à-vis emergency remote teaching, especially in spring 2020, when classes first went online and getting by became the core goal. Regina prioritized emotion labor, positioning Zoom as a means of enacting not primarily pedagogy but feeling rules, i.e. the need to check in on students emotionally. At the same time, she also centers the affective states of the teachers, who are encouraged to choose the technological tool that makes them "happier." She then went on to mention Tik Tok, as something else she was trying out in her own classroom.

In the second interview, where Regina described her decision-making process while preparing her program's multi-section German courses for remote instruction leading up to fall 2020, her thinking on this seemed to have shifted somewhat. She had originally intended to implement all asynchronous instruction, based on her prior experiences with online teaching and what worked. She then changed her mind:

> I got convinced in the summer through training that synchronous was actually really good for accountability and motivation. So, um, through our training and through reading about that, about how synchronous sessions make students feel more connected and how one of the main reasons that people drop online courses is because they don't feel like they're connected to anybody else. They feel alone.

Regina's expression of appreciation that synchronous language teaching via Zoom is "good" is connected to its capacity to facilitate what are judged as positive learner behaviors, i.e., those connected directly to the regulation of student's affective states and their feelings of connection. The technology here is depicted as an agent that has the ability to "make" students feel a certain way, this leaves an additional judgment implied that working with these technologies is good pedagogical behavior.

The impetus to stay connected and check in on the emotional state of students was likewise Erika's stated reason for originally implementing Zoom in the language program she was directing, but she and the instructors she worked with ended up with some ambivalent experiences in this regard.

> [...] it was really hard for some of the instructors, just like utter devastation, seeing students that were clearly not in a good spot when they were Zooming in and, you know, we allowed them to cameras off too, but you could just see with some that they were uncomfortable that they were not in a good spot. And, so, we did. We did some, we canceled some synchronous sessions and exchanged it with individual shorter meetings with each student, which really serve the purpose of a, okay what's going on, and then connecting them with the resources that they needed. So, it had nothing to do with German, but it was very much needed. And I think after we did that instruction felt a little bit better. Like they at least knew who was in danger and of, like, you know, housing insecure food insecurities and so on and so forth.

As Erika depicts it, instructors' affective relationships to Zoom were wound up with students' affective situations. While synchronous Zoom teaching gave instructors an opportunity to view the students' states of well-being and to notice that they were "uncomfortable" and "not in a good spot," it did not afford them with any clear way to act upon that awareness. This led them to schedule shorter meetings with each student on Zoom where they could connect them with the resources they needed, which in turn created an improved affective relationship to the teaching on Zoom. In Erika's depiction, the program director's and the instructors' decisions about how to use the technology is the recipient of judgment that this was "much needed."

Erika and Regina's comments about the place of German, the language of instruction in both their contexts, echo the titular quote from Back et al.'s article "We were told that the content we delivered was not as important," and their finding that many language instructors experienced a feeling of overall disconnect from the classroom practices that they typically valued and prioritized. The tension between the care work prioritized during the pandemic and pedagogical principles was also apparent in Claudia's first interview. Responding to a question about whether she felt that the synchronous classes had gone well, she said,

> I think so, but I think it was very different in terms of target language. So, there was way more English than in my classroom. And there was a lot of care involved, much more care than teaching sometimes where it was really about how are you doing, and kind of just being there with each other rather than really engaging with the German, – Interactive things that I had planned... we did something, but I have no idea what happened in all of the breakout rooms,

> either. I mean, I came back with something, but… it was definitely not the same like sitting in a classroom and being able to just walk through and say, oh, I'm hearing a lot of English there I'm bringing them back to kind of the task at hand.

There is a tension running through Claudia's description of the Zoom teaching, between "really engaging with German" as a pedagogical principal, i.e., judged as an established norm for language teaching, and "care," which relates to the feeling rules that were heightened during the pandemic (see Warner & Diao, 2022). At the same time, the functionality of Zoom teaching, where breakout rooms replaced in-class group work, also interfered with the realization of interactive, engaged tasks in German, which are judged here as the ideal pedagogical behavior for language teaching.

In reference to her role as a mentor for relatively novice instructors, Regina expressed a different but related aspect of the disconnect between pedagogical principles and pandemic teaching practices. Where she encouraged teachers to focus on community-building, by implementing meaningful interpersonal language use, she believed that instructors were often instead asking students to merely practice vocabulary and grammar.

> They don't see a problem with, now go practice. You know, what color is my shirt? You know, and it's like it's like, I'm like, okay – I get that you think that that's an okay exercise because you think, well, I'm just practicing language, but students don't often care for that kind of stuff.

Regina is referencing a long ongoing discussion in the field of second language teaching and learning about meaning-oriented language teaching and expressing her own judgment of approaches that superficially engage learners in acts of communication for the sole purpose of rehearsing specific forms. She also attributes a similar critical stance to learners. But, moreover, she is arguing that meaningful language use is itself a way of enacting pedagogy as care that can be mediated over a platform like Zoom.

For other participants, the failure to realize pedagogy as care seemed more directly associated with the technology itself. Earlier we saw how Rachel adopted Zoom for pragmatic reasons initially. She also later indicated that she had hoped to also be able to maintain connections with her students but that this was not working as she had hoped. "I feel like there's ways of kind of getting to them that we're not translating into Zoom at all," she told us.

> And so, my attempt to perform was way up initially trying to like evoke some kind of reaction. And then I just had to like accept that, okay, now you know. And they don't owe that to me either. It's not their job to perform excitement when they're sitting in their parents' house during pandemic.

The imperative to "get to" students to "evoke some kind of reaction" centers learners' affective states, but the potential to behave in ways that enable educators to regulate student emotions is treated as incompatible with Zoom teaching. The use of graduation ("some kind of") leaves it vague and ambiguous what kind of affect is desired, but it is differentiated from "performing excitement." Performing excitement is less a form of affect and emotion and acts here as more a normative social behavior associated with the classroom. While behaving with emotion and even enthusiasm is not the learners' job, inducing the right kinds of feelings is very much the teachers' job. The result is that Rachel must "accept" the situation of remote teaching, implying an ambivalent affective state in between satisfaction and dissatisfaction.

The idea that Zoom promised connection but in actuality resulted in feelings of disconnectedness was a common theme in the interviews. In answer to a question about how things were going with Zoom, Holly shared that she had a less clear sense of where students were as the semester progressed. This was in large part because students had increasingly opted to turn video cameras off, despite her encouragement that they might leave them on.

> But definitely the trend is that, like, well, even today, when I started my class, one of my classes that normally shows me at least half of their videos. Everybody was just black boxes – when I sent them to their first breakout room. So, like gradually more and more are not turning on their videos. And, so, then that just really changes the dynamic a little bit and, um, so, yes. I find it to be a little bit trickier. Just to even check in with where they are at in their language development. I like Zoom in that it has a lot like a lot of the cool engagement features for Zoom are really helpful for especially for things like comprehension. And they can they can write in the chat. But like there are so many of the engagement features are nonverbal, you know, like they can mark there, they can use the annotation tools and like, write on my screen share and they can do all of these things, but they're all – very little of it is to actually unmute and speak.

Holly noticed a difference between the start of the semester and later on when students started to turn their cameras off, becoming "just" a grid of black boxes on the screen. Like many other participants, Holly's expressed judgment of Zoom teaching based on how it was different from what she had been doing before the pandemic, but here she also sees a change in how students were interacting with the affordances of Zoom in that it became "trickier". She then goes on to express her appreciation of the technology, listing all the positive pedagogical features of Zoom, but at the end returns to absence of physical presence – not only are students not visible but they are not heard.

Ruth was the only participant to reference a critical stance vis-a-vis Zoom that circulated in the US news media with its rise in use during the pandemic, namely that the use of Zoom, as a proprietary platform might be "unethical." The concern here was around privacy issues that might arise when using a video-conferencing software with the potential of recording people's contribution. Although Ruth was the only one to raise this issue directly, this judgment is also tacitly referenced in the insistence from others, like Holly, that students could not be required, only encouraged, to turn cameras on.

Digital Communications Technologies

In addition to Zoom, the teachers we interviewed also named several digital communication tools that they used. These communication platforms that have been mentioned in the interviews include Discord, GroupMe, Slack, WhatsApp, and WeChat (Table 3).

The use of these technologies was often discursively associated with a desire to stay in touch with their students at a moment when the physical mandate to social distance was creating a sense of social and emotional isolation. This relates directly to two of the feeling rules we identified in our

Table 3 Participants' Use of Digital Communications Media

Pseudonym	Interview 1	Interview 2
Claudia	Discord	Discord
Kai	GroupMe, WhatsApp	WhatsApp
Nathaniel	GroupMe, WhatsApp	GroupMe
Regina	WhatsApp	
Ruth		Discord (student-initiated)
Tyler	Slack	
Ying	WeChat (for professional development)	GroupMe (student-initiated)
Yvonne	GroupMe	

earlier research: the need to establish/maintain personal connections to students and to create/maintain a sense of classroom community between students (see Warner & Diao, 2022). For example, Kai explained his rationale for choosing WhatsApp in his teaching:

> And then that also enables communication between me and students on cell phone because, because I kind of have a feeling that computer or email means something different than a cell phone. […] You know that the email platform is more formal, it's more educational. Oh, it's more hierarchical, you know? the teacher and the student. but on a cell phone so, I intentionally and consciously try to kind of lower my social status. You know, you know, I moved down in the power structure. So, kind of, I would sometimes even use some some emoji in some, hey, that kind of language. You know, it's a balance. It's just a balance. it's like, It's not my native language. So I tried not to, you know, be be too too not serious, but but I'm saying is I try to, to let them feel like the teacher is actually closer than they thought.

Through statements of appreciation, Kai discursively constructs a contrast between email/computer and social networking applications (e.g., GroupMe and WhatsApp); while the former is evaluated as "hierarchical" and "serious," the latter is viewed as a "balanced" approach that allowed the instructor to feel "closer" to the students.

Describing his use of the app GroupMe, another educator, Nathaniel, expressed a similar contrast between serious educational technologies and more familiar apps.

> I wanted there to be uh interaction. And I feel like that was lacking with the synchronous and asynchronous. And I also wanted students to have some sort of – not a group atmosphere, but you know, a place they can go. And because they would ask kind of random questions, some of them would start to, like, you know, playfully poke fun at each other, the ones that were friends, they'd be liking certain messages that, you know, there'd be some so that, and so I feel like and they said in that comment that they really enjoyed that, because that was because, you know, they missed being around each other for three days a week, ya know, and so I, I'm, you know, other colleagues used WhatsApp, and there's even programs to use, I just use GroupMe because I was familiar with that. And it Yeah, they, they really enjoyed it. I enjoyed having a daily interaction.

Nathaniel's evaluation that both synchronous and asynchronous remote teaching was somehow *lacking* is contrasted with the student's playful behavior on GroupMe. The aim of using these tools, as described by Nathanial, was to create a particular emotional experience for the students, one that would mimic a sense of "being around each other." Nathanial emphasizes the students' and his own affect at the end of this quote, repeating how much they and he "enjoyed" it.

While the participants named a total of six different tools that they were planning to incorporate in their communication with their students in the first interview, in the second round of interviews the number dropped to only four (see Table 3). A closer analysis of their interview discourse further corroborated this trend. For example, Claudia was "excited" about using Discord in the first interview, because the students were "already there."

> We are hoping that we're just going to get some traffic because people are already there [on Discord]. And so we're doing our office hours there. We're going to move German club into that area we're going to have some channels where… where we all share or leave links, and some other information. We're going to do tutorials there. […] I'm and I'm really looking forward to seeing how that works and… and whether that actually gives us some things that we didn't have when we were face to face. So that's what I'm excited about. I'm nervous that that all is not going to work at all.

Claudia's discussion of Discord in this first interview was saturated with affective expressions, such as "looking forward" and "excited." Although the orientation is overwhelmingly positive, she also admits to being "nervous" at the end. By the second interview, however, Claudia's excitement has seemingly faded. She admitted that "nobody" showed up during the tutorial time on Discord, despite her original expectation that it would provide a convenient access because the students were already using the technology.

> We also offered tutorials through Discord and whenever I do a tutorial, there's nobody there. So, it's okay. They don't have to come, but it was meant to be kind of the space where they can ask additional questions, if you just don't have the time to do in zoom.

Instead of the strong positive affect expressed in the first interview, Claudia's judgment of Discord changed to reluctant acceptance ("it's *okay*"). The qualitative change in her affect reveals another layer of the emotional experience during remote teaching; the humanizing outcome that teachers hoped to achieve through digital communications media was sometimes not well received, because virtual communication requires intentional and deliberate participation not only from the instructors, but also the students. In contrast to GroupMe and WhatsApp, the Discord tutorials planned by Claudia prioritized synchronous, virtually co-present participation. This raises questions about what presence and connectivity meant for students during the pandemic and how their proclivities and desires intersected with educators attempts to enact emotion labor.

In at least two of the emergency remote classes described by our participants the creation of digital communities using communication apps was initiated or managed entirely by their students (Discord for Ruth and GroupMe for Ying). In her second interview, Ying described how this development took place in her class.

> A lot of college students nowadays use GroupMe, and we have like a group chat for our sections. [...] because I guess because I was involved in the group chat, they didn't talk very often, but I know they have a separate group chat amongst students themselves. [...] I created the GroupMe chat on the first day saying like, oh, we're going to use that to do handwriting dictation to to – as the channel for it to ask questions, because I might not be able to check my emails very frequently. So, if you have if you have emergent questions just shoot me a message through through GroupMe and also asking the group chat would be a good way to share answers. So and also I encouraged them to share whatever the you know the happenings in their daily lives, though, like interesting things. No one shares that in the chat.

Ying's approach was similar to Claudia's at the outset, in that she chose a platform, which many of her students were already using, and like Nathanial she hoped to fill in a gap in communication where other technologies like email might be lacking. Ying evaluated this both as a "good" classroom tool, a place where students could post questions and have them answered more quickly, but also as a space for promoting social–emotional connections, sharing "interesting" things, as was emphasized by Kai and Nathanial. However, Ying suggests that the students did not end up sharing these group chats, but that they appeared to do so in private student groups. While the affective associations with digital communications apps may have typically been informal and playful, as we saw in Kai and Nathanial's discussions, Ying's experience points to ways in which these emotions became unstuck in some cases as teachers co-opted these social apps for institutional, educational purposes.

Discussion

The findings of our interview research re-affirm the centrality of emotions and emotion labor in language teaching (Gkonou & Miller, 2019, 2021; Miller & Gkonou, 2018, 2020) and illustrate how feelings rules became even more of a focal concern in remote language education during the pandemic (Warner & Diao, 2022). In the present chapter, we have built upon our earlier findings to consider the particular affective relations associated with those technologies that were seemingly most pervasive during emergency remote teaching, videoconferencing apps (specifically Zoom) and digital communication apps (e.g. GroupMe, WhatsApp, and Discord) as these manifest during the earlier months of the COVID pandemic.

Zoom was adopted by many campuses wholesale, which meant that it became the default technology for many classrooms during emergency remote teaching. As a rapidly adopted medium for emergency remote teaching, Zoom was sticky with ambivalent emotions. With the exception of program directors like Regina, who asked instructors to seek out what was for them the "happier" communications medium, Zoom teaching was for the majority of educators in this study simply a happy medium, an "okay" way to interact and connect during a moment of collective crisis when getting by with what was available and worked fine was deemed a social and pedagogical good (compare Benesch, 2017). This also seemed to lead to an immediate feeling of reassurance experienced by the educators, expressed in the chorus of "we're going to be okay" in the interviews with Rachel, Regina, Erika and others. Many of the participants, even those who were first uncertain about Zoom, saw an opportunity to enact feeling rules because the synchronous video platform allows them to check in on students' emotional states and remain connected with them. At the same time, this was only effective insofar as students were willing to engage; in Holly's case the experience of teaching to rows of black boxes heightened feelings of disconnection.

To augment or in some cases replace the connectivity of the Zoom classroom, most of the participants quickly and creatively adopted freely available digital communications technologies, such as GroupMe, WhatsApp, Discord, etc. In this way the educators went beyond their institutionally endorsed tools (e.g., Zoom) and seized upon technologies which they had identified as more familiar to students from their everyday lives. In some cases (e.g., Kai and Nathanial) this appeared to be a successful way of establishing more informal interactions, while in other cases (e.g., Claudia and Ying) the teachers' initial evaluations of these technologies as *good* did not match the behaviors of students. The result was that students did not engage or show up in the more casual ways desired by the teachers, perhaps because emotional stickiness of the classroom context was simply not enough for the informal, playful attachments students might have to those apps to persevere.

Our findings here rebuke the assumption that the language educators simply felt all at a loss in the context of remote teaching. While some participants felt unprepared to teach on Zoom, they also experienced excitement about the prospect of working with new technologies and their attention to what college students might already be using. These positive feelings were in some cases tempered as the actual experience of remote teaching unfolded and evolved. This is often seen in the data as a contrast between what the educators appreciated about the technological affordances and their judgment of behaviors that arose, e.g., turning off cameras during class. In contrast to some of the earlier studies of language teaching during the pandemic, our findings suggest that the assessment that teachers were unprepared is oversimplified; rather, language educators were learning to work with technologies in new ways on the fly while navigating complex webs of emotional entanglements associated with those same tools – all within the context of unprecedented social and physical precarity. Even in cases where the technologies did seem to support affective connections, the result was sometimes uncomfortable amounts of emotion labor as teachers became stuck to their devices. For example, Nathanial expressed feeling like he was "married to the phone" – an affective attachment that captures the slipperiness between personal and professional time created when feelings rules compel teachers to be continually available.

Conclusion

Technologies are emotionally sticky objects (Ahmed 2004). The teachers' recounts in this study suggest that in some moments, despite educators' intentions to realize a pedagogy of care using Zoom and digital communications apps, the potential affective states and appreciated affordances associated with these tools resisted the movement to the classroom. In a study of digital gaming in the language classroom, Reinhardt et al. (2014) similarly argued that the experience of a digital practice in the classroom is phenomenologically distinct from its use outside of the classroom use. Likewise, digital communication technologies brought not only their technological affordances but their emotional attachments. As a result, the ease of digital connectivity did not always translate into the kinds of social and emotional connection teachers sought to enact through their efforts at digitally mediated emotion labor. A core implication for teacher professional learning is that deliberate reflection on the affective dimensions of technology-mediated teaching and learning must be a part of what it means to prepare educators to work in new modalities.

If the field of second language teaching and learning is to take away lessons from the pandemic about the role of technology in language education, future research must continue to investigate the complex negotiations of affect between teachers, students, and digital tools in online language teaching. The expressions of judgment and appreciation highlighted in our analysis of the educators' discourses around emergency remote teaching show that they were discerning about technology and its potential uses; however, the centrality of affect also points to the reality that any future discussions of how to better prepare teachers must consider not only what different digital tools do but also how they feel. This ought to include not only careful and nuanced reflection on the potential of technology for enacting emotion labor, but also on the nuances of connectivity, that is on the range of affective relationships between connected or disconnected, and how these come into play in different teaching and learning arrangements.

About the Authors

Chantelle Warner is Professor of German Studies and Second Language Acquisition and Teaching at the University of Arizona (Tucson, Arizona). She co-directs the Center for Educational Resources in Culture, Language and Literacy (CERCLL), a National Language Resource Center supported by the US Department of Education. Dr. Warner's research focuses on affective, experiential, and aesthetic dimensions of language use and intercultural learning and second language literacy development. Her current book project argues for an expansion of models of second language literacy to better address the aesthetic and feeling rules that tacitly shape responses to different language uses.

Wenhao Diao is Associate Professor of East Asian Studies and Second Language Acquisition and Teaching at the University of Arizona (Tucson, Arizona), where she also co-directs the Title VI Center for East Asian Studies. She is interested in identities and ideologies that are (re)produced and (re) distributed in Chinese language teaching and learning. Her publications have appeared in journals such as *Applied Linguistics*, *Modern Language Journal*, *System*, among others. She also co-edited *Language Learning in Study*

Abroad: The Multilingual Turn (Multilingual Matters, 2021) and a special issue Study Abroad in the 21st Century for the *L2 Journal* in 2016.

References

Ahmed, Sara. (2004). *Cultural Politics of Emotion*. Edinburgh University Press.

Ahmed, Sara. (2010). Happy Objects. In M. Gregg & G. J. Seigworth (Eds.) *The Affect Theory Reader* (pp. 29–51). Duke University Press.

Alger, M., & Eyckmans, J. (2022). "I took physical lessons for granted": A case study exploring students' interpersonal interactions in online synchronous lessons during the outbreak of COVID-19. *System*, *105*, 1–18. doi: 10.1016/j.system.2021.102716

Appel, C., & Robbins, J. (2021). Language teaching in times of COVID-19: The emotional rollercoaster of lockdown. In J. Chen (Ed.) *Emergency Remote Teaching and Beyond* (pp. 3–22). Springer. https://doi.org/10.1007/978-3-030-84067-9_1

Back, M., Golembeski, K., Gutiérrez, A., Macko, T., Miller, S., & Pelletier, D. (2021). "We were told that the content we delivered was not as important": Disconnect and disparities in world language student teaching during COVID-19, *System*, *103*, 1–11. doi: 10.1016/j.system.2021.102679

Benesch, S. (2017). *Emotions and English language teaching: Exploring teachers' emotion labor.* Routledge. https://doi.org/10.4324/9781315736181

Benesch, S. (2018). Emotions as agency: Feeling rules, emotion labor, and English language teachers' decision-making. *System*,*79*, 60–69. doi: 10.1016/j.system.2018.03.015

Benesch, S. (2019). Feeling rules and emotion labor: A poststructural-discursive approach to English language teachers' emotions. In X. Gao (Ed.), *Second handbook of English language teaching* (pp. 1111–1130). Springer International Handbooks of Education. https://doi.org/10.1007/978-3-030-02899-2_57

Besser, A., Flett, G. L., & Zeigler-Hill, V. (2022). Adaptability to a sudden transition to online learning during the COVID-19 pandemic: Understanding the challenges for students. *Scholarship of Teaching and Learning in Psychology*, *8*(2), 85–105. doi: 10.1037/stl0000198

Cheung, A. (2021). Language teaching during a pandemic: A case study of zoom use by a secondary ESL teacher in Hong Kong. *RELC Journal*, *0*, 1–16. doi: 10.1177/0033688220981784

Cowie, N. (2011). Emotions that experienced English as a Foreign Language (EFL) teachers feel about their students, their colleagues and their work. *Teaching and Teacher Education*, *27*(1), 235–242. doi: doi.org/10.1016/j.tate.2010.08.006

Creswell, J. W. (2013). *Qualitative inquiry & research design: Choosing among five approaches.* Thousand Oaks, CA.

Gilmore, S., & Warren, S. (2007). Emotion online: Experiences of teaching in a virtual learning environment. *Human Relations*, *60*(4), 581–608. doi: 10.1177/001872670707835

Gkonou, C., & Miller, E. (2019). Caring and emotional labour: Language teachers' engagement with anxious learners in private language school classrooms. *Language Teaching Research*, *23*(3), 372–387. doi: 10.1177/1362168817728739

Gkonou, C., & Miller, E. (2021). An exploration of language teacher reflection, emotion labor, and emotional capital. *TESOL Quarterly*, *55*(1), 134–155. doi: 10.1002/tesq.580

Guillén, G., Sawin, T., & Avineri, N. (2020). Zooming out of the crisis: Language and human collaboration. *Foreign Language Annals*, *53*, 320–328. doi: 10.1111/flan.12459

Hakim, B. (2020). Technology integrated online classrooms and the challenges faced by the EFL teachers in Saudi Arabia during the COVID-19 pandemic. *International Journal of Applied Linguistics & English Literature*, *9*(5), 33–39. http://dx.doi.org/10.7575/aiac.ijalel.v.9n.5p.33

Hargreaves, A. (2000). Mixed emotions: Teachers' perceptions of their interactions with students. *Teaching and Teacher Education*, *16* (8), 811–826. doi: 10.1016/S0742-051X(00)00028-7

Hochschild, A. (2012[1983]). *The managed heart: Commercialization of human feeling* (3rd edition). Berkeley: University of California Press.

Hodges, C., Moore, S., Lockee, B., Trust, T., & Bond, A. (2020). The difference between emergency remote teaching and online learning. *Educause*, March 27, 2020. *https://er.educause.edu/articles/2020/3/the-difference-between-emergency-remote-teaching-and-online-learning*.

Jones, A., & Kessler, M. (2020). Teachers' emotion and identity work during a pandemic. *Frontiers in Education*, *5*. doi: 10.3389/feduc.2020.583775

King, J. (2016). "It's time, put on the smile, it's time!": The emotional labor of second language teaching within a Japanese university. In C. Gkonou, D. Tatzl, & S. Mercer (Eds.), *New directions in language learning psychology* (pp. 97–112). International Publishing.

Kohnke, L., & Moorhouse, B. (2022). Facilitating synchronous online language learning through Zoom. *RELC Journal*, *53*(1), 296–301. doi: 10.1177/00336882209372

Krsmanovic, I. (2022). "Unmute, please!": Tertiary lecturers' perceptions on emergency remote English language teaching during COVID-19 pandemics. *European Journal of Interactive Multimedia and Education*, *3*(2), 1–10. http://dx.doi.org/10.30935/ejimed/12272

Lee, S., & Ogawa, C. (2021). Online teaching self-efficacy – How English teachers feel during the Covid-19 pandemic. *Indonesian TESOL Journal*, *3*(1), 1–17. doi: 10.24256/itj.v3i1.1744

Li, J., Xu, Y., Deifell, E., & Angus, K. (2021). Emergency remote language teaching and U.S.-Based college-level world language educators' intention to adopt online teaching in postpandemic times. *Modern Language Journal*, *105*(2), 412–434. doi: 10.1111/modl.12712

Liu, S., Yuan, R., & Wang, C. (2021). "Let emotion ring": An autoethnographic self-study of an EFL instructor in Wuhan during COVID-19. *Language Teaching Research*, 1–21. doi: 10.1177/13621688211053498

Looney, D., & Lusin, N. (2019). Enrollments in languages other than English in United States institutions of higher education, summer 2016 and fall 2016: Final report. Retrieved from https://www.mla.org/content/download/110154/2406932/ 2016-Enrollments-Final-Report.pdf

MacIntyre, P., Mercer, S., Gregerson, T., Hay, A. (2022). The role of hope in language teachers' changing stress, coping, and well-being. *System*, *109*, 1–14. doi: 10.1016/j.system.2022.102881

Maican, M.-A., & Cocorada, E. (2021). Online foreign language learning in higher education and its correlates during the COVID-19 pandemic. *Sustainability*, *13*(2), 1–21. doi: 10.3390/su13020781

Martin, J. R., and White, P. R. R. (2005). *The language of evaluation: Appraisal in English*. Springer.

Martin, J., & White, P. R. R. (2007). *The language of evaluation: Appraisal in English*. Palgrave Macmillan.

McAlinden, M., & Dobinson, T. (2022). Teacher emotion in emergency online teaching: Ecstasies and agonies. In J. Chen (Ed.) *Emergency Remote Teaching and Beyond: Voices from World Language Teachers and Researchers* (pp. 261–287). Springer.

Meirovitz, T., Russak, S., & Zur, A. (2022). English as a foreign language teachers' perceptions regarding their pedagogical-technological knowledge and its implementation in distance learning during COVID-19. *Heliyon*, *8*(4), 1–7. doi: 10.1016/j.heliyon.2022.e09175

Miller, E., & Gkonou, C. (2018). Language teacher agency, emotion labor and emotional rewards in tertiary-level English language programs. *System*, *79*, 49–59. doi: 10.1016/j.system.2018.03.002

Miller, E., & Gkonou, C. (2020). "Critical incidents" in language teachers' narratives of emotional experience. In C. Gkonou, J.-M. Dewaele, & J. King (Eds.). *The emotional rollercoaster of language teaching* (pp. 131–149). De Gruyter. https://doi.org/10.21832/9781788928342-012

Moser, K., Wei, T., & Brenner, D. (2021). Remote teaching during COVID-19: Implications from a national survey of language educators. *System*, *97*, 1–15. doi: 10.1016/j.system.2020.102431

Nias, J. (1996). Thinking about feeling: The emotions in teaching. *Cambridge Journal of Education*, *26*, 293–306. doi: 10.1080/0305764960260301

Noddings, N. (2013). *Caring: A relational approach to ethics & moral education* (2nd edition). University of California Press.

Pham, L. T. T., & Phan, A. N. Q. (2023). "Let's accept it": Vietnamese university language teachers' emotion in online synchronous teaching in response to COVID-19. *Educational and Developmental Psychologist*, *40*(1), 115–124. doi: 10.1177/14782103231178644

Reinhardt, J., Warner, C., & Lange, K. (2014). Digital games as practices and texts: New literacies and genres in an L2 German classroom. In J. Pettes-Guikema, J. & L. Williams (Eds.), *Digital Literacies in Foreign Language Education: Research, Perspectives, and Best Practices* (Calico Monograph) (pp. 159–177). CALICO Monograph Series, V. 12. CALICO.

Resnik, P., & Dewaele, J-M. (2023). Learner emotions, autonomy and trait emotional intelligence in "in-person" versus emergency remote English foreign language teaching in Europe. *Applied Linguistics Review*, *8*, 1–28. https://doi.org/10.1515/applirev-2020-0096

Saldaña, J. (2016). *The coding manual for qualitative researchers* (3rd edition). Thousand Oaks, CA: SAGE.

Tafazoli, D., & Meihami, H. (2022). Narrative inquiry for CALL teacher preparation programs amidst the COVID-19 pandemic: Language teachers' technological needs and suggestions. *Journal of Computers in Education*, *10*, 1–25. https://doi.org/10.1007/s40692-022-00227-x

Yuan, K., & Liu, S. (2021). Understanding EFL instructor identity changes during online teaching in the COVID-19 pandemic: A case study in China. *RELC Journal*, *0*(0), 1–17. http://dx.doi.org/10.1177/00336882211066622

Warner, C., & Diao, W. (2022). Caring is pedagogy: Foreign language teachers' emotion labor in crisis. *Linguistics and Education*, *71*(1–12), 29–51. doi: 10.1016/j.linged.2022.101100

Zembylas, M. (2005). Discursive practices, genealogies, and emotional rules: A poststructuralist view on emotion and identity in teaching. *Teaching and Teacher Education*, *21*(8), 935–948. doi: 10.1016/j.tate.2005.06.005

13 Predicting Success in Difficult Times: A Latent Class Analysis of World Language – Teachers' Online Experience During the COVID-19 Pandemic

Marta Tecedor and Inmaculada Gómez Soler

Introduction

The COVID-19 health crisis prompted an unprecedented global move to online instruction that forced language teachers to redefine their roles as instructors and their relationship with technology. This crisis also highlighted shortcomings regarding teachers' digital skills and their lack of appropriate training and, at the same time, their resilience and ability to adapt their teaching in difficult circumstances. Our study examines teachers' attitudes towards online teaching and their experiences during the first months of the pandemic, a time when their ability to deliver quality instruction under stressful circumstances was under public scrutiny. Teachers faced this challenging time with varying levels of digital skills, access to resources, training and support as discussed in many of the previous chapters. Still, their ability to navigate these circumstances marked not only their own experience but also that of their students. Thus, understanding how teachers interpreted the transition to online teaching is crucial to preparing for future crises—e.g., social unrest (e.g., Gokool & Naidoo, Chapter 3, this volume), natural disasters, health crises—and preempting the challenges that could prompt school closures and require a move towards online teaching.

In the last few decades, the rapid development of information and communication technologies (ICT) has improved and expanded distance education both quantitatively and qualitatively (Bozkurt, 2019). We have also seen the development of frameworks related to teachers' and students' digital competence that serve as roadmaps for digital skill development. For instance, in Europe, the *European Framework for the Digital Competence of Educators* (*DigCompEdu*) (Redecker, 2017) provides guidelines for the development of digital skills with descriptors applicable to all levels of education from early childhood to higher and adult education, including general and vocational education and training, special needs education, and non-formal learning contexts. In the US, the *American Council on the Teaching of Foreign Languages* (ACTFL) developed the *21st Century Skills Map* (ACTFL, 2011) that highlights the importance of information, media and technology literacy for language students and, in turn, for teachers.

Despite these advances and a solid body of research on the effectiveness of online instruction (Hampel & Stickler, 2005; Plonsky & Ziegler, 2016; Stickler & Hampel, 2015), by the time the COVID-19 crisis struck in March 2020, many educators still resisted using educational technology and doubted its effectiveness (Jaschik & Lederman, 2018; Kessler, 2017). Additionally, the pandemic also highlighted teachers' lack of digital competence as many struggled to adapt to an online environment under these challenging circumstances. A number of studies and position papers (e.g., Gacs et al., 2020; Hodges et al., 2020; Lee, 2021; Paesani, 2020; Tarrayo et al., 2023; Xu et al., 2022) have highlighted the distinction between planned and crisis-prompted teaching, stressing that the emergency remote language teaching (ERLT) that took place during the pandemic lacked the systematicity and coherence that characterize planned online teaching.

This study adds to the literature by providing specific training solutions that address the challenges and training shortcomings reported by language educators. The study is framed within the construct of attitudes, which is defined in the field of applied linguistics as an individual's response to, or evaluation of, an object or task (Petty et al., 2003). It is a complex and multifaceted construct that encompasses emotions, beliefs, and behaviors. While some of its sources are situation-specific, others are rooted in past experiences with the task and/or the tools at hand (Bandura, 1991). Training has been shown to challenge and modify teachers' attitudes (Chao, 2015; Ertmer, 2005) and even their own professional identity (Comas-Quinn, 2011). By examining teachers' attitudes towards online teaching during the first months of the pandemic and exploring the factors—type of institution, years of teaching experience, training, etc.—that predict them, this study aims to provide effective and sustainable training initiatives.

Literature Review

Language Teachers' Attitudes Towards Online Teaching and Learning

Despite the fact that online learning has been part of the educational landscape for centuries in different shapes or forms (Kentnor, 2015), teacher reticence towards this teaching mode has been widely documented (e.g., Mitchell et al., 2014). Before the pandemic, for instance, a large-scale survey (2,335 participants) from *Inside Higher Ed* (Jaschik & Lederman, 2018) shed light on this topic. Almost 50% of respondents, which included teachers of all subjects and digital learning leaders, considered face-to-face teaching more effective than online teaching (Jaschik & Lederman, 2018).

In the field of language teaching, a number of post-pandemic studies have documented teachers' challenges with online teaching. Moser et al. (2021) used a survey to examine the challenges experienced by US preK-12 and postsecondary teachers (n=377) and looked into how prior experiences with online teaching shaped their perceptions of ERLT. According to their findings, PreK-12 teachers experienced more challenges, likely due to complications derived from educational inequalities such as students' lack of technology, as well as to issues beyond their control (e.g., in many cases they were mandated not to engage with students in order to prioritize other subjects) that shaped their perceptions of the ERLT. Jin et al. (2021) collected data from 662 world language teachers in the US via a survey to identify factors that had a positive influence on participants' future intention to teach online. Although most participants seemed optimistic about the idea and reported that the ERLT experience helped them value the affordances of online teaching, some reported reaffirming their previous beliefs about online teaching as incompatible with language teaching, less than an ideal teaching environment, and disliked by students. Bachiri and Sahli (2020) examined the experiences of English teachers in Morocco—a society where ICT are not prevalent— through a questionnaire and participant observation. While highlighting some positive outcomes from their distance learning experience such as more creative activities using videos, games, and software-based learning, participants also described challenges related to content, pedagogy, assessment and evaluation. Digital inequality and access to resources were, in this context, crucial issues that manifested in a lack of digital literacy. Junaidi et al. (2022) used an online survey to investigate ESL teachers' (n=124) perspectives and attitudes towards online teaching during the COVID-19 pandemic in Malaysia. The results of the study revealed that despite the challenges reported by participants, e.g., territorial (urban-rural) and digital inequalities (both in terms of infrastructure and resources and also digital literacy), overall they held positive attitudes towards online teaching, and highlighted the support they received from colleagues as one of the most positive aspects of the experience.

Particularly relevant for our study is how experience in online teaching shapes teachers' attitudes towards online learning. Two studies shed light on these issues. Moser et al. (2021) found that teachers without previous experience with online teaching felt less confident in their ability to meet the goals they had set for their students through ERLT, indicating that previous experience with online teaching was an asset for this group of participants. Additionally, Moser et al. (2021) also found that pre-K12 teachers had more difficulty navigating online teaching during the pandemic as compared to their peers in higher education. In Jin et al.'s (2021) study, however, training and support during ERLT were not found to be significant predictors of language teachers' intention to teach online in the future. Additionally, teachers reported a lack of language-specific training, which influenced their feeling of preparedness. These studies reveal that, despite initial reticence regarding online teaching, teachers rose to the challenge of virtual instruction during the global pandemic. Different factors shaped their attitudes towards online teaching—support from colleagues, their previous beliefs and experiences, training, etc.—but these were also highly dependent on the context in which participants operated and the resources and infrastructure available in such contexts.

Language Teachers' Competencies and Training in Online Teaching and Learning

Understanding the skills teachers need to teach online is essential to both assessing current approaches to training and designing new ones that effectively allow teachers to develop said competences. Undoubtedly, online teaching requires different skills than face-to-face teaching, something that was at the core of the struggles teachers faced during the pandemic. Various models (e.g., *DigCompEdu*, *21st Century Skills Map*) have attempted to capture these abilities. One of the most influential is that of Hampel and Stickler (2005), which presents, in a pyramidal form, the seven skills that teachers need to master online teaching: Basic ICT competence; specific technical competence for the software; dealing with the constraints and possibilities of the medium; online socialization; facilitating communicative competence; creativity and choices; and own style. Another prominent model is the TPACK model discussed in chapter two (Jin et al., Chapter 2, this volume).

However, despite the existence of frameworks such as these, which identify the skills that should be developed in training programs, the training that teachers actually receive is not always effective or sufficient. For example, in a study on Spanish teachers in training in the US, Gómez Soler and Tecedor (2018) concluded that training in the field of technology was based mostly on how to use tools to practice formal aspects of the language, indicating that the training related to digital competence is in many cases at an incipient state. When comparing training in language, culture and technology, it was observed that technology training was perceived as less effective and transferable to advanced level courses than training in the area of language, although more effective and transferable than culture training.

Especially relevant for the current study, then, are publications that delineate optimal training practices. In the context of the COVID-19 health crisis, Paesani (2020) described the approach to training received by teachers in the first months of the pandemic as a *survival approach* (p. 293). This training included aspects such as directing teachers to use Zoom, providing them with workshops to learn how to use several online tools, publishing "tip of the day" and success stories, and curating a list of resources. According to the author, although this training played an essential role in avoiding the interruption of classes, it should be interpreted as an emergency measure, not as a model that should be replicated, since it is not a coherent or sustainable approach in the long term. Paesani insisted that effective training must be oriented towards clear objectives in addition to being collaborative, experiential, scaffolded and sustainable. In a pre-pandemic study, Comas-Quinn (2011) highlighted the important role that attitudes play in the reception of training initiatives. The author argued that training, to be effective, must help teachers to accept the identity changes associated with pedagogical model modifications. Thus, Comas-Quinn argued that training should not focus solely on the ability to use specific tools, but rather on helping teachers develop a critical attitude towards technology and learn to independently explore the functional possibilities of any resource that they may find in the future (Chao, 2015). Warner and Diao (Chapter 12, this volume) would add the need for teachers to navigate the emotional and affective relations to technology.

The current study provides a snapshot of what it meant for teachers to transition to online teaching during the first months of the COVID-19 pandemic at a global scale. By exploring teachers' attitudes towards online teaching as well as the training they received during the first months of the health crisis and the challenges they experienced, we aim to offer training-based solutions that can be implemented at a large scale in different countries and settings. The following research questions guide this investigation:

1. What are language teachers' attitudes towards online teaching?
2. What factors predict instructors' attitude towards online teaching?

3. How did training received during the first months of the Covid-19 crisis differ according to attitude group?
4. What challenges did teachers from the different attitude groups experience during the transition to online teaching?

Methods

Participants

A total of 308 FL teachers from 43 countries on five continents completed the survey: Austria, Chile, Colombia, Dominican Republic, Finland, Ghana, Hong Kong, India, Indonesia, Israel, Mexico, Norway, Rumania, South Korea, South Africa (1); Argentina, Portugal (2); Belgium, Greece, Morocco, Tunisia, Turkey (3); Bulgaria, Canada, Hungary, Japan, Jordan, New Zealand, Poland (4); China, France, Russia, Netherlands (5); Czech Republic, Italy, Not reported (6); Brazil, Australia (8); Algeria (11); Germany (15); Spain (21); United Kingdom (31); Ireland (45); US (69).

Regarding languages taught, most of them (n=224) taught Spanish, followed by English (n=23), French (n=13), German (n=4), Italian (n=3), Chinese, Portuguese, Hebrew, Early Irish, Polish (n=1). Twenty-eight participants taught more than one language. Table 1 shows the distribution of participants according to the type of institution, years of experience teaching, and years of experience teaching online.

Table 1 Participants' Institutions and Experience

Institution	Primary and secondary	34.1% (n = 105)
	Language school	21.8% (n = 98)
	University	34.1% (n = 105)
Years teaching language	1–5	23.7% (n = 73)
	6–15	35.1% (n = 108)
	> 15	41.2% (n = 127)
Years teaching online	0 years	71.1% (n = 219)
	1–5 years	18.2% (n = 56)
	6–15 years	6.8% (n = 21)
	> 15	3.9% (n = 12)
Technology training before the pandemic	Yes	31.2% (n = 96)
	No	68.2 % (n = 212)
Technology training during the pandemic	Yes	70.1% (n = 216)
	No	29.9% (n = 92)

Instrument

An online survey designed by the authors (IRIS) was used as a data collection tool. The survey contained 4 sections: Demographics (5 questions); online teaching during COVID-19: Practices and challenges (5 questions); training for online teaching (4 questions); and attitudes about online teaching (16 questions). This last section contained randomized Likert-scale questions in the following domains: enjoyment of online teaching (3 questions); self-efficacy in the virtual environment (5 questions); effectiveness of online teaching (2 questions); transferability of online teaching to post pandemic times (4 questions); effectiveness of the training received (2 questions).

Data Collection

Between June and August 2020, a Google Forms survey was distributed via announcements on social network sites, such as Facebook and Twitter, on distribution lists of associations of world language teachers in different countries, and through emails to schools, universities and headquarters of private language schools.

Data Analysis

To determine the underlying attitude structure toward online teaching, a latent class analysis (LCA) was conducted on the last section of the survey (i.e., attitudes towards online teaching). This statistical procedure models the relationships between observed variables and identifies the number of latent classes that best describes the relationship between them (Garson, 2009), that is, the LCA detects significant trends and classifies participants into groups according to the probability that they will present a similar response pattern in their responses to the survey questions (Monroy, et al., 2010). The analysis typically estimates several models, which are compared using two measures of goodness of fit—the Bayesian Information Criterion (BIC) and the Akaike Information Criterion (AIC). These two measures indicate a better fit to the data the lower their value. Once the model that best described the data was identified, a multinomial logistic regression was used to determine which of the variables were predictive of instructors' attitude toward online learning. Finally, descriptive statistics were used to examine the content of the training received during the first months of the health crisis and the challenges experienced by participants.

Results

RQ1 Language Teachers' Attitudes Towards Online Teaching

Research question 1 examined instructors' underlying attitude structure toward online teaching in five domains: enjoyment, self-efficacy, effectiveness, transferability, and effectiveness of training received. The results from the LCA produced two possible models: one with three classes and one with four. The AIC and BIC indicators produced contradictory results: the AIC selected the four-class model (three-class model = 18397.76; four-class model = 18259.21) and the BIC the three-class model (three-class model = 19389.97; four-class model = 19583.4). Therefore, the conceptual interpretability criterion was used to identify the most appropriate and parsimonious model, that is, the model with the least number of classes. Using this criterion, the three-class model turned out to be not only the easiest to interpret, but the model in which all groups had a high percentage of membership: the model correctly classified 97.4% of the participants according to their attitude towards online teaching: Negative Attitude Class (NegAC) (n=97; 31.5%); Neutral Attitude Class (NAC) (n=145; 47.1%); and Positive Attitude Class (PAC) (n=66; 21.42%).

As can be seen in Figure 1, the results of the analysis revealed that the three classes present similar response profiles, but at different points on the scale: for most of the constructs, the mean response of teachers with a negative attitude is between 1.5 and 2.5 ("I disagree"); for teachers with a neutral attitude the mean response is between 3 and 3.5 ("Neither agree nor disagree"); and for teachers with a positive attitude, the mean is above four ("Agree"). Exceptions to this pattern are found in the construct of "Transferability," for which the average response of participants with negative and neutral attitudes rises slightly (almost to 3 for NegAC and above 3.5 for NAC), indicating that they recognize, to some degree, the value of the knowledge and skills they have acquired during their short experience teaching online. In contrast, the mean response of instructors with a positive attitude decreased slightly, particularly for Transferability 1 (i.e., flipped instruction) and Transferability 4 (i.e., assessment) questions, which could be indicative of their greater understanding of the distinction between planned and crisis-prompted teaching.

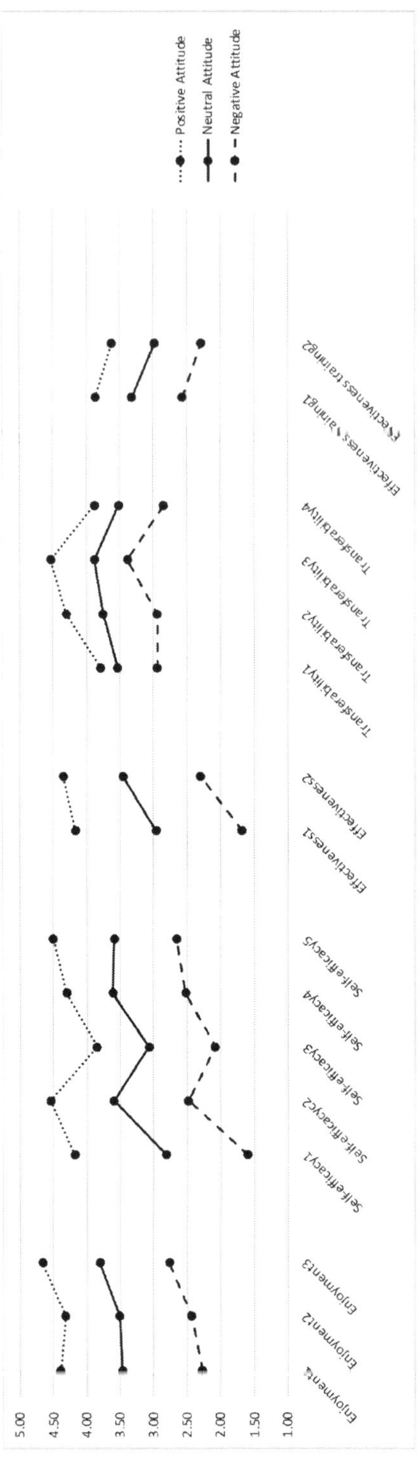

Figure 1 Underlying Participants' Attitude Structure Toward Online Teaching

RQ2 Factors that Predict Instructors' Attitude Towards Online Teaching

The second research question examined the relationship between the independent variables and the three classes. Multinomial logistic regression estimates the probability of participants belonging to one of the three classes depending on the values of each of the independent variables while the values of the other variables in the model remain constant. The results of the analysis revealed that the variables *Teaching experience*, *Training during the pandemic*, and the interaction between *Institution* and *Training before the pandemic* were predictors in the model, while *Years teaching online* was not a significant predictor for any of the classes. Table 2 shows the predictive probabilities for each of the independent variables. The comparisons that were found to be significant in the regression are indicated in bold.

Table 2 Predictive Probabilities by Group

	Positive Attitude		Neutral Attitude		Negative Attitude	
	Probability	CI	Probability	CI	Probability	CI
Teaching experience						
1–5 years	.24	.14–.34	**.55**	.44–.66	.21	.13–.29
6–15 years	.24	.16–.31	**.46**	.37–.56	.30	.23–.38
> 15 years	.18	.12–.24	.31	.33–.5	**.40**	.32–.48
Training during						
Yes	.20	.15–.25	**.55**	.48–.61	.25	.2–.3
No	.23	.15–.31	.29	.2–.38	**.48**	.38–.58
Institution#Training						
before	.05	0–.09	.44	.34–.55	**.51**	.4–.62
Primary & secondary#no	.19	.02–.35	**.57**	.36–.78	.25	.07–.43
Primary & secondary#yes						
	.32	.19–.44	**.59**	.46–.72	.01	.03–.16
Language schools#no	**.54**	.29–.6	.35	.19–.5	.21	.08–.34
Language schools#yes						
	.13	.05–.2	**.44**	.32–.55	**.44**	.33–.55
University#no	**.57**	.29–.65	.32	.22–.55	.14	.01–.27
University#yes						

Teaching Experience

The results from the multinomial logistic regression revealed that participants with more than 15 years of experience had a higher relative risk ratio of belonging to the NegAC than to the NAC or the PAC. Bonferroni posthoc results indicate that these participants were significantly different from those with less than five years of experience (RRR=.31; z=-2.88; p=.008; CI=.12–.77) but not from those with 6 to 15 years of experience (RRR=.59; z=-1.51; p=.26; CI=.27–1.28). The analysis did not yield significant differences between teachers with less than 5 years of experience and those with 6 to 15 years of experience (RRR=.53; z=-1.61; p=.21; CI=.22–1.28). In terms of predictive probability, teachers with more than 15 years of experience had higher probability (i.e., .40) of being assigned to NegAC. In contrast, Instructors with less than 5 years of experience or with 6 to 15 years of experience had a higher probability of being assigned to NAC, .55 and .46 respectively.

Training During the Pandemic

The results of the analysis indicate that instructors who received training during the first months of the COVID-19 sanitary crisis had a higher relative risk ratio of belonging to the NAC than to the NegAC or the PAC. The analysis also revealed that this group was significantly different from the group of participants who did not receive training during the pandemic (RRR=4.24; z=-4.18; p=.000; CI=2.16–8.35). When looking at the results in terms of predictive probability, it can be observed that participants who received training had a higher probability of being assigned to NAC (i.e., .55) than to any of the other two groups. In contrast, participants who did not receive training had a higher probability of being assigned to the NegAC (i.e., .48), than to the NAC or the NPC.

Institution *and* Training Before

The results of the analysis indicate that, overall, teachers who received training before the start of the health crisis on how to teach online expressed a more positive attitude towards this teaching model, while teachers who did not receive training beforehand expressed primarily negative and neutral attitudes. Bonferroni posthoc results indicate that participants working in language schools were significantly different from those working in primary or secondary schools (RRR=.25; z=-2.66; p=.01; CI=.07–.8) and in universities (RRR=.18; z=2.72; p=.01; CI=1.28–12.8). In terms of predictive probability, instructors who work at primary and secondary schools and did not receive training on online teaching before the COVID-19 pandemic had a .51 predictive probability of being assigned to the NegAC. In contrast, those who had received training before the pandemic had a .57 predictive probability of being assigned to NAC. Instructors working at language schools who did not receive training before the pandemic had .59 predictive probability of being assigned to the NAC. If they had received training, they had .54 predictive probability of being assigned to the PAC. Instructors at the tertiary level who had not received training before the beginning of the health crisis had a .44 predictive probability of being assigned to either the NegAC and the NAC. If they had received training, however, they had a .57 predictive probability of being assigned to the PAC.

RQ3 Training During the First Months of the COVID-19 Health Crisis

Research question 3 examined the relationship between the training received during the first months of the pandemic and the three classes. As can be seen in Figure 2, the content of the training, as reported by participants, was pretty similar in all areas: the most reported area of the training was "how to manage the virtual platform", which was reported by around 50% of participants from all three classes, followed by the category "How to create materials for an online setting", reported by around 40% of the participants in all three categories, and the category "How to adapt assessments to the online environment", reported by around 30% of the participants in all three categories. Exceptions to this trend are the categories "Synchronous sessions" and "Motivation". For the former, 51% of instructors in the PAC reported having received training in this area, compared to 37% of the instructors in

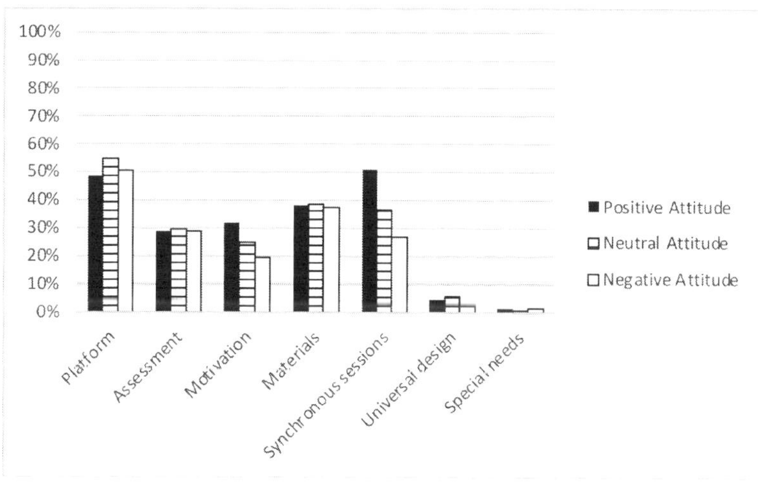

Figure 2 Training Areas

the NAC, and 27% in the NegAC. A similar trend is observed in the latter, although the gap between classes is much smaller: 32% of instructors in the PAC reported having received training on how to motivate students, versus 25% and 20% in the NAC and the NegAC respectively.

RQ4 Challenges Experienced During the First Months of the COVID-19 Health Crisis

Research question 4 explored the relationship between the challenges experienced by instructors during the first months of the pandemic and the three classes. As can be seen in Figure 3, the trend in the area of challenges is clear: the percentage of instructors from the NegAC who reported having experienced difficulties is higher for all categories. They are followed by instructors in the NAC and finally those in the PAC. Particularly noteworthy are the challenges "Motivating students" and "Designing effective online activities"—which were reported by almost 70% of instructors in the NegAC, almost 60% of instructors in the NAC, and around 40% of instructors in the PAC. Special attention must be paid to the category "Making students talk in the synchronous sessions," which was reported by 50% of the participants in the NegAC and the NAC, compared to only 30% of the participants in the PAC. These results indicate that although, as expected, the teachers

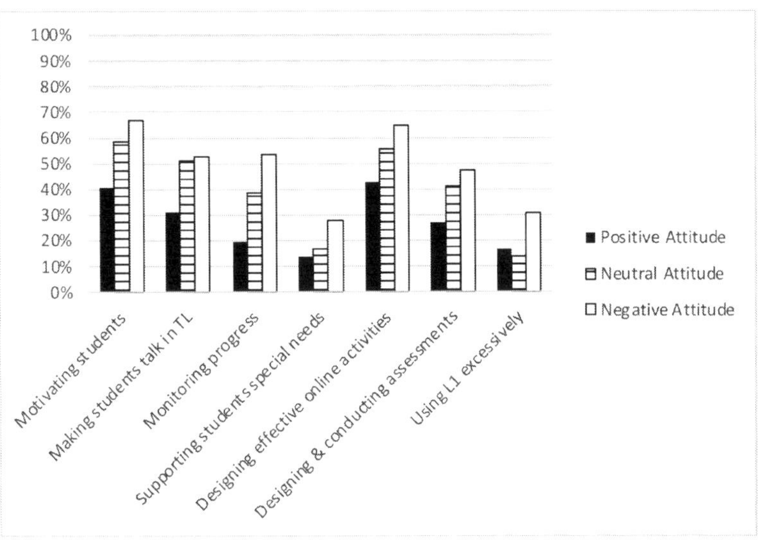

Figure 3 Challenges Experienced by Instructors

who expressed a negative attitude reported experiencing more challenges than the instructors in the other classes, there were challenges reported by all instructors regardless of the class they were assigned to, which helps us identify aspects of the training that require special attention in future teacher training programs.

Discussion

This study explores how language teachers across the world navigated the first months of the COVID-19 crisis. In exploring teachers' attitudes across 43 countries and 5 continents, this research provides us with a global snapshot of how teachers felt at the beginning of the pandemic. Although we acknowledge an overrepresentation of teachers from US and Ireland and towards Spanish language teaching, this study still leverages geographical diversity and offers researchers a more global perspective than previous research in the area of online teacher training.

The study itself was guided by four research questions. The first one examined language instructors' attitudes towards online teaching. The analysis categorized participants into 3 groups according to the nature of their attitudes: positive (21.42%), neutral (47.1%), and negative (31.5%). These results represent an important development with respect to those of Jaschik and Lederman (2018), who found that almost 50% of teachers doubted the effectiveness of online teaching.

Our second research question allowed us to elucidate factors that explained teachers' categorization into each group. Two factors—*Teaching experience* and *Training during the pandemic*—and the interaction between *Institution* and *Training before the pandemic* were found to be predictors of participants' attitudes towards online teaching. The key trends in our analysis are as follows.

First, teachers with more than 15 years of experience tended to have more negative attitudes toward online teaching, while teachers who had less than 5 or between 6 and 10 years of experience were more likely to be categorized as having neutral attitudes. This inverse relationship between years of experience and attitudes towards online teaching is notable insofar as it reveals that teachers with an established teaching career were less open to and comfortable with the possibilities afforded by online teaching. Possible reasons for this could be that the training received by the newer generation of teachers already includes some technological components, which then makes new teachers more open to technology-enhanced teaching. Another possible explanation is that teachers with less experience have a longer career ahead of them, which in turn makes investing in new training/skills a more logical investment. This divide between more and less experienced teachers and their willingness to engage with technology-supported instruction has been reported in the literature (e.g., Orlando, 2014), in some cases correlated with instructor's age (e.g., Cheng, 2017; O'Bannon & Thomas, 2014 [who finds this particularly relevant for older female teachers]).

A second finding was that teachers who did not receive training during the pandemic were more likely to be classified within the negative attitude class, while those who received training during the pandemic expressed more neutral attitudes. As mentioned above, the training received during the pandemic was not the sort that is adequate for planned online instruction. However, this *survival approach to training*, as Paesani (2020) describes it, helped teachers through the initial months of the crisis (with varying levels of success). In other words: having access to this survival training was better than not having it. At the same time, this survival training did not foster positive attitudes, which indicates that a more comprehensive type of training is needed if we expect teachers to develop positive attitudes towards online teaching.

The last significant factor found was the interaction between *Institution* and *Training before the pandemic*. The primary/secondary school teacher group was at a disadvantage with respect to the other two groups (language schools and university teachers). While, for the latter groups, training resulted in a positive attitude, for the former, it only developed neutral attitudes. Similar results have been reported in the literature. For instance, Moser et al. (2021) found this same dichotomy with pre-K12 teachers experiencing greater difficulty with online teaching during the pandemic as compared to their higher education counterparts. While these authors explained their results in terms of the challenges faced by teachers in primary/secondary school settings as well as issues related to digital inequalities among students, the fact that online classes and/or integration of technology in the curriculum have been common for decades in higher education and language schools (Kentnor, 2015) could also be a factor. Thus, there is a higher likelihood that teachers in these types of institutions were already familiar with online teaching or at least had resources in place at their institution they could leverage during the ERLT experience.

Our third research question looked into the type of training teachers received during the first months of the COVID-19 crisis and whether it differed according to attitude group. The results of the study indicate that a greater percentage of participants in the PAC group received training in two areas: management of online sessions and motivating students. While these results do not indicate a causal relationship, they point to the fact that including them into training programs may help foster positive attitudes towards online teaching. Additionally, it is worth noting that two categories—training on Universal Design for Learning and on how to support students with special needs—were almost nonexistent in the reported training components. While this absence may be related to the fact that the training was designed hurriedly to meet the immediate needs of moving to online instruction, these areas of training are nonetheless essential in the development of effective, sustainable, and inclusive online language courses (e.g., Gacs et al., 2020; Hodges et al., 2020).

Our last research question delves into the challenges faced by teachers during the first months of the health crisis. A clear trend emerged with participants in NegAC experiencing more challenges than participants in the NAC and both classes reporting having experienced more difficulties than those in the PAC. However, echoing the results of other post-pandemic studies (e.g., Bachiri & Sahli, 2020; Junaidi, et al., 2022), there were challenges reported by teachers in all attitude classes, particularly "motivating students", "designing effective activities" and "making students talk in synchronous sessions". These three challenges are crucial for the success of any online class and, thus, should be afforded special attention in the design of training initiatives. Some of the other challenges mentioned, such as "designing effective activities," were elements usually included in the survival training; and yet, evidently, that training component was not seen as effective to teachers surveyed in this study, indicating the need for revision to this training component.

Taking these findings as a point of departure, we propose the design of a training program that helps teachers gradually increase their digital competence while at the same time fostering positive attitudes towards online instruction and Computer Assisted Language Learning (CALL). In doing so we argue that technology preparedness equals crisis preparedness, although we acknowledge this is not the only possibility. Specifically, we follow the principles outlined in the literature by proposing specific initiatives that are collaborative, experiential, scaffolded, and sustainable (Paesani, 2020), that assist teachers in the construction of a virtual identity (Comas-Quinn, 2011), and that foster a sense of belonging within a community, a feature that has been identified as especially helpful for teachers with lower digital and teaching skills (Lincoln et al., 2021) and in low-resource areas where support from peers is particularly necessary (Junaidi et al., 2022). These features allow the development of a training program that provides opportunities to engage with others who face similar situations and codify the knowledge—both implicit and explicit—that the community considers valuable within a given point in time. Based on our results, we advise that these training initiatives have a strong focus on three specific aspects: (i) how to manage synchronous sessions effectively, (ii) how to motivate students in a virtual environment, and (iii) how to design effective activities for online teaching.

Mentoring programs make it possible to take advantage of the knowledge of professionals with greater training and experience in digital skills and communicate that knowledge effectively to colleagues with less experience and competence in this area. If it is not possible to have a mentor in our same institution, there are initiatives such as the ACTFL Distance Learning Mentoring Program that is offered free of charge to members of the organization.

Peer observations have been shown to be effective in both traditional (Kissau & King 2015) and virtual settings (Lincoln et al., 2021). The process must be guided by the person observed and can be structured in three phases: a meeting before the observation to determine what feedback is wanted, the observation, and a final meeting to discuss the observation and areas or initiatives for improvement.

Online communities of practice represent a meeting point with other professionals in the field in a relaxed atmosphere in which topics of mutual interest are discussed. Among the advantages of these communities are that they allow different levels of participation and they open the dialogue to perspectives external to the institution of the participant. Some of these communities have sprung up informally on social media, for example the Technology for Language Teaching and Learning Facebook group, but there are also formally instituted communities of practice, such as the aforementioned Distance Learning Mentoring Special Interest Group of ACTFL, or those of professional associations such as the Computer-Assisted Language Instruction Consortium (CALICO) and the European Association of Computer Assisted Language Learning (EuroCALL), which have special interest groups (SIGs) and organize annual conferences during which members have the opportunity to socialize.

Techno-pedagogical workshops, in face-to-face or virtual format, represent a way of being up to date with the new technological advances applied to language teaching. Regardless of the format, it is important to remember that this type of training must go beyond familiarization with specific tools and include a presentation and/or discussion of the pedagogical principles that support their use in the classroom.

All these initiatives must be supported by critical and guided reflection on the part of teachers, who can evaluate what types of tools and approaches could help them meet their goals within their specific contexts. These initiatives are likewise possible in all types of settings as they put teachers and the support they provide each other at the core of the training model. Ideally, such initiatives should be imbued in our day-to-day teaching so that, when a moment of crisis emerges, teachers are not only better equipped to navigate the crisis, but they can also get the support they need from their own community. The suggestions proposed herein should allow teachers to view moments of crisis in their professional careers not as an impasse but as an opportunity to move forward and become better equipped to teach 21st century learners.

Conclusions

This study has explored how language teachers across the world navigated the first months of the COVID-19 crisis. The results reveal that training focused primarily on low-level skills (i.e., technical competence) and that the areas that set participants apart related to the management of online sessions and motivating students, both of which were reported by a higher percentage of participants in the Positive Attitude group. Regarding challenges, participants reported difficulties motivating students, designing effective activities, and encouraging students to talk during synchronous sessions. The triangulation of these data sources allows us to identify areas in the training that should be emphasized to make training more effective and sustainable, and help us be better prepared for moments of crisis.

About the Authors

Marta Tecedor is an assistant professor in Spanish linguistics at Arizona State University. Her primary area of research is computer-assisted language learning. In her current research, she examines how the use of multimedia technologies can be incorporated in the language classroom to promote the development of linguistic, interactional, and intercultural competencies. Her work has appeared in, Foreign Language Annals, Hispania, L2 Journal, ReCALL, Computer-Assisted Language Learning, Language Culture and Curriculum, Journal of Pragmatics, and Applied Linguistics.

Inmaculada Gómez Soler is Assistant Professor at the School of Applied Language and Intercultural Studies, Dublin City University. Her research fits broadly within the discipline of Applied Linguistics and encompasses three main interrelated areas: heritage speaker bilingualism, language teacher development, and language pedagogy. Her recent publications have appeared in Foreign Language Annals, Hispania, Urban Education, and Languages

References

American Council on the Teaching of Foreign Languages [ACTFL]. (2011). *21st Century Skills Map*. Washington, D. C.: Partnership for 21st Century Skills. https://www.actfl.org/sites/default/files/resources/21st%20Century%20Skills%20Map-World%20Languages.pdf

Bachiri, H., & Sahli, R. (2020). The need of distance learning in the wake of COVID-19 in Morocco: Teachers' attitudes and challenges in the English foreign language instruction. *International Journal of Language and Literary Studies*, *2*(3), 240–256. https://doi.org/10.36892/ijlls.v2i3.326

Bandura, A. (1991). Social cognitive theory of self-regulation. *Organizational Behavior and Human Decision Processes, 50*(2), 248–87. https://doi.org/10.1016/0749-5978(91)90022-L

Bozkurt, A. (2019). From Distance Education to Open and Distance Learning: A Holistic Evaluation of History, Definitions, and Theories. In S. Sisman-Ugur, & G. Kurubacak (Eds.), *Handbook of Research on Learning in the Age of Transhumanism* (pp. 252–273). Hershey, PA: IGI Global. https://doi.org/10.4018/978-1-5225-8431-5.ch016

Chao, C. (2015). Rethinking transfer: Learning from CALL teacher education as consequential transition. *Language Learning & Technology, 19*(1), 102–118. http://dx.doi.org/10125/44404

Cheng, K. H. (2017) A survey of native language teachers' technological pedagogical and content knowledge (TPACK) in Taiwan. *Computer Assisted Language Learning*, *30*(7), 692–708. https://doi.org/10.1080/09588221.2017.1349805

Comas-Quinn, A. (2011). Learning to teach online or learning to become an online teacher: An exploration of teachers' experiences in a blended learning course. *ReCALL, 23*(3), 218–232. https://doi.org/10.1017/S0958344011000152

Ertmer, P. A. (2005). Teacher pedagogical beliefs: The final frontier in our quest for technology integration. *Educational Technology, Research and Development, 53*(4), 25–39. https://doi.org/10.1007/BF02504683

Gacs, A., Goertler, S., & Spasova, S. (2020). Planned online language education versus crisis-prompted online language teaching: Lessons for the future. *Foreign Language Annals*, *53*(2), 380–392. https://doi.org/10.1111/flan.12460

Garson, G. D. (2009) "Factor Analysis" from *Statnotes: Topics in Multivariate Analysis*.

Gómez Soler, I., & Tecedor, M. (2018). Foreign Language Teaching Assistant Training: A Contrastive Analysis of Trainers and Trainees' Perspectives. *Hispania*, *101*(1), 38-54. https://doi.org/10.1353/hpn.2018.0083

Hampel, R., & Stickler, U. (2005). New skills for new classrooms: Training tutors to teach languages online. *Computer Assisted Language Learning, 18*(4), 311–326. https://doi.org/10.1080/09588220500335455

Hodges, C., Moore, S., Lockee, B., Trust, T., & Bond, A. (2020). The difference between emergency remote teaching and online learning. *Educause Review.*

Jaschik, S., & Lederman, D. (2018). *2018 Survey of Faculty Attitudes on Technology: A Study by Inside Higher Ed and Gallup*. Inside Higher Ed/Gallup.

Jin, L., Xu, Y., Deifell, E., & Angus, K. (2021). Emergency remote language teaching and US-Based college-level world language educators' intention to adopt online teaching in postpandemic times. *The Modern Language Journal*, *105*(2), 412–434. https://doi.org/10.1111/modl.12712

Junaidi, Y., Hashim, H., & Ismail, H. H. (2022). ESL teachers' perception and attitudes towards the adoption of emergency remote teaching in time of crisis. *Journal of Nusantara Studies (JONUS)*, *7*(2), 221–244. http://dx.doi.org/10.24200/jonus.vol7iss2pp221-244

Kentnor, H. E. (2015). Distance education and the evolution of online learning in the United States. *Curriculum and Teaching Dialogue*, *17*(1), 21–34.

Kessler, G. (2017). Technology and the future of language teaching. *Foreign Language Annals*, *51*(1), 205–218. https://doi.org/10.1111/flan.12318

Kissau, S. P., & King, E. T. 2015. Peer Mentoring Second Language Teachers: A Mutually Beneficial Experience? *Foreign Language Annals*, *48*(1), 143–160. http://dx.doi.org/10.1111/flan.12121

Lee, S. M. (2021). Factors affecting the quality of online learning in a task-based college course. *Foreign Language Annals, 55*(1), 116–134. https://doi.org/10.1111/flan.12572

Lincoln, A., O'Riordan, F., & Buckley, K. (2021). *Peer Observation of Teaching: Can Peer Observation of Teaching Enhance Professional Development Practices within Higher Education? A Literature Scoping Review*. Dublin: Dublin City University. https://doi.org/10.5281/zenodo.4494444

Mitchell, L. D., Parlamis, J. D., & Claiborne, S. A. (2014). Overcoming faculty avoidance of online education: From resistance to support to active participation. *Journal of Management Education*, *39*(3), 350–371. https://doi.org/10.1177/1052562914547

Monroy, L., Vidal, R. S., & Saade A. (2010). *Análisis de Clases Latentes: Una técnica para detectar heterogeneidad en poblaciones*. México, DF: Centro Nacional de Evaluación para la Educación Superior, A.C (CENEVAL).

Moser, K. M., Wei, T., & Brenner, D. (2021). Remote teaching during COVID-19: Implications from a national survey of language educators. *System, 97, 102431.* https://doi.org/10.1016/j.system.2020.102431

O'Bannon, B. W. & Thomas, K. (2014). Teacher perceptions of using mobile phones in the classroom: Age matters! *Computers & Education*, *74*, 15–25. https://doi.org/10.1016/j.compedu.2014.01.006

Orlando, J. (2014). Veteran teachers and technology: Change fatigue and knowledge insecurity influence practice. *Teachers and Teaching, 20*(4), 427–439. https://doi.org/10.1080/13540602.2014.881644

Paesani, K. (2020). Teacher professional development and online instruction: Cultivating coherence and sustainability. *Foreign Language Annals*, *53*(2), 292–297. https://doi.org/10.1111/flan.12468

Petty, R.E., Fabrigar, L. R., & Wegener, D. T. (2003). Emotional factors in attitudes and persuasion, In R. J. Davidson, K. R. Scherer, and H. H. Goldsmith (Eds.): *Handbook of Affective Science*. Oxford: Oxford University Press.

Plonsky, L., & Ziegler, N. (2016). The CALL–SLA interface: Insights from a second-order synthesis. *Language Learning & Technology, 20*(2), 17–37. http://dx.doi.org/10125/44459

Redecker, C. (2017). *European Framework for the Digital Competence of Educators: DigCompEdu*. Sevilla: Joint Research Centre.

Stickler, U., & Hampel. R. (2015). Transforming teaching: new skills for online language learning spaces, In R. Hampel and U. Stickler (Eds.), *Developing Online Language Teaching: Research-Based Pedagogies and Reflective Practices. New Language Learning and Teaching Environments*, (pp. 63–77.) Palgrave Macmillan.

Tarrayo, V. N., Paz, R. M. O., & Gepila, E. C. Jr. (2023). The shift to flexible learning amidst the pandemic: The case of English language teachers in a Philippine state university. *Innovation in Language Learning and Teaching*, *17*(1), 130-143. https://doi.org/10.1080/17501229.2021.1944163

Xu, Y., Jin, L., Deifell, E., & Angus, K. (2022). Chinese character instruction online: A technology acceptance perspective in emergency remote teaching. *System, 100*, 102542. http://dx.doi.org/10.1016/j.system.2021.102542.

14 The Infinite Loop of Change: A Reflection on the Technology-mediated Transformation of a TESOL Program

Elena Schmitt and Anastasia Sorokina

Introduction

During the COVID-19 pandemic, higher education institutions experienced a rapid shift from face-to-face (F2F) classes to emergency online instruction which, for some, later evolved into or reverted back to planned online education (for definitions of emergency remote teaching (ERT) and planned online education see Gacs et al., 2020). As the initial crisis subsided, some universities reintroduced in-person instruction, while others opted to continue offering online or hybrid models. This transition posed challenges for programs as they navigated the changes and sought to engage students in meaningful learning experiences (Mallibhat & Iyer, 2022). In the context of a Master's in TESOL program at a US state university, a comprehensive study was conducted on its journey from F2F to fully online and subsequently to hybrid programming during the pandemic. This chapter focuses on the program's transitional phases and explores the outcomes of learning and teaching across different modalities, encompassing students' academic success, perceptions, levels of interaction, and factors influencing their choice of modality. The analysis is based on three years of data spanning from 2020 to 2023. The implications drawn from these findings contribute to shaping the program's future development.

Literature Review

The COVID-19 pandemic and subsequent lockdowns have had a profound impact on the landscape of teaching and learning in higher education. While online education has been present in higher education for some time, the pandemic rapidly accelerated the adoption of digital technology and online learning. It has become an integral part of the post-pandemic higher education system (Bartholomay, 2021) with projections indicating a doubling of online instruction by 2026 (National Center for Education Statistics, 2023). This shift has led to a surge in research examining the effects of the pandemic on various aspects of higher education, including the use of online tools (Malinowski et al., 2022), the impact of changes on student success (Al Wahhabi & Rajab, 2022), and the future development of online higher education (Keshavarz, 2020). While some studies have touched on specific aspects of TESOL training in the US, such as recounting student-teaching practicum experiences in California (Malinowski et al., 2022), examining TESOL students' emotions and coping strategies during the pandemic (Kang & Nam-Huh, 2022), and exploring the effects of different modalities on TESOL assessment courses in US students (Porter-Szucs & DeCicco, 2022), there is still a lack of definitive answers to questions about the relationship between learning modality and academic achievement, students' perceptions and experiences with online learning, the differences and similarities in the interaction between F2F and online classes, and the factors influencing students' choice of modality.

The Effect of Online and F2F Learning on Academic Achievement

Numerous studies conducted both before and during the pandemic have examined the relationship between students' academic achievement and learning modality. The findings of these studies are varied, with some indicating no significant differences between the two modalities (Paul & Jefferson, 2019), while others suggest a slight advantage of F2F instruction (Sarac & Durakovic, 2022) and others find that online education may be more beneficial (Slover & Mandernach, 2018). For instance, Al Wahhabi and Rajab (2022) investigated the academic achievement measured by the mean GPA of 36 female TESOL students from Saudi Arabia and found a statistically significant difference between F2F and online learning, with online students outperforming their counterparts in F2F classrooms. In contrast, Porter-Szucs and DeCicco (2022) found no significant differences in the learning outcomes measured by final grades and grades on high-stakes and low-stakes assignments of MA TESOL students at a US university during the pandemic. Goertler and Gacs (2018) also discovered no significant differences between F2F and online modalities but noted a higher standard deviation in grades for online students, suggesting that online learning may be more effective for certain individuals but less so for others (see also Gleason & Bartlett, Chapter 9, this volume). Given the variable results of these studies, a definitive answer regarding the impact of learning modality on academic achievement remains elusive.

Students' Experiences in Online and F2F Learning Modalities

Gaining insights into students' experiences and perceptions of online learning compared to F2F instruction is crucial for designing effective online courses and ensuring student success. Consequently, it is unsurprising that this has emerged as a central theme in research during the pandemic. Studies indicate that students hold mixed perceptions of online learning. Altuwairesh (2021) discovered that while most participants expressed satisfaction with their online experiences, they later acknowledged a preference for F2F instruction due to challenges such as motivation, technical issues, and the absence of interaction. Adnan and Anwar (2020) identified the lack of F2F interaction, socialization, and technical difficulties as challenges reported by students in their study of digital and distance learning. Moallem (2015) and Belamghari (2022) highlighted issues of intimacy and non-verbal communication difficulties in online learning. Conversely, Al Wahhabi and Rajab (2022) found that online learning had a positive impact on female MA TESOL students, providing them with additional time to complete their work. Similarly, Hamza Sheerah et al. (2022) reported that students perceived online learning as offering greater flexibility, discipline, and motivation. Some students, particularly those familiar with online learning, older in age, and engaged in full-time employment, reported enjoying distance learning during the pandemic (Maskun et al., 2020; Ojha & Rahman, 2020). Others experienced difficulties due to the lack of social connection and loss of motivation (Vega & Eppendi, 2021). Thu (2020) explored Master of TESOL students' perceptions of online learning and found that students who received proper training in digital technologies held more favorable views of online classes and were more willing to continue with distance learning.

Porter-Szucs and DeCicco (2022) suggested that the quality of instruction, instructor commitment, and institutional support contribute to equitable academic achievement across modalities. Bangert (2006) identified student-faculty interaction, time on task, engagement, and cooperation as factors influencing learners' perceived quality of online courses. Nassuora (2020) found that instructor characteristics, social presence, instructional design, and trust influenced students' perceptions of online learning.

Overall, the available research suggests that online learning offers convenience and flexibility, but the presence of human interaction and thoughtful course design as well as its appropriateness for the delivery format are crucial factors affecting students' perceptions. Therefore, it is imperative to continue investigating students' experiences with online learning during the pandemic and beyond to inform the development of future distance learning programs.

The Role of Interaction in Online and F2F Classes

Educational theorists, including Vygotsky (1987), Piaget, and Bruner, among others, emphasize the importance of interaction in promoting student success through active engagement, social learning, cognitive development, communication skills, motivation, and valuable feedback and guidance. However, interaction in F2F environments has been recognized as distinct from online contexts. Media Naturalness theory (Kock, 2004, 2011) suggests that when individuals perceive online communication as less natural or dissimilar to F2F communication, they may experience reduced feelings of presence, social presence, and social cues, which can impact interaction dynamics. This perceived lack of naturalness can affect the quality and depth of interaction, as well as the development of social relationships in the online class environment.

Pre-pandemic research on interaction and engagement in F2F versus online formats indicates potential significant differences between the modalities. For example, Gao et al. (2009) discovered that while students produced similar amounts of communication in both F2F and online activities, the communication styles differed with more turns and shorter utterances produced by online students.

Pandemic-related research suggests that in-class interaction and engagement during online classes may be different or even inferior to F2F communication, potentially compromising student success (Nguyen et al., 2022). Fish et al. (2023) reported significant differences in student-to-student and student–instructor interactions among graduate students, with less interaction observed in online courses compared to F2F ones.

One possible approach to address the issue of in-class engagement and interaction is through the implementation of the flipped classroom model. The flipped classroom is an innovative teaching approach that reverses the traditional lecture-plus-homework formula (see Lavolette & Asaba, Chapter 10, this volume). It involves students accessing online lectures before class, allowing for active, engaging activities during class time where they can apply their knowledge and skills. Although the design is credited to high school teachers Jonathan Bergmann and Aaron Sams (Arnold-Garza, 2014), variations of this method have been employed by many educators for years (Roehl et al., 2013). The flipped classroom approach has been shown to improve active learning, optimize the use of student-faculty time, enhance academic outcomes, and create an enriched learning environment (Akcayir & Akcayir, 2018). Kostka and Marshall (2020) have demonstrated the precise structuring of a flipped classroom for synchronous online language learning through their Synchronous Online Flipped Learning Approach (SOFLA) (Marshall, 2017). The present study aims to provide a direct comparison of F2F and online courses, and to discuss whether the flipped classroom design can mitigate some of the limitations of online learning while enhancing the quality of in-class interaction and engagement.

Factors that Affect Students' Choice of Modality

Numerous studies have investigated the factors that influence students' decision-making process when choosing between online and F2F modalities. Throughout the pandemic, the literature has highlighted the following key factors: flexibility and convenience (McIntyre et al., 2023; O'Neill et al., 2022), individual learning preferences (Van Wart et al., 2020), comfort with technology (Wang & Lu, 2021), and social interaction (Cadapan et al., 2022). Several studies have statistically ranked these factors based on their importance in students' decision-making processes (Van Wart et al., 2020). However, the specific role of each individual factor in students' choices remains unclear. As the availability of different modalities increases, students rely on a combination of these factors to aid them in their decision-making process necessitating a better understanding of the factors influencing student choice.

Research Questions

Given the unresolved issues in the current literature, this study aims to investigate the following research questions with a specific focus on graduate TESOL studies:

- What were students' experiences with online learning during the early and late stages of the pandemic?

- During and after the pandemic, what factors contribute to students' decision-making process when choosing between online and F2F modalities?
- Does the learning modality (F2F vs. online) have an impact on students' academic performance and level of engagement?
- What are the structural and interactional differences between the in-class components of F2F and online classes?

By addressing these research questions, this study seeks to provide a more comprehensive understanding of students' experiences and preferences regarding online and F2F modalities in the field of graduate TESOL studies.

Methods

Context Overview and Participants

This study was conducted in a medium-sized state university known for its teacher preparation programs, including Bilingual Education and TESOL, which are designated as licensure shortage areas in the state. Prior to the pandemic, the Bilingual/TESOL program attempted to tackle the challenge of educating teachers for the state's growing multilingual population by seeking alternatives to traditional classroom instruction (e.g., video conferencing) and sponsoring students' tuition through federal funding. However, the pandemic exacerbated the problem of access to F2F classes and forced the program to further rethink its delivery. The familiarity of faculty and students with video conferencing and the enhancement of digital technologies in recent years informed the program's response to the crisis (Capra, 2011; Christensen et al., 2011; Hart, 2012). An initial survey of students in the program at the start of the pandemic in 2020 revealed their needs, types of technology available at home, and learning preferences. Based on the results, the program completed the semester with synchronous classes in a flipped format defined by Kostka and Marshall (2020) as "an educational approach in which content that is traditionally presented in class is learned at home, and work that is traditionally completed as homework is done in class" (p. 224). All the courses in the program were taught synchronously online for the rest of the academic year. Starting in the summer of 2021, the program has been able to offer an online and F2F section for each course. Most of the students in the program are in-service teachers between the ages of 20–60 with a median age of 28, and 88% of the students identify as female.

Table 1 Summary of Research Design

	Data Collected	Participants or Analyzed Items
RQ#1 What were students' experiences with online learning during the early and late stages of the pandemic?	Survey	37 participants
	Interview	4 participants
RQ#2 During and after the pandemic, what factors contribute to students' decision-making process when choosing between online and F2F modalities?	Survey	37 participants
	Interview	4 participants
RQ#3 Does the learning modality (F2F vs. online) have an impact on students' academic performance and level of engagement?	Final grades	48 students
	Participation grades	
	PRAXIS II results	
RQ#4 What are the structural and interactional differences between the in-class components of F2F and online classes?	Recorded online and F2F class meetings	Two online class meetings Two F2F class meetings 480 minutes

Data Collection and Analysis

To address the aforementioned research questions, various types of data were collected and analyzed: student surveys, semi-structured interviews with students, students' academic performance, and video recordings of F2F and online class meetings. summarizes the research design.

Surveys and Interviews

The first survey focused on difficulties that students experience in their courses, availability of support, overall satisfaction, specific satisfaction with various course tasks and activities, and engagement was sent out to the students at the onset of the pandemic in March 2020. The main goal was to solicit feedback and incorporate best practices into the learning experiences of the students during the pandemic. The survey which was completed by nineteen students contained a series of open-ended questions and was administered through Google Forms.

The second survey asked students and recent alumni about their experiences in online and F2F courses and their approach to selecting a modality and was sent out in January 2023. The survey contained a variety of open-ended, multiple-choice, and Likert-scale questions and was administered through Google Forms. Eighteen students (six of those who took part in the previous survey and 12 new students) completed the survey. After the second survey, four of the 18 students volunteered to share more about their experiences and what factors they considered when selecting a modality by completing semi-structured interviews. Interviews were conducted via Zoom, recorded, and transcribed. Each interview contained a variety of open-ended questions and lasted between 12–30 minutes. All survey instruments are available on the book's website (https://sites.google.com/msu.edu/2024crisiscall/instruments-and-materials). A content analysis approach was utilized to code and examine survey results and interview responses. Content analysis is an established approach for data processing in social studies that are based on reviewing the data and identifying repeated patterns or themes (Krippendorff, 2004; Neuendorf, 2016). All the data were initially analyzed by the two authors independently, then the analyses were compared and discussed. An inter-rater reliability measure of the Percentage Agreement Method was utilized in this study to reduce bias (Gwet, 2017). This method estimates consistency between raters by calculating the number of agreements; a conservative marker of 90% agreement between the two raters was used in this study (Gwet, 2021; Shrout & Fleiss, 1979).

Academic Performance

Academic performance was measured by the final grades, participation grades, and PRAXIS II results. There are four required courses in the program: *Principles of Bilingual Education*, *TESOL Principles and Practices*, *Introduction to Linguistics*, and *Second Language Acquisition*. Starting in the Fall, 2021 semester, these courses were taught in both online and F2F formats, giving students choice. Both modalities were taught by the same instructor and followed the same course objectives. Academic grades of 48 enrolled students were analyzed using descriptive statistics as well as inferential statistics. The Welch's t-test was used to determine whether the grades in F2F courses were significantly different from those in online courses (Zimmerman, 2004). In addition, students' scores on the external examination results for teacher certification (PRAXIS II in TESOL) were collected. Praxis II in the TESOL exam measures pedagogical and linguistic knowledge for educators who teach English to speakers of other languages. Successful completion of the exam is a requirement for teacher licensure in the state of Connecticut (CT Bureau of Certification, n.d.).

Video Recordings of F2F and Online Classes

We recorded all synchronous online classes on Zoom and used a tripod and iPhone camera to record F2F classes. We randomly selected four recordings, completed at compatible times and covering the same academic content, for transcription and in-depth analysis, resulting in 480 minutes (about 8 hours) of multimedia-rich data. Regularly scheduled Zoom meetings lasted 120 minutes, whereas F2F meetings lasted 150 minutes. Analysis of in-class video recordings of F2F and recordings of online classes was coded using the content analysis approach described above. When the content analysis is applied to in-class recordings, observations help identify emergent patterns, themes, and behaviors (Y. Li & Dorai, 2006) and interpret the data by examining the nature and quality of students' learning and overall experiences.

Results

RQ1: What were Students' Experiences with Online Learning During the Early and Late Stages of the Pandemic?

When discussing early pandemic experiences in the interviews and surveys, students exhibit clear discomfort with online instruction and observe the absence of F2F features in online classes. Specifically, the following themes are salient in their responses:

1. Lack of intimacy and absence of private conversations in online classrooms (e.g., "I wish we had room for a private conversation with each other.")
2. Absence of body language and personal interaction (e.g., "I miss the personal interaction and body language that you get from in-person communication.")
3. The fast pace and overwhelming nature of online classes (e.g., "Online communication can be really fast-paced and overwhelming, with so many notifications and messages coming in all the time. It's hard to keep up.")
4. The lack of immediacy and physical proximity in online communication (e.g., "I find it harder to build relationships and make connections with people online. It feels like there's a barrier between us.")
5. Difficulty with understanding/reading of non-verbal cues (e.g., "Sometimes, the lack of nonverbal cues and tone of voice in online communication can lead to miscommunication and misunderstandings.")

In addition, students express how much they value interpersonal assignments, in-class group activities of F2F classes that include gallery walks, and team tasks like jigsaws and debates. In their responses to questions about late pandemic experiences, students report being more at ease with online classes and even preferring them to F2F instruction. Their comments are less negative and find many positive aspects of the online modality. The following themes emerge:

1. Affordances of sufficient opportunities for engagement in online modality (e.g., "I enjoyed the online meetings; I was able to engage in the same small group and whole class discussion from the comfort of my home.")
2. Recognition of the value of online classes in bringing together people from distant geographical areas ("I recognize the value in being able to bring people together, who are in reality very far apart.")
3. Small class size of online classes (e.g., "Small class size. If Zoom had many people on it, I would probably 'check out' more easily and not necessarily do all the necessary work.") Importantly, online classes have been small (no more than 10 students) due to the number of students who make the online choice as the university does not have any special regulation for online class sizes.

Many responses to the questions regarding preferred online activities in the later stages of the pandemic primarily highlight various interactive and team-based activities and tools such as Padlets, breakout room discussions, Jamboards, and games on WordWall.

RQ 2: During and After the Pandemic, What Factors Contribute to Students' Decision-making Process When Choosing Between Online and F2F Modalities?

The emergency response to the pandemic only allowed for online instruction. Once the pandemic eased, the program was able to offer the required courses in both modalities – F2F and online, thus providing the students with a choice of format.

Reasons for Selecting Online Classes

When analyzing students' survey responses and interviews, three main themes stand out:

1. Convenience ("I live far away… it is really nice to get home after a long day of teaching and not have to go to deal with traffic.")
2. Comfort and enjoyment of learning from home (e.g. "I prefer to take online classes because I can just sit in my pajamas and have a cup of coffee, and it's very comfortable.")
3. Diminished anxiety (e.g., "I'm more relaxed and focused. I don't have to worry about being in a classroom with other people. I can just focus on the material and that's what's important.")

It is noteworthy that when students talk about future (post-pandemic) course selections, they remark on the importance of interaction and professors' accessibility in the online modality. They appreciate the continuous support they receive from their professors and peers.

Reasons for Selecting F2F Classes

When analyzing students' responses on why they select F2F classes, three interconnected themes were observed:

1. Quantity of in-class interactions with peers and professors (e.g., "It is so much easier… to ask questions and interact with professors and classmates in person.")
2. Quality of in-class interactions (e.g., "Discussions in the class feel more organic and I learn a lot more from other students.")
3. Opportunities to establish social connections (e.g., "I did make some relationships with some of the girls. We check in here and there.")

These responses highlight the contrasting preferences and benefits students perceive in online and face-to-face learning environments.

RQ 3: Does the Learning Modality (F2F vs. Online) Affect Students' Academic Performance and Engagement?

An analysis of students' grades indicates that there is no significant variation across modalities. Specifically, according to the Welch's t-test, the course grades did not differ significantly between F2F (M=94.01; SD=4.24) and online classes (M=92.76; SD=6.63), $t(79.1)=1.08$, p=0.3. The difference in participation grades between F2F (M=11.77; SD=1.89) and online (M=11.76; SD=1.87) modalities was also not statistically significant, $t(87.1)=0.03$, p=0.9. Overall, based on the academic performance data, the learning outcomes did not differ between the F2F and online modalities. Despite these similarities, we observed more grade variation in some of the online courses. This is especially noticeable in the standard deviation values: 4.24 for the F2F versus 6.63 for the online modality.

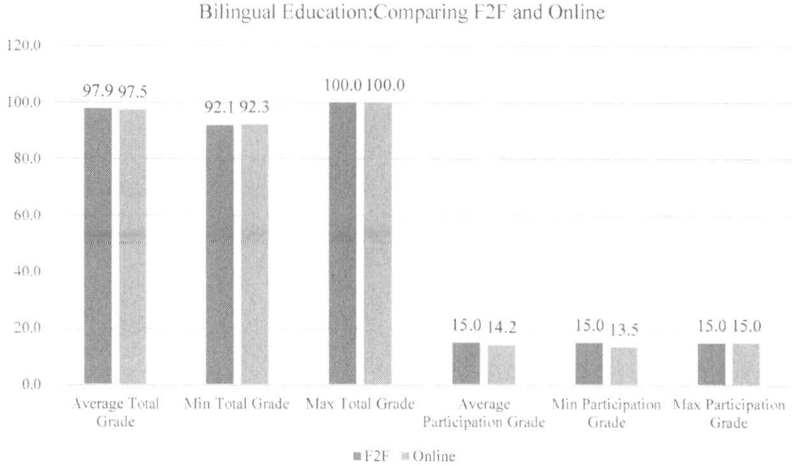

Figure 1 Comparing Academic Grades and Participation for F2F Versus Online Sections of the Bilingual Education Course

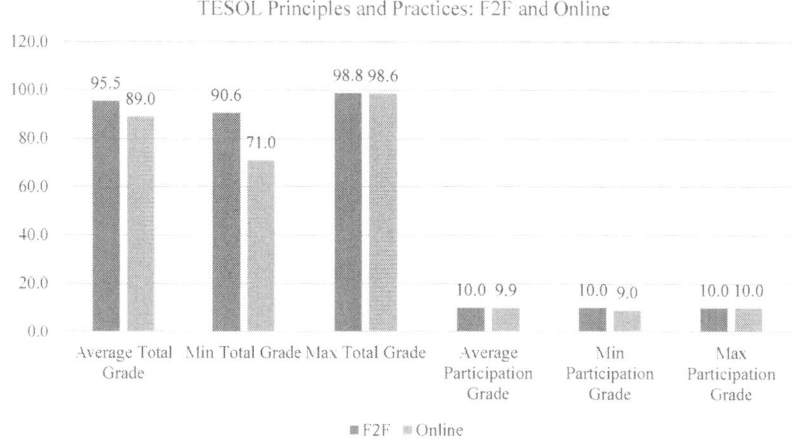

Figure 2 Comparing Academic Grades and Participation for F2F Versus Online Sections of the TESOL Principles and Practices Course

All teacher candidates (100%) who took Praxis II in TESOL in 2020, 2021, and 2022 (i.e., at all stages of the study) passed the test at or above the required score. Thus, regardless of the teaching and learning modality, these students acquired the appropriate knowledge base for their teaching certification.

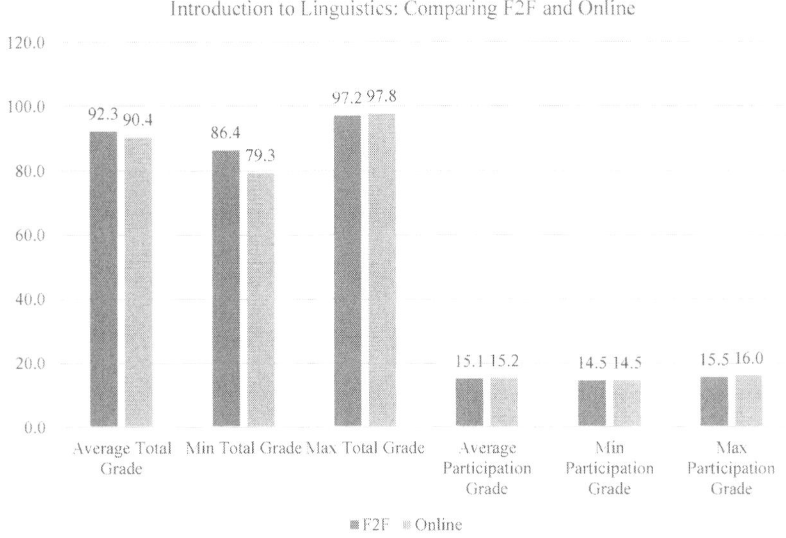

Figure 3 Comparing Academic Grades and Participation for F2F Versus Online Sections of the Introduction to Linguistics Course

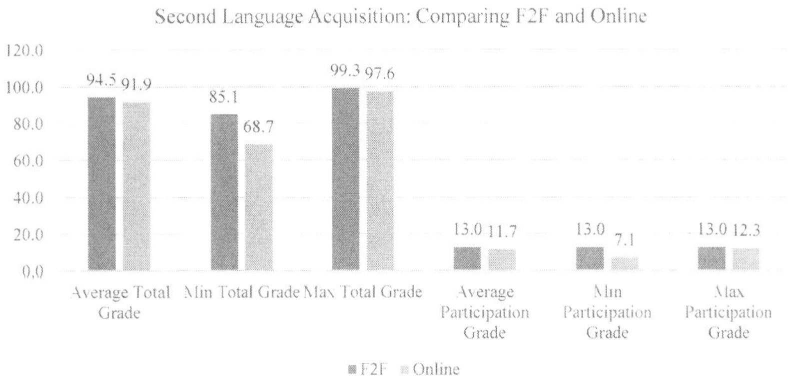

Figure 4 Comparing Academic Grades and Participation for F2F Versus Online Sections of the Second Language Acquisition Course

RQ 4: What are the Structural and Interactional Differences Between the In-class Components of F2F and Online Classes?

Here we provide a side-by-side comparison of the recorded lessons to understand how specifically students engage with peers and instructors within different modalities. We find differences in 1) class formats; 2) lesson structures; and 3) the amount of student and teacher talk. The two modalities show similarities in 1) the instructor's ability to gauge the emotional reactions of students; 2) students' involvement in small group discussions; 3) the overall objectives and activities. The comparative analysis of the formats of online and F2F classes indicates differences reported in Figure 5.

Our analysis reveals that the flipped structure of the online class, where lectures are delivered outside the synchronous meeting time and the in-class time is focused on interactions through student-centered activities, yields more time for discussions and student-to-student interaction than the F2F class, where lectures take up about 43% of the meeting time. Students in the online classes spoke for 80% of the time (about 96 minutes), with the remaining 20% (about 24 minutes) being instructor talk, while in the F2F classes, the instructor spoke for 62% of the time, leaving students with 56 minutes of speaking time (37%). These results are presented in Figures 6 and 7.

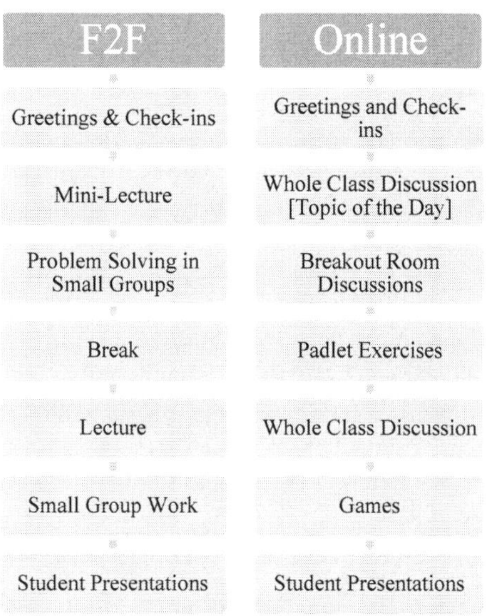

Figure 5 Formats of F2F and Online Class Meetings

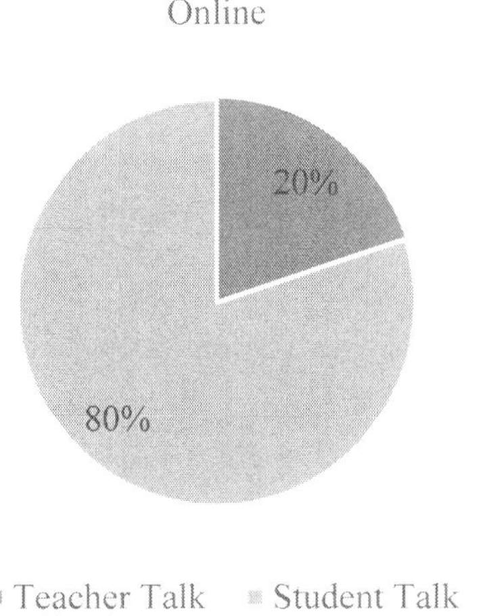

Figure 6 Distribution of Teacher and Student Talk in the Online Modality

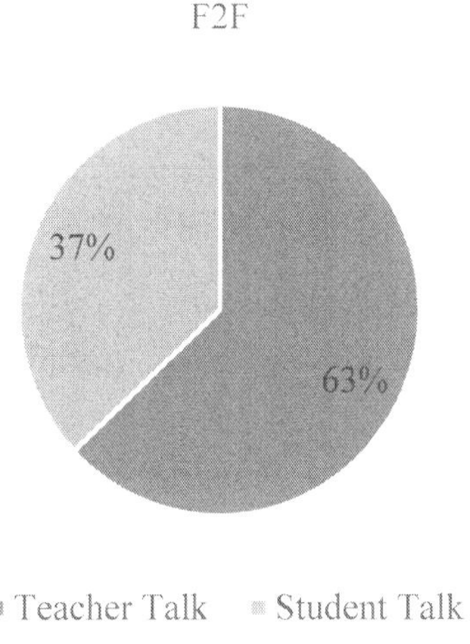

Figure 7 Distribution of Teacher and Student Talk in F2F Modality

The analysis of the lessons shows that students remained engaged throughout a long online lesson as they provided explanations, selected topics for discussion, and utilized appropriate professional jargon. One student remarked, "I was hesitant about taking an online class, but I've actually found it to be just as effective as a face-to-face class. I think it's because our teacher makes such an effort to keep us engaged and connected with each other." This contrasts with F2F classes, where the instructor dominates the communicative space. As another student noted, "I feel like in our in-person classes, we don't get as many chances to speak up or ask questions. The teacher is always talking and we're just listening."

While a more detailed reporting of the results of the video analysis is beyond the scope of this chapter, it is important to note that in both modalities students engage in productive conversations that involve negotiating meaning and using subject-specific vocabulary to achieve desired learning outcomes.

Discussion

Academic Achievement Across Modalities

The most tangible outcomes of this study relate to students' grades and the national licensure exam in both, early and late pandemic. Our results show that students' overall course and participation grades as well as the licensing exam pass rate are similar across online and F2F sections in line with similar findings by Porter-Szucs & DeCicco (2022). However, like Goertler & Gacs (2018) and also Gleason & Barlett (Chapter 9, this volume), we find more grade variation in online courses. We interpret this finding as an indication that some students opt for online classes for reasons of convenience without considering their learning styles, levels of motivation, and experience.

Factors Influencing Modality Selection

Some of the factors influencing modality selection are explicitly mentioned by our informants, while others are implicitly revealed throughout the qualitative findings of the study. Overall, we find many similarities between our TESOL students' experiences in the early pandemic and those reported in the literature. The difficulties faced by the participants (e.g., lack of intimacy, limited non-verbal communication, challenges with non-verbal communication) are not unique and similar problems have been reported by pre-pandemic studies (Moallem, 2015) and early pandemic research (Belamghari, 2022; D. Li, 2022)

While the factor of convenience, which has been extensively documented in both pre-and during-pandemic literature (Lin et al., 2021; Van Wart et al., 2020), undeniably remains the primary motivating force for students in selecting the online modality, a deeper examination of the data reveals that the decision-making process becomes more intricate as additional factors gain significance for students. In 2021, when students were given the option to choose between modalities, they opted for online learning primarily due to the convenience it offered and the desire to minimize physical contact. However, by Fall 2022, as students gained more experience with online learning, additional factors such as the quantity and quality of interactions with peers and professors, the establishment of social connections, and in some cases, students' awareness of their own learning styles became important factors in their selection process.

Role of Interaction in Learning

Research conducted before the pandemic mentions limited opportunities for social interaction in online classes, leading to a higher preference for F2F modalities (Marriott et al., 2004; Smith & Greene, 2013; Wong & Fong, 2014). Blau et al. (2017) attributed the lack of social interaction in online modalities to the absence of essential features found in F2F communication, such as immediacy, spontaneity, physical proximity, nonverbal cues, and a sense of presence. In our study, during the early stages of the pandemic, students expressed criticism towards online socialization as they missed the personal interaction and social connections. They found online communication to be fast-paced, overwhelming, and lacking nonverbal cues, making it challenging to build relationships and establish connections. However, later interviews indicate that opportunities for establishing ties became more sufficient as students recognized the value of "bringing people together, who are in reality very far apart" (student response).

Previous studies conducted in traditional classrooms have consistently reported that teachers tend to dominate the conversation, while students have limited opportunities to speak. For example, Hattie (2012) highlighted that "teachers talk between 70 and 80 percent of class time" (p. 80) and also noted that student engagement increases when teachers talk less. The ratio of student-teacher talk in our online classes was 80/20 compared to 38/62 in F2F classes. In the online classes it included abundant collaboration, engagement, and negotiation of meaning among students, which – building on Swain (2017) – can enhance students' confidence and competence in the subject matter. The findings from our analysis demonstrate that our online classes approximate and even surpass F2F instruction in key aspects of natural interaction as outlined by Weiser et al. (2018). These include real-time interactions via synchronous online modality, the ability to convey non-verbal cues and body language with audio and video tools, collaborative tasks that involve teamwork and group decision-making, a sense of the social presence of all participants, and richness of communication using multimedia that conveys a nuanced range of emotions and information.

Shift in Students' Perceptions

At the onset of the pandemic, students' comments regarding their online experiences were characterized by significant use of negative terms such as lack, absence, overwhelming, and difficulty. It is possible that the students' initial negative perceptions were further exacerbated by the overall stressful and anxiety-inducing context of the pandemic (Saeed et al., 2022). However, in their responses concerning their experiences with coursework during the later stages of the pandemic, students employ more positive language, utilizing terms such as afford, recognize, contribute, and no longer compare online classes to F2F experiences. They express their enjoyment of online meetings and the ability to actively participate in both small-group and whole-class discussions comfortably from their homes. Additionally, they emphasize the significance of peer and faculty support in their online work, noting that professors took the time to conduct wellness check-ins at the beginning of each class. This personal touch and care helped them form connections, alleviate their fears and concerns regarding technology, and foster persistence. This contributed to the positive experiences students have had with technology, which can shape their perception of online learning contexts in a favorable manner (Dison et al., 2022; Thu, 2020).

While students reflect on these differences when asked about their perceptions, they do not verbalize them as factors that contribute to their selection of modality. In reality, when students are offered a choice, their decisions are informed by salient common factors like convenience, comfort, the amount of physical contact, and the importance of the traditional characteristics of the F2F classroom, that are often mentioned in pre-pandemic and post-pandemic literature (Van Wart et al., 2020). As the pandemic progressed, their choices were shaped by a combination of factors: convenience, positive online features, equivalent interaction opportunities, ability to make friends online, and less anxiety when learning from home. As one student explained, "Synchronous online interaction has allowed people to maintain personal connections and engage in real-time interactions, despite being physically apart." Figure 8 illustrates the changes over time.

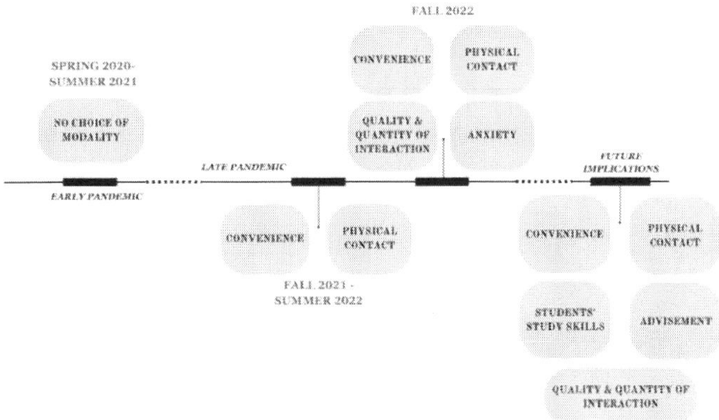

Figure 8 Factors Contributing to the Choice of Online Modality Over Time

Implications

These considerations, as well as the overall results, have implications for language teacher education in the post-pandemic era. (1) Online learning can be a viable long-term alternative to traditional F2F instruction, especially in programs that have students with geographic and temporal limitations. Given the grade variation in online courses, students should be guided in their selection by being fully informed about the differences between F2F and online modalities and the implications of these differences, so that they can assess the suitability of online learning based on their learning style, motivation, and time management skills. Additionally, programs could also investigate additional ways to support students who experience difficulties. (2) Students' preferences for collaboration and interaction indicate the importance of prioritizing the development of learning environments that foster engagement, interactivity, and support, while considering the distinct needs and preferences of online and on-ground learners. (3) Students' perceptions and expressed opinions regarding online learning shift as circumstances and their experience levels change. With experience, students stopped comparing online classes to F2F modalities and instead directed their attention toward recognizing the unique affordances and benefits offered by online learning.

Conclusion

This chapter contributes to the conversation regarding similarities and differences between F2F and online modalities and students' perceptions thereof. Our findings support the notion that online teaching can be just as effective as F2F teaching, particularly when considering design and delivery factors such as interactive technologies, clear communication, and the importance of fostering interaction. Each modality offers unique advantages that can cater to diverse student needs and reach a broader audience, including working professionals and commuters. Overall, the findings suggest that higher education institutions should continue offering both F2F and online course modalities in the post-pandemic era and prioritize the development of interactive and engaging online learning environments that are on par with, or even surpass, the quality of F2F instruction.

About the Authors

Elena Schmitt is a Professor of Applied Linguistics and TESOL in the Department of World Languages and Literatures at Southern Connecticut State University in New Haven, CT. She received a PhD in Linguistics from the University of South Carolina. Elena's research interests include first language attrition, heritage language studies, bilingualism, and language teacher training. Her recent publications appeared in the *International Journal of Bilingualism*, *Bilingualism: Language and Cognition*, and *Linguistic Encyclopedia of Slavic Languages*.

Anastasia Sorokina is an Assistant Professor of Applied Linguistics in the TESOL program, World Languages and Literatures Department at Southern Connecticut State University, New Haven, CT, US. She received a PhD in Education (Applied Linguistics Track) from Temple University. Anastasia's research focuses on the issues of L1 attrition and connections between language loss and bilingual autobiographical memory in immigrant communities that are forced to assimilate. Her publications appeared in the *International Journal of Bilingualism*, *Bilingualism: Language and Cognition*, and the *Russian Journal of Communication*.

References

Adnan, M., & Anwar, K. (2020). Online learning amid the COVID-19 pandemic: St Dents' perspectives. *Journal of Pedagogical Sociology and Psychology*, *2*, 45–51. https://doi.org/10.33902/JPSP.2020261309

Akcayir, G., & Akcayir, M. (2018). The flipped classroom: A review of its advantages and challenges. *Computers & Education, 126,* 334-345. https://doi.org/10.1016/j.compedu.2018.07.021

Altuwairesh, N. (2021). Female Saudi university students' perceptions of online education amid covid-19 pandemic. *Arab World English Journal (AWEJ) Special Issue on Covid 19 Challenges*, 381–397. https://doi.org/10.31235/osf.io/ym7js

Al Wahhabi, G., & Rajab, B. A. (2022). The impact of online learning on the female MA TESOL students' academic performance during the COVID-19 pandemic. *Open Journal of Modern Linguistics*, *12*(3), 313–335. https://doi.org/10.4236/ojml.2022.123024

Arnold-Garza, S. (2014). The flipped classroom teaching model and its use for information literacy instruction. *Communications in Information Literacy*, *8* (1), 7–22. https://doi.org/10.15760/comminfolit.2014.8.1.161

Bangert, A. W. (2006). Identifying factors underlying the quality of online teaching effectiveness: An exploratory study. *Journal of Computing in Higher Education*, *17*(2), 79–99. https://doi.org/10.1007/bf03032699

Bartholomay, D. J. (2021). A time to adapt, not "return to normal": Lessons in compassion and accessibility from teaching during COVID-19. *Teaching Sociology*, *50*(1), 62–72. https://doi.org/10.1177/0092055x211053376

Belamghari, M. (2022). Distance learning amidst the COVID-19 pandemic: Moroccan university students' perceptions. *The Teacher Educator*, *57*(1), 79–95. https://doi.org/10.1080/08878730.2021.2003918

Blau, I., Weiser, O., & Eshet-Alkalai, Y. (2017). How do medium naturalness and personality traits shape academic achievement and perceived learning? An experimental study of face-to-face and synchronous e-learning. *Research in Learning Technology*, *25*. https://doi.org/10.25304/rlt.v25.1974

Bureau of Certification. CT.gov. (n.d.). https://portal.ct.gov/sdecertification

Cadapan, R. R., Tindowen, D. J., Mendezabal, M. J., & Quilang, P. (2022). Graduate school students' self-efficacy toward online learning in the midst of the COVID-19 pandemic. *International Journal of Evaluation and Research in Education (IJERE)*, *11*(2), 555–564. https://doi.org/10.11591/ijere.v11i2.21856

Capra, T. (2011). Online education: Promise and problems. *Journal of Online Learning and Teaching*, *7*, 288–293. https://jolt.merlot.org/vol7no2/capra_0611.pdf

Christensen, C. M., Horn, M. B., Caldera, L., & Soares, L. (2011). *Disrupting college: How disruptive innovation can deliver quality and affordability to postsecondary education.* Lexington, MA: Innosight Institute. https://eric.ed.gov/?id=ED535182

Dison, L., Padayachee, K., De Klerk, D., Conradie, W., MacAlister, F., Moch, S. L., & Krull, G. (2022). Reframing purpose and conceptions of success for a post-Covid-19 South African higher education. *Scholarship of Teaching and Learning in the South*, *6*(1), 33–54. http://dx.doi.org/10.36615/sotls.v6i1.222

Fish, L. A., Snodgrass, C. R. and Kim, J. H. (2023). A comparison of graduate university perspectives of online versus face-to-face during the pandemic. *Journal of International Education in Business*, *16*(2), 129–151. https://doi.org/10.1080/08832323.2023.2224545

Gacs, A., Goertler, S., & Spasova, S. (2020). Planned online language education versus crisis-prompted online language teaching: Lessons for the future. *Foreign Language Annals,* 53, 380-392. https://doi.org/10.1111/flan.12460

Gao, F., Noh, J., & Koehler, M. J. (2009). Comparing student interactions in Second Life and face-to-face role-playing activities. *Visual Communications and Technology Education Faculty Publications*, *22*, 1–18.

Goertler, S. & Gacs, A. (2018). Assessment in online German: Assessment methods and results. *Die Unterrichtspraxis / Teaching German*, *51*(2), 156–174. https://www.jstor.org/stable/90026423

Gwet, K. (2017). *Handbook of Inter-Rater Reliability: The Definitive Guide to Measuring the Consistency of Judgments*. Routledge.

Gwet, K. L. (2021). *Handbook of inter-rater reliability: The definitive guide to measuring the extent of agreement among raters: Vol 2: Analysis of quantitative ratings*. Advanced Analytics, LLC.

Hamza Sheerah, H., Sharma Yadav, M., Elzein Fadl Allah, M. A., & Jalal Abdin, G. (2022). Exploring teachers and students' perceptions towards emergency online learning intensive English writing course during COVID-19 pandemic. *Arab World English Journal (AWEJ) 2nd Special Issue on Covid 19 Challenges*, *2*, 64–84. SSRN Electronic Journal. https://doi.org/10.2139/ssrn.4035984

Hart, C. (2012). Factors associated with student persistence in an online program of study: A review of the literature. *Journal of Interactive Online Learning*, *11*, 19–42. https://www.ncolr.org/jiol/issues/pdf/11.1.2.pdf

Hattie, J. (2012). *Visible learning for teachers: Maximizing impact on learning*. Routledge. https://doi.org/10.4324/9780203181522

Kang, H., & Nam-Huh, Y. (2022). TESOL practicum in the pandemic era: The emotions and strategies of teacher candidates. In C. Pu & W. Wright (Eds.), *Innovating the TESOL practicum in teacher education: Design, implementation, and pedagogy in an era of change* (pp.52–63). Routledge: New York. https://doi.org/10.4324/9781003193937-5

Keshavarz, M. H. (2020). A proposed model for post-pandemic higher education. *Budapest International Research and Critics in Linguistics and Education (BirLE) Journal*, *3*(3), 1384–1391. https://doi.org/10.33258/birle.v3i3.1193

Kock, N. (2004). The psychobiological model: Toward a new theory of computer-mediated communication based on Darwinian evolution. *Organization Science*, *15*(3), 327–348. https://doi.org/10.1287/orsc.1040.0071

Kock, N. (2011). The theory of media naturalness. *Journal of Communication, 61*(5), 823–843.

Kostka, I., & Marshall, H. (2020). Flipped learning in TESOL: Past, present, and future. In Perren, J., Kelch, K., Byun, J., Cervantes, S., & Safavi, S. (Eds.), *Applications of CALL theory in ESL and EFL environments* (pp. 223–243). IGI Global Publishers. https://doi.org/10.4018/978-1-5225-2933-0.ch013

Krippendorff, K. (2004). *Content analysis: An introduction to its methodology*. Sage publications.

Li, D. (2022). The shift to online classes during the Covid-19 pandemic: Benefits, challenges, and required improvements from the students' perspective. *The Electronic Journal of e-Learning, 20*(1), pp. 1–18. https://doi.org/10.34190/ejel.20.1.2106

Li, Y., & Dorai, C. (2006). Instructional video content analysis using audio information. *IEEE transactions on audio, speech, and language processing, 14*(6), 2264–2274. https://doi.org/10.1109/TASL.2006.872602

Lin, C. L., Jin, Y. Q., Zhao, Q., Yu, S., & Su, Y. (2021). Factors influence students' switching behavior to online learning under COVID-19 pandemic: A push–pull–mooring model perspective. *Asia-Pacific Education Researcher*, *30*(3), 229–245. https://doi.org/10.1007/s40299-021-00570-0

Malinowski, D., Abeywickrama, P., & Phillabaum, S. (2022). A turning point in the TESOL practicum: Navigating a forced move from in-person to online practice teaching. In C. Pu & W. Wright (Eds.), *Innovating the TESOL practicum in teacher education: Design, implementation, and pedagogy in an era of change* (pp.36–51). Routledge: New York. https://doi.org/10.4324/9781003193937-4

Mallibhat, K., & Iyer, N. (2022). Program level adaptations during pandemic: Opportunities and faculty perceptions. *EDULEARN Proceedings*, 3138–3145. https://doi.org/10.21125/edulearn.2022.0778

Marriott, N., Marriott, P., & Selwyn, N. (2004). Accounting undergraduates' changing use of ICT and their views on using the Internet in higher education: A research note. *Accounting Education*, *13*(4 supp 1), 117–130.

Marshall, H. W. (2017). The synchronous online flipped learning approach. *FLGI Community Blog*. https://community.flgobal.org/the-synchronous-online-flipped-learning-approach/

Maskun, M., Rusman, T., Suroto, S., & Rahmawati, F. (2020). Student perceptions of online learning. *International Journal of Multicultural and Multireligious Understanding*, *7*(20), 62–73. https://doi.org/10.18415/ijmmu.v7i2.1416

McIntyre, M. M., Medina, P. S., Zhang, J., & Ni, A. (2023). Understanding student intentions to take online courses: A theory-driven examination of adoption factors and prior experience. *Education and Information Technologies*, *28*, 15599–15624. https://doi.org/10.1007/s10639-023-11823-4

Moallem, M. (2015). The impact of synchronous and asynchronous communication tools on learner self-regulation, social presence, immediacy, intimacy and satisfaction in collaborative online learning. *The Online Journal of Distance Education and e-Learning*, *3*(3), 55–77.

Nassuora, Ayman. (2020). Measuring students' perceptions of online learning in higher education. *International Journal of Scientific & Technology Research, 9*(4). 1965–1970.

National Center for Education Statistics. (2023). English learners in public schools. *Condition of Education*. U.S. Department of Education, Institute of Education Sciences. Retrieved 05/31/2023 from https://nces.ed.gov/programs/coe/indicator/cgf.

Neuendorf, K. A. (2016). *The content analysis guidebook*. Sage publications. https://doi.org/10.4135/9781071802878

Nguyen, N. H., Tran, T. L. N., Nguyen, L. T., Nguyen, T. A., & Nguyen, M. T. (2022). The interaction patterns of pandemic-initiated online teaching: How teachers adapted. *System, 105*, 102755. https://doi.org/10.1016/j.system.2022.102755

Ojha, M., & Rahman, M. A. (2020). Do online courses provide an equal educational value compared to in-person classroom teaching? Evidence from US survey data using quantile regression. *Education Policy Analysis Archives, 29*(85), 1–25. https://doi.org/10.14507/epaa.29.5919

O'Neill, D. K., Reinhardt, S., & Jayasundera, K. (2022). What undergraduates say about choosing an online or in-person course: Qualitative results from a large-sample, multi-discipline survey. *Higher Education Research & Development, 41*(4), 1199–1214. https://doi.org/10.1080/07294360.2021.1896484

Paul, J., & Jefferson, F. (2019). A comparative analysis of student performance in an online vs. face-to-face environmental science course from 2009 to 2016. *Frontiers in Computer Science, 1*, 7. https://doi.org/10.3389/fcomp.2019.00007

Porter-Szucs, I., & DeCicco, B. (2022). TriHy: Teaching an MA TESOL class face-to-face, synchronously online, and asynchronously online. *SN Social Sciences, 2*(8), 143. https://doi.org/10.1007/s43545-022-00434-4

Roehl, A., Reddy, S. L., & Shannon, G. J. (2013). The flipped classroom: An opportunity to engage millennial students through active learning. *Journal of Family and Consumer Sciences, 105*, 44. https://doi.org/10.14307/JFCS105.2.12

Saeed, H., Eslami, A., Nassif, N. T., Simpson, A. M., & Lal, S. (2022). Anxiety linked to COVID-19: A systematic review comparing anxiety rates in different populations. *International Journal of Environmental Research and Public Health, 19*(4), 2189. https://doi.org/10.3390/ijerph19042189

Sarac, S., & Durakovic, B. (2022). Analysis of student performances in online and face-to-face learning: A case study from a Bosnian public university. *Heritage and Sustainable Development. 4.* 87–94. https://doi.org/10.37868/hsd.v4i2.91.

Shrout, P. E., & Fleiss, J. L. (1979). Intraclass correlations: Uses in assessing rater reliability. *Psychological Bulletin, 86*(2), 420–428. https://doi.org/10.1037/0033-2909.86.2.420

Slover, E. & Mandernach, B.. (2018). Beyond Online Versus Face-to-Face Comparisons: The Interaction of Student Age and Mode of Instruction on Academic Achievement. *Journal of Educators Online*, *15*(1). http://dx.doi.org/10.9743/jeo2018.15.1.4

Smith, J. J., & Greene, H. C. (2013). Pre-service teachers use e-learning technologies to enhance their learning. *Journal of Information Technology Education: Research*, *12*, 121–140. Retrieved from http://www.jite.org/documents/Vol12/JITEv12ResearchP121-140Smith1223.pdf

Swain, M. (2017). Languaging, agency and collaboration in advanced second language proficiency. *The Modern Language Journal*, *101*(S1), 64–80. http://dx.doi.org/10.1080/03057640500490981

Thu, L. T. (2020). Online learning experience of the master of TESOL students during Covid-19 closures. *Social Sciences*, *10*, 3–10. https://doi.org/10.46223/hcmcoujs.soci.en.10.2.1326.2020

Vygotsky, L. S. (1987). *Mind in society: The development of higher psychological processes*. Harvard University Press.

Van Wart, M., Ni, A., Medina, P., Canelon, J., Kordrostami, M., Zhang, J., & Liu, Y. (2020). Integrating students' perspectives about online learning: A hierarchy of factors. *International Journal of Educational Technology in Higher Education*, *17*(1), 1–22. https://doi.org/10.1186/s41239-020-00229-8

Vega, N. D., & Eppendi, J. (2021). Students' perceptions of online learning in teacher training and education faculty. *Journal of Physics: Conference Series*, *1810*. https://doi.org/10.1088/17426596/1810/1/012061

Wang, Y., & Lu, H. (2021). Validating items of different modalities to assess the educational technology competency of pre-service teachers. *Computers & Education*, *162*, 104081. https://doi.org/10.1016/j.compedu.2020.104081

Weiser, O., Blau, I., & Eshet-Alkalai, Y. (2018). How do medium naturalness, teaching-learning interactions and students' personality traits affect participation in synchronous e-learning? *The Internet and Higher Education*, *37*, 40–51. https://doi.org/10.1016/j.iheduc.2018.01.001

Wong, L., & Fong, M. (2014). Student attitudes to traditional and online methods of delivery. *Journal of Information Technology Education: Research*, *13*, 1–13. Retrieved from http://www.jite.org/documents/Vol13/JITEv13ResearchP001-013Wong0515.pdf

Zimmerman, D. W. (2004). A note on preliminary tests of equality of variances. *British Journal of Mathematical and Statistical Psychology*, *57*(1), 173–181. https://doi.org/10.1348/000711004849222

PART FIVE

LESSONS LEARNED

15 Crisis Response and Crisis Preparedness: Moving Forward

Senta Goertler and Jesse Gleason

The purpose of this book is to use the COVID-19 crisis as an example for crisis preparedness and technology-mediated crisis response and to share lessons for a new normal in language education. In this concluding chapter, we aim to draw from the chapters in this book and move beyond them to define lessons forward for language learning and teaching.

A health crisis first, the COVID-19 pandemic was a global traumatic period not just medically, but also socially, financially, and emotionally. It showcased inequities, and lack of crisis preparedness. In response, technological innovation played a crucial role in mitigation and problem-solving. We refer here to crises rather than crisis, since many crises were co-occurring and often intensifying due to the COVID-19 pandemic. Language education in the United States, for example, has been experiencing a crisis: a changed role in society and education have resulted in enrollment declines, removal of language requirements, shrinking institutional supports, program closures, and reduction in faculty positions (Quinn, 2023). Measures taken by institutions have signaled a devaluation of language education and appear counter to the often proclaimed goals of globalization, multiculturalism, diversity, equity, and inclusion. During ERTL new possibilities and roles of language education were (re)discovered.

At the time of this writing, the COVID-19 crises are still at the forefront of people's minds. In the future, the context and impact of COVID-19 might be less familiar to readers. Hence, we start this chapter with a review of the COVID-19 context more generally before homing in on language learning and teaching. Afterwards, we aim to answer the following: (1) What were the major lived experiences and lessons of the COVID-19 pandemic? (2) What are some recommendations for constructively, productively, and sustainably moving forward?

Given the complexity of the topic, the assumed audience for this volume, and our own professional experience, we limit our discussion to the U.S. contexts. Global perspectives are covered in other chapters within this volume. We limit our discussion to formal education in languages other than English in higher education in the U.S. contexts. Unfortunately, it is beyond the scope of this volume to present the pandemics' (detrimental) effects on multilingual communities, heritage maintenance, Indigenous language revitalization, and interpreting services.

The COVID-19 Crisis Case Study

In March 2020, the global COVID-19 pandemic was officially declared by the World Health Organization. The immediate health impact for many was mild to severe sickness, an increase in death (e.g., 19% in the U.S. by 2022), and at times debilitating long-term health effects (CDC, 2023). Due to issues in infrastructure, the U.S. quickly became the country with the highest number of COVID-19 deaths (CDC, 2023). Table 1 below summarizes a timeline from the Center for Disease Control and Prevention (CDC, 2023).

To mitigate the pandemic, life in 2020 and into 2021 generally moved towards little to no physical contact, which varied in duration depending on the context (CDC, 2023). The move to remote life had consequences across many spheres, all of which impacted different populations differently, often widening the gap between the elite and the marginalized (CDC, 2023). Table 2 below summarizes some of the mitigation measures and impacts based on information provided by the CDC. Most notable for this book is that education in many places moved to forced emergency remote teaching and learning (ERTL), also called "Zoom School" (CDC, 2023).

Table 1 COVID-19 Pandemic Timeline and Data

December 2019	"Pneumonia" cluster reported from Wuhan, China.
January 2020	First COVID-19 death.
February 2020	COVID-19 deaths exceed SARS deaths.
March 2020	COVID-19 a global pandemic. Life moves remote.
August 2020	Third leading cause of death in the U.S.
December 2020	Vaccines available. Restrictions begin to be removed.

Table 2 COVID-19 Mitigation Measures and COVID-19 Impacts

Mitigation Measures	Physical distancing requirements of six feet. Travel bans. Lockdowns and curfews. Mandatory masking. Restrictions on public gatherings. Mandatory testing. Mandatory vaccination. Quarantine and isolation procedures.
Immediate Impacts	Non-essential businesses shut down or moved online. Non-essential services moved remote or canceled. Campus and school closures. Event cancellations. Breakdown in supply chains.
Ripple Effects	Financial • Highest unemployment rate since Great Depression (14.7%). • 52 million people with food insecurities. • Housing insecurities. • Global recession. (Mental) Health • 41% of adults struggled with mental health; 11% with suicidal ideation. • People delayed medical treatment causing complications. Destabilized Home Life • 140,000 children in the U.S. lost a caregiver. Mistrust in Institutions and Governments • Increase in civil unrest.

Governments and their agencies developed relief and aid programs to support individuals, businesses, and institutions to reduce the impact of the pandemic and underlying issues. The crisis brought to light global and societal inequities (Andrew et al., 2020) and compounded crises that had already existed before, as shown in Table 3.

As life moved remote, the lack of technology (skills) became the source of crisis and compounded inequities. Crowd-sourcing and (virtual) collaboration became more common practices as people were removed from their usual professional and personal circles (Kaul & Garg, 2021). Taking health care as an example: apps and databases were developed for tracking the spread of COVID-19, contact tracing, and educating the public (CDC, 2023); the urgency for finding effective treatments, a vaccine, and ways

Table 3 Crises Brought to Light by the COVID-19 Pandemic

Health-care	Inadequate health-care infrastructure (CDC, 2023) • Hospital beds. • Intensive care units. • Essential equipment. • Personal protective devices. • Treatments (medicine, ventilators, etc.). • Number of under- and uninsured.
Technology	• Lack of access to technology and digital literacy needed to participate in remote life (Supovitz & Manghani, 2022). • Inequities in technology access and skills (Ortega, 2017). • Inadequate reliable internet access in low-income and rural communities (Kantamneni, 2020).
Institutions	Governmental Institutions • Mistrust in or disapproval of the way institutions (mis)managed the crises (Edelman, 2021). Educational Institutions • Increased frustration with administrators (Williamson et al., 2018). • Appreciation for departmental support, but frustration with the college and university due to lack of support/timely and transparent communication (Edelman, 2021). • Decreased educator tolerance with administrators and the pay gaps between regular educators and those in administration (Vujnovic & Foster, 2022). • National trend toward unionization (Nakra, 2021). • Educators leaving the profession (Rantz, 2021; Sainato, 2021). • Students taking breaks from education (Morgan & Thompson, 2023).
Inequities	Inequitably experienced health risks (CDC, 2023) • Death rates higher among Black people (e.g., Chicago: Blacks 68% of COVID-19 deaths and only 30% of the population). • American Indian and Alaska Natives at greater risk for severe COVID. • Health-care infrastructure worse for rural and low socio-economic as well as BIPOC communities. • Higher ratios of mental health concerns among essential workers, unpaid caregivers, youth, LBGTQ+, and BIPOC. • Losing caregivers disproportionately impacted BIPOC children. Inequitably experienced mitigation measures (CDC, 2023) • Essential workers continued to have to work in person. • People in high density areas could not keep six feet distance. • Low-income workers without adequate remote working space could not (effectively) work from home. • Low-income workers and minoritized groups were especially impacted by unemployment. • Reduction in social and learning services. • Increase in unpaid caretaking responsibilities. • 5.1 million women left the workforce in response to school closures leading to the lowest participation in salaried work for women since 1986. • Access to support for students and care-taking support for working professionals was inequitably distributed (Blundell et al., 2020). • Isolation led some households to be closer than ever, while in others conflicts (e.g., physical and emotional abuse, divorce and separation, etc) increased (Mineo, 2022).

to mitigate the pandemic prompted unconventional technology-mediated mechanisms of collecting and disseminating data, global and interagency collaborations (CDC, 2023); and telehealth exponentially increased, bringing (mental) health support to communities that may not have had access previously (Shaver, 2022). Technology is not neutral and, at times, it is both the solution and the problem (e.g., Warner & Diao, Chapter 12, this volume).

COVID-19 and Language Learning and Teaching

The context of the pandemic was difficult for many people and disproportionately impacted marginalized groups. Isolation, lacking support, burnout, and mistrust in institutions made pandemic life difficult for learning and teaching regardless of subject matter. In this discussion of education during COVID, we will first summarize issues in education generally before turning to the conditions of language learning and teaching.

Emergency Remote Teaching and Learning (ERTL) Conditions

Emergency Remote Teaching and Learning (ERTL) became one of the prominent terms to describe the triaged trial-by-fire, typically (partially) online formats of education that ever-evolved in responses to constantly changing conditions and guidelines during the pandemic. ERTL was challenging for learners, parents and guardians, educators, administrators, and schools and higher education in general.

School closures meant learners lost access to important services (Abramson, 2022), were removed from their school-affiliated social lives, needed to participate in education from (often) less than ideal circumstances (Mineo, 2022) often in inadequate spaces with inadequate equipment (Fontenelle-Tereshchuk, 2021) with inadequate digital skills (Supovitz & Manghani), which increased their support needs, while in an environment with less support (Lidegran et al., 2021). These circumstances contributed to (inequitable) learning losses (Aguaded et al., 2023; Engzell et al., 2021). Institutions and educators responded with changes in policies, practices, and procedures (Garrote et al., 2021) and using own and government funds to improve infrastructures and training. ERTL impacted the personal development of learners (Checa-Domene et al., 2022), their mental health, and their sense of belonging (van Heerden & Bharuthram, 2023), which led to a sense of missing out on their college/school experience (Hayran & Anik, 2021), delays in getting their careers started (Mockaitis et al., 2022), and long-term financial concerns (Soria et al., 2023).

Supporting learners in crisis while one's self is also in crisis without adequate support, left educators overwhelmed and burned out (Ghanizadeh, 2022). Educators experienced struggles (e.g., adequate work space, transportation, care-taking needs, health care, financial losses, job insecurities due to declining enrollments, etc.), while being tasked to academically and emotionally support their learners (Snow et al., 2023), which took priority (Benesch & Prior, 2023). Not surprisingly, educator workload increased (Mpofu, 2020), while teachers were stripped of their support system (Khalil & Alharbi, 2022) and distanced from their local communities of practice (van Deusen-Scholl, 2020). Not surprisingly, many educators opted to leave the profession, be it through early retirement (Zamarro et al., 2021) or quitting their jobs (Sainato, 2021). Even amongst the group of educators who stayed in the profession, many engaged in quiet quitting, a process in which they stay employed but disengage from their work and their workplace (Gregersen et al., 2021). Yet others were reluctant or even refused to return to in-person work (Rantz, 2021).

Like educators, many students left school or took leaves of absence, resulting in decreased enrollment and retention rates (Morgan & Thompson, 2023), which culminated in various budgetary crises and thereby anxieties about job loss and program closures (Kutch, 2023). Educational leaders and administrators were the beacon of light that educators looked to for guidance, training, and support (Azaz, 2020), and the ones left to fight for positions and programs (Morgan & Thompson, 2023), which meant that ERTL was even more detrimental for program directors, who not only supported learners but also other educators (Mills, 2020).

The Nature of Language Learning

Due to the nature of language education, ERTL posed unique challenges for language learners and educators. Remote formats of teaching and masked teaching at six feet of distance complicated language teaching that has at its core and as its goal spontaneous (oral) communication (Nobrega et al., 2020). Masks and distance made it difficult to read facial expressions, accurately hear, and read lips – all elements crucial for successful communication and thereby language learning (Codreanu & Celik, 2013; Goldin et al., 2020; Landry & Hamel, Chapter 8, this volume; Morris et al., Chapter 11, this volume). Time lags in remote teaching (Gherheş et al., 2021) and the plethora of students who could not or did not want to leave their cameras on (Bedenlier et al., 2020; Calvo-Ferrer, 2022; Walter & Schenker, 2022) further complicated communicative practice and thereby language learning. With travel restrictions and social isolation, the opportunity for immersive experiences – hailed to be essential for achieving high proficiencies – such as education abroad (Griffin, 2023), community engagement (Baumgartner & Schulze, 2023), and/or service learning (Kautz, 2021; Zimotti & Miller DeRutté, Chapter 4, this volume) decreased, putting into question the ability to achieve advanced proficiency levels and/or specialized language skills.

The State of Language Education

Looking at the state of language education in the U.S., there have been significant enrollment declines in languages other than English (LOTE) across post-secondary contexts (Looney & Lusin, 2019) due to persistent erosion of the importance of LOTE coupled with a "monolingual mindset" (Copland & McPake, 2021); ideologies that undervalue multilingualism and thereby language learning (Baker & Wright, 2017); students' personal and systemic barriers, such as unavailability of classes/preferred languages, poor articulation, less room in students' schedules due to credit-heavy vocation-oriented degree programs (Clayton, 2022); and the presentation of university language requirements as chores/obstacles (Diao & Liu, 2020).

In surveying the status of university language requirements, data from the MLA report (Lusin, 2012) show that in 2009–10, only 50.7% of 1,358 four-year institutions had a language requirement, as opposed to 67.5% in 1994–95, and for comparison 88.9% in 1965–66 (Lord, 2020a). Lord (2020a) further cited a more recent albeit smaller-scale survey carried out in 2017 among ADFL member departments, in which 30% of the represented institutions had no language requirement, and of those, close to 40% had previously had one but it had been eliminated. Lord (2020a) points to the connection between the removal of university requirements and shrinking enrollments. Both of these trends put into question the future of language education (Quinn, 2023).

Catalyst for Innovation and Growth in Language Education

With little incentive for students to study languages, it becomes even more important to reduce barriers to language education. The voices in this volume present an opportunity to positively impact practices and programs. Several programs revised curricula and implemented them online as an opportunity to address other issues, offering online courses to reach additional ESL educators to meet the growing multilingual population (e.g., Schmitt & Sorokina, Chapter 14, this volume); changing policies about online education to increase enrollment (Gleason & Bartlett, Chapter 9, this volume); using virtual realities (VR) to bridge the classroom and real world demands of Spanish in healthcare settings (Zimotti & Miller De Rutté, Chapter 4, this volume); and increasing student output through a flipped approach (e.g., Lavolette & Asaba, Chapter 10, this volume). Experience in new modalities contributed to an expansion in receptivity to alternative course modalities, in addition to the creation of different instructional delivery formats (hy-flex courses) (Classen, 2023), which ultimately expands access to language education.

While educators lost their traditional communities of practice, they found new ways and communities, which in some cases led to a greater emphasis on teamwork and collaboration (Sánchez-Gutiérrez et al., Chapter 7, this volume; van Deusen-Scholl, 2020) and changed work conditions/practices for different work arrangements (Greene & Sanderson, 2023). The forced innovation resulted in increased confidence and greater willingness to experiment (Kutch, 2023), which led to greater sustained innovation/creativity (Baumgartner & Schulze, 2023). The tumult opened up opportunities for engagement and self-reflection (Giupponi et al., Chapter 6, this volume; Hamdan et al., 2021); the emotional trauma both required and promoted new ways of managing stress and anxiety (Denzel & Ostrau, 2023); and the challenges in triaged online education heightened appreciation of in-person, F2F modalities which may have previously been taken for granted (Brunow & Kuhn-Brown, 2023). Overall, attitudes toward technology-mediated language learning (CALL) improved (Hamdan et al., 2021). In short, the COVID-19 crisis forced learners, educators, and programs to expand their repertoires (Hussain et al., 2021); become flexible, adaptable, and resilient (Kolovou, 2023); innovate (Classen, 2023); and take agency and make room for agency (Zhu & Chan, 2023).

Lessons Learned for Language Education

In 2020, CALL practitioners and scholars found themselves suddenly in demand to assist others in solving the immediate language education needs (Lord, 2020b). Lessons already learned by CALL practitioners and scholars were (re)discovered by a larger audience such as the possibility of online language education (Amoush & Mizher, 2023; Ghanizadeh, 2022), need for community building in online courses (Kaul & Garg, 2021), issues in access and accessibility (Kantamneni, 2020), barriers to technology literacy and access (Nordmeyer & Bettney, 2022), challenges with copy-right and plagiarism (Gacs et al., 2020), benefits and challenges of synchronous vs. asynchronous modalities (Ocando Finol, 2020), etc. ERTL raised awareness of CALL practices and research; allowed for comparisons between the pre-pandemic perspectives on CALL and those during and post-ERTL; and provided opportunities for longitudinal investigations in ever-changing conditions. ERTL research brought important lessons for navigating the new normal and preparing for future crises.

Crisis-Preparedness

Most institutions, learners, and stakeholders were not fully crisis-prepared. Equity and inclusion were quickly revealed as problems during ERTL. We focus here on digital skills, digital access, support for learners with disabilities, and program bifurcation.

Already before the pandemic, researchers have pointed out the limited access to adequate equipment or high speed internet necessary for audio and video input, software and equipment that allows for the teaching and practicing of non-Roman scripts, essential components of online language learning (Winke & Goertler, 2008). Even individuals who had access, may not have known how to use the equipment (Winke & Goertler, 2008). Students and educators in pre-pandemic online courses participated in online courses from campus or other adequately equipped spaces, yet during the pandemic this could no longer be assumed or required (Fontenelle-Tereshchuk, 2021; Gacs et al., 2020). Inequitably distributed digital access and skills pose(d) a social equity issue (Gleason & Suvorov, 2019; Ortega, 2017; Supovitz & Manghani, 2022).

Educator training in CALL (Kessler, 2018; MacIntyre et al., 2020; Paesani, 2020) and CALL knowledge (Arnold & Ducate, 2015) was insufficient for ERTL. Lack of administrative support influenced educators' experience and their attitude toward online language teaching (Jin et al., Chapter 2, this volume). Since most educators had no experience teaching languages online (Caws et al., 2021) and even those with prior experience teaching online, had to adjust their teaching for ERTL and needed training (Gacs et al., 2020; Moser et al., 2021), educators felt unprepared (Morris, 2022) and needed professional development (Morris et al., Chapter 11, this volume).

Institutional infrastructure was insufficient to support the increase in technology usage and support needs (Gacs et al., 2020). Varied institutional preparedness displayed inequities (Crawford et al., 2020). Not all institutions had appropriate licenses to allow for interactive multimedia course design or may have had data security rules that prohibited tools commonly used in language classes. Not all institutions were able to invest in additional resources to deploy to learners and/or educators or to pay for reimbursements for equipment/internet services. Furthermore, emergency funding made available typically had to be invested in more generally needed resources and not specialized resources for language learning.

In many instances learners and educators with disabilities lost their support services or had them greatly reduced (Abramson, 2022). The triaged conversions of F2F courses came at the expense of students with disabilities (Gacs et al., 2020). While teachers became more aware of inclusion issues and felt that they needed to increase their inclusive pedagogy practices (Rüschoff, Chapter 5, this volume), trainings did not include professional development for supporting learners with disabilities in (language) ERTL (Tecedor & Gómez Soler, Chapter 13, this volume).

Language programs continue to struggle with bifurcation, resulting in contingent faculty and graduate students' having fewer rights. Vulnerable educators may not have had, or felt that they did not have, a choice over modality; may have been forced to return to in-person teaching before they felt safe; and the larger and more frequently meeting courses they typically teach put them at greater health risk. Furthermore, contingent faculty and graduate students are often in shared offices, which are not conducive to online teaching and meetings.

Working through Crisis

There was no rule book for navigating ERTL. Communications from decision-makers were often neither transparent nor clear nor timely creating instability and mistrust but also opportunities for learners and educators to actively make choices in the absence of guidance. Educators and learners developed an appreciation for the agency they were given or were able to take as well as the flexibility of the new context (Rüschoff, Chapter 5, this volume). Some educators felt overwhelmed by the new demands (Sainato, 2021) and others felt greatly empowered to innovate their practice (Baumgartner & Schulze, 2023).

Prior to the pandemic, language educators had already explored different teaching modalities. Delivery formats often included face-to-face (i.e., almost exclusively in person in the same physical space), blended or hybrid (i.e., some of the instruction online and some in person), and online (i.e., most instruction occurring online) (Goertler, 2019). These delivery formats are further differentiated by the synchronicity of the course (asynchronous, synchronous, or mixed) and the distribution of activities (e.g., flipped classroom, where class-time is reserved for interactive components and asynchronous time for new content and concept instruction) (Goertler, 2019).

In ERTL, some programs made no program or institution-wide decisions and others continuously planned and revised together (Sánchez-Gutiérrez et al., Chapter 7, this volume) as they adjusted modalities and curricula. Three modalities gained more traction namely asynchronous components/ courses (Giupponi et al., Chapter 6, this volume); the flipped classroom (Lavolette & Asaba, Chapter 10, this volume; Schmitt & Sorokina, Chapter 14, this volume); and the hy-flex model, where some of the individuals are in the same physical location and others are joining remotely (Lederman, 2022). As learners were removed from their school-affiliated co-curricular experiences and school-affiliated social lives, institutions sought virtual alternatives. Different modalities were explored not just for classes, but also co-curricular activities, service learning, community engagement, education abroad, office hours, tutoring, research activities, meetings, etc.

The constantly changing policies surrounding physical gatherings and the frequent needs for quarantining or sick leaves necessitated flexibility within and beyond modalities. Masked and distanced F2F language classes limited group and pair work options requiring technology-mediated communication (e.g., microphones, texting, etc.). F2F classes needed larger classrooms or split classes into sections to adhere to distancing requirements. Regular class sizes of 20–30 students were often impossible to manage when moved to ERTL formats as smaller class sizes have been seen as crucial for success in synchronous online courses (Payne, 2020). Educators explored different options: reducing class sizes (Rüschoff, Chapter 5, this volume); splitting one course into multiple sections (Landry & Hamel, Chapter 8, this volume; Sánchez-Gutiérrez et al., Chapter 7, this volume); and replacing class sessions with individual speaking appointments (Sánchez-Gutiérrez et al., Chapter 7, this volume; Warner & Diao, Chapter 12, this volume). Institutions continuously changed the rules about modality, adjusted calendars to eliminate or extend breaks, etc. to address the ever-changing circumstances

Assessment practices changed during the pandemic to adjust to the remote format and many seized the moment for alternative assessment formats. Some of these adjustments included: proctored online formal exams, portfolios, project/task-based assessments, interactions as assessments (Giupponi et al., Chapter 6, this volume); self- and peer evaluation (Rüschoff,

Chapter 5, this volume); and replacing formal summative assessments with continuous alternative formative assessments (Rüschoff, Chapter 5, this volume; Sánchez-Gutiérrez et al., Chapter 7, this volume). Digital tools made logistics of assessment more efficient (e.g., automated grading, feedback storage, feedback modalities, etc.) (Giupponi et al., Chapter 6, this volume; Landry & Hamel, Chapter 8, this volume).

Mitigation policies (e.g., distancing, masking, quarantine, etc.) had an impact on expectations and policies. Policies were adjusted: laxer attendance policies; limitations on homework and screen time; removal of fixed due dates; enhanced flexibility with regard to independent study, withdrawal, leave of absence, and pass/fail grading options (Greene & Sanderson, 2023; Kougiourouki & Masali, 2022; Was & Greve, 2021). Generally speaking, expectations were lowered (Garrote et al., 2021). For example, language educators indicated being less stringent about target language use expectations (Lavolette & Asaba, Chapter 10, this volume; Warner & Diao, Chapter 12, this volume). Some of these changes were especially interesting for language classes, where regular engagement with the language and input and output opportunities are necessary for improvement.

Pre-pandemic many educators refused to teach online and/or engage with technology training (Jin et al., Chapter 2, this volume) and could afford to do so due to no imminent needs. The pandemic forced professional development resulting in unprecedented wide-spread educational technology training (Giupponi et al., Chapter 6, this volume). Professional development was needed for the triage phase, for more sustainable revisions and iterations in later ERTL courses, and during the transition to the new normal. Pre-pandemic guidelines for educator CALL knowledge include ACTFL's position paper on CALL (ACTFL, 2017); the European Framework for Digital Competence of Educators (European Commission et al., 2017); and the TESOL Technology Standards (Healey et al., 2011). Quality Matters and the Online Language Consortium adjusted their online education guidelines for ERTL (Gacs et al., 2020).

Moving through the pandemic meant relearning one's trade and reshaping one's working environment, whether educators navigated the challenges of teaching during a pandemic alone through trial and error (Gao & Zhang, 2020), through formal training (Giupponi et al., Chapter 6, this volume), through self-reflection and iterative teacher-researcher practices (Landry & Hamel, Chapter 8, this volume), or with a community of practice be it a new community of practitioners or a community of practice across ranks locally (Sánchez-Gutiérrez et al., Chapter 7, this volume; Tecedor & Gómez Soler, Chapter 13, this volume); relying on social media or blogs (Xu et al., 2022);

shadowing/observing or consulting more experienced CALL practitioners (Jin et al., Chapter 2, this volume; Landry & Hamel, Chapter 8, this volume; Tecedor & Gómez Soler, Chapter 13, this volume); being mentored (Tecedor & Gómez Soler, Chapter 13, this volume); or seeking help from their students (Jin et al., Chapter 2, this volume; Landry & Hamel, Chapter 8, this volume). Overall educators displayed flexibility and creativity in redefining their roles and learning new skills (Rüschoff, Chapter 5, this volume; Warner & Diao, Chapter 12, this volume). Thereby the pandemic contributed to significant professional growth (Gao & Zhang, 2020; Jin et al., Chapter 2, this volume; Rüschoff, Chapter 5, this volume; Sun & Zou, 2022). Educators not only improved their global technological skills, but also their knowledge and skills for detailed pedagogical decisions for technology-mediated language learning and teaching (Jin et al., Chapter 2, this volume).

While many institutions, organizations, and publishers rushed to make resources available, about half of educators were not aware of or did not take advantage of them (Jin et al., Chapter 2, this volume; Walter & Schenker, 2022). Institutions did not create conditions to make it possible for educators to participate in training (e.g., timing of the sessions, lack of compensation, already excessive workload, etc.) and/or for those sessions to support the particular needs for language education (Jin et al., Chapter 2, this volume) leaving trainings often inadequate (Gómez Soler & Tecedor, 2018; Jin et al., Chapter 2, this volume; Moser & Wei, 2023). Training sessions conducted by individuals or institutions closer to language education were perceived more positively (Walter & Schenker, 2022). Hence, the professional organizations (most notably IALLT with its webinars) and the Title VI Language Research Centers played a crucial role in providing just-in-time language teacher training and support.

The continued high levels of burnout at this time suggest that living through the pandemic was difficult - though how so depended on many factors (Garrote et al., 2021). Disconnected from resources and their social networks and support systems (Abramson, 2022) students were not well: Learners felt anxious and lacked motivation (Wilson & Lengeling, 2021); were lonely, lacked certain freedoms, missed interaction in both quality and quantity, and struggled with establishing a sense of community and experiencing belonging (Morris et al., Chapter 11, this volume; Rüschoff, Chapter 5, this volume; Sánchez-Gutiérrez et al., Chapter 7, this volume) - a challenge in all online learning (Schmitt & Sorokina, Chapter 14, this volume; Strambi & Bouvet, 2003). Increased screentime impacted focus (Abramson, 2022; Bradley Ruder, 2019) and led to Zoom-fatigue (Bradley Ruder, 2019; Kohnke & Moorhouse, 2022). From the beginning learners did not always have the necessary adequate space for participation, access to the appropriate technologies, and human support to have a positive and successful learning experience (Zimotti & Miller DeRutté, Chapter 4, this volume). As distance and life in crisis compounded, learners disengaged (Czura & Baran-Łucarz, 2021; Gokool & Naidoo, Chapter 3, this volume) as indicated by low attendance and completion rates, high attrition, and lack of visible participation. The (often times necessary) turned off cameras impacted the experience for not just the student, but also for their peers and educators (Bedenlier et al., 2020) as it was experienced negatively (Walter & Schenker, 2022) and judged as disengagement (Warner & Diao, Chapter 12, this volume). A few innovations appeared to have a positive impact on well-being and/or a sense of belonging: VR tasks (Thrasher, 2022; Zimotti & Miller DeRutté, Chapter 4, this volume); alternative evaluation methods (Rüschoff, Chapter 5, this volume); and online social and community building activities (Landry & Hamel, Chapter 8, this volume).

The additional emotional (Benesch & Prior, 2023), interactional (Maican & Cocorada, 2021), academic, logistical, and technological support needed by learners was shifted to teachers, who became increasingly aware of learners' diverse needs and redesigned their courses and policies accordingly (Rüschoff, Chapter 5, this volume). The changes made teaching more varied and thereby displayed educator resilience, flexibility, and adaptability (Rüschoff, Chapter 5, this volume); yet, increased their workload and emotion labor (Snow et al., 2023; Warner & Diao, Chapter 12, this volume). Constantly changing policies put a strain on sustainability (Morris, 2022) and motivation to innovate (Giupponi et al., Chapter 6, this volume) as staying up-to-date with new tools without training is challenging (Morris, 2022). Educators were confronted with much decision-making leading some to decision fatigue (Mills, 2020) and combined with the technostress contributed to educators' own emotional distress (Landry & Hamel, Chapter 8, this volume; Sánchez-Gutiérrez et al., Chapter 7, this volume; Warner & Diao, Chapter 12, this volume). The demands made of educators at times conflicted with their values as educators (Back et al., 2022): what they were expected/expecting to do and what they were able to do were a mismatch, decreasing their confidence and causing stress and general sense of not being well (Jin et al., 2021; MacIntyre et al., 2022; Warner & Diao, Chapter 12, this volume).

Some educators were able to continuously adapt and move forward and others were removing themselves or disengaging (Ghanizadeh, 2022; Landry & Hamel, Chapter 8, this volume). While some educators felt invigorated and appreciated being forced to re-evaluate their practices (Giupponi et al., Chapter 6, this volume; Rüschoff, Chapter 5, this volume); overall educators were stressed and burned out (Jin et al., 2021; MacIntyre et al., 2020; Warner & Diao, 2022), but with training and time stress and trauma decreased and growth was reported (Jin et al., Chapter 2, this volume; MacIntyre et al., 2022; Warner & Diao, Chapter 12, this volume). As educators experienced ERTL and professional development, they developed a more favorable attitude toward CALL (Gao & Cui, 2022; Jin et al., 2021; Waldvogel & Robayna, 2022; Walter & Schenker, 2022); their emotional distress decreased (MacIntyre et al., 2022) and they came to appreciate the resource sharing and communities of practice that developed during ERTL (Sánchez-Gutiérrez et al., Chapter 7, this volume; Xu et al., 2022).

ERTL Outcomes and By-products

ERTL had an impact and provided an opportunity to take stock of existing policies, procedures, practices, expectations, and goals. It was also a moment in which many saw new possibilities and realized the differences between communication outside of the classroom and communication within the classroom.

The goal of contemporary language learning and teaching is typically communicative competence broadly defined. At the center of communicative competence is interaction and human connection, the format of which is changing with the development of technology. Language users today regularly communicate via text chat in real-time in a way that approximates spoken language in form and usage more so than typically written textual genres (Pateno, et al., 2022). Multimodal input, output, and interaction increases the cues and pragmatic practices that language users need to manage. As these multimodal interactions have become more ubiquitous, these new forms of interaction require adjustments in language curricular goals, pedagogical techniques, and classroom policies. The pandemic helped learners recognize the dissonance between the communicative practices in their classrooms and those outside the classroom and gave educators the impetus to design their educational environments to better match the hybridity and multimodality of today's communications (Giupponi et al., Chapter 6, this volume).

Technology has also shaped education. Naturally, online language education and CALL more generally were not an invention of the pandemic. The pandemic learning conditions simply made the potential of CALL more visible. While few were able to approach the innovations in the first round with a careful review of existing literature or planning, subsequent iteration allowed for a more purposeful and informed, and therefore more successful, process (Giupponi et al., Chapter 6, this volume; Landry & Hamel, Chapter 8, this volume). CALL practitioners and scholars already knew that well-planned CALL is effective for language learning (Plonsky & Ziegler, 2016). Literature reviews, syntheses, and meta-analyses have shown that learning outcomes and performance in online, blended, and face-to-face courses are comparable (Moneypenny & Aldrich, 2016; Blake et al., 2008; Goertler, 2019; Grgurovic et al., 2013). Online language education can be more flexible and adaptive, especially when utilizing individualized paths and intelligent feedback (Goertler, 2019); reduces barriers to language education (Goertler, 2019) and logistical stresses such as long commutes (Gleason & Bartlett, Chapter 9, this volume; Landry & Hamel, Chapter 8, this volume; Morris et al., Chapter 11, this volume; Schmitt & Sorokina, Chapter 14, this volume). Similar to CMC, online course (component)s can more easily be structured to reduce teacher dominance (Schmitt & Sorokina, Chapter 14, this volume). The biggest challenges of online education are (1) the aforementioned stakeholder preparedness; (2) technological issues; (3) lack of a common physical experience; and (4) challenges in building community.

The lack of shared physical experiences and missing non-verbal cues (Schmitt & Sorokina, Chapter 14, this volume) combined with screen sizes and other technological issues (Morris et al., Chapter 11, this volume) reduce comprehensible input and output, tamper the sense of community and increase mis(sed) communication (Landry & Hamel, Chapter 8, this volume). Learning outcomes and/or performance vary more in online courses than F2F courses (Gleason & Bartlett, Chapter 9, this volume; Goertler & Gacs, 2018; Schmitt & Sorokina, Chapter 14, this volume). Factors influencing success in online learning environments are: self-motivation, technology skills (Discenza et al., 2001; Geng et al., 2019); motivation and stress (Heo & Han, 2018); self-regulation and self-directed learning (Gokool & Naidoo, Chapter 3, this volume; Martin et al., 2020); conscientiousness (Arispe & Blake, 2012); personality (Morris et al., Chapter 11, this volume); educators' skills, knowledge, and attitudes (Moser et al., 2021); and course design.

Comparative results between ERTL and non-crisis F2F courses mirror the results from comparisons between online and F2F courses (Gleason et al., 2024; Gleason & Bartlett, Chapter 9, this volume; Merrill et al., 2021). Learners also perceived no significant differences in modalities' effectiveness (Morris et al., Chapter 11, this volume). Interestingly, Gleason and Bartlett (Chapter 9, this volume), found that students in F2F outperformed those in post-ERTL online courses, but the ERTL students outperformed all pre- and post-ERTL groups. These longitudinal results suggest that there might be differences between pre-pandemic, ERTL, and post-ERTL courses regardless of modality. During ERTL learning and teaching conditions were different from pre-pandemic and post-ERTL. Given the number of students and educators who (temporarily) excited education, student and teacher profiles may also have been different.

ERTL required adjustments and inspired creativity and innovation. Most education moved (partially) online and many different formats of online and hybrid learning developed or gained popularity. One promising version of (partially) online education is the flipped classroom, that combines asynchronous and synchronous components thereby taking advantage of the best of both worlds: access to authentic materials, intelligent feedback, immediate feedback, virtual access through CALL and the inter-personal relationship building through a shared physical experience or at least synchronous experience (Lavolette & Asaba, Chapter 10, this volume). Another modality that became more prominent during ERTL with potential for the future were virtual immersions, be it through virtual exchanges or VR. VR benefits include: language learning, learner autonomy, motivation, transcultural competence, authenticity, engagement, safe practice environment, sense of feeling present, and lower anxiety (see also Kaplan-Rakowski & Gruber, 2021; Zimotti & Miller DeRutté, Chapter 4, this volume). VR and virtual immersion hold promise for simulating real world tasks and easing the transition from the classroom to functioning in the targeted language context.

The innovations from ERTL were not just a creative but also a strategic moment. Some used the pandemic to address underlying long-standing issues (Rüschoff, Chapter 5, this volume); others approached the creation of materials purposefully for future use (Lavolette & Asaba, Chapter 10, this volume); yet others used the pandemic to try new delivery formats (Lavolette & Asaba, Chapter 10, this volume; Schmitt & Sorokina, Chapter 14, this volume) or task types (e.g., VR) for use in the future (Zimotti & Miller DeRutté, Chapter 4, this volume); and others - like all authors in this volume - used research to make evidence-based decisions. Educators tried to better meet their students' pedagogical and logistical needs to improve effectiveness (Giupponi et al., Chapter 6, this volume); remove barriers from language education by offering different teaching modalities (Gleason & Bartlett, Chapter 9, this volume); make courses more affordable, and provide more autonomy to learners (Giupponi et al., Chapter 6, this volume).

While online education had been steadily growing (Murphy-Judy & Johnshoy, 2017), the forced remote teaching made some educational institutions recommit to the residential experience and reduce online offerings in comparison to before the pandemic requiring special permission to continue teaching online (Sánchez-Gutiérrez et al., Chapter 7, this volume). Other institutions finally allowed online education and saw its value in increasing enrollments and access (Gleason & Bartlett, Chapter 9, this volume; Schmitt & Sorokina, Chapter 14, this volume). In that senses ERTL became a moment in which institutions, programs, and educators had to renegotiate and redefine their roles and identities.

Many educators, and at times even programs, recognized that in a moment of crisis goals have to be shifted as priorities and conditions changed. The desperate need for community and social and emotional wellbeing experienced by students and teachers alike brought to light the importance of well-being and belonging (Snow et al., 2023). Educators re-evaluated their curricula, teaching techniques, and policies (Rillard, 2020); reduced the workload and content (Baumgartner & Schulze, 2023); adjusted goals from setting stringent language proficiency goals to prioritizing enjoyment with the language and curiosity for the language and culture (Brunow & Kuhn-Brown, 2023); changed assessment practices to accommodate new modalities and take a more holistic and/or developmental approach (Landry & Hamel, Chapter 8, this volume; Rüschoff, Chapter 5, this volume; Sadeghi, 2023); removed expectations for target language use in favor of well-being (Warner & Diao, Chapter 12, this volume); all of which created tension between the pre-pandemic expectation of regular engagement in the target language and language learning and the ERTL modifications that prioritized community building and emotional support goals over language (use) goals (Warner & Diao, Chapter 12, this volume).

Negotiating the New Normal

We start this section with quotes from participants in this volume: "The pandemic 'completely revolutionized our perception of teaching and learning … what we built during the past academic year will be used again.'" (Landry & Hamel, Chapter 8, this volume, p. 166). "We became convinced that school systems should be updated and made more interactive." (Rüschoff, Chapter 5, this volume, p. 103)

Revisiting the State of Language Education

The pandemic prompted reevaluations of current practices and new ideas for cost-effective restructuring (Rilliard, 2020), especially since the increased costs for ERTL and lowered enrollments caused budget constraints leading to budget cuts, hiring freezes, and program closures. Small programs such as language programs and their educators were especially vulnerable, a trend that was exacerbated in language education contexts due to the ongoing decline in enrollment (Looney & Lusin, 2019). Language educators are often ill-protected populations on contingent contracts, who are particularly endangered by institutional cuts.

Unfortunately, the sudden ubiquity of learning technologies and growth in new technologies was (ab)used by some institutions to argue for decreased funding of language programs or complete elimination of language programs in favor of language learning apps or subcontracted/shared courses (Quinn, 2023). These arguments (e.g., West Virginia University) reinforced educator fears of being replaced by technology (Blake, 2001), contributing to the impression that online language education is an administrative agenda to lower costs, increase class sizes, and eliminate faculty (Jin et al., Chapter 2, this volume). Yet, language educators play a crucial role in online education (Hampel & Stickler, 2015) as facilitators and designers (Zimotti & Miller DeRutté, Chapter 4, this volume). Human connection and (in-person) interactions with educators are essential for students' sense of belonging, satisfaction, and success.

Reducing Barriers to Language Education

The lived experiences of the pandemic and new skills and knowledge have changed attitudes, infrastructures, and contexts; creating opportunities to reduce barriers to language education. Now - regardless of modality - we have different techniques, tools, and pathways to facilitate learning in our language programs with and without technology. Educators continue to use their reflections, new knowledge through training, and trial and error to revise their innovations in an iterative process (Giupponi et al., Chapter 6, this volume; Landry & Hamel, Chapter 8, this volume; Sánchez-Gutiérrez et al., Chapter 7, this volume). Hence, as Rüschoff (Chapter 5, this volume) and Giupponi et al. (Chapter 6, this volume) argue, ERTL had an impact on the normalization of educational technology. Further contributing to the normalization were the experiences with and training for online teaching during the pandemic as well as the improvements to infrastructures that individuals and institutions made to allow for remote learning and working. The normalization of technology has led to greater openness to and preparedness for (partially) online language learning, which is essential in increasing access to language education.

Technology can assist in making language courses logistically and financially more affordable. Traditional language courses often met five days a week putting restrictions on students' schedules, which intersected with their needs in their work, personal, and/or academic life (Greene & Sanderson, 2023). Offering alternative modalities reduces logistical burdens and increases access (Goertler, 2019). Generally speaking, educators see an opportunity in asynchronous materials (Giupponi et al., Chapter 6, this volume) due to their logistical flexibility, and the possibility to recycle materials (Lavolette & Asaba, Chapter 10, this volume). However, since learners often must work alone, curriculum design needs to scaffold and pace materials in the absence of an educator as guide and facilitator (Lavolette & Asaba, Chapter 10, this volume). Hence, self-paced asynchronous courses might be better suited for reading knowledge or content courses than lower-level language courses (Morris et al., Chapter 11, this volume). If using synchronous and asynchronous components, care must be taken to provide smooth transitions between online and F2F work (Morris et al., Chapter 11, this volume). If programs want to increase not just one-time enrollments, but also retain students, special care needs to be taken to establish a sense of community in online courses, especially those without a synchronous component. Perhaps inspired by the pandemic, educators and programs committed to developing Open Educational Resources (OER) or their own in-house online materials to reduce costs for attending their classes and customize materials to their learners (Giupponi et al., Chapter 6, this volume), thereby further reducing barriers to language education.

Assessments of any kind are often a hurdle for participation in language education. Making placement testing available on demand online with proctoring software and immediate automated scoring that is embedded in the Registrar's Office software removes barriers to registration. Alternative assessment formats (e.g., project-based, task-based, portfolios, etc.) are perceived as more enjoyable by educators (Giupponi et al., Chapter 6, this volume) and students (Rüschoff, Chapter 5, this volume) and reduce stress. Reducing high stakes summative assessments with creative formative assessments creates a more welcoming environment.

Yet, another barrier to language education are the barriers to curricular support services as well as immersive (co-)curricular experiences. During the pandemic, learners came to appreciate the increased availability of online resources such as online tutoring, advising, self-grading, and additional practice activities, all of which reduce the pressure of having to be in a physical location at a specific moment in time. Alternatives to formerly embodied experiences such as virtual home visits, virtual exchanges, virtual guest speakers, Google Street View excursions are ways to engage with other cultures, places, people, and languages (Kautz, 2021). Immersive VR experiences can bridge to real world tasks (Zimotti & Miller DeRutté, Chapter 4, this volume). Offering support services in a variety of modalities and expanding virtual immersive experiences are great ways to diversify pathways to a language major and/or further language development.

During ERTL, programs changed policies and procedures that made language courses less restrictive (e.g., lenient attendance policies, lower workloads, flexible due dates). Pass/fail options, typically not available to students, encouraged exploration of new subjects and languages. Such options as well as variable credits or flat-rate tuition can further reduce barriers to language education, especially at institutions without language requirements. Students are often afraid when faced with a classroom that is conducted exclusively in the target language. While ACTFL recommends 90% target language use in the classroom, multilingual perspectives on L2 acquisition place a greater value and importance on learners' full linguistics repertoire. Lavolette and Asaba (Chapter 10, this volume), for example, found that the purposeful inclusion of more L1 contributed to student satisfaction, workload, and learning outcomes. Regular target language input and output engagement is seen as an essential component of language learning, which prompts strict attendance policies, heavy regular homework loads, and verbal real-time participation expectations. These effort- or engagement-based components are often weighed highly in final grades. ERTL put into question these practices and ERTL modifications made workload and engagement expectations more feasible.

The survival and thriving of language programs depends on reducing barriers to accessing language education, lowering stressors associated with language learning, providing multiple pathways to successful course completion, and diversifying support services and immersive experiences. For program health, we must also facilitate program-wide engagement and sense of belonging to improve retention.

Engaging, Communicating, and Belonging

Engagement has changed and educators need to learn to communicate in different formats and modalities. This means that they have to relearn how to effectively use teaching spaces (Guillen et al., 2020) and how to communicate/renegotiate feeling rules (Warner & Diao, Chapter 12, this volume). In online classes or meetings, one can find it challenging to see/hear others as well as be seen/heard (Warner & Diao, Chapter 12, this volume). In pre-pandemic language courses, participation was required and defined by attendance in the physical space, and the quality and quantity of target language output. During ERTL physical attendance may no longer have been possible or a requirement and virtual attendance or asynchronous participation became acceptable; non-verbal responses such as nods, head shakes, votes, likes, etc. were seen as forms of participation, especially in lower-level language courses; written answers in a chat or on an assignment sheet may have become equally acceptable as oral answers. In today's world, interaction is mostly technology-mediated and the ERTL encouraged educators to embrace these new forms of interaction in their classrooms (Giupponi et al., Chapter 6, this volume).

Digital spaces have become social spaces, a resource, and the place for interaction, where educators show their presence through their digital footprint (e.g., online feedback, alerts), interactive features (Giupponi et al., Chapter 6, this volume), and ability to facilitate engagement. Incentivization can be an important technique to improve engagement (Gokool & Naidoo, Chapter 3, this volume) and not all engagement needs to be between teacher and student (Lavolette & Asaba, Chapter 10, this volume). Content delivery using an asynchronous medium can oftentimes help students engage more deeply and with more language production by offering them flexibility and freedom to work with the constraints of their multifaceted and complex lives and without the omnipresence of the educator as authority (Schmitt & Sorokina, Chapter 14, this volume).

Building relationships and community and thereby a sense of belonging, can be difficult in a hybrid/hy-flex world. Platforms have to be carefully selected to not only make communication possible, but to allow for the social connections. Warner and Diao's (Chapter 12, this volume) participants used platforms students like in an - not always successful - attempt to build relationships and flatten hierarchies, but found them more effective when used by students without educators. Due to students' emotional needs synchronous formats are preferred (Warner & Diao, Chapter 12, this volume), as even in online courses or remote working contexts, synchronous activities are essential for emotion building. If selecting asynchronous components, they have to be carefully designed.

Technology is not neutral, serving both as a connector and stressor (Jin et al., 2021; Warner & Diao, Chapter 12, this volume). For example, Warner and Diao (Chapter 12, this volume) show how the relation to Zoom changed over time in their participants: from confidence builder in the beginning of ERTL, to a tool for connections further in the pandemic, and a source of frustration in later parts of the pandemic. Zoom/video conferencing meetings have replaced many, especially larger in-person meetings; as they are perceived as time efficient, however, they do require a private quiet space for participation, which especially for graduate students and contingent faculty may not always be an option. The important time to decompress, while walking from one meeting to the next, is lost when you can schedule back-to-back meetings. Informal interactions that are necessary for relationship building are more difficult to design effectively for online meetings. With the ubiquity of hybrid and hyflex learning and working conditions, we need to establish community norms for engagement.

Empowering the People

The pandemic showed people that things could be done differently and empowered them to demand change. Multi-modal or hy-flex options for learning and working have become ways to address diverse needs and desires. The additional flexibility experienced during the pandemic gave people a sense of agency, which they enjoyed and wanted to maintain (Rüschoff, Chapter 5, this volume). Employers are noticing that it is difficult to find employees for positions that require full-time physical presence. Similarly, some reports suggest that continued low attendance in classes is due to learners taking/demanding more agency (Zhu & Chan, 2023).

With increases in agency and autonomy, power dynamics change. During ERTL, learners appreciated being consulted in the redesign efforts, which provided them with agency in their own learning environment (Rüschoff, Chapter 5, this volume). Educators felt empowered to address existing issues with their modifications for ERTL conditions (Giupponi et al., Chapter 6, this volume). The autonomy, flexibility, and agency afforded through the crisis, allowed many educators to delegate power and leadership towards and to their learners (Zhu & Chan, 2023) reshaping classroom power dynamics. A more balanced distribution of power in the classroom results in reciprocity and collaboration, understanding and goodwill (Thi Thanh, 2023). The pandemic also shifted power relations in the workplace. The skill sets and knowledge that were needed prior to ERTL were different from those during ERTL, at times changing expert/leader roles and values of different expertise (Landry & Hamel, Chapter 8, this volume). Some programs created instant collaborative communities with often flattened hierarchies, while others maintained the bifurcated structures that separate graduate students and contingent faculty from the tenure-stream faculty. Sánchez-Gutiérrez et al. (Chapter 7, this volume) described how they flattened hierarchies and created a collaborative spirit and sense of community. Through the pandemic, students and educators alike have developed an increased appreciation of learner and peer voices and perspectives for curricular decisions and pedagogical recommendations (Rüschoff, Chapter 5, this volume).

In light of the ERTL experiences and research results, it behooves us to consider expanding opportunities for the humans in our institutions (learners, educators, administrators, and staff) to be agents in co-constructing the practices, policies, and procedures that best support their needs and define our new normal. Managing people in the physical and a virtual space at the same time is exhausting and requires new skills and community norms. Programs have to make decisions about what activities can be or should be in person, online asynchronous, or online synchronous. Given the plethora of options, it is important that institutions and educators clearly and transparently communicate, which modality their courses will take and why; which work modalities are allowed and under which conditions and for whom; and how tasks and responsibilities will be distributed across modality. Inconsistent, unclear, and often untimely communication during ERTL reduced trust in institutional leaders, which has to be rebuilt, and the new normal has to be collaboratively designed.

Facilitating Language Learning

The role of the (language) educator has changed during the pandemic and needs to be clearly defined and negotiated for the new normal. Two issues came to the forefront: (1) the role of technology vs. the role of educators; and (2) individual and whole human approaches necessitated by the diversity of lived experiences

Any form of CALL changes the role of the teacher as technology provides affordance forcing educators to redefine their roles and their relationship with technology (Tecedor & Gómez Soler, Chapter 13, this volume). Technology – whether in online or face-to-face classrooms – can be used for classroom management, access to authentic materials and virtual experiences, increase accountability, individualization of instruction, streamlining, recyclability of materials, and automate instruction and grading (Giupponi, et al., Chapter 6, this volume). Especially in asynchronous components, the teacher becomes more of a curriculum designer and feedback provider rather than a real-time guide (Lavolette & Asaba, Chapter 10, this volume). Programs must make purposeful choices about tools and provide training on how to use these tools, how to pedagogize the technology (Rapanta et al., 2021), and how to enact social roles. In program and course design a central question is: what roles are best served by technology and which by the teacher?

In synchronous (online and physical) components, especially during ERTL, teachers take on many socio-emotional roles such as the role of a therapist or life coach for students experiencing increasing levels of stress, uncertainty, and anxiety (Snow et al., 2023) and/or those who lose access to important student support services (Andrew et al., 2020). While some feel prepared and appreciate the expansion of their role, others harbor animosity and/or resistance to the new job expectations, for which we are neither trained nor compensated. Teacher-learner roles have been impacted and experienced a shift (Gregersen et al. 2021) leading to questions and rethinking of identities and responsibilities of our educational personae. Because educators so clearly prioritized their students' well-being during ERTL, awareness of the emotional labor in a pedagogy of care and the teacher's role as caretaker has increased, leaving us with important questions about what role educators should play. The care-taking role, so common with educators, cannot be replaced by technology, though at times it can be mitigated through technology (Warner & Diao, Chapter 12, this volume). If we are to continue to play the multitude of roles as educator, advisor, caretaker, mentor, etc., what skills and training are necessary to support us in this work, how it is evaluated and valued, and how do we create sustainable and equitable working conditions in light of this emotional labor?

Given the trauma and inequities that were/are part of stakeholders' lives, a whole human approach to education that is sustainable, trauma-informed, and transformative was/is needed and must guide modified practices, procedures, and policies. During ERTL, we collectively shifted to a more compassionate whole human approach to learning: working with more lenient student-centered policies and a pedagogy of care (Warner & Diao, Chapter 12, this volume). While some have embraced this, and are pushing for continued whole human approaches that acknowledge lived experiences and individualize experiences to meet needs, others may be more cautious or even reject such approaches. Greater flexibility and leniency holds the potential to spark emotional responses from educators, from taking pride in accommodating students to feeling betrayed by students and themselves due to a sense of betraying their standards (Sánchez-Gutiérrez et al., Chapter 7, this volume). We invite educators and programs to take the lessons from ERTL to keep and create more just, equitable, and sustainable working and learning conditions with high but attainable expectations.

Building Resilience and Crisis Preparedness

To enact a whole human approach, preparing stakeholders for crisis, building resilience, and creating an atmosphere of innovation and personal growth are key. Experimentation should be encouraged and failure must be an acceptable outcome. At the core of moving forward constructively, productively, and sustainably are: finding matrices to measure workload that go beyond contact hours and considering best ways to compensate both visible and invisible labor; creating sustainable workloads for all stakeholders; empowering stakeholders to be the experts and drivers of change; providing stakeholders with appropriate infrastructures for teaching, learning, and professional development; and supporting stakeholder well-being and belonging.

In order to better prepare for future crises, there are several needs and opportunities: Institutions and communities need to continue to improve support infrastructure in multiple modalities; offer training and improve infrastructure for technology. Learners not only need to be empowered to take agency in their learning, but also need training in how to become independent, self-directed learners. We must be cognizant to meet our learners where they are in terms of technology, community, modality, and to increase our awareness of their communication and learning needs. Additionally, learners need better strategies and support for time management and self-regulation in online and asynchronous formats (Morris et al., Chapter 11, this volume).

If institutions decide that increased online education is a strategic move forward, given the continued negative attitude toward online language education by educators and the relationship between training and experience with attitudes (Jin et al., Chapter 2, this volume), significant investments in compensated, sustainable, systematic, and collaborative training have to be made. Professional development opportunities should vary in format to address different learning styles and needs. An important goal of training should be fostering agency and teaching educators how to be auto-didacts, so that they have the knowledge, strategies, and resources and seek out the kind of training they need. Hence, training needs to be individualized taking into account where educators are starting out (Landry & Hamel, Chapter 8, this volume). Educators need an environment in which innovation is appreciated, compensated, and celebrated (Giupponi et al., Chapter 6, this volume). To sustainably move forward as Giupponi and colleagues have said: "... is to identify the instructors who will embrace innovation and encourage them so that they can guide the way for others." (Chapter 6, this volume, p. 131).

Rüschoff, Chapter 5, this volume and his colleagues from the larger survey project concluded based on their discussions that preparedness for crises requires educational literacy and adaptability rather than knowledge of specific tools. An important aspect of adaptability is "the ability to redesign or adapt approaches to and means of education in an agile and imaginative way in response to unexpected environmental or other changes." (Rüschoff, Chapter 5, this volume, p. 109). Building on Rüschoff's concepts, we suggest a framework of professional development that focuses on educational literacy and adaptability over specific tools. For example, at Michigan State University, we were able to use the mindset of adaptability and flexibility during the COVID-19 pandemic to adjust to and respond to teaching, learning, and working in the wake of a school shooting based on the lessons learned from ERTL.

The pandemic has shown us that the prior (lived) experience as well as current contextual factors influence how one experiences a crisis and/or traumatic event. This uniqueness means that we have to adjust environments and conditions to fit diverse individual needs. There is no one path forward; but an openness to new ways. At the core is giving permission to fail, to not know the answers, and to be vulnerable. We invite our profession to value these features as opportunities for growth in learning, teaching, and scholarship.

Committing to Language Education

There has been an increased tendency to view language education mainly as a service provider or for student professionalization and marketability within specific industries. Language educators have tried to fight back by emphasizing the scholarly and pedagogical significance of language studies in creating a more equitable and just globally connected world. Yet, the value of language education on U.S. campuses goes beyond the roles identified by those outside and those within language education. At a campus-wide event, we informally asked students, if they took language classes, and if so, what role those classes played in their education. The overwhelming answers were that their language classes - much like their arts and theater classes – gave them a sense of belonging, and were the places where they formed their closest college friendships early on, leading us to believe that language courses play a role in easing transitions to campus and increasing student retention and mental health.

Language teaching holds a unique place in university contexts. Lower level language courses are often attended by students in their first few years of university education. During this time, students typically take large classes, often with hundreds if not thousands of students. Yet, language courses offer them the chance to experience smaller, close-knit classroom settings, which combined with the focus on discussing individual lives and societal issues, make language courses an important environment for defining one's (multilingual and multicultural) identities, building connections on campus and within the world, and establishing their sense of belonging. This important role became even more visible during the pandemic, when students lost (partial or complete) access to many student support and social features and large classes moved to asynchronous formats. The pandemic underlined the important role of language classes and by extension language educators in students' well-being and sense of belonging (Hayran & Anik, 2021). As Morris and colleagues (Chapter 11, this volume) conclude: "In fact, the L2 classroom helped foster social interactions in a time when both social and physical distancing was necessary."

Language educators play a crucial role in learners' personal development, identity formation, well-being, and sense of belonging. This important, if not essential, contribution cannot be measured in the number of majors, enrollments, student credit hours, or any of the other quantitative measures that tend to define university budget allocations. Hence, moving forward we must find ways to make this contribution visible to educational leaders, who may operate under the assumption that language learning needs to be directly applicable to one's future career and professional goals, and can be obtained by using language learning apps. A closer look at data from learners in language courses during the pandemic will allow us to address the language program sustainability crisis. It is disheartening that while educational institutions across the country pronounce their commitment to diversity, equity, and inclusion (DEI) (Cumming et al., 2023); they remove language requirements, programs, and departments, when multilingualism and cultural understanding are necessary ingredients for successful DEI (Sykes, 2021). Furthermore, many DEI goals, such as equitable health-care and education require multilingual trained professionals (Schmitt & Sorokina, Chapter 14, this volume; Zimotti & Miller DeRutté, Chapter 4, this volume) and by extension language programming.

Moving Forward

In this concluding chapter, we documented the COVID-19 context, summarized research on ERTL, shared lessons learned, and made recommendations for designing the new normal. The COVID-19 pandemic was traumatizing and navigating the ever-changing ERTL was hard. As a new normal sets in, many people are still exhausted and burned out (Izquierdo et al., 2021) and counseling services continue to report increased caseloads (Schrimpf et al., 2023). In discussing this book chapter and the body of research on the impact of COVID-19 on higher education with a counselor in a higher education setting, the counselor concluded: "We need change, we cannot self-care our way through this." For those who lived through COVID, we hope this chapter provided you with an acknowledgment of your difficulties. For those who did not experience ERTL, we hope that our chapter helped you understand the context of the pandemic and perhaps understand the origin of policies, procedures, and practices you are experiencing.

The COVID-19 pandemic provoked change and it is impossible to go back to normal or to the "before times." We must use the ERTL lessons to move forward and negotiate our new normal in an iterative and collaborative process. This means being truthful about the challenges and the inequities; continuing to advance innovations that show(ed) potential through evidence-based iterative development processes; and seeking answers to the new questions to establish sustainable and just language education. Undoubtedly, technology will play a variety of roles in this process. We must continue to reduce barriers in language education and argue for its central role in student success and belonging within our shared commitment to diversity, equity, and inclusion.

About the Authors

Senta Goertler (Ph.D., University of Arizona, Second Language Acquisition and Teaching) is Associate Professor of Second Language Studies and German at Michigan State University. Her research focuses on language program administration especially as it intersects with technology and/or education abroad.

Jesse Gleason (Ph.D.) is Associate Professor of Spanish and Applied Linguistics at Southern Connecticut State University in New Haven, CT, where she presently coordinates the Lower-Division Spanish program. Her teaching and research interests include world language education, pedagogy and curriculum, technology-enhanced language learning, and assessment.

References

Abramson, A. (2022, January 1). Children's mental health is in crisis. *Monitor on Psychology*, *53*(1). https://www.apa.org/monitor/2022/01/special-childrens-mental-health

ACTFL. (2017). The role of technology in language learning. Retrieved June 19, 2023 from: https://www.actfl.org/news/the-role-of-technology-in-language-learning).

Aguaded, I., Vizcaíno-Verdú, A., García-Prieto, V., & De-Casas-Moreno, P. (2023). The impact of post-pandemic learning loss on education development: A systematic review. *Review of Communication Research*, *11*, 172–189.

Amoush, K. H., & Mizher, R. A. (2023). Interaction as a predicator for EFL undergraduate university students' satisfaction with online English language courses. *Theory and Practice in Language Studies*, *13*(4), 927–937. https://doi.org/10.17507/tpls.1304.14

Andrew, A., Cattan, S., Costa-Dias, M., Farquharson, C., Kraftman, L., Krutikova, S., Phimister, A., & Sevilla, A. (2020). Inequalities in children's experiences of home learning during the COVID-19 lockdown in England. *Fiscal Studies*, *41*(3), 653–683. https://doi.org/10.1111/1475-5890.12240

Arispe, K., & Blake, R. (2012). Individual factors and successful language learning in a hybrid course. *System*, 40(4), 449–465. https://doi-org.libweb.uwlax.edu/10.1016/j.system.2012.10.013

Arnold, N., & Ducate, L. (2015). Contextualized views of practices and competencies in CALL teacher education research. *Language Learning & Technology*, *19*(1), 1–9. http://llt.msu.edu/issues/february2015/commentary.pdf

Azaz, M. (2020). Language program coordination during the pandemic: Challenges encountered and lessons learned. *Second Language Research & Practice*, *1*(1), 174–178. http://hdl.handle.net/10125/69852

Back, M., Zavala, V., & Franco, R. (2022). "Siempre adistanciados": Ideology, equity, and access in Peruvian emergency distance education for Spanish as a second language. CALICO Journal, 39(1), 79–102. https://doi.org/10.1558/cj.19665

Baker, C. & Wright, W. E. (2017). *Foundations of bilingual education and bilingualism* (6th ed). Bristol, UK: Multilingual Matters.

Baumgartner, K., & Schulze, M. (2023). (Re-)discoveries in a time of disruption. *Die Unterrichtspraxis*, *56*(1), 1–5. https://doi.org/10.1111/tger.12250

Bedenlier, S., Wunder, I., Gläser-Zikuda, M., Kammerl, R., Kopp, B., Ziegler, A. & Händel, M. (2020). "Generation invisible". Higher education students' (non) use of webcams in synchronous online learning. https://doi.org/10.31234/OSF.IO/7BRP6

Benesch, S., & Prior, M. T. (2023). Rescuing "emotion labor" from (and for) language teacher emotion research. *System*, *113*, 102995.

Blake, R. (2001). What language professionals need to know about technology. *ADFL Bulletin*, *2*(3), 3–15.

Blake, R., Wilson, N., Pardo Ballester, C., & Cetto, M. (2008). Measuring oral proficiency in distance, face-to-face, and blended classrooms. *Language Learning and Technology*, *12*(3),114–127. http://llt.msu.edu/vol12num3/blakeetal/

Blundell, R., Costa Dias, M., Joyce, R. and Xu, X. (2020). COVID-19 and inequalities. *Fiscal Studies*, *41*, 291–319, https://doi.org/10.1111/1475-5890.12232.

Bradley Ruder, D. (2019, June 19). Screen time and the brain: Digital devices can interfere with everything from sleep to creativity. Harvard Medical School. https://hms.harvard.edu/news/screen-time-brain

Brunow, B., & Kuhn-Brown, K. (2023). Cultivating social well-being: (re) discovering the impact of positive relationships. *Die Unterrichtspraxis*, *56*(1), 58–62. https://doi.org/10.1111/tger.12233

Calvo-Ferrer, J. (2022). Disposición del alumnado universitario español a conectar su cámara durante la pandemia generada por la COVID-19. [Willingness of Spanish University Students to Connect their Camera during the COVID-19 Pandemic] *Íkala*, *27*(2), 292–311. https://doi.org/10.17533/udea.ikala.v27n2a01

Caws, C., Hamel, M.-J., Jeanneau, C., & Ollivier, C. (2021) Formation en langues et littératie numérique en contextes ouverts. Une approche socio-interactionnelle. Éditions des archives contemporaines. https://doi.org/10.17184/eac.9782813003911

CDC (Center for Disease Control and Prevention) (2023, March 15). CDC Museum COVID-19 timeline. Retrieved from: https://www.cdc.gov/museum/timeline/covid19.html

Checa-Domene, L., Luque de la Rosa, A., Gavín-Chocano, Ó., & Torrado, J. J. (2022). Students at risk: Self-esteem, optimism and emotional intelligence in post-pandemic times? *International Journal of Environmental Research and Public Health*, *19*(19), 12499.

Classen, A. (2023). Productivity and creativity triggered by the COVID-19 pandemic and new technologies. *Die Unterrichtspraxis*, *56*(1), 41–44. https://doi.org/10.1111/tger.12223

Clayton, S. (2022). Systemic and personal factors that affect students' elective language other than English enrollment decisions. (2022). *Foreign Language Annals*, *55*(2), 361–382. http://dx.doi.org/10.1111/flan.12605

Codreanu, T., & Celik, C. C. (2013). Effects of webcams on multimodal interactive learning. *ReCALL*, *25*(1), 30–47. https://doi.org/10.1017/S0958344012000249

Copland, F., & McPake, J. (2021). Building a new public idea about language?: Multilingualism and language learning in the post-Brexit UK. *Current Issues in Language Planning*, *23*(20), 117–136. https://doi.org/10.1080/14664208.2021.1939976

Crawford, J., Butler-Henderson, K., Rudolph, J., Malkawi, B., Glowatz, M., Burton, R., Lam, S. (2020). COVID-19: 20 countries' higher education intra-period digital pedagogy responses. *Journal of Applied Learning & Teaching*, *3*(1), 1–20. https://doi.org/10.37074/jalt.2020.3.1.7

Cumming, T., Miller, M. D. & Leshchinskaya, I. (2023) DEI institutionalization: Measuring diversity, equity, and inclusion in postsecondary education. *Change: The Magazine of Higher Learning*, *55*(1), 31–38, http://doi.10.1080/00091383.2023.2151802

Czura, A. & Baran-Łucarz, M. (2021). "A stressful unknown" or "an oasis?": Undergraduate students' perceptions of assessment in an in-class and online English phonetics course. *Ikala, Revista de Lenguaje y Cultura*, *26*(3), 623–641. http://dx.doi.org/10.17533/udea.ikala.v26n3a09 http://www.scielo.org.co/pdf/ikala/v26n3/0123-3432-ikala-26-03-623.pdf

Denzel, H. & Ostrau, N. (2023). Responding to the mental health crisis among our language-learning community: A report on the pilot project FLOW (foreign languages offering well-being). *Unterrichtspraxis*, *56*(1), 21–24. https://doi.org/10.1111/tger.12246

Diao, W., & Liu, H. Y. (2020). Starting college, quitting foreign language: The case of learners of Chinese language during secondary-postsecondary transition. *Journal of Language, Identity & Education*, *20*(2), 75–89. https://doi.org/10.1080/15348458.2020.1726753

Discenza, R., Howard, C., & K Schenk, K. (2001). The design and management of effective distance learning programs. Hershey: IGI Global. https://doi.org/10.4018/978-1-930708-20-4

Edelman, R. (2021, January 13). Pandemic fuels culture of institutional mistrust. *World Economic Forum*. https://www.weforum.org/agenda/2021/01/pandemic-mistrust-government-global-survey/

Engzell, P., Frey, A., & Verhagen, M. D. (2021). Learning loss due to school closures during the COVID-19 pandemic. *Proceedings of the National Academy of Sciences*, *118*(17), e2022376118.

European Commission, Joint Research Centre, Redecker, C. & Punie, Y. (2017). *European framework for the digital competence of educators – DigCompEdu*. Retrieved June 19, 2023 from: https://data.europa.eu/doi/10.2760/159770

Fontenelle-Tereshchuk, D. (2021). 'Homeschooling' and the COVID-19 crisis: The insights of parents on curriculum and remote learning. *Interchange*, *52*(2), 167–191. https://doi.org/10.1007/s10780-021-09420-w

Gacs, A., Goertler, S., & Spasova, S. (2020). Planned online language education versus crisis-prompted online language teaching: Lessons for the future. *Foreign Language Annals*, *53* (2), 380–392. https://doi.org/10.1111/flan.12460

Gao, Y., & Cui, Y. (2022). English as a foreign language teachers' pedagogical beliefs about teacher roles and their agentic actions amid and after COVID-19: A case study. *RELC Journal*. https://doi.org/10.1177/00336882221074110

Gao, LX, & Zhang, LJ. (2020). Teacher learning in difficult times: Examining foreign language teachers' cognitions about online teaching to tide over COVID-19. *Frontiers in Psychology*, *11*. https://www.frontiersin.org/articles/10.3389/fpsyg.2020.549653/full

Garrote, A., Niederbacher, E., Hofmann, J., Rösti, I., & Neuenschwander, M. P. (2021). Teacher expectations and parental stress during emergency distance learning and their relationship to students' perception. *Frontiers in Psychology*, *12*, 712447.

Geng, S., Law, K. M. Y. & Niu, B. (2019). Investigating self-directed learning and technology readiness in blending learning environment. *International Educational Technology in Higher Education 16*, . https://doi.org/10.1186/s41239-019-0147-0

Ghanizadeh, A. (2022). Higher education amid COVID-19 pandemic: Contributions from resilience, positive orientation and grit. *Journal of Applied Research in Higher Education*, *14*(4), 1670–1685. https://doi.org/10.1108/JARHE-05-2021-0189

Gherheş, V., Şimon, S. y Para, I. (2021). Analysing students' reasons for keeping their webcams on or off during online classes. *Sustainability*, *13*(6), 3203. https://doi.org/10.3390/su13063203

Gleason, J. & Suvorov, R. (Eds.) (2019). Moving forward with CALL to promote Social Justice. *CALICO Journal*, *36*(1). https://doi.org/10.1558/cj.37162

Gleason, J., Cardone, R., & Bartlett, A. (2024). The impact of the pandemic on student Spanish language proficiency. *Language Learning and Technology*. http://dx.doi.org/10.35542/osf.io/g4qd8

Goertler, S. (2019). Normalizing online learning: Adapting to a changing world of language teaching. In N. Arnold & L. Ducate (Eds.), *Engaging language learners through CALL: From theory and research to informed practice* (pp. 51–92). Equinox.

Goertler, S. & Gacs, A. (2018). Assessment in online German: Assessment methods and results. *Die Unterrichtspraxis / Teaching German*, *51*(2), 156–174. https://www.jstor.org/stable/90026423

Goldin, A., Weinstein B. E., & Shiman N. (2020). How do medical masks degrade speech perception? *Hear. Rev.*, *27*(5), 8–9.

Gómez Soler, I., & Tecedor, M. (2018). Foreign language teaching assistant training: A contrastive analysis of trainers and trainees' perspectives. *Hispania*, *101*(1), 38–54. https://doi.org/10.1353/hpn.2018.0083

Greene, A., & Sanderson, T. (2023). *Remote works: Managing for freedom, flexibility, and focus*. Berrett-Koehler.

Gregersen, T., Mercer, S., & MacIntyre, P. D. (2021). Language teacher perspectives on stress and coping. *Foreign Language Annals*, *54*(4), 1145–1163. https://doi.org/10.1111/fl1n.12544

Grgurovic, M., Chappele, C., & Shelley, M. (2013). A meta-analysis of effectiveness studies on computer technology-supported language learning. *ReCALL*, *25*(2). https://doi.org/10.1017/S0958344013000013

Griffin, K. (2023). Study abroad programs in transition from pandemic to endemic. *L2 Journal*, *15*(2), 160. https://doi.org/10.5070/L215260153

Guillen, G., Sawin, T. & Avineri, N. (2020). Zooming out of the crisis: Language and human collaboration. *Foreign Language Annals*, *53*, 320–328. DOI: 10.1111/flan.12459

Hamdan, K. M., Al-Bashaireh, A. M., Zahran, Z., Al-Daghestani, A., Al-Habashneh, S., & Shaheen, A. M. (2021). University students' interaction, Internet self-efficacy, self-regulation and satisfaction with online education during pandemic crises of COVID-19 (SARS-CoV-2). *International Journal of Educational Management*. https://doi.org/10.1108/IJEM-11-2020-0513

Hampel, R., & Stickler, U. (Eds.). (2015). *Developing online language teaching: Research-based pedagogies and reflective practices.* Palgrave Macmillan. https://doi.org/10.1057/9781137412263

Hayran, C., & Anik, L. (2021). Well-being and fear of missing out (FOMO) on digital content in the time of COVID-19: A correlational analysis among university students. *International Journal of Environmental Research and Public Health*, *18*(4), 1974.

Healey, D., Hanson-Smith, E., Hubbard, P., Ioannou-Georgiou, S., Kessler, G., & Ware, P. (2011). *TESOL technology standards: Definition, implementation, integration.* Alexandria, VA: TESOL.

Heo, J., & Han, S. (2018). Effects of motivation, academic stress and age in predicting self-directed learning readiness (SDLR): Focused on online college students. *Education and Information Technologies*, *23*, 61–71. https://doi.org/10.1007/s10639-017-9585-2

Hussain, R., Ilyas, U., & Ilyas, A. (2021). Agency in Computer-Assisted Language Learning (CALL): Learning to use language for a sustainable post-COVID-19 society. *Sustainable Business and Society in Emerging Economies*, *3*(3), 397–409. https://doi.org/10.26710/sbsee.v3i3.2048

Izquierdo, J., María del Carmen, S. C., Verónika De la, C. V., & Rubén Zapata Díaz. (2021). University language instructors' preparedness for technology-mediated instruction and burnout during the COVID-19 pandemic. *Íkala*, *26*(3), 661–695. https://doi.org/10.17533/udea.ikala.v26n3a11

Jin, L, Xu, Y., Deifell, E., & Angus, K. (2021). Emergency remote language teaching and U.S.-based college-level world language educators' intentions to adopt online teaching in postpandemic times. *Modern Language Journal*, *105*(2), 412–434. http://dx.doi.org/10.1111/modl.12712

Jin, L., Deifell, E., & Angus, K. (2022). Emergency remote language teaching and learning in disruptive times. *CALICO Journal*, *39*(1), i–x. https://doi.org/10.1558/cj.20858

Kantamneni, N. (2023). The impact of the COVID-19 pandemic on marginalized populations in the United States: A research agenda. *Journal of Vocational Behavior*, *119*, 103439. https://doi.org/10.1016/j.jvb.2020.103439

Kaplan-Rakowski, R., & Gruber, A. (2021). One-on-one foreign language speaking practice in high-immersion virtual reality. In Y.J. Lan & S. Grant (Eds.), *Contextual language learning – Real language learning on the continuum from virtuality to reality* (pp. 187–202). Springer. https://doi-org.ezproxy2.library.colostate.edu/10.1007/978-981-16-3416-1_9

Kaul, P. & Garg, P. K. (2021). Crowdsourcing and global collaboration during COVID-19 pandemic: A silver lining. *Journal of Surgical Oncology*, *123*(5), 1204–1205. https://doi.org/10.1002/jso.26417

Kautz, E. A. (2021). Sustainability, study abroad, and curricular revisions in the face of global crises. *Die Unterrichtspraxis*, *54*(2), 314–328.

Kessler, G. (2018). Technology and the future of language teaching. Foreign Language Annals, 51(1), 205–218. https://doi.org/10.1111/flan.12318

Khalil, L., & Alharbi, K. (2022). A descriptive study of EFL teachers' perception toward e-learning platforms during the Covid-19 pandemic. *Electronic Journal of e-Learning*, *20*(4), 336–359. https://doi.org/10.34190/ejel.20.4.2203

Kohnke, L., & Moorhouse, B. L. (2022). Facilitating synchronous online language learning through Zoom. *RELC Journal*, *53*(1), 296–301. https://doi.org/10.1177/0033688220937235

Kolovou, P. (2023). Teaching resilience in fragile times. *Unterrichtspraxis*, *56*(1), 25–29. https://doi.org/10.1111/tger.12247

Kougiourouki, M., & Masali, Z. (2022). Homework during Emergency Remote Education (ERE) due to Covid-19 pandemic: Teachers' perceptions. *American Journal of Educational Research*, *10*(7), 452–458.

Kutch, L. M. (2023). Disruptive innovation for language teaching in a multimodal format. *Die Unterrichtspraxis*, *56*(1), 68–72. https://doi.org/10.1111/tger.12243

Lederman, D. (2022). HyFlex learning: Pros, cons, and the future. *Insider HigherEd.* https://www.insidehighered.com/quicktakes/2022/10/21/hyflex-learning-pros-cons-and-future

Leung, D., Lee, C., Wang, A. H., & Guruge, S. (2023). Immigrants' and refugees' experiences of access to health and social services during the COVID-19 pandemic in Toronto, Canada. *Journal of Health Services Research & Policy*, *28*(1), 34–41. https://doi.org/10.1177/13558196221109148

Lidegran, I., Hultqvist, E., Bertilsson, E., & Börjesson, M. (2021). Insecurity, lack of support, and frustration: A sociological analysis of how three groups of students reflect on their distance education during the pandemic in Sweden. *European Journal of Education*, *56*(4), 550–563.

Looney, D., & Lusin, N. (2019). Enrollments in languages other than English in United States institutions of higher education, summer 2016 and fall 2016: Final report. Modern Language Association. www.mla.org/content/download/110154/2406932/2016-Enrollments-Final-Report.pdf

Lord, G. (2020a). Is the sky falling (again)? Observations on the language requirement in U.S. higher education. *ADFL Bulletin*, *46*(1), 114–122.

Lord, G. (2020b). The dark clouds of COVID-19 (and the unexpected silver linings). *Second Language Research & Practice*, *1*(1), 155–158. http://hdl.handle.net/10125/69848

Lusin, N. (2012). *The MLA Survey of Postsecondary Entrance and Degree Requirements for Languages Other Than English, 2009–10*. Modern Language Association, March 2012. www.mla.org/content/download/3316/ file/requirements_survey_200910.pdf.

MacIntyre, P.D., Gregersen, T., & Mercer, S. (2020). Language teachers' coping strategies during the COVID-19 conversion to online teaching: Correlations with stress wellbeing and negative emotions. *System*, *94*, 1–12. https://doi.org/10.1016/j.system.2020.102352

MacIntyre, P., Mercer, S., Gregersen, T., & Hay, A. (2022). The role of hope in language teachers' changing stress, coping, and well-being. *System*, *109*, 102882. https://doi.org/10.1016/j.system.2022.102881

Maican, M.-A. & Cocorada, E. (2021). Online foreign language learning in higher education and its correlates during the COVID-19 pandemic. *Sustainability*, *13* (2), 1–21. doi: 10.3390/su13020781

Martin, F., Stamper, B., & Flowers, C. (2020). Examining student perception of their readiness for online learning: Importance and confidence. *Online Learning*, *24*(2), 38–58. https://doi.org/10.24059/olj.v24i2.2053

Merrill,J., Dengub, E., & Pastushenkov, D. (2021). Language gains in intensive synchronous online and face-to-face Russian immersion programs: A Comparison. *Russian Language Journal*, *71*(2), 87–120.

Mills, N. (2020). Language program direction during COVID-19: Collective memories of the extraordinary. *Second Language Research & Practice*, *1*(1), 159–163. http://hdl.handle.net/10125/69849

Mineo, L. (2022, June 29). 'Shadow pandemic' of domestic violence. *Harvard Gazette.* https://news.harvard.edu/gazette/story/2022/06/shadow-pandemic-of-domestic-violence/

Mockaitis, A. I., Butler, C. L., & Ojo, A. (2022). COVID-19 pandemic disruptions to working lives: A multilevel examination of impacts across career stages. *Journal of Vocational Behavior*, *138*, 103768

Moneypenny, D. B., & Aldrich, R. S. (2016). Online and face-to-face language learning: A comparative analysis of oral proficiency in introductory Spanish. *Journal of Educators Online*, *13*(2), 105–133. https://doi.org/10.9743/jeo.2016.2.2

Morgan, W. J., & Thompson, A. S. (2023). "My friend Travis says...": A look at enrollment trends in language classes in the United States. *Foreign Language Annals*, *56*(2), 259–279. https://doi.org/10.1111/flan.12683

Morris, K. (2022). Language teaching in the time of COVID-19: Insights from experienced and pre-service teachers. In J. LeLoup & P. Swanson (Eds.), *Handbook of research on effective online language teaching in a disruptive environment* (pp. 1–23). IGI Global. http://doi.org/10.4018/978-1-7998-7720-2

Moser, K. & Wei, T. (2023). Professional development in collaborative online spaces: Supporting rural language teachers in a post-pandemic era. *The New Educator*, *19*(1), 1–32. https://doi.org/10.1080/1547688x.2023.2174279

Moser, K. M., Wei, T., & Brenner, D. (2021). Remote teaching during COVID-19: Implications from a national survey of language educators. *System*, *97*, 102431. https://doi.org/10.1016/j.system.2020.102431

Mpofu, N. (2020). Online and in the classroom, COVID-19 has put new demands on teachers. *The Conversation.* https://theconversation.com/online-and-in-the-classroomcovid19-has-put-new-demands-on-teachers-147202

Murphy–Judy, K., & Johnshoy, M. (2017). Who's teaching which languages online? IALLT Journal of Language Learning Technologies, 47, 137–167. https://doi.org/10.17161/iallt.v47i1.8570

Nakra, P. (2021). COVID-19 disrupts U.S. higher education industry reimagining the future. *Journal of Higher Education Theory & Practice*, *21*(6), 140–147. https://doi-org.scsu.idm.oclc.org/10.33423/jhetp.v21i6.4382

Nobrega, M., Opice, R., Lauletta, M. M., & Nobrega, C. A. (2020). How face masks can affect school performance. *International Journal of Pediatric Otorhinolaryngology*, *138*, 110328. https://doi.org/10.1016/j.ijporl.2020.110328

Nordmeyer, J. & Bettney, E. (2022). Equity for multilingual learners: A global network response to the pandemic. *Current Issues in Comparative Education*, *24*(2), 119–122.

Ocando Finol, M. (2020, March 26). Asynchronous vs. synchronous learning: A quick overview. https://www.brynmawr.edu/news/asynchronous-vs-synchronous-learning-quick-overview

Ortega, L. (2017). New CALL-SLA research interfaces for the 21st century: Towards equitable multilingualism. *CALICO Journal*, *34*(3), 283–316. https://doi.org/10.1558/cj.33855

Paesani, K. (2020). Teacher professional development and online instruction: Cultivating coherence and sustainability. *Foreign Language Annals*, *53*, 292–297.

Pateno, G. M., Cotejo, D. G., & Bongcales, M. (2022). The growing popularity of netspeak among millennials: An analysis of the emerging lingo on facebook messenger. *Webology*, *19*(3), 1978–1990.

Payne, S. J. (2020). Developing L2 productive language skills online and the strategic use of instructional tools. *Foreign Language Annals*, *53*, 243–249. https://doi.org/10.1111/flan.12457

Plonsky, L., & Ziegler, N. (2016). The CALL–SLA interface: Insights from a second-order synthesis. *Language learning & Technology*, *20*(2), 17–37. Retrieved from http://llt.msu.edu/issues/june2016/plonskyziegler.pdf

Quinn, R. (2023, August 11). West Virginia's unprecedented proposed cuts become clear. *Inside Higher Ed.* https://www.insidehighered.com/news/faculty-issues/tenure/2023/08/11/west-virginia-universitys-unprecedented-proposed-cuts-become

Rantz, J. (2021, March 10). Even after cutting in line for vaccines, teachers won't return to work. *Newsweek.* https://www.newsweek.com/even-after-cutting-line-vaccines-teachers-wont-return-work-opinion-1574615

Rapanta, C., Botturi, L., Goodyear, P., Guárdia, l. & Koole, M. (2021). Balancing Technology, Pedagogy and the New Normal: Post-pandemic Challenges for Higher Education. *Postdigital Science and Education*, *3*, 715–742. https://doi.org/10.1007/s42438-021-00249-1

Rilliard, M. (2020). Adaptability 2.0: Tackling the challenge of the COVID-19 crisis. *Second Language Research & Practice*, *1*(1), 179–182. http://hdl.handle.net/10125/69853

Sadeghi, K. (Ed.). (2023). *Technology-assisted language assessment in diverse contexts: Lessons from the transition to online testing during Covid-19.* Routledge.

Sainato, M. (2021, October 4). 'Exhausted and underpaid': teachers across the US are leaving their jobs in numbers. *The Guardian.* https://www.theguardian.com/world/2021/oct/04/teachers-quitting-jobs-covid-record-numbers

Schmitt, E. (2014). Seat time versus proficiency: Assessment of language development in undergraduate students. In J. Norris & N. Mills (Eds.), *Innovation and accountability in language program evaluation* (pp. 110 –130). Cengage.

Schrimpf, A., Bleckwenn, M., & Braesigk, A. (2023). COVID-19 continues to burden general practitioners: Impact on workload, provision of care, and intention to leave. *Healthcare, 11*(3), 320. https://doi.org/10.3390/healthcare11030320

Shaver, J. (2022). The state of telehealth before and after the COVID-19 pandemic. *Primary Care*, *49*(4), 517–530. https://doi.org/10.1016/j.pop.2022.04.002

Snow, J. L., Dismuke, C., Carter, H., & Holloway, S. (2023). The emotional work of being a teacher educator and persisting through a pandemic. *Teaching and Teacher Education, 127*, 104098.

Soria, K. M., Horgos, B., & Shenouda, J. D. (2023). Disparities in college students' financial hardships during the covid-19 pandemic. *Journal of Student Affairs Research and Practice*, *60*(1), 31–48.

Strambi, A., & Bouvet, E. (2003). Flexibility and interaction at a distance: A mixed-model environment for language learning. Language, Learning and Technology, 7(3), 81–102. https://www.lltjournal.org/item/10125-25215/

Sun, W., & Zou, B. (2022). A study of preservice EFL teachers' acceptance of online teaching and the influencing factors. *Language Learning & Teaching*, *26*(2), 38–49.

Supovitz, J. A., & Manghani, O. (2022). The role of inequity in school responses to the COVID-19 pandemic. *Peabody Journal of Education*, *97*(3), 257–273.

Sykes J. M. (2021). Editor's message. *Foreign Language Annals*, *54*, 565-566. https://doi.org/10.1111/flan.12581

Thi Thanh, H. P. (2023). Prolonged online learning: An exploratory mixed-methods study on EFL learners' needs and need satisfaction: Online learning: Needs and need satisfaction. *International Journal of Emerging Technologies in Learning (Online)*, *18*(4), 186–201. https://doi.org/10.3991/ijet.v18i04.35759

Thrasher, T. (2022). The impact of virtual reality on L2 French learners' language anxiety and oral comprehensibility: An exploratory study. *CALICO Journal*, *39* (2). https://doi.org/10.1558/cj.42198

van Deusen-Scholl, N. (2020). The resilience of a community of practice during the COVID-19 crisis. *Second Language Research & Practice*, *1*(1), 144–148. http://hdl.handle.net/10125/69846

van Heerden, M., & Bharuthram, S. (2023). 'It does not feel like I am a university student': Considering the impact of online learning on first-year students' sense of belonging in a 'post pandemic' academic literacy module. *Perspectives in Education*, *41*(3), 95–106.

Vujnovic, M., & Foster, J. (2022). Bringing the F.U.D to thin the ranks. In *Higher Education and Disaster Capitalism in the Age of COVID-19* (Palgrave Critical University Studies, pp. 57–104). Switzerland: Springer International Publishing AG.

Waldvogel, D. A., & Robayna, T. (2022). Teaching languages virtually during a global pandemic: Perspectives from post-secondary language educators. *Dimension*, 57–79. DOI

Walter, D., & Schenker, T. (2022). Surviving or thriving? Experiences and job satisfaction of language instructors in the USA during the COVID-19 pandemic. *Journal of Language Teaching*, *2*(11), 1–14. https://doi.org/10.54475/jlt.2022.014

Warner, C. & Diao, W. (2022). Caring is pedagogy: Foreign language teachers' emotion labor in crisis. *Linguistics and Education*, *71*, 1–12. https://doi.org/10.1016/j.linged.2022.101100

Was, C. A., & Greve, M. (2021). Undergraduate student goal orientations and the impact of COVID-19: Student effort following the pandemic shutdown. *Educational Research: Theory and Practice*, *32*(1), 23–29.

Williamson, T., Hughes, E., & Head, P. (2018). An exploration of administrative bloat in American higher education. *Planning for Higher Education*, *46*(2), 15–22.

Wilson, A., & Lengeling, M. (2021). Language learning in the time of Covid-19: ELT students' narrated experiences in guided reflective journals. *Ikala, Revista de Lenguaje y Cultura*, *26*(3), 571–585. http://www.scielo.org.co/pdf/ikala/v26n3/0123-3432-ikala-26-03-571.pdf

Winke, P. M., & Goertler, S. (2008). Did we forget someone? Students' computer access and literacy for CALL. *CALICO Journal*, *25*(3), 482–509.

Xu, Y., Jin, L., Deifell, E., & Angus, K. (2022). Facilitating technology-based character learning in emergency remote teaching. *Foreign Language Annals*, *55*(1), 72–97. https://doi.org/10.1111/flan.12541

Zamarro, G., Camp, A., Fuchsman, D., & McGee, H. (2021, September 16). Pandemic prompts more teachers to consider early retirement or new career. *The Conversation*. https://theconversation.com/pandemic-prompts-more-teachers-to-consider-early-retirement-or-new-career-166871

Zhu, R., & Chan, S. S. Y. (2023). The clash between CLIL and TELL: Effects and potential solutions of adapting TELL for online CLIL teaching. *Applied Sciences*, *13*(7), 4270. https://doi.org/10.3390/app13074270

Index